INTERNATIONAL THEORY

International Theory

Critical Investigations

Edited by

James Der Derian
Professor of Political Science
University of Massachusetts at Amherst

Foreword by Adam Watson

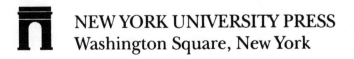

NEW YORK UNIVERSITY PRESS
Washington Square, New York

Selection, editorial matter, and Chapters 1 and 14
© James Der Derian 1995
Foreword © Adam Watson 1995
For individual chapters please see the Acknowledgements.

First published in the U.S.A. in 1995 by
NEW YORK UNIVERSITY PRESS
Washington Square
New York, N.Y. 10003

Library of Congress Cataloging-in-Publication Data
International theory : critical investigations / edited by James Der
Derian.
p. cm.
Includes bibliographical references and index.
ISBN 0–8147–1861–2 (cloth) — ISBN 0–8147–1862–0 (pbk.)
1. International relations—Philosophy. I. Der Derian, James.
JX1391.I639 1995
327. 1—dc20   94–7501
                                                         CIP

Printed in Great Britain

Contents

Preface

This book is the product of a dialogue and a debt. The dialogue emerged from a transatlantic and transdisciplinary encounter, cutting across British and North American schools of international theory, and traversing the belated first contact between International Relations and critical, interpretive approaches which have already taken root in the humanities and social sciences. The debt originated from an early subvention of that dialogue by Hedley Bull, who took me on as a neophyte student of International Relations after I confessed to a chronic inability to distinguish an independent from a dependent variable during a brief pursuit of IR at McGill University. From him I learned – and agreed – that the most important dialogues to enjoin in international theory were between philosophical-historical approaches and behavioralist-methodological ones, between a normative inquiry and a value-free social science, and between a skeptical criticism and a progressivist research program. But it was also in a dialogue of disagreement with Bull that I learned much, for he forced me to test and temper my early engagement with continental philosophy by a combination of analytical rigor and informed skepticism that no subsequent critic has since matched. I believe it is ample testimony to the philosophical power and ethical value of Bull's disposition that he was able to guide and support students through journeys into intellectual territories that he found alien to his own.

For that I am in debt to Bull and to those who shaped his thinking, as well as to those dissident thinkers who continue to refigure my own. By pairing the early diplomatic investigations of Bull, Wight, and other classical international theorists with contemporary critical ones, I hope to repay a portion of that debt. Call it a dialogue, a tutorial, or an intertext, one can never escape the debtor's prison of influence. I imagine mine as a neo-victorian, post-modern panopticon, with Hedley Bull absent from the watchtower but still effective, and Michel Foucault providing the illusory means ('This is not a ladder') to climb the walls of a discipline's power. Therein, of course, lies the irony, for as Foucault shows us prisons 'work' not by eliminating crime, but by producing new categories of delinquency. So too with the prison-house of IR. Hence, this book should not be read as a potential cure but as one more (morbid) symptom of an international society that can not rid itself of prison-states. It should be bought in the knowledge that all royalties will go to Amnesty International, to help treat those symptoms.

There are many others to thank, but I will limit the naming ritual to just a few. I am grateful for the invitation, many years back, of William Connoly and Steven Lukes to contribute a volume to their series on *Readings in Social and Political Theory*. Throughout the elephantine gestation of this book Niko Pfund from New York University Press has been patient, supportive, and full of good advice. Tim Farmiloe, Clare Andrews, and Keith Povey from Macmillan were diplomatic and critical at the right moments. Andrew Hurrell, Adam Roberts, and Adam Watson early on provided valuable advice on the selection and gathering of materials. Mary Bull and Gabriele Wight offered encouragement and guidance through the labyrinth of permissions. Closer to home, Neta Crawford, Eric Einhorn, Peter Haas, M.J. Peterson, Nicholas Xenos, and Yasmin Boroumand have all added their voice to the dialogue and I thank them for it.

JAMES DER DERIAN

Foreword

By making these papers available in one volume, James Der Derian performs a very useful service to the study of international relations and to the thoughtful general reader. This is not just another collection of familiar teaching texts. A sequential and contrapuntal argument runs through the differing chapters, so that, taken together, they become a statement of Der Derian's own evolving perspective and of his unresolved concerns.

Der Derian has his intellectual tap-roots in the British Committee for the Theory of International Politics. There is in his chapters a dialogue between the realism of the disenchanted academics and practitioners of the era of the cold war and decolonization after World War II, and their successors who see an advantage in the philosophical and historical approach of classical realism but who also want to go beyond it, to explore the less Eurocentric history which was a principal aim of the Committee and a more emancipatory, less state-bound political approach.

In order to put Der Derian's perspective in its intellectual context, it may be useful to set out what the British Committee contributed to the study of international relations.

It is a truism that theorizing about politics reflects the political problems of its time and place. By 1950, and certainly after the Suez débacle of 1956, it was clear that the self-destruction of European power and authority in two great wars, and the re-emergence of non-European civilizations from colonial tutelage, had led to the fitful establishment of a new global international society, organized largely by means of rules and institutions inherited from its European predecessor and based nominally on multiple sovereign independences and in practice on a bipolar power struggle and a self-styled Third World. It seemed important to both academics and practitioners in Britain to take a fresh and realistic look at the European and other states systems, in order to see what light a comparative study might throw on the unfamiliar world order that was taking shape.

Therefore, when the Rockefeller Foundation offered Herbert

Butterfield, Professor of Modern History at Cambridge and
Master of Peterhouse, the funding for a committee to study
these questions, he together with Professor Martin Wight
set up the British Committee for the Theory of International Politics. The Committee met three weekends a year,
usually at Peterhouse, and was composed of members from
several disciplines, including practitioners like myself. Guests
were also invited, ranging from George Kennan to Garret
Fitzgerald. Members wrote papers for the Committee, which
they modified after discussion. Three sets of these papers
have been published: *Diplomatic Investigations: Essays in the
Theory of International Politics* (after which Der Derian's book
is named, and from which Wight's and the first of Bull's
essays are taken); *Systems of States* by Wight; and *The Expansion of International Society* edited by Bull and myself. Two
individual books, Bull's *The Anarchical Society: a Study of Order
in International Politics,* and my own *The Evolution of International Society: a Comparative Historical Analysis,* also owe much
to the Committee's deliberations.

The Committee concentrated on the study of *states systems.* This indispensable German concept goes back to
Pufendorf's *De Systematibus Civitatum* (1675) and to Heeren's
monumental *History of the European States System and its
Colonies* during the Napoleonic wars. Butterfield and Wight
insisted on the importance of the cultural issue from the beginning. Butterfield's paper 'The Historic States Systems' stated:

> The salient fact about the international systems so far
> studied is that . . . the effective forces making for some
> sort of combination may be the elements of an anteced-
> ent common culture. Granted that a states system is al-
> ready in existence, it may not be difficult to add to it
> new units . . . that are of a quite alien culture.[1]

Hudson's paper on the Chinese society of the warring
states, and mine on the classical Indian society of the
Arthashastra, from which two chapters of my *Evolution of
International Society* are partly derived, also illustrated the
importance of a cultural matrix for a society of states.

What did we mean, or come to mean, by a states system
and an international society? After some discussion, and led
by Hedley Bull, the Committee inclined towards a mecha-

nistic definition of a states system. When a number of states, or political entities, are so involved with one another that each, in the classical phrase, is obliged to take account of the others and shape its behaviour accordingly, then these political entities form a system, in the way that the sun and the planets form a solar system. We recognized that, as technology makes the contemporary world shrink, and states become ever more interdependent, so the impersonal network of interests and pressures that binds the system together gets ever tighter.

It seemed to Pufendorf and particularly to Heeren that not any group of states formed a system. Heeren defined a *Staatensystem* as 'the union of several contiguous states resembling each other in their manners, religion and degree of social improvement and cemented together by a reciprocity of interests'[2] – in other words a cultural unity. The Committee preferred a more objective criterion. Bull proposed, and the rest of us agreed, that when independent states locked into a system put into place rules and institutions and observe certain codes of conduct, in order to manage the network of interests and pressures and especially when they share certain values, we should say that these states have created an international society. Such rules and institutions, and the accumulated lessons of practical experience, can be seen in Toynbee's terms as the response of governments to the challenge of living locked into a system.

However, the concept of a society as the conscious response of states to the pressures of a system is inadequate in its simple form. The Committee saw that Bull's definition skirted the fundamental cultural issue. 'Europe' was a society in a much profounder sense: what Toynbee called European civilization and Spengler the Western culture. The eighteenth century saw Europe not as an 'anarchical society' of independent entities that had worked out a *modus vivendi*, let alone a sort of permanent catfight, but as a family or commonwealth of states largely ruled by related princes. Some went rather further: Voltaire called it a 'grande république partagée entre plusieurs états';[3] and Gibbon said 'a philosopher may be permitted to consider Europe as one great republic'.[4] The exclusive political correctness of sovereign statehood had not yet been established. And of course the Committee noted that as we watched, Europeans were coming to think of themselves again as one great republic. The rules, institutions and values of the European international society were a distillation of European culture.

Important as the European society of states seemed to the Committee, Europe's relations with the rest of the world appeared equally or even more relevant to its efforts to understand the contemporary scene. For the system into which the European states were increasingly tightly locked had from the beginning been wider than their society. The European republic did not include the great Ottoman empire. The Ottomans played a major role in the system: they occupied about a quarter of geographical Europe; and both their military and economic strength was such that all the states of the European society felt obliged to shape their policies accordingly. Their generally anti-hegemonial policy towards the European society helped to break the aims of the Habsburgs and ensured the establishment of Protestant states, and later contributed to the defeat of Napoleon. But they were culturally alien to the European republic, and did not accept its rules and institutions, and especially not its values. They and the Europeans therefore worked out a separate and more limited set of rules and institutions to regulate their close involvement; which hardly went beyond the substantial minimum required to facilitate their intercourse. The Ottomans in their heyday were able to formulate the rules largely according to their own imperial practice; but as the Europeans grew stronger they increasingly modified the rules in their own favor.

When in the nineteenth century the industrial and technical revolution enabled the Europeans (including Russia and the United States) to extend the net of their system over the whole world, they applied the regulatory arrangements they had developed with the Ottomans to other areas of different cultures that they did not administer, from China to Morocco. Then gradually they admitted other noncolonized polities to their club as member states, as and when those states conformed or promised to conform to European 'standards of civilization,' ranging from commercial law to what we now call human rights.

It seemed to the Committee worth considering what sort

of arrangements might prevail in an uncolonized and many-cultured world if the Europeans had not used their nineteenth-century military and economic superiority to impose their standards on all of it, and if after World War II the two superpowers, Russia and America, refrained from pushing their domestic values and practices on to states with other cultural traditions. For it seemed – and still seems – possible that 'greater Europe' including America and Russia might continue to disengage from Asian and African countries, which would then reassert their cultural identity while continuing to share modern technology and to be bound in the tightening net of the global economic and strategic system. Could our multicultural world be moving towards one system but a number of separate societies?

To understand what was happening in the 1960s and 1970s (and is now happening in the ex-Soviet Union) and to understand what may happen next in the non-European world, which is one of Der Derian's chief concerns, we need a thorough study of the differences between the more intimate arrangements, based on a common culture, that determined the relations between governments and individuals of the member states of the European *grande république*, and the much more aloof, purely regulatory agreements that governed their relations with independent states in the rest of the world, and especially the Ottoman empire, before the era of administrative colonialism.

Bull and I were especially interested in these questions; and in the flood tide of European expansion over the rest of the world, and its subsequent ebb, which has left behind a global system managed, for the present at least, by a global international society still formed in the European cultural matrix. When I and later he took over the chairmanship, the Committee agreed to focus its attention on this set of issues, which became the central themes of *The Expansion of International Society*. We noted the racial and cultural basis of the revolt against the West, which with the parallel revolt against the Soviet Union constitutes a general alienation from, and rejection of, what the rebels often call white domination, white doctrines and white practices. Bull's list of successive themes of the revolt against the West in his chapter in *Expansion* placed as the climax, after the struggle for equal sovereignty, the anti-colonial revolution and the struggles for racial equality and economic justice, the ultimate insistence on cultural liberation – 'the reassertion of their traditional and indigenous cultures'.[5]

Those who rebelled against Western and Soviet dominance, and especially the Western-educated governing elites of the newly independent member states, insist that the central feature of the worldwide international society, its constituent legitimacy, is sovereign independence, consecrated by membership of the United Nations, and its corollary of non-interference in their internal affairs. But the northern industrialized world, including Japan, is moving beyond independent statehood to ideas of a world economy and more exacting standards of human rights. The demand in 'developing' countries for improved standards of living leads their governments to seek increasing economic aid and improved terms of trade from the donor countries; which in return, directly and through organizations like the World Bank and the IMF, insist on Western standards of economic practice and, led by the United States, also standards of human rights. These Western demands are the modern equivalent, and indeed the linear continuation, of the nineteenth-century demands for observance of Western standards of civilization as the price of admission to international society. They are welcome to many people in non-Western countries, but unwelcome to governments. So the pressures of a tightening world system and the institutions and practices of an ever more integrated society are cracking open the walls between independent states, in ways that reduce both their external and internal independence in practice to no more than a *de facto* autonomy, while leaving intact the symbolic sovereignty of statehood.

Among the principal Western solvents of independence, human rights and feminist themes in international relations occupy an important place in this volume. There is in it a thought-provoking latent tension between the emergence of a less Eurocentric view of history and the common weal, and the Western, especially American, assumption that certain values and behavior of Western provenance have a universal validity and should be universally enforced.

This brings us to the question which came to interest

me most: the role of hegemony in international societies, and their relation to more tightly knit suzerain and imperial societies. It gradually and steadily became clearer to me during the quarter century of the Committee's meetings and since, that hegemony is an integral and inevitable feature of all systems of independent and quasi-independent states because, even when the political entities involved are all equal juridically according to the rules of the corresponding society, some are very much more equal than others in practice; and moreover this status of the great powers is usually recognized, with varying legitimacy, in the operation of the society. The degree of hegemony varies, of course, and it may be exercised by one power, by a diarchy or by a concert of great powers. When one compares the known systems along a spectrum of integration, hegemony shades without any clear dividing line into dominion and then empire, where the propensity to autonomy corresponds to the propensity to hegemony in the lesser integrated part of the spectrum.

According to the prevailing intellectual fashion in Europe and the Third World in the age of decolonization, independent statehood was the instant right of every dependent territory. No other status was any longer considered legitimate; and empires, zones of influence and even hegemony were widely regarded as too reprehensible for objective study. Wight and I uneasy about exclusive concentration on independent states. The attempt to stretch every political entity on the Procrustean bed of sovereign statehood was carried to absurd lengths during the period of decolonization, when tiny territories – what De Gaulle with military bluntness called the 'dust of empires' – were made full members of international society for want of any intermediate status, without the experience or the resources to play a meaningful part.

Wight rejected and helped the Committee to free itself from what he called 'the intellectual bias imposed by the sovereign state.' His view that societies of states operated within a cultural framework was developed from Toynbee's concern with distinct civilizations and their contacts in time and space. Wight wanted to look not only at the European republic but also at 'suzerain systems' where one state had a recognized primacy in the system, and at systems which included autonomous though not independent states; and then to compare all the systems. He essays for the Committee published as *Systems of States* were first steps towards that goal.

Butterfield and Bull, and the Irish diplomat Noel Dorr, were more specifically concerned with the value and the workings of sovereignty and multiple independences. Indeed the word 'international' implies an anarchy in the literal sense, and tends to limit the study of states systems to those whose sovereign members recognise the same independence of all the others. Bull limited his study of our present international system, *The Anarchical Society*, in that way: 'In terms of the approach being developed here,' he wrote, 'only what Wight calls an international states system is a system at all'.[6] However, he accepted Wight's point that the European society and the present world-wide one, in spite of their constituent legitimacy of absolute independence, were in fact 'a succession of hegemonies,' and he welcomed my interest in hegemony and my aim to produce a comparative analysis of all the main states systems, whether based on theoretical independence or not.

Herbert Butterfield had the most original mind on the Committee. He was particularly interested in the subtle accumulation of experience in managing and adjusting the relations between states, with what made the formal rules and institutions of an international society work – what Alberto Coll in his book on Butterfield[7] calls the wisdom of statecraft. Butterfield and Wight described this line of inquiry in their introduction to the volume of papers written for the Committee, *Diplomatic Investigations*: 'The underlying aim . . . is to clarify the principles of prudence and moral obligation which have held together the international society of states throughout its history, and still hold it together.'[8]

Maxims of prudence, the sense of responsibility and the other intangibles that make up the management of an international society are the products of a common cultural atmosphere, or a dominant one in more expanded societies. The process of 'holding a society of states together,' of managing change and of providing a mantle of gradual legitimation for adjustments to the rules and institutions, is largely determined by the practice of the member states. It is especially important at this time of transition. The significance of practice in international societies is described as follows by Andrew Hurrell of Oxford University, in his chapter in *Regime Theory and International Relations* (1993).

> International regimes are necessarily intersubjective phenomena whose existence and validity is created and sustained in the interrelationship of their subjects . . . Such a view . . . suggests the need for a hermaneutic or interpretivist methodology which seeks to recreate the historical and social processes by which rules and norms are constituted and a sense of obligation engendered. We can still try to understand what this sense of obligation consists of, not in general terms but on a specific case-by-case basis.[9]

The Committee would have agreed warmly with the argument.

James Der Derian says in his Introduction: 'Before all else I believe that international theory only progresses when voices of authority are engaged by voices that go against the grain.' That is precisely the spirit that animated the British Committee. It is welcome to see Der Derian continuing it, and so furthering the development of international theory.

ADAM WATSON

Notes

1. Text available in the library of the Royal Institute of International Affairs, St James's Square, London SW1. See also Watson, *Evolution of International Society*, p. 5.
2. Heeren, *History of the European States System*, Preface.
3. Voltaire, *Histoire du Règne de Louis XIV*, ch. 2.
4. Gibbon, *Decline and Fall of the Roman Empire*, ch. 38, general observations.
5. Bull, H., *The Expansion of International Society*, p. 223.
6. Bull, H., *The Anarchical Society*, p. 11.
7. Coll, A., *The Wisdom of Statecraft: Sir Herbert Butterfield and the Philosophy of International Politics*, Duke University Press, (1985).
8. Butterfield, H. and Wight, M., *Diplomatic Investigations*, p. 13.
9. Hurrell, A., *Regime Theory in International Relations*, p. 64.

Acknowledgements

The author and publishers wish to thank the following for permission to reproduce the following copyright material:

George Allen & Unwin, for Chapters 2 and 5, from H. Butterfield and M. Wight (eds), *Diplomatic Investigations* (1966).

Praeger, for Chapter 3, from H. Morgenthau, *Truth and Power: Essays of a Decade, 1960–1970* (1970).

Millennium Journal of International Studies, for Chapter 4, from J.A. Tickner, 'Hans Morgenthau's Principles of Political Realism: A Feminist Reformation' (1988), and for Chapter 12, from R.B.J. Walker, 'History and Structure in the Theory of International Relations' (1989).

International Organization, for Chapter 7, from A. Wendt, 'Anarchy is What States Make of it: The Social Construction of Power Politics' (1992).

Oxford University Press, for Chapter 8, from Brian Porter (ed.), *The Aberystwyth Papers: International Politics 1919–1969* (1972).

Daedalus, for Chapter 9, from S. Hoffmann, 'An American Social Science: International Relations' (1977).

International Studies Quarterly, for Chapter 10, from H. Alker and T. Biersteker 'The Dialectics of World Order: Notes for a Future Archeologist of International *Savior Faire*' (1984), and for Chapter 11, from R. Keohane, 'International Institutions: Two Approaches' (1988).

Notes on the Contributors

Hayward Alker has been Professor of Political Science since 1968. He also taught at Yale, Michigan, Geneva, FLACSO (Santiago, Chile), Uppsala and Stockholm Universities. He was the first Olaf Palme guest Professor in Sweden, and was the 1992–93 President of the International Studies Association. Currently, he coordinates (with Kumar Rupesinghe of International Alert) the Conflict Early Warning Systems Research Programme of the International Social Science Council. A collection of his essays entitled *Rediscoveries and Reformulations: Humanistic Methodologies for International Studies* is in press. He is working with Tahir Amin, Thomas Biersteker and Takashi Inoguchi on the summary volume of the *Dialectics of World Order* project, from which the present chapter also arose.

Richard Ashley is Professor of Political Science at Arizona State University and author of *The Political Economy of War and Peace* as well as numerous articles in journals and edited volumes.

Thomas Biersteker is the Henry R. Luce Professor of International Relations and Political Science at Brown University. He received his BA. from the University of Chicago in 1972 and his MS and PhD. from the Massachusetts Institute of Technology, in 1975 and 1977. He is the author of *Distortion or Development?* (1981), *Multinationals, the State, and Control of the Nigerian Economy* (1987) and *Dealing with Debt: International Financial Negotiations and Adjustment Bargaining* (1993). He has also published extensively on different aspects of international relations theory and is currently co-editing a book on the social construction of state sovereignty.

Hedley Bull, FBA, who died in 1985, was Montague Burton Professor of International Relations at the University of Oxford, and Fellow of Balliol College, from 1977 to 1985.

His works include *The Control of the Arms Race* (1961). *The Anarchical Society* (1977) and (ed with Adam Watson) *The Expansion of International Society* (1984)

James Der Derian is Professor of Political Science at the University of Massachusetts at Amherst. He studied at McGill University, was a Rhodes Scholar at the University of Oxford, and has taught at Columbia University, the University of Southern California, and the Gardner and Lancaster State Prisons. He is the author of *On Diplomacy: A Genealogy of Western Estrangement, Antidiplomacy: Spies, Terror, Speed and War,* and (co-editor with Michael Shapiro) of *International/Intertextual Relations: Postmodern Readings of World Politics.* He is currently writing a book on war games, the media, and US foreign policy called *Virtual Security.*

Jean Bethke Elshtain is the Centennial Professor of Political Science and Professor of Philosophy at Vanderbilt University. She is the author of many books, including *Public Man, Private Woman: Women in Social and Political Thought; Meditations on Modern Political Thought; Power Trips and Other Journeys; Women and War and Democracy on Trial.* She is the editor of *The Family and Political Thought;* co-editor of *Women, War and Feminism;* and co-author of *But Was It Just? Reflections on the Morality of the Persian Gulf War.* Elshtain is the author of some 200 articles and essays in scholarly journals and journals of civic opinion.

Stanley Hoffman is Douglas Dillon Professor of the Civilization of France at Harvard University, where he has taught since 1955. He has been the Chairman of the Center for European Studies at Harvard since its creation in 1969. His books include *Contemporary Theory in International Relations* (1960), *The State of War* (1965), *Gulliver's Troubles* (1968), *Decline or Renewal: France since the 30s* (1974), *Primacy or World Order* (1978), *Duties Beyond Borders* (1981), *Dead Ends* (1983), and *Janus and Minerva* (1986). He is co-author of *The Fifth Republic at Twenty* (1981), *Living with Nuclear Weapons* (1983), *The Mitterrand Experiment* (1987), *The New European Community: Decisionmaking and Institutional Change* (1991), and *After the Cold War* (1993). He is currently working, with Professor Michael Smith of the University of Virginia, on a book on ethics and international relations. He is also preparing a book on French nationalism, past and present.

Robert Keohane is Stanfield Professor of International Peace, Harvard University. He is the author of *After Hegemony: Cooperation and Discord in the World Political Economy* (1984) and (with Joseph S. Nye) of *Power and Interdependence; World Politics in Transition* (1977, 2nd edn 1988). His recent books include *International Institutions and State Power: Essays in International Relations Theory* (1989), and (with Gary King and Sidney Verba) *Designing Social Inquiry: Scientific Inference in Qualitative Research* (1994).

Hans Morgenthau was Albert A. Michelson Distinguished Service Professor of Political Science and Modern History as the University of Chicago, and Leonard Davis Distinguished Professor of Political Science at City College of the City University of New York. He is best known for his book *Politics Among Nations*. Among his many publications are *Scientific Man versus Power Politics, In Defence of the National Interest, Politics in the Twentieth Century,* and *A New Foreign Policy for the United States*.

J. Ann Tickner is Associate Professor of Political Science at the College of the Holy Cross. She is the author of *Self-Reliance Versus Power Politics: The American and Indian Experiences in Building Nation States* and *Gender in International Relations: Feminist Perspectives on Achieving Global Security*.

R.B.J. Walker teaches international relations and political theory at the University of Victoria, British Columbia. His most recent book is *Inside/Outside: International Relations Theory as Political Theory*. He is also the author of *One World, Many Worlds*, editor of *Culture, Ideology, and World Order*, and co-editor of *Towards a Just World Peace*.

Adam Watson is Professor Emeritus of International Affairs at the University of Virginia, and has been a British Ambassador and Assistant Under-Secretary of State, Chairman of the British Committee on the Theory of International Politics and Director General of the International Association for Cultural Freedom.

Alexander Wendt is Assistant Professor of Political Science at Yale University. He is interested in identity formation in world politics, and is currently writing a book entitled *Social Theory of International Politics*.

Martin Wight (1913–72) was a Scholar at Hertford College, Oxford, taught briefly at Haileybury, England, was a member of research teams at Nuffield College, Oxford and twice at the Institute of International Affairs, Chatham House, London. He was University Reader at the London School of Economics from 1949 to 1961, spent the academic year 1956–57 as Visiting Professor at Chicago University and as Dean of European Studies and Professor of History he worked at the newly founded University of Sussex from 1961 until his death. He was author of *The Development of the Legislative Council 1606–1945; Power Politics* (1946); *The Gold Coast Legislative Council* (1947); *Attitude to Africa* (with W. Arthur Lewis, Michael Scott and Colin Legum) (1951); *British Colonial Constitutions* 1947 (1952); *Diplomatic Investigations* (edited and contributed to with Herbert Butterfield) (1966); *Systems of States* (edited by Hedley Bull); *Power Politics* (edited by Hedley Bull and Carsten Holbraad) (1978); and *International Theory: The Three Traditions* (edited by Gabriele Wight and Brian Porter) (1991).

1 Introduction: Critical Investigations
James Der Derian

> Everyone is a Realist nowadays, and the term in this sense
> needs no argument.
> (Martin Wight, *International Theory*)

Realism. Historical, social, philosophical, political, economic,
artistic, cinematic, literary, legal realism. Machiavellian,
Hobbesian, Rousseauian, Hegelian, Weberian, Kissingerian
realism. Optimist, pessimist, fatalist realism. Naive, vulgar,
magical realism. Technical, practical, empirical realism.
Classical and scientific realism. Structural, structurationist,
poststructuralist realism. Minimalist, maximalist, fundamentalist, potentialist realism. Positivist, post-positivist, liberal,
neoliberal institutionalist, radical, radical interpretivist
realism. Critical, nuclear, epistemic realism. Sur-, super-,
photo-, anti-, neo-, post-realism. And now on your computer screens and supermarket tabloid racks, hyper-realism.

Clearly, realism is protean in form, eclectic in style. Yet
in the discipline of International Relations the meaning of
realism has more often than not been presented as uniform,
self-evident and transparent – even by those critics in debates great and not-so-great who have questioned its historical relevance, political function, or heuristic value.[1] Cast
from idealism's failure to stop Hitlerism, congealed by the
bipolar exigencies of the Cold War, tempered by a disciplinary scholasticism, modern IR realism for something short
of a *longue durée* came in one shape only, the standardized
'traditional'. True, a made-in-American alloy, 'neorealism',
bearing the insignia of progress, parsimony, and microeconomic method, emerged from the theory doldrums of
the 1970s. Nonetheless, when measured against this opening backdrop of a multiplicity of realisms, the purported
differences within and between realism and neorealism in
IR, for which so much ink and not a few drops of figurative

1

blood have been spilled, appear as so much hair-splitting. Indeed, when measured against the amount of literal blood-letting that has been done in realism's name, the debate over the differences seems obscenely academic.

So why yet another book on realism? Arguments could be made that there still exist gaps in our knowledge of the subject, or that there are always some new phenomena or events against which the claims of realism must be tested. These arguments, made in the service of a research program or a particular problematic of realism, are certainly sound and often persuasive.[2] But I do not intend to rehearse or to rely on them. Instead, this collection does something new with something old, by reinvestigating realism through a dialogue between classical international theory and critical theoretical challenges to it.[3] It signals the arrival if not yet the acceptance of a broader range of plural realisms for a newly multipolar, multicultural International Relations.

However, were I to rank the reasons, the primary purpose of this collection is to honor ancestors and mentors. It begins where Herbert Butterfield, Martin Wight, Hedley Bull, Michael Howard, Adam Watson and other classical realists began, with their 'diplomatic investigations' into the limits and possibilities of international theory.[4] On a professional level this collection offers tribute to the 'English' school of realism (so-called, in spite of the odd South African and Australian in its ranks), by providing access to seminal essays that have long been out of print yet continue to exercise a profound influence on the field.[5] On a more particular and personal level, it seeks to repay an intellectual debt to Hedley Bull.

However, one of the more valuable things I learned from Bull was not to allow excessive debt to inhibit new and possibly risky undertakings. Hence the strategy to couple classical with critical investigations, in order to call into question the natural hegemony of traditional realism. The intent is to reopen the dossier, out of the suspicion that the full story of realism can not be told without an understanding of the philosophy as well as politics of representation that imbrue every powerful discourse in IR. This is not a call to check the papers of specific realists; I leave that to the self-appointed guardians of the discipline. Rather it is to investigate the manner and meaning of the construction of a collective identity, of an international theory with traditional realism at the core against which peripheral theoretical differences were to be constituted.

To be sure, these particular thinkers at different times and in different writings displayed a range of interests and beliefs, assisted by an erudite grasp of history, that traveled widely and deeply across the theory spectrum. Indeed, a small cottage-industry quickly sprung up, seeking to place each of them like a peg in a hole somewhere in – or more frequently, somewhere in between – Wight's famous triad of realist, rationalist, and revolutionist traditions. However, Wight's own statement on the subject, taken from the conclusion to his lecture course at LSE on the three traditions, attests to a restlessness of mind and theory that defies all efforts to put them to a final rest:

> I find my own position shifting round the circle. You will have guessed that my prejudices are Rationalist, but I find I have become more Rationalist and less Realist through rethinking this question during the course of giving these lectures. If I said Rationalism was a civilizing factor, Revolutionism a vitalizing factor, and Realism a controlling disciplinary factor in international politics, you might think I was playing with words, but I hope I have shown that there is more substance to international theory than that.[6]

It should be equally obvious that the Martin Wight of his classic 68-page pamphlet *Power Politics* (1946) is not the same Wight of *Diplomatic Investigations* (1966); nor the Hedley Bull of *The Control of the Arms Race* (1961) the Bull of *Justice in International Relations* (1983). Perhaps it is simply the case in IR that good Machiavellians grow up to become better Grotians. And if one adds a gendered, Oedipal explanation to the mix, then critical investigations are also generational in nature – and perhaps patricidal in execution.

But if we are to focus on what these thinkers held in common, and hold for the final Chapter 14 the matter of distinctions and discontinuities, then the realist tag sticks better than most. Or as Martin Wight somewhat presumptuously put it, 'Everyone is a Realist nowadays, and the term in this sense needs no argument.[7] This is true, to the extent that they (and even most of their contemporary critics) accepted (some explicitly, others implicitly) the centrality of the sovereign state, the pervasiveness of power, the inevitability of conflict, and the over-arching problem of anarchy in world politics. And although they investigated and appreciated mediating and alternative traditions informed by the work of international jurists like Grotius, Vattel, and Oppenheim, and cosmopolitan philosophers like Augustine, Kant, and Marx, they re-presented them from realist positions.[8] Most importantly, they all were philosophical realists, to the extent that they believed theory to reflect 'things as they really are.' Hence, from the beginning their conception of international theory helped to reconstruct a modern form of realism at – and *as* – the center of International Relations.

This is one reason to pair international theory and critical investigations, because – and this might grate on the ear of purists in either camp – of their joint recognition that there is no natural center to international relations. Each recognizes that international societies, institutions, and regimes have been historically constructed – and often tragically deconstructed – out of the desire for order and the fear of anarchy. Where they differ is the degree to which anarchy is conceived as the threat and order as the task; or put less charitably, whether the will to order produces the very effect of anarchy.

A critical investigation of international theory does not aim to resolve these differences. At best, the dialogical form can help us to negotiate the ambiguities, paradoxes, and yes, sometimes hostilities of disparities that seem incompatible, at times even incommensurable. The task is not simple, for international theory in its earliest coinage was decidedly two-faced about dialogue. Like Janus, international theory guarded with deserved (yet ultimately damaging) prestige the portals of International Relations by a forward/backward gaze, admitting only the history that confirmed its own powers of narration; like the ideal diplomat, it sang the virtues of compromise and synthesis, and consecrated the *via media* by an artful depiction of what hazards lie at the polar extremes; and like true statesmen, it tempered its harder, Machiavellian edges by a Grotian rhetoric (in the positive, constructive sense) of order built upon rational intercourse, institutional cooperation, and legal mediation. But the paramount obstacle to critical investigation lies in the relationship of international theory to the *ultima ratio* of realism. For the most part (Wight's early pacifism comes to mind here as an exception), international theory helped realism maintain its value as the common currency of international relations because it did not trouble the 'naturalness' of its relationship to violence. To accept realism, as international theory did, as the reflection rather than construction of world politics, was to accept things as they were: the necessitous conditions of anarchy and (at least in its early English form) of evil; the permanence of alienation and the sanction to use force against it; and the universality of a will to power that seduced statesmen and would-be advisers to the prince. As a result, international theory all too often followed the path of least ethical resistance toward fatalism, dogmatism, and cynicism.

This is not to beg the question that all politicians and scholars now face: will a critical investigation of international theory make the next generation 'better off' than the last? The opening contentious essay-question by Martin Wight in Chapter 2, 'Why is there no International Theory?,' anticipated this bellwether question. The title conveys his belief that international theory is in a sorry state of recurrence and repetition because of the absence of the kind of sovereignty and domestic order which made political theory possible.[9] Hence, why there is no *body* of international theory (the title of an early draft of the essay) is positively adduced for the un-progressive, non-cumulative, necessarily speculative nature of the beast.[10]

If it amounts to anything, a critical investigation is an attempt 30 years on to render a serious response to Wight's question. It does not provide a definitive answer, but it does try to set up through the structure of a series of trialogues (with apologies to Jesse Jackson and the guardians of the English language) the opportunity for a learned continuation of the conversation. Admittedly, a trialogue is duller than Hedley Bull's polemical defense of international theory as a classical approach, or Richard Ashley's forceful sweeping of neorealism into the error-bin of history.[11] But by maintaining an equidistance from an authoritative answer or an ultimate destination for international theory, a trialogue can give us a sense of where we have been as well as how much further we have to go.

In other words, this investigation does not aim like a beeline towards the truth of realism, or move along one track towards a model solution to the problems of world politics. It offers a triangulation for an international theory that has begun to travel to foreign, uncharted lands. It provides, I hope, a way to assess and appreciate progress not by the linear path or homogeneous company some might wish it to keep, but by its relationship to the differences, discontinuities, and contingencies that make up world politics. Perhaps then we will be able to newly judge realism, not by the accuracy of its reflection but by the ethics of its construction of the world.

This is born out by the core texts of international theory, two of which (Chapters 2 and 5), written by Martin Wight and Hedley Bull, appear in this collection, respectively opening Parts I and II. They are the products of early meetings of the British Committee on the Theory of International Politics. Founded by a small group of IR scholars, historians, and diplomats, and funded by the Rockefeller Foundation, this group asked the 'big questions' of International Relations over a 25-year period (1959–1984).[12] In 1966, some of its early presentations were published in *Diplomatic Investigations*, the highly influential collection edited by Butterfield and Wight. The first two essays of *Diplomatic Investigations*, 'Why is there no International Theory?' by Wight, and 'Society and Anarchy in International Relations' by Bull, provide an early pass at many of the tenets that came to make up the classical tradition in international theory, that is, a combination of historical inquiry, philosophical speculation, and normative (often legal) theory. These essays set out the key issues of world politics that form the major part divisions of this volume: theory and tradition, anarchy and sovereignty, discipline and power, reason and history.[13]

Wight and Bull have been selected not just for the foundation of classical thinking which they provide, but for their speculative and self-reflexive attitudes which allow for supplementary readings. There is nothing parsimonious or hermetic about these texts. Hence, Hans Morgenthau is able to use a review article of Wight, 'The Intellectual and Political Functions of Theory' (Chapter 3), to make some piercing criticisms of the 'abstract', 'unhistorical', and 'apolitical' nature of IR theory in the United States as it made the turn toward behavioralism in the 1960s. The result is a surprisingly ethical defense of political realism. Similarly, J. Ann Tickner is able to take advantage of this ethico-political opening in Morgenthau, to challenge and supplement it with a feminist critique (Chapter 4) which reveals the decidedly *non*-universal and *non*-objective nature of the gendered and socially constructed principles of political realism.

Their central concerns and constructions of theory and tradition form the launch-point for a dialogue with contemporary critical thinkers. It will become apparent that some of these thinkers wish to redeem and recover, others to repudiate and reject classical realism. They all, however, respect its power and willingness to look at the world, in Richard Ashley's words, as 'an open-ended, always hazardous contest among plural cultural possibilities, of which the domestic experience of modern culture is surely only one.'[14] Ashley in Chapter 6 takes Bull seriously by returning to and then dismantling 'the fact of anarchy' and the authoritative myth of the 'domestic analogy' which enforces it. Alexander Wendt in Chapter 7 offers a North American berth for the transatlantic voyage of the anarchy problematic, interpellating all sides of the contemporary debates between realists and liberals, rationalist and reflectivists, modern and post-modern constructivists with the arduously substantiated challenge that 'anarchy is what states make of it.'

These theoretical provocations are followed in Part III by a series of essays by Hedley Bull, Stanley Hoffmann, and Hayward Alker and Thomas Biersteker (Chapters 8–10) on the power and the state of the discipline of IR. From differing perspectives they offer an historical review of modern IR theory as well as a sociological explanation for the persistence of realist theory. The essays were chosen not just for their comprehensive grasp of the field, but for their forceful arguments about the strengths and shortcomings of the various historical challenges to realism, like the emergence of idealist, behavioralist, and radical/marxist approaches. These are scholars who have thought long and hard about the condition of the discipline, who have attained the stature and security to tell it like it is, and who have the vision and courage to say just how difficult it will be to make it better.

Part IV, on 'Reason and History', follows up on the theme of how disciplinary practices and pressures shape theoretical inquiry in IR, but takes the debate a step further to include important new questions of epistemology, ontology, and morality. Chapter 11, by Robert Keohane, advocates the pursuit of knowledge and progress in IR through a rationalist approach, and acknowledges the emergence of a 'reflectivist' approach which has been quick to critique others but slow to develop its own research programs. Rob Walker, in Chapter 12, responds to the methodological questions raised by Keohane, but goes on to discuss the ethical and political issues that emerge when questions of identity are brought into international theory. This missing element of ontology is picked up by Jean Bethke Elshtain in Chapter 13, who gives it a feminist twist and inserts it with subversive effect into the major debates in IR about rationality and equality, power and sovereignty, violence and justice.

The final chapter in Part V (Chapter 14) is not a conclusion but a reopening of the debate to include poststructuralist questions about realism that have been neglected in IR – to the detriment, I believe, of international theory.

In sum, the aim of this collection is not to solve problems, synthesize opposites, or let a hundred weeds flourish – as positivistic, dialectic, or eclectic approaches might promote – but to reinvestigate the beginnings as well as the legacy of international theory through a dialogue with critical interpretations. It is up to the reader to decide if this represents a de-centering, a deconstruction, or merely a de-evolution of international theory.

I should leave it at that, but I cannot leave unspoken what usually, in the name of objectivity and professionalism, is. Obviously my choice of essays reflects my own training, intellectual attitudes, and political beliefs. But before all else I believe that international theory only progresses when voices of authority are engaged by voices that go against the grain. Some might see this to be the ruin of a good finish, others the scar of a new branch of knowledge. But for those who still prefer their international theory to come in straight planks, I end this introduction (and belabored metaphor) with Isaiah Berlin misquoting Immanuel Kant: 'Out of the crooked timber of humanity no straight thing was ever made.'[15]

Notes

1. Some of the more notable signposts of this debate include: Reinhold Neibuhr, *Moral Man and Immoral Society: A Study in Ethics and Politics* (New York: Scribner's, 1932); E. H. Carr, *The Twenty Years' Crisis: 1919–1939* (London: Macmillan, 1939); Hans Morgenthau, *Politics Among Nations: The Struggle for Power and Peace* (New York: Knopf, 1948); John Herz, *Political Realism and Political Idealism* (Chicago: University of Chicago Press: 1951); H. Bull, 'International Theory: the Case for a Classical Approach,' *World Politics* (April 1966), pp. 361–377; and J. David Singer, 'The Incompleat Theorist: Insight Without Evidence,' *Contending Approaches to International Politics* (Princeton: Princeton University Press, 1969), pp. 63–86.

   Two narrative reviews of the seminal figures of realism offer more insights than most analytical accounts: Michael J. Smith, *Realist Thought from Weber to Kissinger* (Baton Rouge: Louisiana State University Press, 1986); and Joel H. Rosenthal, *Righteous Realists: Political Realism, Responsible Power, and American Culture in the Nuclear Age* (Baton Rouge: Louisiana State University Press, 1991).

   For a range of 'post-realist' perspectives see: Richard Ashley, 'Political realism and human interests,' *International Studies Quarterly*, 25, pp. 204–236, and 'The Poverty of Neo-Realism,' *International Organization* (Spring 1984), pp. 225–286; R. B. J. Walker, 'Realism, Change, and International Political Theory,' *International Studies Quarterly* (March 1987), pp. 65–86; Anders Stephanson, *Kennan and the Art of Foreign Policy* (Cambridge, MA: Harvard University Press, 1989); Friedrich Kratochwil, *Rules, Norms and Decisions: On the Conditions of Practical and Legal Reasoning in International Relations and Domestic Affairs* (Cambridge: Cambridge University Press, 1991); J. Ann Tickner, *Gender in International Relations* (New York: Columbia University Press, 1992); David Campbell, *Writing Security* (Minneapolis, MN: Minnesota University Press, 1992); Roger Epp, 'Power Politics and the Civitas Terrena: The Augustinian Sources of Anglo–American Thought in International Relations,'

Ph.D. dissertation (Kingston, Ontario: Queen's University, June 1990); Costas Constantinou, '*Theorias*: Reflections on the Question Concerning Diplomacy,' Ph.D. dissertation (Lancaster, England: University of Lancaster, 1993).

To forestall the assumption of a coherent school of 'Realism' in International Relations – and admittedly, for expository convenience – I use the lower case 'realism' throughout this essay to signify its many and sometimes conflicting meanings. Only when the context of the argument fails to give a sufficient understanding of which realism is being discussed, I resort to the upper case 'Realism' to refer to a putative school of thought in IR.

2. For a sample of internal critiques, see Robert Keohane, 'Realism, Neorealism, and the Study of World Politics,' *Neorealism and its Critics*, pp. 1–26; and Barry Buzan, Charles Jones, and Richard Little, *The Logic of Anarchy: Neorealism to Structural Realism* (New York: Columbia University Press, 1993). For a cutting attack on realism's failure to comprehend let alone predict the end of the cold war – and its blithe refusal to assess the significance of its incomprehension – see Richard Falk's review of *Governance without Government: Order and Change in World Politics*, James Rosenau and Ernst-Otto Czempiel (eds.) (New York: Cambridge University Press, 1992), in *American Political Science Review*, 87 (2) (June 1993), pp. 544–545.

3. For those who will go no further without a definition, 'international theory' is, according to lectures presented by Wight and Bull, respectively, 'the political philosophy of international relations'; and 'the leading ideas that have governed and do govern our thinking about International Relations or World Politics ... how we relate them to their historical context and examine their truth and their bearing on our present political concerns, in relation to past practice and to present practice.' See Martin Wight, *International Theory: The Three Traditions*, Gabriele Wight and Brian Porter (eds.) (Leicester and London: Leicester University Press, 1991), p. 1; and Hedley Bull, lecture notes to *Theory and Practice of International Relations 1648–1789*.

4. See *Diplomatic Investigations*, Herbert Butterfield and Martin Wight (eds.) (London: George Allen & Unwin, 1966); Hedley Bull, *The Anarchical Society: A Study of Order in World Politics* (New York: Columbia University Press, 1977); Michael Howard, *The Causes of War* (Cambridge, MA: Harvard University Press, 1983); Adam Watson, *The Evolution of International Society: A comparative historical analysis* (New York: Routledge, 1992). For those seeking distinctions and differences within the group, and within the individuals who made it up, I recommend the essays edited by J. D. B. Miller and R. J. Vincent, *Order and Violence: Hedley Bull and International Relations* (Oxford: Clarendon Press, 1990).

5. On the meta-question which this introduction ducks, of the defects, merits, and even the existence of the 'English School' of IR, see Roy E. Jones, 'The English school of international relations,'

Review of International Studies, 7 (1981), pp. 1–12; Hidemi Suganami, 'The Structure of Institutionalism: an anatomy of British mainstream international relations,' *International Relations,* 7 (1983); Sheila Grader, 'The English school of international relations: evidence and evaluation,' *Review of International Studies,* 14 (1988), pp. 29–44; N. J. Rengger, 'Serpents and Doves in Classical International Theory,' *Millennium Journal of International Studies* 17 (2) (Summer 1988), pp. 215–226; and the Special Issue on 'Beyond International Society,' *Millennium Journal of International Studies,* 21 (3) (Winter 1992).

6. Martin Wight, *International Theory: The Three Traditions,* Gabriele Wight and Brian Porter (eds.) (Leicester and London: Leicester University Press, 1991), p. 268.

7. Wight, *International Theory,* p. 15.

8. On the philosophical meanings of realism, see Chapter 14.

9. See Martin Wight's Chapter 2 in this collection, 'Why is there no International Theory?', pp. 15–35.

10. This echoes Hedley Bull's interpretation from his 'Martin Wight and the theory of international relations,' *British Journal of International Studies,* 2 (1976), pp. 101–116; reprinted in Wight, *International Theory,* pp. ix–xxiii.

11. See Hedley Bull, 'International Theory: The Case for a Classical Approach;' and Richard Ashley, 'The Poverty of Neorealism.' For what I have found to be the best – and most eloquent – defense of dialogue over against polemic, see M. Foucault, 'Polemics, Politics, Problemizations,' *The Foucault Reader,* Paul Rabinow (ed.) (New York: Pantheon, 1984), pp. 381–383.

12. For a discussion – as well as a continuation – of the work of the British Committee, see Hedley Bull, 'Martin Wight and the Theory of International Relations,' *British Journal of International Studies* (July 1976), and his introductions to Martin Wight, *Systems of States,* Hedley Bull (ed.) (Leicester: Leicester University Press, 1977), and Martin Wight, *Power Politics,* Hedley Bull and Carsten Holbraad (eds.) (Harmondsworth: Penguin, 1979); Adam Watson, *The Evolution of International Society;* and Roger Epp, 'Power Politics and the Civitas Terrena: The Augustinian Sources of Anglo-American Thought in International Relations.'

13. On the making of a tradition in International Relations, see James Der Derian, 'Introducing Philosophical Traditions in International Relations,' *Millennium Journal of International Studies,* 17 (2) (Summer 1988), pp. 189–193.

14. Richard Ashley's Chapter 6, 'The Powers of Anarchy: Theory, Sovereignty, and the Domestication of Global Life', p. 98.

15. Isaiah Berlin, *The Crooked Timber of Humanity* (New York: Vintage, 1992), p. vii.

Part I
Theory and
Tradition

2 Why is There No International Theory? (1966)*
Martin Wight

'Political theory' is a phrase that in general requires no explanation. It is used here to denote speculation about the state, which is its traditional meaning from Plato onwards. On the other hand, the phrase 'international theory' does require explanation. At first hearing, it is likely to be taken as meaning either the methodology of the study of international relations, or some conceptual system which offers a unified explanation of international phenomena – 'the theory of international relations.' In this paper neither of these is intended. By 'international theory' is meant a tradition of speculation about relations between states, a tradition imagined as the twin of speculation about the state to which the name 'political theory' is appropriated. And international theory in this sense does not, at first sight, exist.

Some qualification, of course, is needed. There are many theoretical writings about international relations; some of them bear names as eminent as Machiavelli or Kant; and in the twentieth century they have become a flood.[1] Yet it is difficult to say that any of them has the status of a political classic. This is a problem that besets the teacher of International Relations if he conceives of International Relations as a twin subject, distinct from but parallel with, the subject commonly known as Political Science or Government. Political Science has its tensions and internecine conflicts, to be sure, but it is in some sense held together by Political Theory, or as it is sometimes called the History of Political Ideas. The student of Government, however

* H. Butterfield and M. Wight (eds), *Diplomatic Investigations* (London: George Allen & Unwin), pp. 17–34.

else he may be misled, is given an introduction to the tradition of speculation and the body of writings about the state from Plato to Laski. But the student of International Relations cannot, it seems, be similarly directed to classics in his branch of politics, of the stature of Aristotle or Hobbes or Locke or Rousseau. Is it because they do not exist?

The question may be put in a different way. The teacher of International Relations is often given the impression that his subject sprang fully-armed from the head of David Davies or of Sir Montague Burton. But if he seeks to trace it further back, behind the memorable Endowment whereby Andrew Carnegie left ten million dollars for 'the speedy abolition of war between the so-called civilized nations' (to be applied when this end was achieved to other social and educational purposes), he finds himself involved in obscurity. In the nineteenth century and earlier, there is no succession of first-rank books about the states-system and diplomacy like the succession of political classics from Bodin to Mill. What international theory, then, was there before 1914? And if there was any, is it worth rediscovering?

One answer to the question is plain. If political theory is the tradition of speculation about the state, then international theory may be supposed to be a tradition of speculation about the society of states, or the family of nations, or the international community. And speculation of this kind was formerly comprehended under International Law. The public law of Europe in the eighteenth century has been described as 'an amalgam of formulae, jurisprudence, political speculation and recorded practice.'[2] (Indeed, the very speculative breadth of international lawyers did something to create their reputation as futile metaphysicians among practical men, even after the influence of positivism disciplined them to neglect metalegal questions.) When Tocqueville gave his presidential address to the Académie des Sciences Morales et Politiques in 1852, he made one of the earliest attempts to place the study of international relations among the political and social sciences. He distinguished on the one side the study of the rights of society and of the individual, what laws are appropriate to particular societies, what forms of government to particular circumstances, citing as examples the names of Plato, Aristotle, Machiavelli, Montesquieu, Rousseau. He continued:

> D'autres essayent le même travail à l'égard de cette société des nations où chaque peuple est un citoyen, société toujours un peu barbare, même dans les siècles les plus civilisés, quelque effort que l'on fasse pour adoucit et régler les rapports de ceux qui la composent. Ils ont découvert et indiqué quel était, en dehors des traités particuliers, le droit international. C'est l'oeuvre de Grotius et de Puffendorf.[3]

It is, he says, to the classical international lawyers that we must look in the first place for any body of international theory before the twentieth century.[4]

It is worth asking where else international theory is found. We might answer in four kinds of writing:

(a) Those whom Nys called the irenists – Erasmus, Sully, Campanella, Crucé, Penn, the Abbé de St. Pierre, and Pierre-André Gargaz. When Melian Stawell wrote a book on *The Growth of International Thought* for the Home University Library, writers of this kind provided her central line of progress from the Truce of God to the Kellogg Pact. But it is hard to consider them as other than the curiosities of political literature. They are not rich in ideas; the best of them grope with the problem of how to secure common action between sovereign states, and thus gain a mention in the prehistory of the League of Nations.[5]

(b) Those whom it is convenient to call the Machiavellians: the succession of writers on *raison d'état* of whom Meinecke is the great interpreter. In a footnote about the followers of Botero, Meinecke says, 'There are real catacombs of forgotten literature here by mediocrities.'[6] He does not so mean it, but one suspects that the phrase will cover all the writers in his own book apart from those who are notable in another sphere, whether as statesmen, like Frederick, or as philosophers, like Hegel, or as historians, like Ranke and Treitschke. Botero and Boccalini, Henri de Rohan and Gabriel Neudé, Courtilz de Sandras and Rousset: can we see in them forgotten or potential classics? One difficulty in answering is that they are inaccessible except to the scholar, and this perhaps itself conveys the answer.

(c) The *parerga* of political philosophers, philosophers and historians. As examples of this kind might be named Hume's Essay on 'The Balance of Power,' Rousseau's *Project of Perpetual Peace*, Bentham's *Plan for an Universal Peace*, Burke's *Thoughts on French Affairs* and *Letters on a Regicide Peace*, Ranke's essay on the Great Powers, and J. S. Mill's essay on the law of nations. Apart from the classical international lawyers, these are the most rewarding source in the quest for international theory. Is it more interesting that so many great minds have been drawn, at the margin of their activities, to consider basic problems of international politics, or that so few great minds have been drawn to make these problems their central interest? The only political philosopher who has turned wholly from political theory to international theory is Burke. The only political philosopher of whom it is possible to argue whether his principal interest was not in the relations between states rather than – or even more than – the state itself, is Machiavelli. With him, the foreign and domestic conditions for the establishment and maintenance of state power are not distinguished systematically; and this alone – without other reasons – would have justified his being annexed, by detractors and admirers alike, as the tutelary hero of International Relations. In this class, again, it would be necessary to place such miscellaneous political writers as Bolingbroke, whose *Letters on the Study and Use of History* contain a primitive philosophy of international politics, or Mably, whose *Principes des Négociations* is one of the more enduring pieces of his large output, or the Gentz of *Fragments upon the Balance of Power*.

(d) The speeches, despatches, memoirs and essays of statesmen and diplomatists. To illustrate speeches and despatches as a source of international theory, one might cite the authority of Canning over a generation of British foreign policy – for instance, the classic despatch of 1823 containing his doctrine of guarantees. To illustrate memoirs, Bismarck's *Gedanken und Erinnerungen*, perhaps the supreme example. To illustrate essays, Lord Salisbury's early essays on foreign affairs in the *Quarterly Review*.

It is clear, therefore, that international theory, or what

there is of it, is scattered, unsystematic, and mostly inaccessible to the layman. Moreover, it is largely repellent and intractable in form. Grotius has to be read at large to be understood; the only possible extract is the Prolegomena, which gives a pallid notion of whether or why he deserves his reputation. Students cannot be expected to tackle Pufendorf's *De jure naturae et gentium libri octo,* nor even his *De officio hominis et civis juxta legem naturalem libri duo.* There is little intellectual nourishment in the Abbé de St. Pierre, or Hume on the balance of power; and Bismarck's international theory has to be distilled with care from the historical falsehoods in which it is seductively enclosed.

Yet these are external matters. I believe it can be argued that international theory is marked, not only by paucity but also by intellectual and moral poverty. For this we must look to internal reasons. The most obvious are, first, the intellectual prejudice imposed by the sovereign state, and secondly, the belief in progress.

Since the sixteenth century, international society has been so organized that no individuals except sovereign princes can be members of it, and these only in their representative capacity. All other individuals have had to be subjects or citizens of sovereign states. By a famous paradox of international law, the only persons emancipated from this necessity are pirates, by virtue of being *hostes humani generis.* Erasmus could still wander about Europe without bothering himself where his ultimate temporal allegiance was due. Scaliger and Casaubon already learned, two and three generations later, that the only safe way to be citizens of the intellectual world was to exchange a disagreeable allegiance for one less disagreeable. The main difference in the age of Einstein and Thomas Mann has been that change of allegiance has become impossible for an increasingly large proportion of the human race. Even Mr. Hammarskjöld, we must suppose, will retire to write his memoirs as a Swedish citizen under the shelter of the world's fourth air force.[7] Even the Pope, to take the supreme instance, believed his position in international society anomalous and insecure until he had re-established himself as sovereign of a territorial state.

The principle that every individual requires the protection

of a state, which represents him in the international community, is a juristic expression of the belief in the sovereign state as the consummation of political experience and activity which has marked Western political thought since the Renaissance. That belief has absorbed almost all the intellectual energy devoted to political study. It has become natural to think of international politics as the untidy fringe of domestic politics (as Baldwin thought of them in Cabinet), and to see international theory in the manner of the political theory textbooks, as an additional chapter which can be omitted by all save the interested student. The masterpiece of international politics is the system of the balance of power, as it operated from the time of Elizabeth down to that of Bismarck; but if we ask why the balance of power has inspired no great political writer to analysis and reflection, the answer surely is that it has flourished with the flourishing of the modern state, and has been seen as a means to that end. Even today, when circumstances have made the study of international relations fashionable, they are often still thought of and even taught as 'foreign affairs' or 'problems of foreign policy' (meaning our foreign policy, not Nasser's or Khrushchev's), and the world's present predicament will be described in some such parochial phrase as 'the crisis of the modern state.' Professor Morgenthau, who has had a great influence among international relationists in the United States since 1945, has consistently maintained that 'a theory of international politics must be focused on the concept of the national interest.'[8] Practical problems of international politics are often described in terms of building a bigger and better state – a European Union or an Atlantic Community or an Arab Union, without seeing that such an achievement would leave the problems of inter-state politics precisely where they were. Few political thinkers have made it their business to study the states-system, the diplomatic community *itself.*

It might be a good argument for subordinating international theory to political theory, to maintain that the division of international society into separate states is a temporary historical phase, emerging out of the medieval unity (however this be characterized) and destined to be replaced by a world state. In his inaugural lecture at Ox-

ford, Zimmern remarked on the historical conditions that
make International Relations a topical subject in place of
International Government.[9] And it may seem one of the
weaknesses of the concluding volumes of Toynbee's *Study
of History*, that he resists the logic of his own analysis and
supposes that Western civilization will defy all his precedents
by achieving a stable international anarchy instead of a
universal empire. But this is how international theorists have
usually talked. They have seen the maintenance of the states-
system as the condition for the continuance of the existing
state – a small-scale field of political theory. They have not
been attracted by the possibility of maximizing the field of
political theory through establishing a world state. None
of the successive attempts by a single Great Power to achieve
international hegemony has produced any notable international (or political) theory. 'The monarchy of the World'
was apparently a phrase used by Spanish diplomats under
Philip II, but the idea was never embodied in a serious
treatist.[10] Still less was any such thing inspired by Louis XIV
or Napoleon.

Formal international theory has traditionally resisted the
case for a world state. At the very outset, Vitoria uncon-
sciously took over Dante's conception of *universalis civilitas
humani generis*, and strengthened it into an affirmation that
mankind constitutes a legal community, but he repudiated
the Dantean corollary of a universal empire,[11] Grotius and
Pufendorf did the same, with the argument that a world
empire would be too large to be efficient.[12] For seventeenth-
century writers this was a reasonable assumption: they saw
the Spanish monarchy manifestly incapable of maintaining
its intercontinental responsibilities, the Empire disintegrat-
ing, the French and English monarchies having to undergo
fundamental reconstruction. In the eighteenth century, when
the necessity of the balance of power has become a commonplace of pamphlet literature, a different and perhaps
a contrary argument appears – that a world state might be
so efficient as to be intolerable. For Kant as for Gibbon the
division of mankind into many states is the guarantee of
freedom; not only for states themselves, through the balance of power, but for individuals also, for whom it means
the possibility of foreign asylum.[13] After the middle of the

nineteenth century American experience provides a new argument against a super-state; that it would simply transform the admitted evil of international war into civil war, so that the advantage would be nil. 'Even if it were possible to leap over so many intermediate stages, and to set up a world government,' said Sir Llewellyn Woodward recently, 'the political result might be to substitute civil war for international war or, on the other hand, to surrender our existing safeguards of public and private liberty to a centralized executive authority of unparalleled and irresistible strength.'[14] Hence an almost uniform assumption among international theorists up to 1914 that the structure of international society is unalterable and the division of the world into sovereign states is necessary and natural. Nor is it unfair to see the League and the United Nations as the expression of a belief that it may be possible to secure the benefits of a world state without the inconveniences of instituting and maintaining it. If in the twentieth century crude doctrines of world imperialism have become influential is it not partly because they have found a vacuum in international theory to fill? One of the very few reasoned arguments for a world state was put forward by Middleton Murry, when America had the atomic monopoly. He drew a different moral from the American Civil War.

> There is a manifest analogy between the situation which forced Lincoln's reluctant but unshakable decision to compel the Southern states to remain in the Union, and the situation today. A modern Lincoln would apply himself to making the issue crystal-clear to his fellow-countrymen, and if he could find means, to the Russian people also. The issue is world-union or world-anarchy; world-union or world-slavery. The rulers of Russia, he would say, cannot be permitted to refuse world-union, and thereby to condemn the world to anarchy and slavery. If they will not consent, they must be compelled to come in.[15]

This is interesting, not only as an example of the union between pacifist convictions and what might be called a realist attitude to international politics; but also because the argument never had the slightest chance of being listened to by those to whom it was addressed.

The ascendancy of political theory over international theory
can be illustrated in another way. Since the society of states
came into recognizable existence in the sixteenth century,
the three most powerful influences on its development have
been the Reformation and Counter-Reformation, the French
Revolution, and the totalitarian revolutions of the twentieth
century. But none of these upheavals has produced any
notable body of international theory; each has written only
a chapter of political theory. To put it crudely, the Reformation and Counter-Reformation were concerned with Church
and state, the French Revolution with the state simply,
Communism and Fascism with the state and society. In the
end, all these revolutionaries found themselves operating
in international politics in a big way, but it requires wide
reading and considerable discrimination to elicit the principles or theories of international politics by which they
believed they were guided. The Jesuits are the exception:
for they had the old equipment of the supreme temporal
power to refashion. But what was Calvin's international
theory? In some of his sermons it is possible to discern a
conception of a *civitas maxima* whose absolute monarch is
God, with the princes of the earth as His lieutenants; but
it is a pale thing beside the vigorous intervention and subversion undertaken by his foreign policy in practice, whose
principles get a kind of formulation in the last part of the
Vindiciae contra Tyrannos. It is only when it begins to slide
into the casuistry of *raison d'état* that Calvinist international
theory acquires richness or subtlety, and then it ceases to
be distinctively Calvinist. It is even more difficult to find
any Jacobin international theory. The Rights of Man were
transformed into universal conquest without, it seems, any
theorizing more sophisticated or less negative than the statement by Genêt which Fox quoted in the House of Commons: 'I would throw Vattel and Grotius into the sea
whenever their principles interfere with my notions of the
rights of nations.'[16]
    The same may be said of Communism. It is a theory of
domestic society, a political theory, which since Russia after Lenin's death came to acquiesce for the time being in
remaining the only Socialist state in international society,
has been tugged and cut about to cover a much wider range

of political circumstances than it was designed for. Marx and Lenin saw the three principal contradictions of capitalism as, first, the struggle between proletariat and bourgeoisie in the advanced industrial states; secondly, the struggle between these imperialist states themselves, as exemplified by the First World War; thirdly, the struggle between the colonial masses and their alien exploiters. This was the hierarchy of importance that they gave to these three struggles, and it is a commonplace that the course of events has reversed the order, so that the struggle between proletariat and bourgeoisie in the Western world has almost ceased, and the struggle between the colonial peoples and their imperialist masters and former masters has become the main theme of international politics. According to Mr. Deutscher, it was Trotsky who first saw that this was happening, and who coined the phrase about the path to London and Paris lying through Calcutta and Peking.[17] Neither Marx, Lenin nor Stalin made any systematic contribution to international theory; Lenin's *Imperialism* comes nearest to such a thing, and this has little to say about international politics. The absence of Marxist international theory has a wider importance than making it difficult to recommend reading to an undergraduate who wants to study the principles of Communist foreign policy in the original sources. It creates the obscurity, so fruitful to the Communists themselves, about what these principles actually are: so that only an expert sovietologist can usefully discuss what Lenin really said (and where) about the inevitability of conflict between the socialist and capitalist camps, and how this doctrine has been revised by Malenkov and Khrushchev. Perhaps it is a misconception, however, to say that all these revolutionary political theories are primarily concerned with the state. It may be truer to see them as attempts to reconstitute that older political phenomenon, a universal church of true believers; and in the light of such an undertaking the realm of the diplomatic system and sovereign states and international law is necessarily irrelevant, transitory, trivial, and doomed to pass away. At the heart of Calvinism and Jacobinism there was something like the exaltation and impatience with international politics which Trotsky showed, when he defined his task on becoming the Soviet Republic's first Foreign Commissar: 'I shall publish a few revolutionary proclamations and then close shop.'[18]

And secondly, international politics differ from domestic politics in being less susceptible of a progressivist interpretation. In Western Europe, at least, national histories considered in isolation do show evidence of progress – even when, as in the case of Germany, they are marked by recurrent catastrophe. There has been growing social cohesion, growing interdependence among the people, growth of state power, increasing flexibility in its operation, increasing wealth and its better distribution, diffusion of culture among the masses, the softening of manners, perhaps the lessening of violence – everything that the Victorians believed was inevitable. If Sir Thomas More or Henry IV, let us say, were to return to England and France in 1960, it is not beyond plausibility that they would admit that their countries had moved domestically towards goals and along paths which they could approve. But if they contemplated the international scene, it is more likely that they would be struck by resemblances to what they remembered: a state-system apportioned between two Great Powers each with its associates and satellites, smaller Powers improving their position by playing off one side against the other, universal doctrines contending against local patriotism, the duty of intervention overriding the right of independence, the empty professions of peaceful purpose and common interest, the general preference for going down to defeat fighting rather than consenting to unresisted subjugation. The stage would have become much wider, the actors fewer, their weapons more alarming, but the play would be the same old melodrama. International politics is the realm of recurrence and repetition; it is the field in which political action is most regularly necessitous. This, I take it, is what Burke means when he says that because commonwealths are not physical but moral essences, the internal causes which affect their fortunes 'are infinitely uncertain and much more obscure, and much more difficult to trace, than the foreign causes that tend to raise, to depress, and sometimes to overwhelm a community.'[19]

If this is indeed the character of international politics, it is incompatible with progressivist theory. Therefore international theory that remains true to diplomatic experience will be at a discount in an age when the belief in progress is prevalent. This may be illustrated by the penetrating observations upon international politics that are to be found scattered about in earlier political writers. Here is an eighteenth-century description of the competition in armaments:

Une maladie nouvelle s'est répandue en Europe; elle a saisi nos princes, et leur fait entretenir un nombre désordonné de troupes. Elle a ses redoublements, et elle devient nécessairement contagieuse; car, sitôt qu'un Etat augmente ce qu'il appelle ses troupes, les autres soudain augmentent les leurs: de façon qu'on ne gagne rien par là que la ruine commune. Chaque monarque tient sur pied toutes les armées qu'il pourroit avoir si ses peuples étoient en danger d'être exterminés; et on nomme paix cet état d'effort de tous contre tous. (Il est vrai que c'est cet état d'effort qui maintient principalement l'équilibre, parce qu'il éreinte les grandes puissances.) Aussi l'Europe est-elle si ruinée, que les particuliers qui seroient dans la situation où sont les trois puissances de cette partie du monde les plus opulentes, n'auroient pas de quoi vivre. Nous sommes pauvres avec les richesses et le commerce de tout l'univers; et bientôt, à force d'avoir des soldats, nour n'aurons plus que des soldats, et nous serons comme les Tartares.[20]

In its exaggeration as well as its perception, this passage written during the War of the Austrian Succession has a timeless quality when read during the Cold War. One seeks to separate the truth from the changing circumstances, asking how far industrialism may have altered the economic burden of armaments, and so on. But no sooner is one in the posture of recognizing a perennial truth in Montesquieu's words, than all one's progressivist instincts revolt. By now, we say, we have seen the arms race run its full cycle sufficiently often to know what it means; our protest is born of knowledge and experience and not, like his, of intuition alone; because our knowledge is greater our strength to break the circle is greater; and to accept Montesquieu's words as a description of our own predicament would be treason to mankind, because it implies the fatalistic doctrine that what has been will be.

In progressivist international theories, the conviction usually precedes the evidence. And when the conviction is analyzed or disintegrates, one is apt to find at the centre of it what might be called the argument from desperation. This is already used by Kant, who first channelled the doctrine of progress into international theory through his *Eternal Peace*. Having established the three definite articles of an eternal peace, he argues that such a peace is guaranteed by Nature herself, who wills that we should do what reason presents to us as a duty; *volentem ducit, nolentem trahit*. And she effects this by means of the commercial spirit, which cannot coexist with war, and sooner or later controls every nation.[21] 'In this way Nature guarantees the conditions of perpetual peace by the mechanism involved in our human inclinations themselves.[22] But a little later, in discussing the disagreement between morals and politics in relation to eternal peace, he seems to reach the ultimate point of his argument, and to take a flying leap beyond it:

> The process of creation, by which such a brood of corrupt beings has been put upon the earth, can apparently be justified by no theodicy or theory of Providence, if we assume that it never will be better, nor can be better, with the human race. But such a standpoint of judgment is really much too high for us to assume, as if we could be entitled theoretically to apply our notions of wisdom to the supreme and unfathomable Power. We shall thus be inevitably driven to a position of despair in consequence of such reasonings [zu solchen verzweifelten Folgerungen werden wir unvermeidlich hingetrieben], if we do not admit that the pure principles of right and justice have objective reality and that they can be realized in fact.[23]

It is surely not a good argument for a theory of international politics that we shall be driven to despair if we do not accept it. But it is an argument that comes naturally to the children of Hegel (and Kant) when they are faced with defeat. Communists, as the Germans neared Moscow, and Nazis, as the Russians returned upon Germany, alike cried that defeat was unthinkable because if they were defeated history would be meaningless. 'To imagine for a moment the possibility of Hitler's victory meant to forego all reason; if it were to happen then there could be no truth, logic, nor light in the development of human society, only chaos, darkness and lunacy; and it would be better not to live.'[24] We shall conquer, because it lies in the logic of history, because a higher destiny wills it, . . . because without our victory history would have lost its meaning; and history is not meaningless.[25]

Perhaps the prevalent belief that nuclear weapons have transformed international politics, giving the Great Powers something to fear more than they fear one another, and so making war impossible, has a similar root. It is clear, at least, that it is the latest in a series of optimistic constructions going back more than a hundred years. In the nineteenth century, public opinion was given the first place as transformer of international politics; in the twentieth century it has usually been the fear of war. The argument that the hydrogen bomb has made war impossible usually contains two propositions: first, that war waged with the new weapons will destroy civilization; secondly, that it is therefore too horrible to happen. Joad used it in 1939 in respect of the bombing aeroplane.[26] Bloch used it in 1900 in respect of mass armies, quick-firing artillery, small-bore rifles, and smokeless powder.[27]

It may be an illusion produced by treating the material selectively; but it sometimes seems that whereas political theory generally is in unison with political activity, international theory (at least in its chief embodiment as international law) sings a kind of descant over against the movement of diplomacy. Political theory is in a direct relation with political activity –whether justifying recent developments as Hooker did the Anglican settlement and Locke the Glorious Revolution, or providing a programme of action that the next generation carries out, as Bentham did for administrative reform in England or Marx and the other socialist writers for the working-class movement. But international law seems to follow an inverse movement to that of international politics. When diplomacy is violent and unscrupulous, international law soars into the regions of natural law;

when diplomacy acquires a certain habit of co-operation, international law crawls in the mud of legal positivism. It was in 1612, in the armistice between the Western European wars of religion and the Thirty Years' War, that Suarez enunciated his belief that mankind 'constitutes a political and moral unity bound up by charity and compassion.'[28] The old view that Grotius had a humanizing influence on the later stages of the Thirty Years' War no longer has any credit. 'Undoubtedly, the general picture of international relations in the two centuries which followed the publication of *De Jure Belli ac Pacis*,' Lauterpacht has written, 'was not one pointing to any direct influence, in the sphere of practice, of the essential features of the Grotian teaching.'[29] International theory did not approximate to international practice until the doctrine of natural law had become completely subjectivized in Wolff and Vattel, and transformed into a doctrine of autonomy of the national will, a counterpart of the theory of the rights of man. Frederick the Great's reign might be taken as the point of intersection of theory and practice. It saw the last stage of naturalism pass over into positivism, and the first great work of positivist jurisprudence, J. J. Moser's *Versuch des neuesten europäischen Volkerrechts*, which came as near to codifying *Realpolitik* as any work of international law can do, was published in 1777–80. Moser set the prevailing tone of nineteenth-century theory. Yet it is curious that a theory which starts from the axiom of legal self-sufficiency, separating the law both from the other normative spheres and from its social context – which sees the will of sovereign states as the exclusive source of international law, and defines international law as nothing but such rules as states have consented to – should have flourished in an age when the conception of Europe as a cultural and moral community acquired a new vigour, and the diplomatic system of the Concert maintained standards of good faith, mutual consideration and restraint higher probably than at any other time in international history. 'Chaque Nation a ses droits particuliers; mais l'Europe aussi a son droit; c'est l'ordre social qui le lui a donné,' ran a protocol of the London Conference on Belgium of 1831.[30] It is surely a deeper theory of international law than the consensual principle could offer. With the signing of the

League Covenant (if not indeed with the Hague Conferences) the relation of theory and practice was once more reversed, and positivist jurisprudence itself by an agreeable irony followed its naturalist predecessor into altitudes of fiction through the multiplication of worthless agreements in the age of Mussolini and Hitler.

The tension between international theory and diplomatic practice can be traced to the heart of international theory itself. It may be seen in the identification of international politics with the precontractual state of nature by the classical international lawyers. This identification was apparently first made by Hobbes, and was carried from him into the law of nations by Pufendorf. But already in Hobbes one can detect an inconsistency. He describes the state of nature, when men live without a common power to keep them all in awe, as a condition of war of every man against every man; and forestalling the argument that such a condition never existed, he points to the relations of sovereign states as exemplifying it. But he adds this sentence: 'But because they uphold thereby (viz., by their 'posture of war'), the industry of their subjects; there does not follow from it, that misery, which accompanies the liberty of particular men.'[31] This is empirically true. Competition in armaments secures full employment as well as bringing war; tariff barriers protect as well as obstruct. Or at least it has been empirically true until the present day, when for the first time we may be beginning to ask whether there may not follow from international anarchy as much misery as follows from civil anarchy. But it is theoretically odd. It introduces an ambiguity into the conception of the state of nature which becomes a persistent feature of international theory. For individuals, the state of nature, whether it is imagined in Hobbesian or Lockean terms, leads to the social contract. For sovereign states, it does no such thing. International anarchy is the one manifestation of the state of nature that is not intolerable. The coexistence of states, said Pufendorf, 'lacks those inconveniences which are attendant upon a pure state of nature.[32] Woolff conceived of international society as a *civitas maxima*, of which states were citizens, but this was a deliberate fiction constructed to support the theory of an international legal order. Vattel gives the fullest account of the ambiguity.

'It is clear that there is by no means the same necessity for a civil society among Nations as among individuals. It cannot be said, therefore, that nature recommends it to an equal degree, far less that it prescribes it. Individuals are so constituted that they could accomplish but little by themselves and could scarcely get on without the assistance of civil society and its law. But as soon as a sufficient number have united under a government, they are able to provide for most of their needs, and they find the help of other political societies not so necessary to them as the state itself is to individuals.'[33]

It was left to nineteenth century writers such as Laurent and Oppenheim to crown the argument by pointing out that sovereign states are more moral than individuals.

There is a profound difference between individuals and nations; the former have their vices and their passions which are continually leading them to do wrong; the others are fictitious beings whose agents are generally the most intelligent and most ethical of their time. And even where intelligence and morality are lacking, public opinion contains them and will increasingly contain them within the limits of duty.[34]

It may seem puzzling that, while the acknowledged classics of political study are the political philosophers, the only acknowledged counterpart in the study of international relations is Thucydides, a work of history. And that the quality of international politics, the preoccupations of diplomacy, are embodied and communicated less in works of political or international theory than in historical writings. It would be possible to argue that the highest form of statecraft, both in the end pursued and in the moral and intellectual qualities required, is the regulation of the balance of power, as seen in Lorenzo the Magnificent or Queen Elizabeth, Richelieu or William III, Palmerston or Bismarck. But to understand this statecraft one can turn to no work of international theory; in the way, for example, that to understand the Founding Fathers one reads *The Federalist*. One turns rather to historical writing; to Ranke or Sorel. Works of international history, whether of wide chronological

range (for example, Seeley's *Growth of British Policy*,
Mattingly's *Renaissance Diplomacy*, or Hudson's *The Far East
in World Politics*), or detailed studies (for example, Sumner's
Russia and the Balkans, Wheeler-Bennett's *Brest-Litovsk*, or
even Sorensen's account of Kennedy's handling of the Cuba
crisis), convey the nature of foreign policy and the working of the states-system better than much recent theoretical writing based on the new methodologies. It is not simply
that historical literature is doing a different job from systems analysis. Historical literature at the same time does
the same job – the job of offering a coherent structure of
hypotheses that will provide a common explanation of phenomena; but it does the job with more judiciousness and
modesty, and with closer attention to the record of international experience. So one might venture tentatively to put
forward the equation:

Politics: International Politics = Political Theory:
Historical Interpretation

By another intellectual route, Henry Adams came to a similar
conclusion. 'For history, international relations are the only
sure standards of movement; the only foundation for a map.
For this reason, Adams had always insisted that international
relations was the only sure base for a chart of history.'[35]

What I have been trying to express is the sense of a kind
of disharmony between international theory and diplomatic
practice, a kind of recalcitrance of international politics to
being theorized about. The reason is that the theorizing
has to be done in the language of political theory and law.
But this is the language appropriate to man's control of
his social life. Political theory and law are maps of experience or systems of action within the realm of normal relationships and calculable results. They are the theory of the
good life. International theory is the theory of survival. What
for political theory is the extreme case (as revolution, or
civil war) is for international theory the regular case. The
traditional effort of international lawyers to define the right
of devastation and pillage in war; the long diplomatic debate in the nineteenth century about the right of intervention in aid of oppressed nationalities; the Anglo–French
argument in the nineteen twenties about which precedes

the other, security or disarmament; the controversy over appeasement; the present debate about the nuclear deterrent – all this is the stuff of international theory, and it is constantly bursting the bounds of the language in which we try to handle it. For it all involves the ultimate experience of life and death, national existence and national extinction.

It is tempting to answer the question with which this paper begins by saying that there is no international theory except the kind of rumination about human destiny to which we give the unsatisfactory name of philosophy of history. The passage from Kant quoted above illustrates the slide-over into theodicy that seems to occur after a certain point with all international theory. At all events, it is necessary to see the domain of international theory stretching all the way from the noble attempt of Grotius and his successors to establish the laws of war, at one extreme, to de Maistre's 'occult and terrible law' of the violent destruction of the human species at the other.[36] 'La terre entière, continuellement imbibée de sang, n'est qu'un autel immense ou tout ce qui vit doit être immolé sans fin, sans mesure, sans relâche, jusqu'à la consommation des choses, jusqu'à l'extinction du mal, jusqu'à la mort de la mort'[37] – which de Maistre, at least, supposed to be political theology. An extra-galactic examiner in tellurian international theory might well hold that the writer of this answer, however curious the language in which it was couched, deserved a mark over some other candidates for not misrepresenting the historical record.

Notes

1. For recent writings there is a valuable critical study in Stanley H. Hoffman, *Contemporary Theory in International Relations* (Englewood Cliffs, NJ: Prentice-Hall, 1960).
2. Sir Geoffrey Butler and Simon Maccoby, *The Development of International Law* (London: Longmans, 1928), p. 7.
3. *Oeuvres*, vol. ix, pp. 120–1.
4. It may be worth adding that international law gained academic recognition in Britain well before political theory. The Chichele Chair of International Law and Diplomacy at Oxford and the Whewell Chair of International Law at Cambridge were founded in 1859

and 1866 respectively, and the Gladstone Chair of Political Theory and Institutions and the Cambridge Chair of Political Science only in 1912 and 1928.

5. They have now been admirably surveyed by F. H. Hinsley, *Power and the Pursuit of Peace* (Cambridge: Cambridge University Press, 1963), part i.
6. F. Meinecke, *Machiavellism* (English trans, London: Routledge, 1957), p. 67, n. 1.
7. The sentence was written in 1958.
8. H. J. Morgenthau, *Dilemmas of Politics* (Chicago: University of Chicago Press, 1958), p. 54. Cf. *In Defense of the National Interest* (New York: Knopf, 1951).
9. A. E. Zimmern, *The Study of International Relations* (Oxford: Clarendon Press, 1931), pp. 13–14.
10. Bohdan Chudoba, *Spain and the Empire 1519–1643* (Chicago: University of Chicago Press, 1952), p. 190.
11. Dante, *De Monarchia*, book i, ch. 2. Vitoria, *De Potestate Civili*, section xxi, para. 4; and *De Indis recenter inventis Relectio prior*, section III, first title. Vitoria nowhere mentions Dante.
12. Grotius, *De jure belli ac pacis*, book II, ch. xxii, section 13; Pufendorf, *Elementa jurisprudentiae universalis*, book II, obs. v. 1.
13. Gibbon, *Decline and Fall of the Roman Empire*, ch. iii, last paragraph; Kant *Eternal Peace*, first addendum, 2.
14. *The Listener* (August 5, 1954), p. 207.
15. J. M. Murry, *The Free Society* (Dakers, 1948), p. 63.
16. House of Commons (January 21, 1794) (*Speeches during the French Revolutionary War Period*, Everyman's Library, p. 124).
17. Isaac Deutscher, *The Prophet Armed* (Oxford: Oxford University Press, 1954), pp. 457–458.
18. *Ibid.*, p. 327.
19. *Letters on a Regicide Peace*, No. 1, third paragraph (*Works*, ed. H. Rogers Holdsworth, 1842, vol. ii, p. 275).
20. *De l'Esprit des Lois*, book xiii, ch. 17.
21. The best English translation is still that by W. Hastie, in *Kant's Principles of Politics* (Clark, 1891).
22. Hastie, p. 115.
23. Hastie, p. 136; *Werke* (Academy edition), vol. viii, p. 380. Cf. *Idee zu einer allgemeinen Geschichte*, ninth principle: 'Denn was hilfts, die Herrlichkeit und Weisheit der Schöpfung im vernunftlosen Naturreiche zu preisen und der Betrachtung zu empfehlen, wenn der Theil des grossen Schauplatzes der obersten Weisheit, der von allem diesem den Zweck enthält, – die Geschichte des menschlichen Geschlechts – ein unaufhörlicher Einwurf dagegen bleiben soll, dessen Anblick uns nöthigt unsere Augen von ihm mit Unwillen wegzuwenden und, indem wir verzweifeln jemals darin eine vollendete vernünftige Absicht anzutreffen, uns dahin bringt, sie nur in einer andern Welt zu hoffen?' (*Werke*, vol. viii, p. 30; Hastie, p. 28).
24. Evgeny Krieger, *From Moscow to the Prussian Frontier* (London: Hutchinson, 1945), p. 8: November 1941.

25. Goebbels, speech in the Berliner Sportpalast (October 3, 1943) (*Völkischer Beobachter* (October 4, 1943).

26. C. E. M. Joad, *Why War?* (Harmondsworth: Penguin, 1939), pp. 50, 52.

27. Ivan Bloch, *Modern Weapons and Modern War* (London: Grant Richards, 1900).

28. *De Legibus*, book II, ch. xix, section 9.

29. The Grotian Tradition in International Law', *British Year Book of International Law* (1946), p. 16.

30. See C. K. Webster, *Foreign Policy of Palmerston* (London: Bell, 1951), vol. i, pp. 109, 132.

31. *Leviathan*, ch. xiii.

32. *De jure naturae et gentium*, book II, ch. ii, section 4.

33. *Le Droit des Gens*, preface.

34. Francois Laurent, *Etudes sur l'histoire de humanite*, vol. i (2nd edn., 1879), p. 42. I owe this quotation to Walter Schiffer, *The Legal Community of Mankind* (New York: Columbia University Press, 1954), p. 160.

35. *The Education of Henry Adams* (New York: Modern Library, 1931), p. 422.

36. *Soirées de St. Pétersbourg*, 7me entretien (Paris: Emmanuel Vitte, 1924, vol. ii, p. 14); cf. *Considérations sur la France,* ch. iii.

37. *Soirées de St. Pétersbourg*, 7me entretien (Paris: Emmanuel Vitte, 1924, vol. ii, p. 25).

3 The Intellectual and Political Functions of Theory (1970)*

Hans Morgenthau

In the April 1960, issue of *International Relations*, Professor Martin Wight, then of the London School of Economics and Political Science, published a paper that bore the title 'Why Is There No International Theory?' (see Chapter 2 in this volume). While I cannot, of course, subscribe to the unqualified negativism of the title for both personal and professional reasons, I find the paper a most illuminating and penetrating discussion of the problem. Its fourteen pages contain more insights into the intellectual issues posed by theoretical concern with international relations than a whole shelf of books and articles that, following the fashion of the day, spin out theories about theories of international relations and embark upon esoteric methodological studies on how to approach such theory-making.

Professor Wight finds elements of an international theory in writings of international lawyers, such as Grotius and Pufendorf; the so-called 'irenists,' seekers after a peaceful international order, such as Erasmus, Sully, Campanella, Crucé, Penn, the Abbé de St. Pierre; the Machiavellians rediscovered by Meinecke; the *parerga* of political philosophers, philosophers, and historians, such as Hume's 'The Balance of Power,' Rousseau's *Projet de Paix Perpétuelle*, Mably's *Principes des Négociations*; and finally the speeches, dispatches, memoirs, and essays of statesmen and diplomatists, such as Gentz's *Fragments on the Balance of Power*[1] or

* Hans Morgenthau, *Truth and Power: Essays of a Decade, 1960–1970* (New York: Praeger), pp. 248–261.

Bismarck's memoirs. Professor Wight concludes that 'international theory is marked, not only by paucity but also by intellectual and moral poverty. For this we must look to internal reasons. The most obvious are the intellectual prejudice imposed by the sovereign State, and the belief in progress.'

According to Professor Wight, the sovereign state has been the focus of Western political thought and experience since the Reformation. Almost all intellectual energies devoted to political studies have been absorbed by it. He writes: 'It has been natural to think of international politics as the untidy fringe of domestic politics . . . and to see international theory in the manner of the political theory textbooks, as an additional chapter which can be omitted by all save the interested student.' Political theory, centered upon the state and its survival within the existing state system, has prevailed over international theory, wherein the state system itself is studied as a phenomenon that owes its existence to the historical process and is destined to be superseded by it. This is what Wight calls 'a small-scale field of political theory.' International theorists 'have not been attracted by the possibility of maximising the field of political theory through establishing a world State. Nor is it unfair to see the League and the United Nations as the expression of a belief that it may be possible to secure the benefits of a world State without the inconveniences of instituting and maintaining it.' Wight finds it significant that none of the three most powerful influences on the development of the modern state system – the Reformation and Counter-Reformation, the French Revolution, and the totalitarian revolutions of the twentieth century – has brought forth a coherent body of international theory.

The other impediment to the development of an international theory Professor Wight finds in the fact that

the character of international politics is incompatible with progressivist theory. Thus international theory that remains true to diplomatic experience will be at a discount in an age when the belief in progress is prevalent. If Sir Thomas More or Henry IV, let us say, were to return to England and France in 1960, it is not beyond plausibility that they would admit that their countries had moved domestically toward goals and along paths which they could approve. But if they contemplated the international scene, it is more likely that they would be struck by resemblances to what they remembered. International politics is the realm of recurrence and repetition; it is the field in which political action is most regularly necessitous.

Yet when the modern mind comes face to face with this immutable character of international politics, it revolts and takes refuge in the progressivist conviction that what was true in the past cannot be true in the future; for if it were, mankind would be in desperate straits. This is what Wight calls 'the argument from desperation.' Thus 'whereas political theory generally is in unison with political activity, international theory (at least in its chief embodiment as international law) sings a kind of descant over against the movement of diplomacy . . . International law seems to follow an inverse movement to that of international politics.' This tension between international theory and international reality is already obvious in the identification of international politics with a precontractual state of nature assumed by the classical international lawyers. Yet while the state of nature among individuals leads to the social contract, establishing authority over, and peace and order among, them, international theory sees no need for a similar development among states.

Wight finds it odd that,

> while the acknowledged classics of political study are the political philosophers, the only counterpart in the study of international relations is Thucydides, a work of history. And that the quality of international politics, the preoccupations of diplomacy, are embodied and communicated less in works of political or international theory than in historical writings. There are out of date books like Seeley's *Growth of British Policy*, which were second-rate at best, that might be thought to convey the nature of foreign policy and the working of the State-system better than much recent literature concerned with the games theory, decision-making, politicometrics and psychological concepts.

Wight summarizes his position by pointing to

> a kind of recalcitrance of international politics to being
> theorized about. The reason is that the theorizing has to
> be done in the language of political theory and law. But
> this is the language appropriate to man's control of his
> social life. Political theory and law are maps of experi-
> ence or systems of action within the realm of normal re-
> lationships and calculable results. They are the theory
> of the good life. International theory is the theory of
> survival. What for political theory is the extreme case
> (as revolution or civil war) is for international theory the
> regular case.

Thus in the end, international theory 'involves the ultimate
experience of life and death, national existence and national
extinction.' What we call international theory, then, amounts
to a kind of philosophy of history.

It hardly needs pointing out that my position coincides
in large measure with that of Professor Wight.[2] I take, indeed, a more sanguine view of the possibility of international theory than he does, finding that possibility in the
very fact that 'international politics is the realm of recurrence and repetition.' It is this repetitive character of international politics, that is, the configurations of the balance
of power, that lends itself to theoretical systematization. I
would also hesitate to equate international theory with
philosophy of history. Theory is implicit in all great
historiography. In historians with a philosophic bent, such
as Thucydides and Ranke, the history of foreign policy
appears as a mere demonstration of certain theoretical assumptions which are always present beneath the surface of
historical events to provide the standards for their selection and to give them meaning. In such historians of international politics, theory is like the skeleton, which, invisible
to the naked eye, gives form and function to the body. What
distinguishes such a history of international politics from
a theory is not so much its substance as its form. The historian presents his theory in the form of a historical recital, using the chronological sequence of events as a
demonstration of his theory. The theoretician, dispensing
with the historical recital, makes the theory explicit and

uses historic facts in bits and pieces to demonstrate his theory.

Yet both Wight's and my orientation are historical, and it is this historical orientation that sets us apart from the present fashionable theorizing about international relations. This theorizing is abstract in the extreme and totally unhistoric. It endeavors to reduce international relations to a system of abstract propositions with a predictive function. Such a system transforms nations into stereotyped 'actors' engaging in equally stereotyped symmetric or asymmetric relations. What Professor Wight has noted of international law applies with particular force to these theories: the contrast between their abstract rationalism and the actual configurations of world politics.[3] We are here in the presence of still another type of progressivist theory. Its aim is not the legalization and organization of international relations in the interest of international order and peace but the rational manipulation of international relations and, more particularly, of military strategy in the interest of predictable and controlled results. The ideal toward which these theories try to progress is ultimately international peace and order to be achieved through scientific precision and predictability in understanding and manipulating international affairs.

In view of their consistent neglect of the contingencies of history and of the concreteness of historical situations that all these theories have in common, they are destined to share the fate of their progressivist predecessors: They must fail both as guides for theoretical understanding and as precepts for action. However, the practical consequences of their theoretical deficiencies are likely to be more serious than those of their predecessors.

The straits in which the Western democracies found themselves at the beginning of World War II were, in good measure, the result of the reliance upon the inner force of legal pronouncements, such as the Stimson Doctrine, which refused to recognize territorial changes brought about by violence; of legal agreements, such as the Kellogg–Briand Pact and non-aggression treaties; and of international organizations, such as the League of Nations, which were incapable of collective action. The scientist theories of our day pretend to be capable of manipulating with scientific precision a society of sovereign nations that use weapons of total destruction as instruments of their respective foreign policies. With that pretense, these theories create the illusion that a society of sovereign nations thus armed can continue the business of foreign policy and military strategy in the traditional manner without risking its destruction. They create the illusion of the viability of the nation-state in the nuclear age. If statesmen should take these theories at their pseudoscientific word and act upon them, they would fail, as the statesmen of the interwar period failed when they acted upon the progressivist theories of their day.

It is significant that, until very recently, no explicit theory of international relations has existed; nobody even considered the possibility of writing a theory of international relations. This is a very significant fact, which ought to give us pause. For certainly theoretically inclined, reflective people have been aware, since the beginning of history, of the existence of international relations, the facts of foreign policy, the fateful results of good and bad foreign policies, the significance of success or failure in foreign policy. And certainly we have not grown so much wiser in recent years or so much more acute in self-awareness that we have all of a sudden started to think in theoretical terms of one of the crucial facts of human existence, recognized as such by prophets, statesmen, historians, and political philosophers for thousands of years. There must be a profound reason why, until very recently, nobody has thought of writing an explicit theory of international relations. Certainly, it could not have been the backwardness of Plato and Aristotle or Hobbes and Locke which prevented them from developing such a theory.

The first reason why there has been no theory, but only history, of international relations is to be found in the philosophic outlook that prevailed until the end of the Napoleonic Wars. Until then, the relations among nations were regarded as a fact of nature that was beyond the power of man to change. The relations among nations were considered a datum of history and a state of nature, resulting from the nature of man; nothing could be said in terms of a specific theory of international relations about their characteristics and about their manipulation. Given this outlook, the best theory could do was what political philosophy actually did, that is, to describe the state of nature and the rudimentary legal order existing, or assumed to exist, among nations.

As long as man believed that the relations among nations were beyond human control, beyond reform by the human will, there was no place in the intellectual scheme of things for a theory of international relations. In this respect, international theory found itself in the same position as social theory in general. As long as people believed that poverty, for instance, was a natural state, which man had to accept without being able to change it, social philosophy could do no more than affirm this natural condition. As long as this state of mind persisted, there was no possibility for the development of a social theory, a social theory of change at least. What *The Times* said in mid-nineteenth century of the misery of the unemployed – 'There is no one to blame for this; it is the result of Nature's simplest laws!' – people said of international relations. Thus the intellectual possibility of a theory of international relations depended upon the recognition that the relations among nations are not something which is given to man, which he has to accept as given, and which he must cope with as best he can; rather, it is that the relations among nations have been created by the will of man and therefore can be manipulated and changed and reformed by the will of man.

The second reason why theoretical concern with international relations was so late in emerging lies in the reformist orientation that characterized theoretical thinking on foreign policy in the nineteenth and the first decades of the twentieth century. The main theoretical concern during that period was not with understanding the nature of international relations but with developing legal institutions and organizational devices that would supersede the type of international relations then existing. 'Power politics' itself as a synonym for foreign policy was then a term of opprobrium, referring to something evil, not to be understood but to be abolished. Woodrow Wilson during and after World War I provides a classic and most impressive example of that position: he was interested not in understanding the operation of the balance of power but in getting rid of it, in reforming international relations in such a way that one did not need to resort any more to the balance of power. Franklin D. Roosevelt and Cordell Hull shared that position. As long as such a negative orientation toward the nature of international relations and foreign policy persisted, it was both intellectually and morally impossible to deal in a theoretical, that is, an objective, systematic manner, with problems of international relations.

The third and permanent factor, which does not make a theory of international relations altogether impossible but strictly limits its development and usefulness, is to be found in the very nature of politics, domestic and international. There is a rational element in political action that makes politics susceptible to theoretical analysis, but there is also a contingent element in politics that obviates the possibility of theoretical understanding.

The material with which the theoretician of politics must deal is ambiguous. The events he must try to understand are, on the one hand, unique occurrences: they happened in this way only once and never before or since. On the other hand, they are similar; for they are manifestations of social forces. Social forces are the product of human nature in action. Therefore, under similar conditions, they will manifest themselves in a similar manner. But where is the line to be drawn between the similar and the unique? The political world appears to the theoretical mind as a highly complicated combination of numerous systems of multiple choices, which, in turn, are strictly limited in number. The element of irrationality, insecurity, and chance lies in the necessity of choice among several possibilities multiplied by the great number of systems of multiple choice. The element of rationality, order, and regularity lies in the limited number of possible choices within each system of multiple choice. Viewed with the guidance of a rationalistic, blueprinted map, the social world is, indeed, a chaos of contingencies. Yet it is not devoid of a measure of rationality if approached with the modest expectations of a circumspect theory.

To take, as an example, three current situations, we may

say that the situations in Laos, Cuba, and Berlin provide American foreign policy with a limited number of rational choices. For some strange reason, these choices generally number three. What a theory of international relations can state is the likely consequences of choosing one alternative as opposed to another and the conditions under which one alternative is more likely to occur and be successful than the other. Theory can also say that under certain conditions one alternative is to be preferred to another. But all these theoretical analyses are contingent upon factors that either occur without our knowing or have consequences beyond our foresight.

For instance, there is the crucial problem of nuclear war. It is possible to develop a theory of nuclear war, as Herman Kahn has done in his book *On Thermonuclear War*, which assumes nuclear war to be just another kind of violence, greater in magnitude but no different in kind from the types of violence with which history has acquainted us. It follows from this assumption that nuclear war is going to be much more terrible than conventional war, but not necessarily intolerable, provided we take the measures which will enable us to survive it. In other words, once you start with this theoretical assumption of the nature and the consequences of a nuclear war, you can logically arrive at Mr Kahn's conclusion that the foreign policy of the United States does not need to limit itself to trying to avoid nuclear war, but that the United States must also prepare to survive it. And then it becomes perfectly legitimate to raise the question, provided 100 million Americans were to be killed in a nuclear war and nine-tenths of the economic capacity of the United States were to be destroyed, 'How do we enable the survivors to rebuild the United States with the remaining one-tenth of economic capacity?'

The contingent element in this theory of nuclear war is its utter uncertainty, and this uncertainty is typical of all levels of theoretical analysis and prediction in the field of politics, domestic and international. Even if one were to accept all its estimates of deaths and material destruction and of the rate of material recovery, this theory would have to be uncertain about the human reaction to the kind of human and material devastation which nuclear war is likely to bring about. Obviously, if a highly complex human society could be visualized to operate like a primitive ant society, its recuperative ability could be taken for granted. If one-third of the ants of one anthill have been destroyed together with nine-tenths of the material of the anthill, it is safe to conclude that the remaining ants will start all over again, building up the anthill and reproducing until the next catastrophe will force them to start once more.

But it is a moot question whether a human society has this type of mechanical recuperative ability. Societies have a breaking point as do individuals, and there may be a point beyond which human endurance does not carry human initiative in the face of such unprecedented massive devastation. Perhaps, under the impact of such devastation, civilization itself will collapse.

It is at this point that theoretical understanding of international relations reaches its limits. It can develop different alternatives and clarify their necessary preconditions and likely consequences. It can point to the conditions that render one alternative more likely to materialize than the other. But it cannot say, with any degree of certainty, which of the alternatives is the correct one and will actually occur.

This is but an extreme example of the utter uncertainty of theorizing about foreign policy beyond the clarification of alternative policies and of their possibilities and possible consequences. The Munich settlement of 1938 is another case in point. In retrospect, of course, we all know from practical experience that it was a failure, and from that experience we have developed the theoretical categories that demonstrate that it was bound to be such a failure. But I remember very well the near unanimity with which the Munich settlement was approved by theoreticians and practitioners of foreign policy and by the man in the street as well. The Munich settlement was generally regarded at the time of its conclusion as a great act of statesmanship, a concession made to a would-be conqueror for the sake of peace. E. H. Carr so regarded it then, and A. J. P. Taylor so regards it now. The flaw in that reasoning, which few people were, and perhaps could be, aware of at the time, was again the neglect of the contingencies inherent in political prediction. That which reveals itself as a simple truth in retrospect was either completely unknown in prospect or else could not be determined by anything but an uncertain hunch.

Apply the reasoning with which I have just analyzed the Munich settlement of 1938 to a hypothetical Berlin settlement of 1962. One of the alternatives for American foreign policy, which theoretical analysis can isolate, is to make certain concessions to the Soviet Union that change the modalities of the West's presence in Berlin but leave that presence itself intact. Another alternative, also revealed by theoretical analysis, is to stand on the Western right to be in Berlin and refuse to make any concessions, because whatever concessions we make will of necessity be followed by other concessions; step by step, then, our presence in West Berlin will be whittled down until it becomes untenable.

A third alternative assumes that our presence in Berlin is *a priori* untenable. It holds that the symbolic value of our presence in Berlin with regard to the unification of Germany has really been bypassed by history because the division of Germany has become definitive. Sooner or later, we must recognize this fact and adapt our policies to it. Especially in view of the risks involved and the odds against success, there is no point in maintaining a symbol that has no longer any active function to perform.

A theoretical argument can be made for any of those three alternatives, and nobody can say in advance with any degree of certainty which of the courses of action indicated by the alternatives is correct in theory, is sound in practice, or is likely to be a choice for actual policy. Only in retrospect, judging from the nature and the results of the action chosen, can we answer these questions. This limitation of theoretical analysis is inherent in the very subject matter of international relations, and this subject matter places insuperable limits on the development of a rational theory of international relations. It is only within those limits that theoretical thinking on international relations is theoretically and practically fruitful. Within these limits, a theory of international relations performs the functions any theory performs, that is, to bring order and meaning into a mass of unconnected material and to increase knowledge through the logical development of certain propositions empirically established.

While this theoretical function of a theory of international relations is no different from the function any social theory performs, its practical function is peculiar to itself. The practical function of a theory of international relations has this in common with all political theory: It depends very much upon the political environment within which the theory operates. In other words, political thinking is, as German sociology puts it, *standortgebunden*, that is to say, it is tied to a particular social situation. And we find that all great and fruitful political thought, which we still remember because of its greatness and fruitfulness, has started from a concrete political situation with which the political thinkers had to come to terms for both intellectual and practical reasons. Edmund Burke is a typical example of how great and fruitful political theory develops from concrete practical concerns. It is not being created by a professor sitting in his ivory tower and, with his publisher, looking over a contract that stipulates the delivery of a manuscript on the 'Theory of International Relations' by a specified date. It is developed out of the concern of a politically alive and committed mind with the concrete political problems of the day. Thus, all great political theory, from Plato and Aristotle and the Biblical prophets to our day, has been practical political theory, political theory that intervenes actively in a concrete political situation with the purpose of change through action.

A theory of international relations can perform four different practical functions by approaching political reality in four different ways. I shall try to exemplify these four different ways with my own experience as a theoretician of international relations, attempting to come to terms with the issues of international relations and of American foreign policy, in particular, since the end of World War II.

I had my first experience as a theoretician of international relations under the Truman–Acheson administration of America's foreign policy. Theory then provided a theoretical justification for what the policy-makers were doing, one may say, instinctively – what they were doing pragmatically on a mere day-by-day basis.

By 1947, the new pattern of American foreign policy was set. It manifested itself in four political innovations: the Truman Doctrine, containment, the Marshall Plan, and the

American alliance system. These policies have in common the permanent assumption, by the United States, of responsibilities beyond the limits of the Western Hemisphere. The heart of that new policy was the policy of containment. Yet the policy of containment was never officially formulated. It grew as an almost instinctive reaction to the threat of Russian imperialism. It called a halt to the territorial expansion of Russian power beyond the line of military demarcation drawn, at the end of World War II, between the Soviet orbit and the Western world.

There was no theory in support of these new policies. It was only as an afterthought that theoreticians developed a doctrine in the form of a theoretical framework that gave rational justification to the new policies. The policy-makers 'played it by ear;' they did what they thought they needed to do under the circumstances. They embarked upon courses of action that at the time appeared to them almost inevitable in view of their knowledge of the threat and of their objectives. It was only as a kind of intellectual reassurance that a theory of American foreign policy was developed that put the stamp of rational approval upon policies already established.

The function of the theoretician of international relations under the two Eisenhower Administrations, dominated by the foreign policy of John Foster Dulles, was of an entirely different nature. It was a function that had many precedents in the history of political thought. One can even go so far as to say that it is one that political theories have traditionally performed. Theory here developed a coherent system of thought, which was supposed to embody the sound principles of foreign policy. The actual conduct of American foreign policy was judged by the standards of that theory and frequently found wanting. Criticism directed at that theory was similarly judged and justified or found wanting, as the case might have been, by the standards of the theory. I remember very vividly that whenever I published an article critical of the foreign policy of Mr Dulles, I found nowhere more enthusiastic approval of that criticism than in the Department of State. Theory here provided a rational framework for a non-orthodox, critical political position either within the government or outside it. Theory gave a rational justification to that position.

The situation in which the theoretician of international relations has found himself since the Kennedy Administration took office on January 20, 1961, is, of course, quite extraordinary. What is the function of the outside theoretician when the government itself is staffed in the command posts of foreign policy by theoreticians? It stands to reason that he has become in good measure technologically obsolete. I have, since January 20, 1961, reflected with a great deal of embarrassment upon this change of position. Hardly anybody asks my advice now, because the people in government know at least as much as I do, and probably some are convinced that they know much more – and perhaps they actually do.

What, then, is the function of the academic theoretician of international relations in a society in which foreign policy itself is determined by theoretically conscious policy-makers? There is still a function to be performed. For it is in the very nature of the conduct of foreign policy in a democracy that what theoreticians regard to be the sound principles of foreign policy must be adapted to the preferences of public opinion and to the pressures of domestic politics, and thereby corrupted and distorted. I remember the statement I once heard a former Secretary of State make to the effect that he had always regarded it as his function to give the President advice on the basis of what he thought the principles of a sound American foreign policy required, leaving it to the President to decide how much of those sound principles could be safely put into practice in view of the state of domestic public opinion and the pressures of domestic politics.

Thus, the actual foreign policies pursued by a government staffed even by theoreticians are bound to fall short, from time to time, of the requirements of a pure theoretical understanding of what American foreign policy ought to be. It is here that the theoretician of foreign policy must perform the function of an intellectual conscience which reminds the policy-makers as well as the public at large of what the sound principles of foreign policy are and in what respects and to what extent actual policies have fallen short of those principles.

There is a final task – and perhaps it is the most noble of all – that a theory of international relations can and must perform, particularly in an age in which the very structure of international relations has radically changed. It is to prepare the ground for a new international order radically different from that which preceded it. Theoretical analysis can show that the principle of political organization that has dominated the modern world from the French Revolution of 1789 to this day is no longer valid. The sovereign nation-state is in the process of becoming obsolete. That is to say, the fact of nuclear power, together with the modern technologies of transportation and communications, which transcends the ability of any nation-state to control and harness it and render it both innocuous and beneficial, requires a principle of political organization transcending the nation-state and commensurate with the potentialities for good or evil of nuclear power itself. Theoretical analysis can show that the availability of nuclear power as an instrument of foreign policy is the only real revolution that has occurred in the structure of international relations since the beginning of history, because it has radically changed the relationship between violence as a means of foreign policy and the ends of foreign policy.

Until the end of World War II, there existed a rational relationship between violence as a means of foreign policy and the ends of foreign policy; that is to say, the policy-maker could rationally ask himself whether he should pursue the aims of his country by peaceful means or whether he ought to go to war. If he chose the latter alternative and if he lost the war, his nation lost in general only a bearable fraction of its human and material resources. If he won, then the risks taken were justified by the victory gained. This rational relationship between violence as a means and the ends of foreign policy has been obliterated by the availability of nuclear power. Nuclear power provides governments with a destructive force transcending all possible rational objectives of foreign policy. For all-out nuclear war is likely to obliterate the very distinction between victor and vanquished and will certainly destroy the very objective for which such a war would be fought. It is here that a theory of international relations has a creative and vital task to perform, a task that has been performed throughout history by the political theories of domestic politics. It is at this point that the realistic and utopian approaches to politics in general, and to international relations in particular, merge.

It is a legitimate and vital task for a theory of politics to anticipate drastic changes in the structure of politics and in the institutions which must meet a new need. The great political utopians have based their theoretical anticipation of a new political order upon the realistic analysis of the empirical *status quo* in which they lived. Today, political theory and, more particularly, a theory of international relations, starting from the understanding of politics and international relations as they are, must attempt to illuminate the impact nuclear power is likely to exert upon the structure of international relations and upon the functions domestic government performs. Further, it must anticipate in a rational way the intellectual, political, and institutional changes that this unprecedented revolutionary force is likely to require.

There is another function of international theory, which is not so much intellectual as psychological in nature and is of interest primarily to the sociology of knowledge. It is to provide a respectable shield that protects the academic community from contact with the living political world. That function is performed by much of the methodological activities carried on in academic circles, with sometimes fanatical devotion to esoteric terminology and mathematical formulas, equations, and charts, in order to elucidate or obscure the obvious. These activities can be explained psychologically by the fear of many academics to come into too close a contact with the political world, to become controversial in consequence, and to be contaminated in their objective scholarship by contact with political reality. By engaging in activities that can have no relevance for the political problems of the day, such as theorizing about theories, one can maintain one's reputation as a scholar without running any political risks. This kind of international theory, then, is consummated in theorizing for theorizing's sake, an innocuous intellectual pastime engaged in by academics for the benefit of other academics, without effect upon political reality and unaffected by it.

In conclusion, it may be said that the nature of a theory of international relations and the intellectual and political functions a theory of international relations performs and ought to perform are not, in essence, different from the nature of general political theory and the functions such theories have performed since the beginning of history. The fact that we have only in recent years turned toward explicit theoretical reflection about international relations is, in good measure, due to our recognition that international relations is not something to be taken for granted but something to be understood and to be changed and, more particularly, to be changed beyond the present limits of its political structure and organization. Here lies, indeed, the ultimate theoretical and practical justification of our interest in a theory of international relations. Threatened by the unsolved political problems of the day, we have come to think more and more in terms of a supranational community and a world government, a political organization and structure that transcend the nation-state. Reflecting on a theory of international relations, the politically conscious theoretician cannot help reflecting upon the political problems whose solution requires such novel structures and types of organization.

Notes

1. Classified by Wight in the preceding category.
2. I am referring, of course, primarily to *Politics Among Nations*, 4th edn. (New York: Knopf, 1967), more particularly to Chapters 11–14, 17, 19, and 29, dealing with the balance of power, the nation-state, and world government, respectively.
3. See for instance, the special issue on "The International System," *World Politics*, 16(1) (October 1961), and the critique of this type of thinking in Irving Louis Horowitz, 'Arms, Policies and Games,' *The American Scholar*, 31(1) (Winter, 1961–1962), pp. 94 ff.

4 Hans Morgenthau's Principles of Political Realism: A Feminist Reformulation (1988)*

J. Ann Tickner

> It is not in giving life but in risking life that man is raised above the animal: that is why superiority has been accorded in humanity not to the sex that brings forth but to that which kills.
>
> (Simone de Beauvoir)[1]

International politics is a man's world, a world of power and conflict in which warfare is a privileged activity. Traditionally, diplomacy, military service, and the science of international politics have been largely male domains. In the past, women have rarely been included in the ranks of professional diplomats or the military: of the relatively few women who specialize in the academic discipline of international relations, few are security specialists. Women political scientists who do international relations tend to focus on areas such as international political economy, North–South relations and matters of distributive justice.

Today, in the United States, where women are entering the military and the foreign service in greater numbers than ever before, rarely are they to be found in positions of military leadership or at the top of the foreign policy establishment.[2] One notable exception, Jeane Kirkpatrick, who was US ambassador to the United Nations in the early 1980s, has described herself as 'a mouse in a man's world.' For in spite of her authoritative and forceful public style and strong conservative credentials, Kirkpatrick maintains that she failed

* *Millennium: Journal of International Studies*, 17(3) (Winter), pp. 429–440.

to win the respect or attention of her male colleagues on matters of foreign policy.[3]

Kirkpatrick's story could serve to illustrate the discrimination which women often encounter when they rise to high political office. However, the doubts as to whether a woman would be strong enough to press the nuclear button (an issue raised when a tearful Patricia Schroeder was pictured sobbing on her husband's shoulder as she bowed out of the 1988 US presidential race) suggest that there may be an even more fundamental barrier to women's entry into the highest ranks of the military or of foreign policy-making. Nuclear strategy, with its vocabulary of power, threat, force, and deterrence, has a distinctly masculine ring;[4] moreover, women are stereotypically judged to be lacking in qualities which these terms evoke. It has also been suggested that, although more women are entering the world of public policy, they are more comfortable dealing with domestic issues such as social welfare that are more compatible with their nurturing skills. Yet the large number of women in the ranks of the peace movement suggests that women are not uninterested in issues of war and peace, although their frequent dissent from national security policy has often branded them as naive, uninformed or even unpatriotic.

In this article I propose to explore the question why international politics is perceived as a man's world and why women remain so under-represented in the higher echelons of the foreign policy establishment, the military and the academic discipline of international relations. Since I believe that there is something about this field which renders it particularly inhospitable and unattractive to women, I intend to focus on the nature of the discipline itself rather than on possible strategies to remove barriers to women's access to high policy positions. As I have already suggested, the issues that get prioritized in foreign policy are issues with which men have had a special affinity. Moreover, if it is primarily men who are describing these issues and constructing theories to explain the workings of the international system, might we not expect to find a masculine perspective in the academic discipline also? If this were so, then it could be argued that the exclusion of women has operated not only at the level of discrimination but also through a process of self-selection which begins with the way in which we are taught about international relations.

In order to investigate this claim that the discipline of international relations – traditionally defined by realism – is based on masculine world view, I propose to examine Hans Morgenthau's six principles of political realism. I shall use some ideas from feminist theory to show that the way in which Morgenthau describes and explains international politics, and the prescriptions that ensue, are embedded in a masculine perspective. Then I shall suggest some ways in which feminist theory might help us begin to conceptualize a world view from a feminine perspective and to formulate a feminist epistemology of international relations. Drawing on these observations, I shall conclude with a reformulation of Morgenthau's six principles. Male critics of contemporary realism have already raised many of the same questions about realism that I shall address. However, in undertaking this exercise, I hope to link the growing critical perspective on international relations theory and feminist writers interested in global issues. Adding a feminist perspective to its discourse could also help to make the field of international relations more accessible to women scholars and practitioners.

HANS MORGENTHAU'S PRINCIPLES OF POLITICAL REALISM: A MASCULINE PERSPECTIVE?

I have chosen to focus on Hans Morgenthau's six principles of political realism because they represent one of the most important statements of contemporary realism from which several generations of scholars and practitioners of international relations have been nourished. Although Morgenthau has frequently been criticized for his lack of scientific rigor and ambiguous use of language, these six principles have significantly framed the way in which the majority of international relations scholars and practitioners in the West have thought about international politics since 1945.[5]

Morgenthau's principles of political realism can be summarized as follows:

1. Politics, like society in general, is governed by objective laws that have their roots in human nature which is unchanging: therefore it is possible to develop a rational theory that reflects these objective laws.

2. The main signpost of political realism is the concept of interest defined in terms of power which infuses rational order into the subject matter of politics, and thus makes the theoretical understanding of politics possible. Political realism stresses the rational, objective and unemotional.

3. Realism assumes that interest defined as power is an objective category which is universally valid but not with a meaning that is fixed once and for all. Power is the control of man over man.

4. Political realism is aware of the moral significance of political action. It is also aware of the tension between moral command and the requirements of successful political action.

5. Political realism refuses to identify the moral aspirations of a particular nation with the moral laws that govern the universe. It is the concept of interest defined in terms of power that saves us from moral excess and political folly.

6. The political realist maintains the autonomy of the political sphere. He asks 'How does this policy affect the power of the nation?' Political realism is based on a pluralistic conception of human nature. A man who was nothing but 'political man' would be a beast, for he would be completely lacking in moral restraints. But, in order to develop an autonomous theory of political behavior, 'political man' must be abstracted from other aspects of human nature.[6]

I am not going to argue that Morgenthau is incorrect in his portrayal of the international system. I do believe, however, that it is a partial description of international politics because it is based on assumptions about human nature that are partial and that privilege masculinity. First, it is necessary to define masculinity and femininity. According to almost all feminist theorists, masculinity and femininity refer to a set of socially constructed categories that vary in time and place rather than to biological determinants. In the West conceptual dichotomies such as objectivity vs. subjectivity, reason vs. emotion, mind vs. body, culture vs. nature, self vs. other or autonomy vs. relatedness, knowing vs. being and public vs. private have typically been used to describe male/female differences by feminists and non-feminists alike.[7] In the United States, psychological tests conducted across different socio-economic groups confirm that individuals perceive these dichotomies as masculine and feminine and also that the characteristics associated with masculinity are more highly valued by both men and women alike.[8] It is important to stress, however, that these characteristics are stereotypical; they do not necessarily describe individual men or women who can exhibit characteristics and modes of thought associated with the opposite sex.

Using a vocabulary which contains many of the words associated with masculinity as I have defined it, Morgenthau asserts that it is possible to develop a rational (and unemotional) theory of international politics based on objective laws that have their roots in human nature. Since Morgenthau wrote the first edition of *Politics Among Nations* in 1948, this search for an objective science of international politics, based on the model of the natural sciences, has been an important part of the realist and neo–realist agenda. In her feminist critique of the natural sciences, Evelyn Fox Keller points out that most scientific communities share the 'assumption that the universe they study is directly accessible, represented by concepts shaped not by language but only by the demands of logic and experiment.'[9] The laws of nature, according to this view of science, are 'beyond the relativity of language.' Like most feminists, Keller rejects this view of science which, she asserts, imposes a coercive, hierarchical and conformist pattern on scientific inquiry. Feminists in general are sceptical about the possibility of finding a universal and objective foundation for knowledge that Morgenthau claims is possible. Most share the belief that knowledge is socially constructed: since it is language that transmits knowledge, the use of language and its claims of objectivity must continually be questioned.

Keller argues that objectivity, as it is usually defined in our culture, is associated with masculinity. She identifies it as 'a network of interactions between gender development, a belief system that equates objectivity with masculinity, and a set of cultural values that simultaneously (and cojointly) elevates what is defined as scientific and what is defined as masculine.'[10] Keller links the separation of self from other, an important stage of masculine gender development, with this notion of objectivity. Translated into scientific inquiry this becomes the striving for the separation of subject and object, an important goal of modern science and one, which Keller asserts, is based on the need for control; hence objectivity becomes associated with power and domination.

The need for control has been an important motivating force for the modern realism. To begin his search for an objective, rational theory of international politics, which could impose order on a chaotic and conflictual world, Morgenthau constructs an abstraction which he calls political man, a beast completely lacking in moral restraints. Morgenthau is deeply aware that real man, like real states, is both moral and bestial but, because states do not live up to the universal moral laws that govern the universe, those who behave morally in international politics are doomed to failure because of the immoral actions of others. To solve this tension, Morgenthau postulates a realm of international politics in which the amoral behavior of political man is not only permissible but prudent. It is a Hobbesian world, separate and distinct from the world of domestic order, in which states may act like beasts, for survival depends on a maximization of power and a willingness to fight.

Having long argued that the personal is political, most feminist theory would reject the validity of constructing an autonomous political sphere around which boundaries of permissible modes of conduct have been drawn. As Keller maintains, 'the demarcation between public and private not only defines and defends the boundaries of the political but also helps form its content and style.'[11] Morgenthau's political man is a social construct which is based on a partial representation of human nature. One might well ask where the women were in Hobbes' state of nature; presumably they must have been involved in reproduction and childrearing, rather than warfare, if life was to go on for more than one generation.[12] Morgenthau's emphasis on the conflictual aspects of the international system contributes to a tendency, shared by other realists, to de-emphasize elements of co-operation and regeneration which are also aspects of international relations.[13]

Morgenthau's construction of an amoral realm of international power politics is an attempt to resolve what he sees as a fundamental tension between the moral laws that govern the universe and the requirements of successful political action in a world where states use morality as a cloak to justify the pursuit of their own national interests. Morgenthau's universalistic morality postulates the highest form of morality as an abstract ideal, similar to the Golden Rule, to which states seldom adhere: the morality of states is an instrumental morality which is guided by self-interest. Morgenthau's hierarchical ordering of morality contains parallels with the work of psychologist Lawrence Kohlberg. Based on a study of the moral development of eighty-four American boys, Kohlberg concludes that the highest stage of human moral development (which he calls stage six) is the ability to recognize abstract universal principles of justice; lower on the scale (stage two) is an instrumental morality concerned with serving one's own interests while recognizing that others have interests too. Between these two is an interpersonal morality which is contextual and characterized by sensitivity to the needs of others (stage three).[14]

In her critique of Kohlberg's stages of moral development, Carol Gilligan argues that they are based on a masculine conception of morality. On Kohlberg's scale, women rarely rise above the third or contextual stage but Gilligan claims that this is not a sign of inferiority, but of difference. Since women are socialized into a mode of thinking which is contextual and narrative, rather than formal and abstract, they tend to see issues in contextual rather than in abstract terms.[15] In international relations, the tendency to think about morality either in terms of abstract, universal and unattainable standards or as purely instrumental, as Morgenthau does, detracts from our ability to tolerate cultural differences and to seek potential for building community in spite of these differences.

Using examples from the feminist literature, I have suggested that Morgenthau's attempt to construct an objective, universal theory of international politics is rooted in assumptions about human nature and morality that, in modern Western culture, are associated with masculinity. Further evidence that Morgenthau's principles are not the basis for a universalistic and objective theory is contained in his frequent references to the failure of what he calls the 'legalistic-moralistic' or idealist approach to world politics which he claims was largely responsible for both the World Wars. Having laid the blame for World War II on the misguided morality of appeasement, Morgenthau's *realpolitik* prescriptions for successful political action appear as prescriptions for avoiding the mistakes of the 1930s rather than as prescriptions with timeless applicability.

If Morgenthau's world view is embedded in the traumas of World War II, are his prescriptions still valid as we move further away from this event? I share with other critics of realism the view that, in a rapidly changing world, we must begin to search for modes of behavior different from those prescribed by Morgenthau. Given that any war between the major powers is likely to be nuclear, increasing security by increasing power could be suicidal.[16] Moreover, the nation-state, the primary constitutive element of the international system for Morgenthau and other realists, is no longer able to deal with an increasingly pluralistic array of problems ranging from economic interdependence to environmental degradation. Could feminist theory make a contribution to international relations theory by constructing an alternative, feminist perspective on international politics that might help us search for more appropriate solutions?

A FEMINIST PERSPECTIVE ON INTERNATIONAL RELATIONS

If the way in which we describe reality has an effect on the ways we perceive and act upon our environment, new perspectives might lead us to consider alternative courses of action. With this in mind, I shall first examine two important concepts in international relations, power and security, from a feminist perspective and then discuss some feminist approaches to conflict resolution.

Morgenthau's definition of power, the control of man over man, is typical of the way power is usually defined in international relations. Nancy Hartsock argues that this type of power as domination has always been associated with masculinity since the exercise of power has generally been a masculine activity; rarely have women exercised legitimized power in the public domain. When women write about power they stress energy, capacity and potential says Hartsock, and she notes that women theorists, even when they have little else in common, offer similar definitions of power which differ substantially from the understanding of power as domination.[17]

Hannah Arendt, frequently cited by feminists writing about power, defines power as the human ability to act in concert, or action which is taken in connection with others who share similar concerns.[18] This definition of power is similar to that of psychologist, David McClelland's portrayal of female power which he describes as shared rather than assertive.[19] Jane Jaquette argues that, since women have had less access to the instruments of coercion, women have been more apt to rely on power as persuasion; she compares women's domestic activities to coalition-building.[20]

All of these writers are portraying power as a relationship of mutual enablement. Tying her definition of female power to international relations, Jaquette sees similarities between female strategies of persuasion and strategies of small states operating from a position of weakness in the international system. There are also examples of states' behavior which contain elements of the female strategy of coalition-building. One such example is the Southern African Development Co-ordination Conference (SADCC) which is designed to build regional infrastructures based on mutual co-operation and collective self-reliance in order to decrease dependence on the South African economy. Another is the European Community, which has had considerable success in building mutual co-operation in an area of the world whose history would not predict such a course of events.[21] It is rare, however, that co-operative outcomes in international relations are described in these terms, though

Karl Deutsch's notion of pluralistic security communities might be one such example where power is associated with building community.[22] I am not denying that power as domination is a pervasive reality in international relations, but sometimes there are also elements of co-operation in inter-state relations which tend to be obscured when power is seen solely as domination. Thinking about power in this multidimensional sense may help us to think constructively about the potential for co-operation as well as conflict, an aspect of international relations generally downplayed by realism.

Redefining national security is another way in which feminist theory could contribute to new thinking about international relations.[23] Traditionally in the West, the concept of national security has been tied to military strength and its role in the physical protection of the nation-state from external threats. Morgenthau's notion of defending the national interest in terms of power is consistent with this definition. But this traditional definition of national security is partial at best in today's world.[24] When advanced states are highly interdependent, and rely on weapons whose effects would be equally devastating to winners and losers alike, defending national security by relying on war as the last resort no longer appears very useful. Moreover, if one thinks of security in North–South rather than East–West terms, for a large portion of the world's population, security has as much to do with the satisfaction of basic material needs as with military threats. According to Johan Galtung's notion of structural violence, the lowering of life expectancy by virtue of where one happens to be born is a form of violence whose effects can be as devastating as war.[25] Basic needs satisfaction has a great deal to do with women, but only recently have women's roles as providers of basic needs, and in development more generally, become visible as important components in devising development strategies.[26] Traditionally the development literature has focused on aspects of the development process which are in the public sphere, are technologically complex and are usually undertaken by men. Thinking about the role of women in development and the way in which we can define development and basic needs satisfaction to be inclusive of women's roles and needs are topics which deserve higher priority on the international agenda. Typically, however, this is an area about which traditional international relations theory, with its prioritizing of order over justice, has had very little to say.

A further threat to national security, more broadly defined, which also has not been on the agenda of traditional international relations, concerns the environment. Carolyn Merchant argues that a mechanistic view of nature, contained in modern science, has helped to guide an industrial and technological development which has resulted in the environmental damage that is now becoming a matter of global concern. In the introduction to her book. *The Death of Nature*, Merchant suggests that, 'Women and nature have an age-old association – an affiliation that has persisted throughout culture, language, and history.'[27] Hence she maintains that the ecology movement, which is growing up in response to these environmental threats, and the women's movement are deeply interconnected. Both stress living in equilibrium with nature rather than dominating it; both see nature as a living non-hierarchical entity in which each part is mutually dependent on the whole. Ecologists, as well as many feminists, are now suggesting that only with such a fundamental change in the way we view the world could we devise solutions that would allow the human species to survive the damage which we are inflicting on the environment.

Thinking about military, economic and environmental security in interdependent terms suggests the need for new methods of conflict resolution which seek to achieve mutually beneficial, rather than zero-sum, outcomes. One such method comes from Sara Ruddick's work on 'maternal thinking.'[28] Ruddick describes 'maternal thinking' as focused on the preservation of life and the growth of children; to foster a domestic environment conducive to these goals, tranquillity must be preserved by avoiding conflict where possible, engaging in it non-violently and restoring community when it is over. In such an environment the ends for which disputes are fought are subordinated to the means by which they are resolved. This method of conflict resolution involves making contextual judgments rather than appealing to absolute standards and thus has much in common with Gilligan's definition of female morality.

While non-violent resolution of conflict in the domestic sphere is a widely accepted norm, passive resistance in the public realm is regarded as deviant. But, as Ruddick argues, the peaceful resolution of conflict by mothers does not usually extend to the children of one's enemies, an important reason why women have been ready to support men's wars.[29] The question of Ruddick then becomes how to get 'maternal thinking', a mode of thinking which she believes can be found in men as well as women, out into the public realm. Ruddick believes that finding a common humanity among one's opponents has become a condition of survival in the nuclear age when the notion of winners and losers has become questionable.[30] Portraying the adversary as less than human has all too often been a technique of the nation-state to command loyalty and increase its legitimacy in the eyes of its citizens but such behavior in the nuclear age may eventually be self-defeating.

We might also look to Gilligan's work for a feminist perspective on conflict resolution. Reporting on a study of playground behavior of American boys and girls, Gilligan argues that girls are less able to tolerate high levels of conflict, more likely than boys to play games which involve taking turns and in which the success of one does not depend on the failure of another.[31] While Gilligan's study does not take into account attitudes toward other groups (racial, ethnic, economic, or national), it does suggest the validity of investigating whether girls are socialized to use different modes of problem-solving when dealing with conflict, and whether such behavior might be useful to us in thinking about international conflict resolution.

TOWARD A FEMINIST EPISTEMOLOGY OF INTERNATIONAL RELATIONS

I am deeply aware that there is no one feminist approach but many which come out of various disciplines and intellectual traditions. Yet there are common themes in these different feminist literatures that I have reviewed, which could help us to begin to formulate a feminist epistemology of international relations. Morgenthau encourages us to try to stand back from the world and to think about theory-building in terms of constructing a rational outline or map that has universal applications. In contrast, the feminist literature reviewed here emphasizes connection and contingency. Keller argues for a form of knowledge, which she calls 'dynamic objectivity,' 'that grants to the world around us its independent integrity, but does so in a way that remains cognizant of, indeed relies on, our connectivity with the world,'[32] Keller illustrates this mode of thinking in her study of Barbara McClintock whose work on genetic transposition won her a Nobel prize after many years of marginalization by the scientific community.[33] McClintock, Keller argues, was a scientist with a respect for complexity, diversity and individual differences whose methodology allowed her data to speak rather than imposing explanations on it.

Keller's portrayal of McClintock's science contains parallels with what Sandra Harding calls an African world view.[34] Harding tells us that the Western liberal notion of rational economic man, an individualist and a welfare maximizer, similar to rational political man upon which realism has based its theoretical investigations, does not make any sense in the African world view where the individual is seen as part of the social order acting within that order rather than upon it. Harding believes that his view of human behavior has much in common with a feminist perspective. If we combine this view of human behavior with Merchant's holistic perspective which stresses the interconnectedness of all things including nature, it may help us to begin to think from a more global perspective which appreciates cultural diversity but at the same time recognizes a growing interdependence which makes anachronistic the exclusionary thinking fostered by the nation-state system.

Keller's 'dynamic objectivity,' Harding's African world view and Merchant's ecological thinking all point us in the direction of an appreciation of the 'other' as a subject whose views are as legitimate as our own, a way of thinking that has been sadly lacking in the history of international relations. Just as Keller cautions us against the construction of a feminist science, which could perpetuate these same exclusionary attitudes, Harding warns us against schema which contrast people by race, gender or class and which originate within projects of social domination. Feminist thinkers generally dislike dichotomization and the distancing of subject from object that goes with abstract thinking, both of which, they believe, encourage a we/they attitude so characteristic of international relations. Instead this literature points us toward constructing epistemologies which value ambiguity and difference, qualities that could stand us in good stead as we begin to build a human or ungendered theory of international relations containing elements of both masculine and feminine modes of thought.

MORGENTHAU'S PRINCIPLES OF POLITICAL REALISM: A FEMINIST REFORMULATION

In the first part of this article I used feminist theory to develop a critique of Morgenthau's principles of political realism in order to demonstrate how the theory and practice of international relations may exhibit a masculine bias. I then suggested some contributions which feminist theory might make to reconceptualizing some important concepts in international relations and to thinking about a feminist epistemology. Drawing on these observations, I will now conclude with a feminist reformulation of Morgenthau's six principles of political realism, outlined earlier in this paper, which might help us to begin to think differently about international relations. I shall not use the term realism since feminists believe that there are multiple realities: a truly realistic picture of international politics must recognize elements of co-operation as well as conflict, morality as well as *realpolitik*, and the strivings for justice as well as order.[35] This reformulation may help us begin to think in these multidimensional terms:

1. A feminist perspective believes that objectivity, as it is culturally defined, is associated with masculinity. Therefore, supposedly 'objective' laws of human nature are based on a partial masculine view of human nature.

Human nature is both masculine and feminine: it contains elements of social reproduction and development as well as political domination. Dynamic objectivity offers us a more connected view of objectivity with less potential for domination.

2. A feminist perspective believes that the national interest is multidimensional and contextually contingent. Therefore it cannot be defined solely in terms of power. In the contemporary world the national interest demands cooperative rather than zero-sum solutions to a set of interdependent global problems which include nuclear war, economic well-being and environmental degradation.

3. Power cannot be infused with meaning that is universally valid. Power as domination and control privileges masculinity and ignores the possibility of collective empowerment, another aspect of power often associated with feminity.

4. A feminist perspective rejects the possibility of separating moral command from political action. All political action has moral significance. The realist agenda for maximizing order through power and control prioritizes the moral command of order those of justice and the satisfaction of basic needs necessary to ensure social reproduction.

5. While recognizing that the moral aspirations of particular nations cannot be equated with universal moral principles, a feminist perspective seeks to find common moral elements in human aspirations which could become the basis for de-escalating international conflict and building international community.

6. A feminist perspective denies the validity of the autonomy of the political. Since autonomy is associated with masculinity in Western culture, disciplinary efforts to construct a world view which does not rest on a pluralistic conception of human nature, are partial and masculine. Building boundaries around a narrowly defined political realm defines political in a way that excludes the concerns and contributions of women.

In constructing this feminist alternative, I am not denying the validity of Morgenthau's work. Adding a feminist perspective to the epistemology of international relations, however, is a stage through which we must pass if we are to begin to think about constructing an ungendered or human science of international politics which is sensitive to, but goes beyond, both masculine and feminine perspectives. Such inclusionary thinking, which, as Simone de Beauvoir tells us, values the bringing forth of life as much as the risking of life, is becoming imperative in a world where the technology of war and a fragile natural environment are threatening human existence. This ungendered or human discourse becomes possible only when women are adequately represented in the discipline and when there is equal respect for the contributions of both women and men alike.

Notes

An earlier version of this paper was presented at the symposium on Women and International Relations at the London School of Economics in June 1988. I am grateful to Hayward Alker, Jr. and Susan Okin for their careful reading of the manuscript and helpful suggestions.

1. Quoted in Sandra Harding, *The Science Question in Feminism* (Ithaca, NY: Cornell University Press, 1986), p. 148.
2. In 1987 only 4.8 per cent of the top career Foreign Service employees were women. Statement of Patricia Schroeder before the Committee on Foreign Affairs, US House of Representatives, *Women's Perspectives on US Foreign Policy: A Compilation of Views* (Washington, DC: US Government Printing Office, 1988), p. 4. For an analysis of women's roles in the American military, see Cynthia Enloe, *Does Khaki Become You? The Militarisation of Women's Lives* (London: Pluto Press, 1983).
3. Edward P. Crapol (ed.), *Women and American Foreign Policy* (Westport, CT: Greenwood Press, 1987), p. 167.
4. For an analysis of the role of masculine language in shaping strategic thinking see Carol Cohn, 'Sex and Death in the Rational World of Defense Intellectuals,' *Signs; Journal of Women in Culture and Society*, 12 (4) (Summer 1987), pp. 687–718.
5. The claim for the dominance of the realist paradigm is supported by John A. Vasquez, 'Colouring it Morgenthau: New Evidence for an Old Thesis on Quantitative International Studies,' *British Journal of International Studies*, 5 (3) (October 1979), pp. 210–228. For a critique of Morgenthau's ambiguous use of language, see Inis L. Claude Jr., *Power and International Relations* (New York: Random House, 1962), especially pp. 25–37.

6. These are drawn from the six principles of political realism in Hans Morgenthau, *Politics Among Nations: The Struggle for Power and Peace*, 5th revised edn (New York: Alfred Knopf, 1973), pp. 4–15. I am aware that these principles embody only a partial statement of Morgenthau's very rich study of international politics, a study which deserves a much more detailed analysis than I can give it here.

7. This list is a composite of male/female dichotomies which appear in Evelyn Fox Keller, *Reflections on Gender and Science* (New Haven, CT: Yale University Press, 1985) and Harding, *The Science Question*.

8. Inge K. Broverman, Susan R. Vogel, Donald M. Broverman, Frank E. Clarkson and Paul S. Rosenkranz, 'Sex-Role Stereotypes: A Current Appraisal,' *Journal of Social Issues* 28 (2) (1972), pp. 59–78. Replication of this research in the 1980s confirms that these perceptions still hold.

9. Keller, *Reflections*, p. 130.

10. *Reflections*, p. 89.

11. *Reflections*, p. 9.

12. Sara Ann Ketchum, 'Female Culture, Womanculture and Conceptual Change: Toward a Philosophy of Women's Studies,' *Social Theory and Practice*, 6 (2) (Summer 1980), pp. 151–62.

13. Others have questioned whether Hobbes' state of nature provides an accurate description of the international system. See, for example, Charles Beitz, *Political Theory and International Relations* (Princeton, NJ: Princeton University Press, 1979), pp. 35–50, and Stanley Hoffmann, *Duties Beyond Borders* (Syracuse, NY: Syracuse University Press, 1981), chapter 1.

14. Kohlberg's stages of moral development are described and discussed in Robert Kegan, *The Evolving Self: Problem and Process in Human Development* (Cambridge, MA: Harvard University Press, 1982), chapter 2.

15. Gilligan's critique of Kohlberg appears in Carol Gilligan, *In a Different Voice: Psychological Theory and Women's Development* (Cambridge, MA: Harvard University Press, 1982), chapter 1.

16. There is evidence that, toward the end of his life, Morgenthau himself was aware that his own prescriptions were becoming anachronistic. In a seminar presentation in 1978, he suggested that power politics as the guiding principle for the conduct of international relations had become fatally defective. For a description of this seminar presentation, see Francis Anthony Boyle, *World Politics and International Law* (Durham, NC: Duke University Press, 1985), pp. 70–4.

17. Nancy C. M. Hartsock, *Money, Sex and Power: Toward a Feminist Historical Materialism* (Boston, MA: Northeastern University Press, 1983), p. 210.

18. Hannah Arendt, *On Violence* (New York: Harcourt, Brace & World, 1969), p. 44. Arendt's definition of power, as it relates to international relations, is discussed more extensively in Jean Bethke Elshtain,

'Reflections on War and Political Discourse: Realism, Just War, and Feminism in a Nuclear Age,' *Political Theory* 13 (1) (February 1985), pp. 39–57.

19. David McClelland, 'Power and the Feminine Role,' in David McClelland, *Power, The Inner Experience* (New York: Wiley, 1975), chapter 3.

20. Jane S. Jaquette, 'Power as Ideology: A Feminist Analysis,' in Judith H. Stiehm, *Women's Views of the Political World of Men* (Dobbs Ferry, NY: Transnational Publishers, 1984), chapter 2.

21. These examples are cited in Christine Sylvester, 'The Emperor's Theories and Transformations: Looking at the Field Through Feminist Lenses,' in Dennis Pirages and Christine Sylvester (eds.) *Transformations in the Global Political Economy* (New York: Macmillan, 1988).

22. Karl W. Deutsch, *Political Community and the North Atlantic Area* (Princeton, NJ: Princeton University Press, 1957).

23. 'New thinking' is a term that is also being used in the Soviet Union to describe foreign policy reformulations under Gorbachev. There are indications that the Soviets are beginning to conceptualize security in the multidimensional terms described here. See Margot Light, *The Soviet Theory of International Relations* (New York: St. Martin's Press, 1988), chapter 10.

24. This is the argument made in Edward Azar and Chung-in Moon, 'Third World National Security: Toward A New Conceptual Framework,' *International Interactions*, 11 (2) (1984), pp. 103–35.

25. Johan Galtung, 'Violence, Peace, and Peace Research,' in Johan Galtung, *Essays in Peace Research*, vol. 1 (Copenhagen: Christian Ejlers, 1974), chapter 1.4.

26. See, for example, Gita Sen and Caren Grown, *Development, Crises and Alternative Visions: Third World Women's Perspectives* (New York: Monthly Review Press, 1987). This is an example of a growing literature on women and development which deserves more attention from the international relations community.

27. Carolyn Merchant, *The Death of Nature: Women, Ecology and the Scientific Revolution* (New York: Harper & Row, 1982), p. xv.

28. Sara Ruddick, 'Maternal Thinking,' and Sara Ruddick, 'Preservative Love and Military Destruction: Some Reflections on Mothering and Peace,' in Joyce Treblicot, *Mothering: Essays in Feminist Theory* (Totowa, NJ: Rowman & Allanheld, 1984), chapter 13–4.

29. For a more extensive analysis of this issue, see Jean Bethke Elshtain, *Women and War* (New York: Basic Books, 1987).

30. This type of conflict resolution bears similarities to the problem solving approach of Edward Azar, John Burton and Herbert Kelman. See, for example, Edward E. Azar and John W. Burton, *International Conflict Resolution: Theory and Practice* (Brighton: Wheatsheaf Books, 1986) and Herbert C. Kelman, 'Interactive Problem Solving: A Social-Psychological Approach to Conflict Resolution,' in W. Klassen (ed.), *Dialogue Toward Inter-Faith Understanding*, (Tantur/Jerusalem: Ecumenical Institute for Theoretical Research, 1986), pp. 293–314.

31. Gilligan, *In Different Voice*, pp. 9–10.
32. Keller, *Reflections*, p. 117.
33. Evelyn Fox Keller, *A Feeling for the Organism: The Life and Work of Barbara McClintock*, (New York: Freeman, 1983).
34. Harding, *The Science Question*, chapter 7.
35. 'Utopia and reality are . . . the two facets of political science. Sound political thought and sound political life will be found only where both have their place,' E. H. Carr, *The Twenty Years' Crisis, 1919–1939* (New York: Harper & Row, 1964), p. 10.

Part II
Anarchy and Sovereignty

5 Society and Anarchy in International Relations (1966)*
Hedley Bull

I

Whereas men within each state are subject to a common government, sovereign states in their mutual relations are not. This anarchy[1] it is possible to regard as the central fact of international life and the starting-point of theorizing about it.[2] A great deal of the most fruitful reflection about international life has been concerned with tracing the consequences in it of this absence of government. We can, indeed, give some account in these terms of what it is that distinguishes the international from the domestic field of politics, morals and law.

One persistent theme in the modern discussion of international relations has been that as a consequence of this anarchy states do not form together any kind of society; and that if they were to do so it could only be by subordinating themselves to a common authority. One of the chief intellectual supports of this doctrine is what may be called the domestic analogy, the argument from the experience of individual men in domestic society to the experience of states, according to which the need of individual men to stand in awe of a common power in order to live in peace is a ground for holding that states must do the same. The conditions of an orderly social life, on this view, are the same among states as they are within them: they require that the institutions of domestic society be reproduced on a universal scale.

The present essay has two purposes. First, to examine

* H. Butterfield and M. Wight (eds.), *Diplomatic Investigations* (London: George Allen & Unwin), pp. 35–60.

the opinion that anarchy in international relations is incompatible with society, or that the progress of the latter has been, or necessarily will be, a matter of the degree to which government comes to prevail. And secondly, to determine the limits of the domestic analogy and thus establish the autonomy of international relations.

It might be thought that the opinions I propose to consider are to be found at the present time only among the small group of people who advocate the establishment of a world government. This is far from being the case. The feeling of unease about the system of sovereign states is a deep-rooted one in Western thinking about international relations. It exists not only among those who explicitly espouse the elimination of this system, but also where we might least expect to find it, in the pronouncements of the servants of sovereign states themselves, by whose daily acts the system is preserved. These pronouncements often betray a sense of inadequacy of the anarchical system, a lack of confidence in its situations, a tendency guiltily to disguise their operation of the system or to apologize for doing so. The League of Nations and the United Nations we are invited to see not as diplomatic machinery in the tradition of the Concert of Europe, but as first steps towards a world state. Military alliances, in this manner of speaking, become regional security systems; exclusive political groupings, like Little Europe or the British Commonwealth, experiments in world order; war, police action. Men of affairs, even while in their actions they are seeking them, in their words are sometimes suggesting that solutions cannot in the long run be found within the framework of the existing system. Whether by a social contract among the nations or by conquest, whether gradually or at once, whether by a frontal assault on national sovereignty or a silent undermining of its foundations, the problem of international relations, if it is soluble at all, is taken to be in the last analysis the problem of bringing international relations to an end.

The view that anarchy is incompatible with society among nations has been especially prominent in the years since World War I. It was World War I that gave currency to the doctrine of a 'fresh start' in international relations and set the habit of disparaging the past. Nineteenth-century thought had regarded both the existence of international society and its further consolidation as entirely consistent with the continuation of international anarchy. The ideas of 1919 were in part a mere extension of the liberal, progressive strand of this nineteenth-century anarchist view: the strengthening of international law, the creation of new procedures for arbitration, the establishment of permanent institutions for cooperation among sovereign states, a reduction and limitation of armaments, the pressure of public opinion, the aspiration that states should be popularly based and that their boundaries should coincide with the boundaries of nations. But there was now voiced also a view that is not to be found in Cobden or Gladstone or Mazzini: a rejection of international anarchy itself, expressed on the one hand in the view that the true value of the League and the United Nations lay not in themselves, but in their presumed final cause, a world government; and on the other hand in the endorsement of world government as an immediately valid objective, and a depreciation of the League and its successor as destined to 'failure' on account of their preservation of state sovereignty.

The twentieth-century view of international anarchy is not, however, something new. Such a doctrine was stated at the outset of modern international history and has since found a succession of embodiments. The European system of sovereign states did not, of course, arise as a result of the outward growth and collision of hitherto isolated communities. Its origin lay in the disintegration of single community: the waning on the one hand of central authorities, and on the other hand of local authorities, within Western Christendom, and the exclusion of both from particular territories by the princely power. Throughout its history modern European international society has been conscious of the memory of the theoretical imperium of Pope and Emperor and the actual imperium of Rome. When in the sixteenth and early seventeenth centuries the question was raised of the nature of relationships between sovereign princes and states, order and justice on a universal scale were readily associated with the idea of universal state: not merely because the supremacy of the prince was observed to be a condition of order within the confines of the state, but also because order throughout Western Christendom as a whole was associated with the vanished authority of the Papacy and the Holy Roman Empire. The idea that international anarchy has as its consequence the absence of society among states, and the associated but opposite idea of the domestic analogy, became and have remained persistent doctrines about the international predicament.

The first of these doctrines describes international relations in terms of a Hobbesian state of nature, which is a state of war. Sovereign states, on this view, find themselves in a situation in which their behavior in relation to one another, although it may be circumscribed by considerations of prudence, is not limited by rules or law or morality. Either, as in the Machiavellian version of this doctrine, moral and legal rules are taken not to impinge on the sphere of action of the state: the political life and the moral life being presented as alternatives, as in the theory of quietism. Or, as in the Hegelian version, moral imperatives are thought to exist in international relations, but are believed to endorse the self-assertion of states in relation to one another, and to be incapable of imposing limits upon it. In this first doctrine the conditions of social life are asserted to be the same for states as they are for individuals. In the case of Hobbes, whose views we shall examine more closely, government is stated to be a necessary condition of social life among men, and the same is said to hold of sovereign princes. But the domestic analogy stops short at this point; it is not the view of Hobbes, or of other thinkers of this school, that a social contract of states that would bring the international anarchy to an end either should or can take place.

The second doctrine accepts the description of international relations embodied in the first, but combines with it the demand that the international anarchy be brought to an end. Where the domestic analogy is employed to buttress this doctrine, it is taken further, to embrace the concept of the social contract as well as that of the states of nature. This search for an alternative to international anarchy may be sustained by the memory of an alternative actually experienced, as in the backward-looking tradition of a return to Roman or to Western Christian unity. The other variety, the forward-looking tradition of which we may take Kant to be representative, finds its sustenance in the belief in human progress, in possibility of achieving in the future what has not been achieved in the past.

Even as these two doctrines were taking shape there was asserted against them both the third possibility of a society of sovereign states; and along with it the beginnings of the idea that the conditions of order among states were different from what they were among individual men. Like the two doctrines against which it has been directed, this third doctrine consists in part of a description of what is taken to be the actual character of relations between states, and in part of a set of prescriptions. The description is one which sees sovereign states in intercourse with one another as consciously united together for certain purposes, which modify their conduct in relation to one another. The salient fact of international relations is taken to be not that of conflict among states within the international anarchy, as on the Hobbesian view; nor that of the transience of the international anarchy and the availability of materials with which to replace it, as on the Kantian view; but co-operation among sovereign states in a society without government. The prescriptions which accompany this account of the nature of international relations enjoin respect for the legal and moral rules upon which the working of the international society depends. In place of the Hobbesian view that states are not limited by legal or moral rules in their relations with one another, and the Kantian view that the rules to which appeal may be had derive from the higher morality of a cosmopolitan society and enjoin the overthrow of international society, there are asserted the duties and rights attaching to states as members of international society.

Two traditions, in particular, have advanced this third conception of an international society. One is the body of theory to which modern international law is the heir, which depicts states as constituting a society in the course of showing them to be bound by a system of legal rules: whether these rules are thought to derive from natural law or positive law, whether the subjects of the rules are taken to be states or the men who rule them, and whether the rules are regarded as universally valid, or as binding only upon the states of Christendom or Europe. In the systems of six-teenth-century writers like Victoria and Suarez, and of seventeenth-century thinkers like Grotius and Pufendorf, the idea of the domestic analogy was still strong; the alternative notion of the uniqueness of international society was fully worked out only by the positivist international lawyers of the nineteenth century. The other tradition is that of the analysis of the political relations of states in terms of the system of balance of power. According to such analyses states throughout modern history have been engaged in the operation of a 'political system' or 'states-system,' which makes its own demands upon their freedom of action and requires them in particular to act so as to maintain a balance of power. In so far as such theories have presented the balance of power as a product of policies consciously directed towards it, and in so far as they have asserted that states are obliged to act so as to maintain it, they must be taken also to embody the idea of international society and of rules binding upon its members. In the sixteenth and seventeenth centuries the predominant theories of the law of nations and of the balance of power were held by different groups of persons and in their respective content were largely antithetical. But in the eighteenth century the two streams converged, as in the writings of Vattel international law came to take account of the balance of power, and in the writings of Burke and later Gentz the political maxim enjoining the preservation of a balance of power came to be defined in a more legalistic way. In the nineteenth century the predominant doctrines moved close together: although it may still be doubted whether either theory can be reconciled to the other without sacrifice of an essential part of its content.

It is the validity of this third conception of an international society, either as a description of the past or as a guide for the present and the future, that is called in question by the doctrine that the international anarchy is, or has become, intolerable. It is not my purpose to vindicate the idea of an international society, nor to argue against the desirability or feasibility of a universal state. In my view the questions with which this essay deals do not lend themselves to clear-cut answers, one way or the other: the future course of history is liable to be richer in its possibilities than our categories for theorizing about it can comprehend. But it would seem important to examine carefully an idea that has stood for so long at the centre of the theory and practice of modern international relations before concluding that it should be cast aside. It is proposed to consider the idea of international society first in relation to the doctrine that states find themselves in a Hobbesian state of nature; and then in relation to the doctrine that they should attempt to emerge from it by constructing a universal state.

II

The identification of international relations as a variety of the Hobbesian state of nature derives from Hobbes himself. Hobbes' account of relations between sovereign princes is a subordinate part of his explanation and justification of government among individual men. As evidence for his speculations as to how men would live were they to find themselves in a situation of anarchy, Hobbes mentions the experience of civil war, the life of certain American tribes and the facts of international relations:

> But though there had never been any time wherein particular men were in a condition of warre one against another; yet in all times Kings, and Persons of Soveraigne authority, because of their Independency, are in continual jealousies, and in the state and posture of Gladiators; having their weapons pointing, and their eyes fixed on one another; that is, their Forts, Garrisons and Guns, upon the Frontiers of their Kingdomes; and continual Spyes upon their neighbors; which is a posture of war.[3]

The situation in which men live without a common power to keep them in awe has three principal characteristics, in Hobbes' account. In it there can be no industry, agriculture, navigation, trade or other refinements of living, because the strength and invention of men is absorbed in providing security against one another. There are no legal or moral rules: 'The notions of Right and Wrong, Justice and Injustice have there no place ... It is consequent also to the same condition, that there can be no Propriety, no Dominion, no *Mine and Thine* distinct; but only that to be every mans, that he can get; and for so long, as he can keep it.'[4] Finally, the state of nature is a state of war: war understood to consist 'not in actual fighting; but in the known disposition thereto, during all the time there is no assurance to the contrary;' and to be 'such a warre, as is of every man, against every man.'[5]

It may be claimed for the Hobbesian view of international relations as conflict among sovereign states that it distils certain qualities that are present in the situation of international anarchy at all times and in all places and that in certain areas and at certain moments seem to drive all other qualities away. It may be claimed also for that other description of international relations as a potential community of mankind that it draws attention to qualities similarly permanent and universal: those arising from the bonds which men have in common as men, and in relation to which the division of mankind into sovereign states must be regarded as something accidental and transient, whether the relations of these states are taken to consist chiefly in conflict or in collaboration. But there is a great area of international experience which is not taken into account by either theory; and which can be accommodated only by the doctrine that there exists in the international anarchy a society of sovereign states.

The theorists of international society have been able to question the applicability to relations between states of each of the three elements in Hobbes' account of the state of nature. In the first place they have often remarked that sovereign states do not so exhaust their strength and invention in providing security against one another that industry and other refinements of living do not flourish. States do not as a rule invest resources in war and military preparations to such an extent that their economic fabric is ruined; even if it may be argued that the allocation of resources to war and armaments is not the best allocation from the point of view of economic development. On the contrary the armed forces of the state by providing security against external attack and internal disorder, establish the conditions under which economic improvement may take place within its borders. The absence of universal government and the fragmentation among sovereign states of responsibility for military security is not incompatible, moreover, with economic interdependence. The relative economic self-sufficiency of states as compared with individuals, has often been taken to explain why states are able to tolerate a looser form of social organization than that enjoyed by individuals within the modern state. At the same time, these theorists may point to the mutual advantages which states derive from economic relationships; and argue that trade, symbolic as it is of the existence of overlapping through different interests, is the activity most characteristic of international relationships as a whole.

As regards the second feature of the Hobbesian state of nature, the absence in it of notions of right and wrong, it is a matter of observation that this is not true of modern international relations. The theorist of international society has often begun his inquiries, as Grotius did, by remarking the extent to which states depart from rules of law and morality, and by uttering a protest against this situation in asserting the binding character of the rules. However, he has also been able to draw attention to the recognition of legal and moral rules by statesmen themselves, and to traditions of positive law and morality which have been a continuous feature of international life. International action which, although it is contrary to recognized principles of international law and morality, is accompanied by pretexts stated in terms of those principles, attests the force in international relations of notions of right and wrong, just as does action which conforms to them. By contrast, action which in addition to involving a violation of the legal and moral rules of international society is accompanied by no legal and moral pretext, action which, to use Grotius' terms, is 'not persuasive' as well as 'not justifiable,' is widely taken by legal theorists to be quite uncharacteristic of the behavior of members states of modern international society (as well as to be hostile to its working in a way in which illegal behavior accompanied by a pretext is not).

The element in the Hobbesian state of nature which appears most clearly to apply to international relations is the third. It is the fact of war which appears to provide the chief evidence for the view that states do not form a society. On the one hand, if we take the modern state to illustrate the idea of a society, one of it salient features is that in it, apart from certain residual rights of self-defence, the private use of force is proscribed. But on the other hand, it cannot be denied that sovereign states in relation to one another are in a state of war, in Hobbes' sense that they are disposed to it over a period of time. It must be conceded also that this war is one of all against all. At any single moment in the history of the modern states-system, it is true, certain states will not be disposed to war against certain other states. That is to say, certain pairs of states will be pursuing common purposes and will be allied to one another; certain other pairs of states will be pursuing purposes which are different but do not cross, and will therefore treat one another with indifference; and certain pairs of states, although they have purposes which are conflicting, nevertheless share such a sense of community that (as now among the English-speaking states) war is not contemplated as a possible outcome of the conflict. But if we consider the states-system not at a single moment but in motion throughout the whole of its life (say, from 1648) then we shall find that every state that has survived the period has at some point or other been disposed to war with every other one.

The theorist of international society has sought to deal with this difficulty not by denying the ubiquity of war, but by questioning the relevance of the model of the modern state. If sovereign states are understood to form a society of a different sort from that constituted by the modern state – one, in particular, whose operation not merely tolerates certain private uses of force but actually requires them – then the fact of a disposition to war can no longer be regarded as evidence that international society does not exist. Theorists of the law of nations and of the system of balance of power have thus sought to show that war does not indicate the absence of international society, or its breakdown, but can occur as a part of its functioning. Thus some international legal writers have seen in war a means by which the law of international society is enforced by individual members; others have seen in it a means of settling political conflicts. Theorists of the balance of power have seen war as the ultimate means by which threats to the international equilibrium are redressed. It may even be argued, in line with these theories, that the element in international relations of a 'war of all against all' so far from being detrimental to the working of international society, is in a certain sense positively favourable to it. For if the enforcement of law depends upon the willingness of particular law-abiding states to undertake war against particular law-breaking ones, then the prospects of law enforcement will be best if every state is willing to take up arms against any state that breaks the law. The fact that at any one time certain states are unwilling to contemplate war with certain other states, either because they are allied to them, or because they are indifferent to one another's policies, or because they are bound by a particular sense of community, is an obstacle to the enforcement of international law. In the same way the balance of power is best preserved if states are willing to take up arms against any state that threatens the balance, to focus their attention upon its recalcitrance in this respect and to disregard all special claims it may have on them.

If, then, we were tempted to compare international relations with a pre-contractual state of nature among individual men, it might be argued that we should choose not Hobbes' description of that condition, but Locke's. In the conception of a society without government, whose members must themselves judge and enforce the law, which is therefore crude and uncertain, we can recognize the international society of many thinkers in the tradition of international law. And although Locke's speculations about life of men in anarchy will leave us dissatisfied, we may turn to modern anthropological studies of actual societies of this kind, which have been 'forced to consider what, in the absence of explicit forms of government, could be held to constitute the political structure of a people.'[6] Such studies widen our view of the devices for cohesion in a society, and suggest a number of parallels in the international field.

There are a number of these which are worth exploring. One, which has received some attention from international lawyers is the principle of the 'hue and cry.' Another is the place of ritual. Another is the principle of loyalty – among kinsmen in primitive society, among allies in international society. International society and certain sorts of primitive society would seem also to be alike in respect of the function performed within them by the principle that might is right. This we are inclined to dismiss as the contrary of a moral principle, a mere way of saying that the question of right does not arise. This, indeed, is what, according to Thucydides, the Athenians said to the Melians: they did not appeal to the principle that might is right, but said that the question of right arose only when the parties were equal, which in this case they were not. Yet in international relations the parties are frequently not equal, and the society of states has had to evolve principles which will take account of this fact and lead to settlements. The rule that the will of the stronger party should be accepted provides a means of going directly to what the outcome of a violent struggle would be, without actually going through that struggle. To say that the principle that might is right fulfils a function in international society is not to provide a justification of it or to regard it as a necessary element in international life; but it is to argue that the working of a social order may be recognized even in a feature of relations between states sometimes taken to demonstrate the absence of any kind of order.[7]

We must, however, at some point abandon the domestic analogy altogether. Not only is this because the attempt to understand something by means of analogies with something else is a sign of infancy in a subject, an indication of lack of familiarity with our own subject matter. But also because international society is unique, and owes its character to qualities that are peculiar to the situation of sovereign states, as well as to those it has in common with the lives of individuals in domestic society. One of the themes that has accompanied the statement of the idea of international society has been that anarchy among states is tolerable to a degree to which among individuals it is not. This has been recognized in some measure even by those who originated the description of international relations in terms of the Hobbesian state of nature.

In the first place, as we have noted, it is not consequent

upon the international anarchy that in it there can be no industry or other refinements of living; unlike the individual in Hobbes' state of nature, the state does not find its energies so absorbed in the pursuit of security that the life of its activities is that of mere brutes. Hobbes himself recognizes this when having observed that persons of sovereign authority are in 'a posture of war,' he goes on to say: 'But because they uphold thereby the industry of their subjects, there does not follow from it that misery which accompanies the liberty of particular men.'[8] The same sovereigns that find themselves in the state of nature in relation to one another have provided with particular territories, the conditions in which the refinements of life can flourish.

In the second place states have not been vulnerable to violent attack to the same degree that individuals are. Spinoza, echoing Hobbes in his assertion that 'two states are in the same relation to one another as two men in the condition of nature,' goes on to add 'with this exception, that a commonwealth can guard itself against being subjugated by another, as a man in the state of nature cannot do. For, of course, a man is overcome by sleep every day, is often afflicted by disease of body or mind, and is finally prostrated by old age; in addition, he is subject to other troubles against which a commonwealth can make itself secure.'[9] One human being in the state of nature cannot make himself secure against violent attack; and this attack carries with it the prospect of sudden death. Groups of human beings organized as states, however, may provide themselves with a means of defence that exists independently of the frailties of any one of them. And armed attack by one state upon another has not brought with it a prospect comparable to the killing of one individual by another. For one man's death may be brought about suddenly, in a single act; and once it has occurred, it cannot be undone. But war has only occasionally resulted in the physical extinction of the vanquished people. In modern history it has been possible to take Clausewitz's view that 'war is never absolute in its results' and that defeat in it may be merely 'a passing evil which can be remedied.' Moreover, war in the past, even if it could in principle lead to the physical extermination of one or both of the belligerent peoples, could not be thought capable of doing so at once in the course of a single act. Clausewitz, in holding that war does not consist of a single instantaneous blow, but always of a succession of separate actions, was drawing attention to something that in the past has always held true and has rendered public violence distinct from private. It is only in the context of recent military technology that it has become pertinent to ask whether war could not now both be 'absolute in its results' and 'take the form of a single, instantaneous blow,' in Clausewitz's understanding of these terms; and whether therefore violence does not now confront the state with the same sort of prospect it has always held for the individual.[10]

This second difference, that states have been less vulnerable to violent attack by one another than individual men, is reinforced by a third contingency of great importance; that in so far as states have been vulnerable in this sense they have not been equally so. Hobbes builds his account of the state of nature upon the proposition that 'Nature hath made men so equal, in the faculties of body and mind . . . [that] the weakest has strength enough to kill the strongest.'[11] It is this equal vulnerability of every man to every other that, in Hobbes' view, renders the condition of anarchy intolerable. In modern international society, however, there has been a persistent distinction between Great Powers and small. Great Powers have been secure against the attacks of small Powers; and have had to fear only other Great Powers, and hostile combinations of Powers. We have only to think of the security enjoyed by Great Britain in the nineteenth century to appreciate that the insecurity which is a feature of the Hobbesian state of nature, in so far as it exists in international society, is not distributed equally among all its members. It is interesting to find Gentz writing of 'the European Commonwealth' that 'The original inequality of the parties in such a union as is here described is not an accidental circumstance, much less a casual evil; but is in a certain degree to be considered as the previous condition and foundation of the whole system.'[12] A footnote follows: 'Had the surface of the globe been divided into equal parts, no such union would ever have taken place; and an eternal war of each against the whole is probably the only

event we should have heard of.' If Great Powers are relatively safe from attack and do not stand in need of the protection of a central authority, then by the same token they
are themselves in a position to attack others and to withstand the pressures which other states may seek to bring
to bear upon them. If an even distribution of strength among
states would seem unfavourable to the development of international society, it is also true that great discrepancies
in strength may obstruct its working or even prove irrecon-
cilable with it. One of the central contentions of theorists
of the balance of power has been that if international society is to be maintained, no one state may be in a position
to dominate the rest. Other writers have gone beyond this,
to assert with Gentz himself, in a doctrine in which the
principle of the balance of power becomes difficult to disentangle from that of collective security, 'That if that system is not merely to exist, but to be maintained without
constant perils and violent concussions, each member which
infringes it must be in a condition to be coerced, not only
by the collective strength of the other members, but by
any majority of them, if not by one individual.'[13] Ancillon,
writing sixteen years later, saw the same principle at work
in the early development in Italy of the principle of equilibrium: 'Le voisinage d'un grand nombre d'états, trop
inégaux pour résister l'un à l'autre, y avait fait saisir, suivre
et appliquer de bonne heure ces maximes de prudence qui
servent de sauvegarde au droit, et qui allaient passer de ce
petit sur un théâtre sur un théâtre plus vaste.'[14]

A fourth point of contrast that has often been remarked
is that states in their economic lives enjoy a degree of self-
sufficiency beyond comparison with that of individual men.
Thus while it has been one of the themes of theorists of
international society to stress the mutual dependence of states
in trade, at the same time their relative economic independence of one another, by contrast with individuals, has provided support for the argument that states are able to tolerate
a form of society looser than that which is crowned by a
government.

As against the Hobbesian view that states find themselves
in a state of nature which is a state of war, it may be argued, therefore, that they constitute a society without a

government. This society may be compared with the anarchical society among individual men of Locke's imagin-
ing, and also with primitive anarchical societies that have
been studied by anthropologists. But although we may
employ such analogies, we must in the end abandon them,
for the fact that states form a society without a government reflects also the features of their situation that are
unique. The working of international society must be understood in terms of its own, distinctive institutions. These
include international law, diplomacy and the system of balance of power. There may be others which should be ranked
alongside these; it is arguable, for example, that collaboration among the Great Powers to manage the affairs of
international society as a whole and impart to them a degree of central direction – seen in operation in the series
of conferences from Westphalia to Potsdam, and finding its
most perfect embodiment in the Concert of Europe – also
represents such an institution, even though it has functioned
only intermittently.

III

The idea that sovereign states find themselves in a Hobbesian
state of nature, as well as standing on its own as a description of what international politics is like, is also to be found
linked to demands for the establishment of a universal state.
In doctrines like that of Kant in *Perpetual Peace*, the Hobbesian
domestic analogy is applied to international relations, but
in this case taken further to embrace not only the idea of
the state of nature but also that of the social contract.

The Kantian view of international relations involves a dilemma. If states are indeed in a Hobbesian state of nature,
the contract by means of which they are to emerge from it
cannot take place. For if covenants without the sword are
but words, this will be true of covenants directed towards
the establishment of universal government, just as it will
hold true of agreements on other subjects. The difficulty
with the Kantian position is that the description it contains of the actual condition of international relations, and
the prescription it provides for its improvement, are incon-

sistent with one another. Action within the context of continuing international anarchy is held to be of no avail; but
at the same time it is in the international anarchy that the
grand solution of the international social contract is held
to take place.

The advocate of a universal state can show his scheme
to be feasible as well as desirable only by admitting that
international relations do not resemble a Hobbesian state
of nature; that in it covenants without the sword are more
than words and the materials may be found with which to
bring about collaboration between sovereign governments.
But to make this admission is to weaken the case for bringing
the international anarchy to an end. For the establishment
of a universal government cannot then be regarded as a
sine qua non of the world order. If a Hobbesian description
of the international state of nature is abandoned for a
Lockean one, then the case for a fundamental change is
simply that which Locke presents for a contract of government: that to crown the anarchical society with a government would be to render it more efficient.

However, such a case might still be a quite formidable
one. It may rest essentially on something which the Lockean
description of international society itself admits: that in it
the private use of force is tolerated or even in certain circumstances required. The international society described by
the international lawyers and the theorists of balance of
power is one in which war has a permanent and perhaps
even a necessary place. The argument for proceeding from
anarchy to government may therefore be stated, as Kant
states it, in terms of the possibility and desirability of perpetual peace.

It is a facile view according to which a universal state
would abolish war because war is a relationship between
sovereign states and sovereign states would have been abolished. Either we may take war to mean any kind of organized violence between large groups of human beings, in which
case the statement is false. Or we may understand the term
in the narrow sense of a contention between sovereign states,
in which case although the statement is true it is misleading. War in this latter sense comprises only one area of the
spectrum of possible violence; if the elimination of war in

this special sense of public war were to occasion the re-establishment of the various forms of private war, this could not necessarily be counted a gain.

If, however, a universal state should be understood as providing, just as does the system of sovereign states, a particular solution to the problem of the management of violence, rather than a means of transcending it, this is not to say that it is an inferior solution. It may be argued that the propensities for violence that are inherent in any form of political organization on a world-scale, will be better managed through the medium of a single authority entrusted with the legitimate exercise of force, than through many such authorities; just as this is the case in the smaller geographical context of the nation-state. Such an argument might well be sustained; yet the traditional arguments upholding international society against universal government would first have to be met.

These arguments have often rested on a preference for liberty in international relations over order or security: the liberty of states and nations from domination by a central power, and of individuals from the reach of a tyrannical government whose ubiquitous authority must deny them the right of foreign asylum. It may well be replied to this that order or security is the prime need of international society, and that liberty should if necessary be sacrificed to it. International anarchy, however, may be preferred on grounds of order also.

Government, involving as it does a legal monopoly of the use of force, provides a means for maintaining order; but it is also a source of dissension among conflicting groups in society, which compete for its control. If government authority, once it is captured, may be wielded so as to deny the resort to force by private individuals or groups, it is also the case that the existence of the governmental mechanism constitutes a prize in political conflict, which raises the stakes in such conflict to a level above that it would otherwise be. In the typical modern nation-state order is best preserved when conflict takes the form of a competition between the contending forces for control of a single government, rather than that of competition among governments. Yet the political community is also familiar in which the reverse is the case; in which the dangers to order arising from the coexistence of sovereign governments are less than those involved in the attempt to hold hostile communities in the framework of a single polity. The partition of India in 1947 had this *rationale*. It is possible also to view the problem of order in the world community in this way. Formidable though the classic dangers are of a plurality of sovereign states, these have to be reckoned against those inherent in the attempt to contain disparate communities within the framework of a single government. It is an entirely reasonable view of world order at the present time that it is best served by living with the former dangers rather than by attempting to face the latter.

Notes

1. Anarchy: 'Absence of rule; disorder; confusion' (*OED*). The term here is used exclusively in the first of these senses. The question with which the essay is concerned is whether in the international context it is to be identified also with the second and the third.
2. A number of the leading ideas in this essay derive, in a process in which they may have lost their original shape, from Martin Wight; and a number of others from C. A. W. Manning.
3. Hobbes, *Leviathan*, ch. xiii (London: Dent, Everyman edn, 1953), p. 65.
4. Hobbes, *Leviathan* (1953), p. 66.
5. Hobbes, *Leviathan* (1953), p. 64.
6. M. Fortes and E. E. Evans-Pritchard, *African Political Systems* (Oxford: Oxford University Press, 1940), p. 6.
7. On the functioning of the principle that might is right in primitive and in international society, see Ernest Gellner, 'How to Live in Anarchy,' *The Listener* (April 3, 1958), pp. 579–583.
8. Hobbes, *Leviathan* (1953), p. 65.
9. Spinoza, *Tractatus Politicus*, ch. iii, para. 11 (*The Political Works*, A. G. Wernham (ed.) (Oxford: Clarendon Press, 1958), p. 295).
10. I have deliberately excluded from this essay any consideration of how far recent military technology should lead us to alter the answers that have been given to these questions in the past.
11. Hobbes, *Leviathan* (1953), p. 63.
12. Friedrich von Gentz, *Fragments upon the Balance of Power in Europe* (London: Peltier, 1806), p. 63.
13. Gentz, *Fragments* (1806), p. 62.
14. J. P. F. Ancillon, *Tableau des Révolutions du Système Politique de l'Europe, depuis la Fin du Quinzième Siècle* (Paris: Anselin et Pochard, 1823), vol. i, pp. 262–263.

6 The Powers of Anarchy: Theory, Sovereignty, and the Domestication of Global Life (1988)

Richard Ashley

INTRODUCTION AND OVERVIEW

The late Hedley Bull once observed that international anarchy, the absence of common government among states, may properly be regarded 'as the central fact of international life and the starting-point of theorizing about it.' 'A great deal of the most fruitful reflection about international life,' he wrote, 'has been concerned with tracing the consequences in it of this absence of government.'[1] Today, two decades after Bull offered this assessment, nearly every theorist addressing problems of global collaboration and international order would seem to agree.

Among these theorists, the 'fact of anarchy' necessarily occupies the foreground of serious discourse. These theorists are interested in the political practices and the international institutional developments that might make possible collaborative global responses to transnationally experienced dilemmas of economy, ecology, equity, and security. Like Bull, these theorists also recognize that global political collaboration, when and if it occurs, cannot be explained by reference to sheer imperatives for global collaboration, no matter how urgent or widely perceived these imperatives might be. The greater the importance one attaches to international order, most might say, the greater the need to respect the anarchic quality of international life, the absence of a central agency capable of effecting, administering, and enforcing rational global designs for order. How can there be governance *in the absence of a government*? How can order be constructed *in the absence of an orderer?* How can cooperation be facilitated *under a condition of anarchy?* The theorist knows that just these questions, with just these inflections, must be given pride of place in any serious inquiry into the problem of global collaboration.

These questions have recently gained a special place and prominence in North American scholarship, where they are echoed anew by what is no doubt the most influential of contemporary discourses in international theory: a discourse of the *anarchy problematique.* This distinctive discourse is not well typified by pointing to individual scholars or to individual works, as if a scholar or a text might be a singular paradigm unto itself. The names and specific writings of Waltz, Keohane, Krasner, Jervis, Lake, Ruggie, Oye, Axelrod, Lipson, Aggarwal, Young, Conybeare, and so on might be invoked as a signifying gesture, but if so, it must be understood that what is signified is the disciplined conversation *among* these authors and writings, not their individual asides.[2]

Perhaps the best way to typify this discourse is to point to a tension that appears to animate it. On the one hand, contributions to this discourse presuppose an elaborated understanding of international anarchy that is often associated with a particular reading of Political Realism.[3] According to this understanding, the world is to be understood not only in terms of the *absence* of a central agency of rule but also in terms of the *presence* of a multiplicity of states, understood as sovereign centers of decision presiding over their respective domestic societies and charged with the responsibility of deciding, legitimating, and administering macroeconomic policy therein. Since this condition of anarchy occurs against the background of interdependence – where cross-national transactions are economically and politically consequential and where there is no natural tendency for one state's self-interested policies to contribute to the enablement of others' best laid plans – it defines a 'cooperation problem' that is taken to be fundamental to international life. International order is always precarious, always in jeopardy of fragmenting into a relation of pure antagonism among states. On the other hand, contributions to this discourse do not acquiesce to 'terrors of anarchy' or find therein a rationale for a state's heroic pursuit of paramount power. Nor do they rehearse idealist longings for an institution that would emerge to fill the anarchic void simply because that void so desperately needs to be filled. Instead, they express a resolve to put reason to work in the mitigation of anarchy's dangers.

Robert Keohane ably expresses this tension and its implications for research and theory:

> Realism is better at telling us why we are in such trouble than how to get out of it. It argues that order can be created from anarchy by the exercise of superordinate power: periods of peace follow establishment of dominance in Gilpin's 'hegemonic wars.' Realism sometimes seems to imply, pessimistically, that order can *only* be created by hegemony. If the latter conclusion were correct, not only would the world economy soon become chaotic (barring a sudden resurgence of American power), but at some time in the foreseeable future, global nuclear war would ensue.
>
> Complacency in the face of this prospect is morally unacceptable. No serious thinker could, therefore, be satisfied with Realism as the correct theory of world politics . . . [T]he conditions of terror under which we live compel us to search for a way out of the trap.
>
> . . . We need to respond to the questions that Realism poses but fails to answer: How can order be created out of anarchy without superordinate power; how can peaceful change occur?[4]

To be regarded as a 'serious thinker' in this North American theoretical discourse on international collaboration, one must join in posing questions such as these. One is 'morally' bound to address oneself to the anarchy problematique.

HEDLEY BULL AND THE DOMESTIC ANALOGY

Now it might be easy to imagine Hedley Bull rejoicing in this theoretical turn among today's leading North American theorists. After all, for more than a quarter of a century the author of *The Anarchical Society* was himself centrally concerned with the question of order in the distinctive context of international anarchy. For much of that period, as it happens, he labored under the impression that his undertaking was alien to the behavioralist projects of his North American counterparts. He was convinced that North American behavioralists were caught up in the conceit that they are 'founders of a wholly new science' and that, as a result, they were ever ready to 'dismiss the classical theories of international relations as worthless.'[5] Against this background, would not Bull have been gratified to learn that today's North American theorists have belatedly discovered the sort of classic questions that had long interested him, including especially the question of order in international anarchy? Would he not have been pleased to be joined by North American theorists in his attempt to 'establish the autonomy of international relations'?[6] Would he not have been cheered by the fact that North American scholars now are obliged to cite the classic literatures in which the questions of order and anarchy are posed?

I suspect not. One might well imagine Bull smiling upon contemporary North American theorizing on the anarchy problematique, but in fairness to him, one must understand his expression, not so much as a smile of gratification, but as a sardonic grin, a grin expressing a hint of irony. The irony is simple enough, Today's theorists of the anarchy problematique do seem at last to be in the business of posing the classic questions. They do pose questions concerning rules, norms, and principles of order that, upon a glance, might be construed as the same questions of lasting concern to Bull. At the same time, however, today's theorists manage to pose their question in a way that replicates an interpretive disposition that Bull himself long criticized.

Specifically, I have in mind Hedley Bull's persistent efforts to diagnose and to escape a longstanding impasse in modern-day theory and practice bearing on the question of international collaboration. Central to that impasse – and central to his attempts to escape it – was what Bull called the 'domestic analogy.'[7] Repeatedly, over the course of more than 20 years, Bull complained that theorizing on the question of international anarchy tends to rely uncritically on idealized models of order and agency – models he called 'Hobbesian' and 'Kantian' – first worked out in the interpretation and legitimation of the domestic orders in which the modern culture of the 'West' finds its place. He worried that international theory, relying upon one or another model of domesticated order, becomes a parasite of the theories by which this modern culture knows itself to be the unique and universal source of truth in history. He worried, too, that international theorists thereby sacrifice the ability to grasp global life as it really is: an open-ended, always hazardous contest among plural cultural possibilities, of which the domestic experience of modern culture is surely only one.[8]

Most crucially, Bull was concerned that reliance upon such an idealized model grounded in the domestic experience of modern culture excuses the theorist 'from the discipline of looking at the world' and encourages a kind of 'dogmatism' upon the part of those who attribute 'to the model a connection with reality it does not have.'[9] Insofar as the idealized model is mistaken for an adequate representation of global politics, it takes on 'an air of authority which is often quite misleading as to its standing as a statement about the real world' of global politics.[10] More than misleading, Bull felt, the authority accorded the model is positively 'dangerous.' For once an authorized model anchored in modern domestic experience is mistaken for a standard of truth in itself, it becomes a device by which non-conforming ambiguities and contingencies of 'anarchical society' may be stigmatized, refused a meaningful place in the discourse of theory, excluded from serious consideration and, where especially recalcitrant, targeted as problems to be corrected or controlled. Viewed in light of such a model, 'international anarchy' cannot betoken a distinctive domain of plural possibilities worthy of being understood. 'International anarchy' can be recognized only as a dangerous void of meaning – a region of conduct known only for its lack of the truth contained in the model of domestic order.

This was Bull's lament, his diagnosis of the impasse in modern theory of international relations. Developing and extending this line of reasoning, I want to suggest that it applies in an especially compelling fashion to contemporary North American theoretical discourse bearing upon global collaboration and framed by the anarchy problematique. Radicalizing Bull's lament, I want to question the *practical political significance* of this discourse.

ELEMENTS OF A POST-STRUCTURALIST ATTITUDE

My idiom, though, is not Bull's. My locutions are not recognizably those of Machiavelli, Meinecke, Satow, Mattingly, Wight, or others of the 'classical tradition' of international theory and practice in which Bull worked. My locutions are more nearly those of Foucault, Kristeva, and Derrida – poststructuralist figures who take their metaphors from notions of 'text' and 'dialogue' as well as from notions of 'battlefield' and 'armed engagement.' In its general form and in its political content, my analysis of the workings of the 'domestic analogy' in theoretical discourse on the anarchy problematique effects a poststructuralist attitude.

Reflecting this poststructuralist attitude, my analysis of this discourse stresses its place and function in the life of modernity. By 'modernity' I do not mean to invoke a homogeneous cultural reality – a pure presence existing independent of practice in history. I mean instead an attitude or set of attitudes – a *regime* of highly mobile knowledgeable orientations and practical dispositions – that since its emergence has struggled actively against attitudes of 'countermodernity,' most often successfully, but very often not. I mean a regime that gives pride of place to one practical disposition above all others – a disposition that, as it happens, renders modernist theory and practice distinctly unable to come to terms with the intrinsic ambiguity, contestedness, and dependence upon arbitrary practice of prevailing modes of subjectivity, objectivity, and conduct in global life. This is the practical disposition to privilege an historically constituted voice of 'reasoning man' as the sovereign center and unquestioned origin of truth and meaning in history. More specifically, and as I shall explain, this is the disposition to privilege some historically imposed *limitation* of human knowing and doing as essential to 'reasoning man's' sovereign being and, as such, as the already present transcendental *foundation* and source of humans' capacities for the autonomous use of reason in history. In saying that theoretical discourse on the anarchy problematique is a modernist discourse, I shall be saying that it participates in this regime. I shall be saying that it finds its center in some historical limitations which it takes to be foundational to 'reasoning man's' sovereign being.

When one understands that the modernist regime is centered upon the sovereignty of 'reasoning man,' one is already positioned to understand the crucial role that the construct of domestic society plays for this regime and for the discourses that participate in it. In theoretical discourse on the anarchy problematique as in the modernist regime more generally, the construct of domestic society is chronically, necessarily, and unassailably privileged. It is so privileged because domestic society is taken to signify the historical presence of a possibility condition that must be present if in history one is to invoke the sovereignty of 'reasoning man.' In particular, domestic society is taken to signify some real historical limitations on knowing and doing that reasoning man has a duty to obey, and that can be encoded in law and backed by the coercive means of the state, because they are taken to supply the already present transcendental conditions of reasoning man's will to total knowledge, freedom, and mastery over himself and his history. In brief, domestic society signifies the limits in space and time in which modern reasoning man can secure the absolute foundations that his will to total knowledge requires.

In keeping with Bull's lament, then, my analysis focuses upon the practical political significance of knowledge in world politics, including especially that knowledge intimately bound up with the modern construct of domestic society. As a poststructuralist analysis, however, the argument to follow departs from Bull's lament in at least three closely related respects:

1. Bull's lament reduces the question of knowledge to a matter of the representation, as in a model, of a referent reality. It interrogates the practical significance of knowledge solely in terms of the extent to which a representational model adequately informs (or, contrariwise, misleads, blinds, or constrains) the conduct of knowing

agents in the various domains of an already structured world. By contrast, my analysis looks to knowledgeable practices as *productive* relations of *power.*[11] It looks to the way in which knowledgeable practices work in history to control ambiguity, privilege some interpretations over others, limit discourse, discipline conduct, and produce subjective agents and the institutional structures of their experience.

2. Bull's lament presupposes a boundary between two domains of human conduct – one domestic and subordinated to the sovereign state, and the other international and noteworthy for the absence of a sovereign center – across which analogies might be drawn, whether for good or for ill. My poststructuralist analysis requires no such limiting presupposition. It puts this boundary in question. It regards this boundary – and, with it, the modern constructs of domestic society and sovereign state, on the one hand, and international anarchy, on the other – as problematical effects whose production in history is never finally completed, always dependent upon knowledgeable practices that potentially traverse all bounds.

3. Bull's lament understands the 'domestic analogy' – the arbitrary imposition of an idealized domestic experience in the interpretation of global history – as an interpretive mistake that modern theorists too often make. It regrets especially the resulting blindness to the unabated contest of plural cultural possibilities in international history. My analysis regards domestic society as a construct that defines practically the bounded space and time in which the modern sovereign, 'reasoning man,' can establish his hegemony as the timeless origin of truth and meaning in history. It understands the arbitrary privileging of a construct of domestic society, not as an incidental interpretive error, but as a knowledgeable practice whose successful replication is at once dependent upon blindness to history and crucial to a never completed process of *domestication* upon which the experience of modernity depends.

Taken together, these three departures from Bull's lament define an analytic premise of sorts: the very production of the experience of modernity in global life – including the subjective agents and objectified institutions of domestic experience and the boundaries separating domestic from international – never ceases to depend upon the way in which knowledgeable practices – theoretical practices among them – discipline the indeterminacy and equivocity of history, imposing structure upon it.

My attempt to assess the practical political significance of theoretical discourse on the anarchy problematique reflects this premise. I shall not approach this discourse as if it were a set of abstract intellectual representations produced from some intellectual vantage point external to history. Eschewing the attitude of a critic of theory, my analysis of this discourse proceeds as a 'case study' into a specific site and mode of conduct that participates within a particular historical regime, a modernist regime, whose command over a space and a time is dependent upon the replication of certain knowledgeable practices to impose boundaries and 'domesticate' the chance, contingency, and ambiguity of a pluralistic history. As a 'case study' into a site of modernist practice, my analysis will be less concerned with what this discourse *says* about history than it will be with what its knowledgeable practices *do* in history. In this discourse's replications of the productive knowledgeable practices of the modernist regime, my analysis will find illustrations of the widely circulated practices by which the recalcitrant and ambiguous domains of global life are subordinated to a narrative of 'domestication.' In the dilemmas and paradoxes that this discourse encounters, my analysis will find illustrations of the more general paradoxes encountered by the modernist regime.

THE DOMESTICATION OF GLOBAL LIFE: SOME ANALYTIC THEMES

This poststructuralist analysis will take time to produce. For now, as a way of providing an orientation and introducing key terms, it is useful to anticipate a number of overlapping themes that will be developed in the course of my analysis. I have six themes in mind.

Heroic Practice and a Narrative of Domestication

My analysis will find its focus neither in actors' subjective intentions nor in objectively structured social institutions but in a specific knowledgeable practice that comes into play whenever and wherever the modernist regime encounters an ambiguous proliferation of interpretations that resists decisive resolution. This knowledgeable practice has a name. Although it bears a close resemblance to the domestic analogy, I shall call it a *heroic practice* for reasons that will later become plain. A heroic practice is a 'double-voiced' practice – a practice so-called because it turns on a dichotomy.[12] It turns on a hierarchical opposition of *sovereignty* versus *anarchy*, where the former term is privileged as a regulative ideal.

In the one 'voice,' a heroic practice invokes *sovereignty,* conceived as a transcendental origin of power that is not in itself a political power because it is also the timeless and universal source of all that can be meaningful and true in history. A heroic practice invokes this sovereign identity of truth and power as the regulative ideal and necessary origin of an already present state of domestic being. It refers to a time and place of domestic being that has its origin in sovereignty, that is already present within history, and that provides within its bounds the necessary *historical* ground of conduct that shall count as meaningful and true. Here, within this domestic time and place, all conflicts of interpretation that bear upon the making of history are taken to be decidable – they are taken to be susceptible to precise and undisputed resolution – by appeal to the decisive truth of sovereignty. Here, where power is always grounded in truth, there is no question of knowledgeable conduct that would secure power independent of universal truth.

In the second 'voice,' a heroic practice invokes a fear of *anarchy*. It situates the real historical presence of domestic being in opposition to a fearsome time and place of ambiguity, contingency, and chance where conflicts of interpretation are intrinsically undecidable – a region of conduct where the sovereign truth is not reliably honored but put in question. Here consequential practices are not taken to be rich in truth and meaning. They are not practices to be listened to and understood. Detached from the presumption of grounding in the universal truth of sovereignty, consequential conduct in the region of anarchy can be recognized solely as a matter of power – an arbitrary power that is also a dangerous power because it threatens to intrude upon and disrupt the historically-lived truth of domestic being. A heroic practice thus invokes anarchic dangers that must be excluded from the time and place of domestic being. It invokes dangers that can be brought under control only when practice, grounded in the already present domestic order, imposes upon the region of anarchy the sovereign truth it lacks.

This double-voiced heroic practice is not a psychological structure, an autonomous moral code, a deep grammar of society, or a representational model that functions to describe the structures and boundaries of an already domesticated society. It is a mobile, iterable productive principle of a constitutive political process – a modern *economy of power* – that works to discipline conduct in widely scattered sites.[13] It is a practical principle that circulates within a diffuse economy of power; that is replicated in different ways, using different resources, in innumerable local settings, from the most 'social' to the most 'solitary;' and that works therein to focus relations of authority, effect sovereign centers of interpretation, arrest ambiguity, stabilize meaning, invest individuals with rights and obligations, impose boundaries of normalized conduct, define and elaborate problems and anomalies, mobilize discourse toward the production of promised solutions and, in all of this do what must be done if the modernist regime is to be secured as a time-bound extrapolitical regime of truth. *It disciplines the chance, contingency, and ambiguity of historical doing in the domestication of modern being.*

Theoretical Practice and the Active Enclosure of History

I shall be arguing that theoretical discourse on the anarchy problematique participates in the modern economy of power by which a multivalent narrative of domestication is

globally imposed. As I shall show, this discourse relies upon
and replicates the double-voiced heroic practice. It brings
it to bear upon regions of ambiguous and contingent practices – regions of 'international politics' – that resist domestication and that are recognized as anarchic therefore.
From this it does not follow that theoretical discourse on
the anarchy problematique is in itself a unique font of power
that makes history through its own conceptual contrivances.
It does follow that this theoretical discourse participates
in, contributes to, and does not question or resist a far-
reaching process of enclosure.

To be sure, this is the sort of closure that the most familiar varieties of critical theory have made it their business to question and overturn. A modern economy of power
does not fix discourse within a sealed ideological horizon,
represent a 'given order' as an unproblematic condition,
and invite a complacent, unquestioning attitude toward that
order. Far from portraying an unproblematic order, theoretical discourse on the anarchy problematique does what
its name implies: it functions to effect a specific problematization of life. Far from inviting complacency, it does what
replications of the heroic practice always do: it incites discourse to recognize and focus upon anarchic dangers and
to explore a variety of means by which domestic resources
might be mobilized and collaboratively deployed to remedy
or arrest these dangers.

Yet if this problematization is opposed to closure on the
model of quietism, it can hardly be mistaken for a readi-
ness to enjoy and cultivate the indeterminate play of plural
interpretations in international history. On the contrary, as
I shall show, this problematization is a way of mobilizing
and focusing social resources in an *active process of enclosure*: a process by which contingencies and ambiguities of
global history are marked as deviant and fearsome, cast as
technical problems requiring collaborative solutions, excluded
from legitimate *political* discourse, made the objects of control
or rehabilitation from the standpoint of sovereign centers,
and thereby subordinated to a multivalent narrative of domestication whose political content is suspended beyond question and criticism.

The Sovereignty of 'Man' and the Centering of Heroic Practices

If the unity of this global process is difficult to grasp at first, it is largely because theoretical discourse on the anarchy problematique poses the problem of global collaboration as one of 'order in the absence of an orderer.' Consistent with this familiar formulation, the heroic practices that are put to work in this discourse and that contribute to the domestication of global life can be said to be 'decentered' and 'pluralistic' in one important respect. They do not require or refer to the existence of a unique and central subjective *agency* of global rule manifesting God-like powers. Instead, these heroic practices find their empirical foci in a multiplicity of domestic domains, each of which is subordinated to the sovereign *subjectivity* of a state, each of which provides within its bounds the *objective* grounds of normal and warranted conduct, and each of which is understood to be *autonomous* in just this sense: conduct grounded in a domestic society is not directed by or answerable to a suprastate agency that audibly pronounces a universal law or that visibly commands the discipline of those who do not conform.

As I shall stress, however, the decentering contemplated by this discourse and effected by a modern economy of global power is far from total. To say that the heroic practices that impose a global narrative of domestication have no need for a *visible* central agency engaging in conspicuous *acts* of global discipline is not to say that these practices dispense with the presupposition of a sovereign source of truth and power that arches the totality of global life. On the contrary, as I shall indicate, the heroic practices replicated in a modern economy of global power – and replicated, too, by theoretical discourse on the anarchy problematique – retain the presupposition of sovereignty as a universal regulative ideal. They invoke the presence of some sovereign source of truth and power, itself independent of political practice in history, from which derives the differentiated totality of multiple sovereign states and domestic societies. Indeed, they earn the name 'heroic' practices precisely because they invoke the distinctly modern sovereign figure, the figure of *man*. Heroic practices invoke the sovereignty of reasoning man whose voice would displace the Word of God as the source of truth and meaning in the world.[14]

The point is a crucial one. It is necessary to pause long enough to clarify what is being said. The principal thesis may be summarized:

> The heroic practices at work within a modern economy of power, including the heroic practices of theoretical discourse on the anarchy problematique, are centered in a modern construct of sovereignty. They speak and move from the standpoint of a universal figure of *reasoning man* – man who is at one with the public discourse of 'reasonable humanity.' More specifically, they invoke a figure of reasoning man who is involved in history and who is invested with a will and a capacity to find in the very facticity of his historical limitations the transcendental foundations of the knowledge that will permit him to achieve in history a promised total freedom, a total mastery of himself and his existence.[15] Thus, although heroic practices might refer to the 'sovereignty of the state over domestic society,' they are not ultimately state-centric. They accord 'sovereignty' to the state as an agency of action only on the condition that the transcendental foundations of man's free, public, and universalizing use of reason are established as the fundamental principle of state conduct, the objective of state policy, and the ground of state legitimation.

Densely packed, this thesis may be decomposed and elaborated by way of four propositions.

The first proposition suggests that in its general form, the modern construct of sovereignty invoked by heroic practices is not centered upon God or upon monarchy but upon man.[16] The modern construct of sovereignty entails a humanist hegemony:

Proposition 1:
Not beholden to Classical epistemology, the modern construct of sovereignty is not dependent upon the Classical assumption that 'God had arranged a chain of being and

arranged language in preestablished correspondence with it.'[17] It thus dispenses with the Classical belief that man and his institutions must find their preestablished and functional place, alongside other objects, within some fixed table of being.[18] As a modern construct, sovereignty invokes the heroic figure of modern reasoning man who is himself the origin of language, the maker of history, and the source of meaning in the world. It invokes the heroic figure of reasoning man who knows that the order of the world is not God-given, that man is the origin of all knowledge, that responsibility for supplying meaning to history resides with man himself, and that, through reason, man may achieve total knowledge, total autonomy, and total power.

The second proposition indicates that although modernist discourse invests the sovereign figure of man with a will and a capacity to transcend those historical conditions that would deny his total freedom, it does not constitute sovereign man as a spectator situated outside of history, therefrom to comprehend history clearly and in its totality. It constitutes a figure of man who is problematically involved in history:

Proposition 2:
The heroic figure of man invoked by the construct of sovereignty confronts – and knows himself to confront – the problem of his involvement in history. Upon exercising his powers of reason, he sees plainly that he is enmeshed in language and in history, indeed, that he is an *object* of language and history. If man is the transcendental condition of the possibility of all knowledge, he also knows himself to be an empirical fact among facts to be examined and conceptualized. If he is a potentially lucid cogito, he also knows himself to be surrounded by domains of darkness and ambiguity that resist the penetration of his thought. And if he is the source of history, he also knows himself as the product of a long history whose beginnings he can never finally fathom.[19] Here, then, is the problem that the heroic figure of man confronts. Since man is the origin of universal truth and meaning, he can and must aspire fully to deny his finitude, to transcend his historical limitations, and to achieve total knowl-

edge; but since man is enmeshed in history, his very knowledge reveals him in his finitude, in the sheer facticity of the historical reality that bears down upon him, determines him, and limits him in what he can here and now do and know.[20]

In its general form, then, the modern sovereign is a universal figure of reasoning man who is situated in history and who must confront his historical limitations with courage lest he despair of his promised transcendence.

The third proposition suggests that the figure of sovereign man need not lose courage in the face of his historical limitations because these limitations are not exterior and imposed upon him, as if from some extra-human force. In modernist discourse, they are limitations *of* man, and through reason, man can turn them to his advantage:

Proposition 3:
The sovereignty of man over history can be heralded because the limitations he confronts are limitations *of* man or imposed or decreed *by* man. Knowing this, the heroic figure of reasoning man is disposed to look upon the factual limitations of historical experience, and he is disposed to discriminate between those that are elemental to what he necessarily and objectively is, as rational human being, and those that are the historical consequences of what man, in history, contingently does. He knows that the former limitations – those that are essential to man – can be obeyed without fear that they in any way compromise his autonomy. More than that, reasoning man knows that he has an *obligation* to obey them because they are the transcendental conditions of the possibility of reasoning man's autonomy and power. They can be taken to provide the transcendental conditions of man's reason, man's total knowledge, man's capacities to assert total mastery over himself and over the contingency and chance of his experience. By knowing these essential limitations, and by knowing to obey them, man can be totally free.

The modern construct of sovereignty thus invokes the heroic figure of reasoning man who, by acknowledging those essential limitations he is obliged not to criticize but only to obey, affirms the absolute foundations upon which he shall ground his reason, his will to truth, his courageous struggle to transcend all those historical contingencies that would deny his infinite powers. It invokes a figure of man who recognizes some specific limitations on his *doing* and *knowing*, not as external constraints, but as virtually constitutive of his autonomous *being* in history.

The fourth proposition links the general form of sovereignty, in the modern construction, to the question of the sovereignty of the state. It suggests that in modernist discourse, the sovereign figure of man, defined in terms of a necessary limitation, supplies the constitutive principle of both (a) the modern state, as sovereign *subject* of rational collective action, and (b) domestic society, as *object* domain subordinated to the state's sovereign gaze:

Proposition 4:

In modernist discourse, the sovereignty of the state, including the duty to obey the law it speaks, does not derive from any source external to man. Rather, the state's sovereignty obtains in its establishing as the principles of its law those historical limitations that modern reasoning man knows to be the necessary conditions of his free use of reason. It consists, more succinctly, in subordinating *raison d'état* to the reason of man, making the former the guarantee of the possibility conditions of the latter. Reasoning man, in obeying the law of the state, will thus not surrender any part of his freedom; he will obey the limitations that supply the condition of his autonomous reason. In turn, domestic society will be recognized as that domain of human interaction in which just this relation can be sustained. It is the time and place in which sovereign man willingly submits himself as an *object* of the state's authority because he knows that the state obeys and defends the conditions of his will to total knowledge.

In modernist discourse, then, the state will be recognized as a sovereign subject of social action that reasoning man is obliged to honor insofar as the disciplines and boundaries imposed in the name of the state can be understood, not as arbitrary constraints, but as necessary to the taming of all those historical contingencies that threaten the transcendental conditions of humanity's autonomous exercise of reason. Domestic society will be recognized as that bounded domain wherein the state, as sovereign subject of social action, effectively objectifies human conduct, compelling conformity to those limitations that reasoning man knows to be foundational to his very being.

These four propositions develop a thesis that, as I say, is crucial to my argument here – a thesis that goes to the general form of sovereignty invoked by heroic practices within a modern economy of global power. They suggest that heroic practices are centered in and profess to speak the voice of a universal sovereign, reasoning man. They suggest, too, that heroic practices, in giving voice to the universal sovereignty of man, must recognize some historical limitations of man's knowing and doing as the already present transcendental foundations of man's universal reason. And they suggest that these essential limitations, however they may be defined, are taken to supply the already extant principle in terms of which the sovereignty of the state and the reach of domestic society may be recognized. When theoretical discourse on the anarchy problematique speaks of a world consisting of multiple states and domestic societies, I shall say, it is always the voice of such a universal sovereign that it speaks. Not the sovereignty of the state but the sovereignty of reasoning man is the center it invokes.

The Historicity of Sovereignty: Paradigm and Paradox

If one can detect the echoes of Immanuel Kant in this distinctively modern form of sovereignty, it is not of course by accident. In my attempt to characterize the sovereign center of the heroic practices by which global life is domesticated, I deliberately rely upon Kantian locutions; and I do so because it was with Kant at the end of the eighteenth century that 'man' was introduced to philosophy as the active being who is at once involved in history and the unified and unifying source of history's order and meaning.[21] I rely upon Kantian locutions for another reason, though. It is possible to put Kant's locutions to further use in order to highlight yet a fourth theme. The general *form* of the sovereignty of man leaves open the question of *content*. To say that the sovereignty of man is practically defined in terms of some recognized identity between (a) some historical limitation on what man knows and does and (b) the essential condition of man's sovereign being is not to impose any constraint on the specific limitations that will be recognized, in history, as essential to the sovereignty of man.

Four important consequences follow. One is that modernist discourse is open in principle to a variety of interpretations of the sovereign man that it puts at its center and whose voice it speaks. The liberal's 'possessive individual man,' the Marxist's 'laboring man in his sociality,' the romantic ecologist's 'man in harmony with nature,' the Christian humanist's 'man in brotherhood with man' – there are in principle as many possible interpretations as there are possible historical limitations that might be erected as absolute foundations of free and rational human being.

A second consequence is that modernist discourse, while everywhere invoking an absolute and universal sovereign presence, is always in jeopardy of fragmenting into a number of violently opposed discourses, each of which speaks a distinctive sovereign voice, each of which knows its voice as a voice of universal domestic truth, each of which knows all others only as the fearsome negation of the truth it speaks, and each of which renders others the objects of its heroic practices of discipline. Such conflicts are no doubt the most consequential conflicts of modern global life, but they are not conflicts between states, and they are not conflicts that could possibly be settled by interstate war. They are conflicts that traverse all political boundaries because they are conflicts over the interpretation of sovereignty by which states, domestic societies, and their political boundaries shall be defined.

A third consequence is that, over time, the prevailing interpretation of the absolute sovereignty of man can change in ways that dramatically alter the character of international relations. With change in the interpretation of the essential limitations defining the sovereignty of man, it remains possible that modern political life on a global scale will continue to be configured as a multiplicity of states and domestic societies, but the constitutive principle by which the subjectivity of the states and the objectivity of domestic societies are practically differentiated and limited will be transformed.

A fourth consequence is that the *historically effective* centering of a global narrative of domestication – the kind of centering that would make possible the stabilized integration of dispersed heroic practices in the coproduction of a multiplicity of states and domestic societies across which conduct is mutually enabling rather than disabling – requires the imposition of what I shall call a *paradigm of sovereignty*.

As the term will be used here, a paradigm of sovereignty is a specific, historically fabricated, widely circulated, and practically effective interpretation of man as sovereign being. It is an interpretation that is sparse in detail, silently affirmed, and yet powerful in its potential effects. Sparse in detail, a paradigm of sovereignty is an interpretation that does no more than privilege certain historical limitations on what man knows and does as the transcendental foundations of man's free use of reason and, hence, as the limitations that man, in the name of his freedom, has a duty never to question and always to obey. Silently affirmed, a paradigm of sovereignty is not a law, prohibition, or external constraint on the autonomy of subjects of action but an unquestioned condition of empowerment of all those sovereign subjects who are competent and free to reflect upon questions of law, prohibition, and constraint. Powerful in its potential effects, a paradigm of sovereignty supplies an iterable 'principle of thrift' that functions to discipline the proliferation of meanings within all the far reaches of a modern economy of global power.[22]

Viewed as a functional principle of thrift, a paradigm of sovereignty is indispensable to a collaborative project of unsurpassed consequence: the 'conductorless orchestration' of dispersed practices in the domestication of global life.[23] In the terminology of Foucault, a paradigm of sovereignty provides the indispensable principle that makes possible a 'strategy' of global domestication in the absence of a 'knowing strategist.' To summarize, a paradigm of sovereignty provides a simple functional principle of interpretation

- that can be circulated widely across a range of disparate times and circumstances;
- that can be put to work in diverse and ambiguous sites to settle contests of interpretation regarding the essential hegemonic truth already present in any time, place, or person;
- that can establish in multiple sites the hegemonic grounds in terms of which anarchic dangers can be recognized and upon which heroic practices might locally pivot;
- that can be replicated in this way to establish the essential difference and the essential identity between individual states as sovereign subjects of political action and corresponding domestic societies as well-bounded object domains; and
- that can thereby make possible the concerting of dispersed, autonomous practices toward the imposition of a collective intention, an overall will, a strategic direction that sovereign subjects perceive to exist in itself, beyond all intentionality.

This strategic effect is of course the domestication of time, space, and political subjectivity in global life. It is, more specifically, a mode of domestication in which the limits inscribed in a paradigm of sovereignty are recapitulated as the universally self-evident structural boundaries and conditions of rational political conduct. Thanks to the fabrication and circulation of a paradigm of sovereignty, local instances of heroic practice can be orchestrated, and their effects can be concerted in a global process of domestication even though circumstances of practice vary widely, even though the people involved do not deliberately co-ordinate their conduct, even though there is no central agency to pronounce a universal program or to direct these practices toward an end, and even though the effects of domestication produced are regarded, not as objects of political will, but as the self-evident conditions and boundaries of life on a global scale.

Considering how consequential a paradigm of sovereignty is for the conduct of modern global politics, one might think that the question of the fabrication and imposition of such a paradigm would be the central analytic question addressed by contemporary theorists interested in matters of global conflict and collaboration. In fact, as we shall see, theoretical discourse on the anarchy problematique has not entertained the question of a paradigm of sovereignty as a matter deserving of critical scrutiny. It does just the reverse. It invokes a paradigm of sovereignty while immunizing from critical analysis the paradigm it invokes.

As I shall indicate, theoretical discourse on the anarchy problematique starts from the premise that there *are* at any time a multiplicity of states and domestic societies, where the paradigmatic differences between state and society and between domestic society and anarchy are not questioned but simply assimilated as part of the premise. Three analytic dispositions derive from this premise:

- Having nullified the question of difference, analysts are able to conclude that modern international politics exhibits a sameness that is basic to its history. International politics appears as no more and no less than an eternal struggle of multiple sovereign states in anarchy, and in turn, the sheer continuity of this struggle is cited as ground for the belief that the struggle among states is the 'structural' basis of international life to which all programs of collaboration must ultimately bow.
- Analysts define international political problems and dangers in terms of the way in which historical happenings transgress boundaries already in place, destabilize structures of state authority already given, and pit state against state as mutual objects of violent means.
- Analysts reduce the question of global collaboration to a question of how sovereign subjects, including states recognized as sovereign, might deliberate their options and coordinate their practices in the attempt to solve problems or bring dangers under control.

When one inquires into the derivation of such a premise, however, it becomes evident that this discourse must rely upon a paradigm of sovereignty even as it must exclude from criticism the paradigm upon which it relies. It is only by invoking such a paradigm, after all, that theorists are able to acknowledge the polyphony of human conduct in history, to observe that interpretations conflict, to be aware that all pronounced boundaries are transgressed in practice, to witness resistances to every purportedly legitimate act, to know that every universalizing law has its exceptions, to note ambiguities and indeterminacy surrounding all totalizing representations and, nevertheless, to make the extraordinary claim that is contained in their very premise of inquiry: that they are able cut through the undecidable ambiguities and decide the presence and boundaries of states and domestic societies as they really are. They are able to know the differentiated reality of states and domestic societies in their multiplicity – their essences, their purposes or interests, their real boundaries, the dangers they encounter, the problems they confront, their constraints, and the power at their disposal to arrest these dangers, solve these problems, and collaboratively refashion their constraints. Only by identifying one's perspective with an unquestioned paradigm of sovereignty could one regard such a claim as an unproblematic starting point of inquiry. Only among others who subscribe to one's paradigm could one expect such a claim to be taken seriously, as a statement at once truthful and powerful, and not as the arbitrary political intervention it is.

It will not be my intention, however, to scold theoretical discourse on the anarchy problematique for its failure to attend to the arbitrary knowledgeable practices that condition its putatively neutral analyses. As noted, I am much more interested in what this discourse does, as a specific site of practice in a modern economy of power. And what it does, in its reliance upon a paradigm it refuses to put in question, is illustrate a more general paradox that is chronically encountered by all of those practices that participate in the domestication of global life.

Two points describe the paradox. The first is that a paradigm of sovereignty does not exist on its own, over and above the temporality of events. Although a paradigm of sovereignty can be said to supply a functional principle, and a crucial one at that, we must avoid the functionalist error of concluding that the function it is said to perform is of itself a basis for ascribing to it a coherence and a self-sufficiency it does not and cannot have.[24] A paradigm of sovereignty must be fabricated in history and through practice, and it must be daily and everywhere fabricated anew in the face of local resistances that would put it in question. It cannot be constituted through the imposition of some totalizing vision from some standpoint outside of history – no such standpoint exists. It cannot be engendered through some great inaugural conjuncture, thereafter to be the already completed paradigm of an epoch – there is no secure and universally acknowledged place for it to reside. Fabricated through the fusion of disparate cognitive resources available within a culture, a paradigm of sovereignty never ascends to its own plane. It can be said to 'exist' at all only to the extent that it 'works' in history and through practice. And it can be said to 'work' only to the extent that the heroic practices pivoting upon it succeed in disciplining the indeterminacy of local sites, incorporating those interpretations that can be assimilated to it and excluding those 'dangerous' interpretations that resist.

The second point is that a paradigm of sovereignty, to be effective, must be regarded as originary unproblematic, given for all time, and hence, beyond criticism and independent of politics. As a limitation on doing and knowing, it must be recognized as something transcendental and foundational within man – something that is always and everywhere already there, prior to the heroic practices which invoke it. It must be summoned as a real presence that is beyond reasoned inquiry because it is in itself the possibility condition of reason. Although it is arbitrarily imposed in history, through practice, and to the exclusion of alternative interpretations, it cannot be recognized as the arbitrary political construction it is.

Here, then, is the paradox. A paradigm of sovereignty is an effect that is problematically produced in history and through practice and that is never independent of practices ongoing here and now; but the production of this effect is at the same time a problem that modern subjects can never directly encounter as a problem to be deliberated and solved. For to deliberate the task is to fail in the task. It is to render political what must be taken to be beyond politics. It is to render historical what must be taken as independent of history. It is to render problematical and in need of analysis what must be taken as the unproblematic and

unquestioned foundation without which it would be impossible to undertake the kind of analysis that permits one clearly
to identify the dangers of politics and the means by which
they might be controlled. Never to be confronted without
extreme embarrassment, it is a task whose performance must
always start from the premise that it has *already* been successfully performed. A paradigm of sovereignty must be
produced through practices that rely on the shared understanding that it is always already in place.

Theoretical Practice and the Politicization of Narrative of Domestication

It is against a background such as this, I shall argue, that
we may begin to appreciate the practical political significance
of theoretical discourse on the anarchy problematique. For
this discourse has brought the modernist regime to a point
where a paradigm of sovereignty, hitherto taken for granted,
is in jeopardy of being recognized as a problem in its own
right. When we interrogate some of the recent theoretical
turns and elaborations of this discourse – the turn to a
theory of hegemonic stability, the opening to non-state actors, and to turn to international regimes – we shall find
that it brings into focus three specific problems that are
irreducible to technical problems. First, this discourse draws
attention to a problem of the *subjectification of the state*:

> How, despite a contest of interpretations and practices
> that cross all boundaries and put all grounds in ques-
> tion, are states constituted as sovereign subjects of ac-
> tion, each recognized to be competent to profess some
> autonomous set of legitimate interests and each em-
> powered to mobilize some range of social resources in its
> name?

Second, this discourse brings into view a corresponding problem of the *objectification of domestic society*:

> How are practices orchestrated and interpretations
> oriented such that it becomes possible to constitute a
> multiplicity of political spaces, each understood as a self-
> evident realization of domestic society, each understood

to be bounded and set apart from an external anarchy,
and each subordinated to the sovereign presence of a state?

Third, this discourse calls attention to a problem that arches
and joins the previous two, namely, the problem of the *in-
scription of a paradigm of sovereignty*:

> How is a paradigm of sovereignty fixed in its widely cir-
> culated and ascribed content so that it might be reliably
> put to work in the orchestration of global practices, thus
> to make possible the constitution of a multiplicity of
> sovereign state subjects and corresponding domestic so-
> cieties, each adapted to specific and changing circum-
> stances, and the several mutually enabling rather than
> disabling in their normalized conduct? How is this poss-
> ible given that there is no state whose every practice can
> be taken to provide a pure exemplar of sovereign subjec-
> tivity, no society that can be taken to provide a homogene-
> ous exemplar of domestic objectivity, no autonomous norm
> already in place, no single voice of authority that speaks
> unambiguously what this paradigm must be?

This threefold problematization, I shall want to say, is far
from a trivial event in the history of the modernist regime.
As the foremost modernist discourse theorizing the question of global collaboration, theoretical discourse on the
anarchy problematique has put in doubt the familiar foundations of heroic practice in international politics: the state
as subject, the domestic society as object domain, the paradigm of sovereignty itself. It renders these foundations problematical, displacing the question of *what* the foundations
of modern life are with the question of *how* foundations
might be imposed. And it thereby brings the modernist
regime face to face with a paradoxical problem that has
long been deferred – the paradoxical problem mentioned
just a moment ago:

> If it is no longer possible effectively to invoke the pres-
> ence of a paradigm of sovereignty as a hegemonic unity
> of truth and power – if this paradigm is destabilized and
> put in question – how might it be possible to produce
> some new or re-formed foundation that modern subjects

will know to honor, that they will take for granted as
part of their normalized understandings of the necessary
truth of life, and that will enable them to replicate the
heroic practice on the global scale, in the temporal compass, and across the diverse and finely detailed aspects of
life that now threaten to elude domestication and to pro-
liferate in their anarchic dangers? How, amidst the contingencies of our circumstances, might we deliberately
make the paradigm of man that we must know ourselves
already to be?

There are obvious risks in encountering such a problem.
To encounter it, as this discourse has done, is not just to
put into question a familiar paradigm of sovereignty purportedly at work in global politics, thereby to politicize
any future replication of heroic practices that would invoke this paradigm. It is also to risk calling attention to
the arbitrariness, contingency, and political content of any
attempt to constitute a new paradigm in its place. It is as
if this discourse, having reached this point, now opens the
way to an *inversion* of the hierarchical opposition upon which
heroic practices turn and upon which the domestication of
global life depends: an opposition in which the sovereignty
of reasoning man, as a hegemonic origin of truth and power,
is privileged over the anarchic dangers encountered in the
indeterminacy and ambiguity of history. It is as if this discourse is now perilously close to recognizing that man's
sovereignty, far from being a privileged term beyond question, is never more than a product of the undecidable contest of interpretations that modernist discourse recognizes
as the hallmark of a dangerous 'anarchy.'

Theoretical Practice and a Modern 'Aesthetics of Experience'

In my attempt to assess the practical political significance
of this theoretical discourse, I shall not draw the conclusion that might seem to follow from its confrontation with
this paradoxical problem. I shall not conclude that one
finds in this discourse the unmistakable signs of a coming
transformation in world politics. Tempting though the con-

clusion may be, one cannot read this discourse as a sign
that the modernist regime has lost its moorings, depleted
its cultural resources, and exhausted its powers; that heroic practices, with the paradigm of sovereignty now problematic, can no longer be effective in taming the resistances
of a pluralistic history; that contingency and chance will
soon overwhelm heroic practices of discipline; that a modernist narrative of global domestication is therefore fast
approaching its culmination; and that a new, more pluralistic, more openly politicizing kind of practice is about to
flourish. One cannot read theoretical discourse on the anarchy problematique in this way because this discourse,
upon producing its threefold problematization of the familiar foundations of heroic practices, has exhibited a most
extraordinary practical response. It has fashioned itself as
a quite different kind of sign.

As I shall note, this discourse has not explicitly pursued
the paradoxical problem encountered as a result of its threefold problematization. It has not inverted the sovereignty/
anarchy opposition, thus to give pride of place to the question that would politicize the narrative of global domestication. It has not posed the question of *how*, amidst the
contingencies and ambiguities of a pluralistic history, a paradigm of sovereignty is arbitrarily fabricated and imposed
as an unquestioned metaphysical foundation of heroic practice. Rather, having rendered familiar foundations problematical, participants in this discourse have begun eagerly to
explore the various categories and remembrances of modern
culture in a search for some alternative unity of truth and
power that might be said to be a foundational reality already in place and that, as such, might be *found* to provide a new paradigm of sovereignty already present, a new
ground of heroic practices of global politics.

Even now, participants in this discourse are variously heard
to say that this foundation is to be 'found' in an arching
institution of the modern states-system, a deep structure of
capitalist society, a transcendent ethical code, the universal need to avoid thermonuclear war, the cyclical rhythms
of modern life, some evolutionary metaphor, the market-
gazing eye of Adam Smith's impartial spectator, the assumptions and methods of 'successful' disciplines, the

imperatives and prerogatives of scientific inquiry, or an international regime of norms, rules, rights, and procedures. It is not difficult to imagine others 'finding' a foundation in ancient Greek moral teachings, the civic humanist tradition, Christian values, a Golden Age, a liberal doctrine of human rights, or a code of satyagraha. Others, in the manner of John Dewey, might 'find' it in some supposedly universal 'ungrounded hope' that the diverse impulses of life will be harmonized into a purpose befitting a human community.[25] And still others might 'find' a foundation in some newly 'revealed' synthesis of cultural texts such as these. Such a buzzing diversity of activity surely belies any conclusion that the modernist regime has finally spent its cultural reserves, that heroic practices cannot be successfully replicated to discipline history, and that a narrative of domestication is therefore at an end.

And therein, it seems to me, is the practical political significance of theoretical discourse on the anarchy problematique. As I shall contend, its significance is no longer primarily as a work of theory. Its significance is that of a practical and prescriptive text whose primary function is not unlike that of the speeches, dialogues, treatises, and precepts offered by the moral teachers of the past. *Its function is to offer instruction, by example and expressed opinion, on a specific 'aesthetic of existence' or 'art of life.'* In the words of Foucault, this discourse teaches 'those intentional and voluntary actions by which [persons] not only set themselves rules of conduct, but also seek to transform themselves, to change themselves in their singular being, and to make their life into an *oeuvre* that carries certain aesthetic values and meets certain stylistic criteria.'[26] In particular, it joins other social scientific disciplines in teaching modern persons *how, as a matter of respected style and ethical integrity, to go about the problematization and elaboration of themselves as sovereign subjects competent to deploy the heroic practice even as they are estranged from the familiar foundations of the world in which they live.* It extends these lessons to international relations, showing its readers how these lessons might be here applied. And its principal teaching can be expressed in three maxims that together describe a practice of austerity in the construction of an ethical self:

1. Participate in the 'syncretic pageantry' of one's culture, be open to the 'jolly relativity of every system,' and explore and assimilate cultural resources wherever one may find them.[27]
2. Be ready at any time to invent oneself as one who speaks a sovereign voice that one chooses to hold beyond questioning, that respected others will likewise choose to affirm and take seriously, that promises to provide a perfect simulation of a perfected world in which all differences of a culture are reconciled and all ambiguities are resolved, and that promises to be powerful enough to exclude or remedy all those resistances that refuse to be so reconciled.
3. Whenever there is confusion or doubt, always subordinate the first maxim to the second.

In brief: conduct, elaborate, and administer oneself as one who is ever preparing to subdue culture's diverse resources, ever ready to invent oneself anew as a universal sovereign subject who puts these resources to work in promised replications of heroic practices.

I will not say that this particular aesthetics of existence is wrong. In the manner of Bull, I highlight what seems to me to be the very considerable danger attending its ritualization in contemporary theories of international collaboration. Most generally, I point to dangers inherent in the displacement of the *political* question of modernity – an analytic question that theorists of the anarchy problematique have helped us to confront in the sphere of international politics – onto a tranquilizing plane of aesthetic discourse that gives price of place to questions of art, stylistic judgment, ethics, and moral responsibility on the part of cultured individuals. Somewhat more specifically, I believe that instruction in this particular aesthetics of existence cultivates not realism but a politically stultifying 'hyperrealism' among the North American women and men who are its primary students.[28]

Theoretical discourse on the anarchy problematique now wavers at the brink of posing the paradoxical question of *how*, in history, a paradigm of sovereignty is arbitrarily imposed. Its great merit is that it has brought international theoretical discourse to this point. Its most courageous political act is that, in so doing, it has risked the considerable scorn of the national security estate for which population, territory, and sovereign state are an inviolable ensemble, questioned only at one's peril. Yet upon risking this contempt and reaching this point, I shall want to say, theoretical discourse on the anarchy problematique now hesitates. Having problematized the foundations behind it, this discourse cannot back away from the brink and return to the celebration of these foundations without either effecting a collective amnesia regarding its past accomplishments or publicly acknowledging that its purported grounds are fake; but beyond the brink it sees in the 'how questions' it encounters an anarchic abyss whose depths cannot be fathomed because there, with the politicization and historicization of all sovereign voices, heroic practices cannot be effectively put to work to tame contingency and effect the certainty of a domesticated ground. And so, unable to imagine an alternative to heroic practice, this discourse now quavers at the point to which it has taken us. Averting its gaze from the 'how questions' it confronts, it busies itself with the fashioning of an aesthetics of existence that instructs us as to the austere style of modern doing and being appropriate to this place and time of quavering.

This discourse fashions an art of life that teaches us how we may sustain self-discipline, how not to lose faith in the promise of heroic practice, indeed, how we must explore all the heroic promises still couched here and there in our culture in the hope that in some combination of these promises we shall find a sovereign reality so real that only the most idealistic would dare to deny it, a sovereign truth so true that only the most false would dare to defy it. This aesthetics of hyperreal existence is, of course, a way of postponing indefinitely an encounter with the real dangers of modern global politics. It simulates, but defers posing as an analytic question, what is going on in modern global politics. It simulates the deferral of the sort of question that must be repeatedly deferred if a modern economy of power is to be sustained.

These deferred questions, and not answers, dominate any analyses. Perhaps the foremost of these is how, at this point

to which a theoretical discourse has taken us, one may
theorize the problem of moving beyond it without ascend-
ing into one or another form of hyperrealism. For example, can one find, hidden away at the peripheries of modern
life, the rudiments of practices that do not replicate the
heroic practice – that might in fact effectively resist it under
some circumstances? Might these resistant practices provide the productive principles of a 'new economy of power'
in global life? Might this new economy of power make way
for a new mode of subjectivity that is not so inclined to
celebrate the universal sovereignty of man and not so fear-
ful of the ambiguities that sovereign man cannot tame? Might
this new economy of power cultivate the undecidability of
being and the proliferation of meaning as effective techniques of power? These questions express a historical readi-
ness for international theory to comprehend and to give voice
to new interpretations and narrations of the anarchy
problematique.

Notes

1. Hedley Bull, 'Society and Anarchy in International Relations,' in
   H. Butterfield and M. Wight (eds.), *Diplomatic Investigations* (London:
   Allen and Unwin, 1966), p. 35. See chapter 5 in this volume.
2. The naming of names is perhaps a necessary gesture, if only to
   point broadly 'over there,' but it is also an arbitrary one. Equally
   arbitrary is the naming of typifying texts. I would point to the
   October 1985 Special Issue of *World Politics*, 38(1), Kenneth Oye
   (ed.); Robert Jervis, 'Cooperation Under the Security Dilemma,'
   World Politics, 30 (January 1978); Oran Young, 'Anarchy and
   Social Choice: Reflections on the International Polity,' *World Politics*, 30 (2) (January 1978); Robert Axelrod, *The Evolution of Cooperation* (New York: Basic Books, 1984); Robert O. Keohane, *After
   Hegemony: Cooperation and Discord in the World Political Economy*
   (Princeton: Princeton University Press, 1984); most, though not all,
   contributions to the volume *International Regimes* edited by Stephen
   Krasner (Ithaca, New York: Cornell Univeristy Press, 1983).
3. As I shall stress, theoretical discourse on the anarchy problematique
   is beholden to a neo-realist interpretation of Political Realism. For
   my analysis of this interpretation and its limits, see Richard K.
   Ashley, 'The Poverty of Neorealism,' *International Organization*, 38
   (2) (Spring 1984).
4. Robert O. Keohane, 'Theory of World Politics: Structural Realism

and Beyond,' in R. O. Keohane (ed.), *Neorealism and Its Critics* (New York: Columbia University Press, 1986), pp. 198–199.

5. Hedley Bull, 'International Theory: The Case for a Classical Approach,' in Klaus Knorr and James N. Rosenau (eds.), *Contending Approaches to International Politics* (Princeton: Princeton University Press, 1969), p. 28.

6. Hedley Bull, 'Martin Wight and the Theory of International Relations. The Second Martin Wight Memorial Lecture,' *British Journal of International Studies*, 2 (2) (1976).

7. Bull, 'Society and Anarchy,' p. 35 and *passim*.

8. Bull, 'Society and Anarchy' and *The Anarchical Society: A Study of Order in World Politics* (New York: Columbia University Press, 1977), pp. 46, 49–51.

9. Bull, 'International Theory,' p. 31.

10. Bull, 'International Theory,' p. 31.

11. An important contribution of post-structuralist argument, most especially Foucault's, is to put in question the disposition to view power as essentially negative, that is, as a constraint on freedom. As I shall be stressing, power must be viewed as productive, and among the things that knowledgeable practices of power produce are subjects of social action and the conditions of their autonomy. See especially Michel Foucault, *The History of Sexuality, Volume I: An Introduction*, trans. Robert Hurley (New York: Random House, 1978).

12. The notion of heroic practice presented here derives primarily from a reading of Foucault's notion of 'disciplinary practices' as presented in his *Discipline and Punish: The Birth of the Prison*, trans. Alan Sheridan (New York: Pantheon, 1977). As will become evident in a moment, I use the name 'heroic' practice in order to stress the centering of this modern practice on the modern sovereign: the figure of reasoning man who would assume the powers that had been ascribed to God in the Classical Age. On the notion of 'dialogized' or 'double-voiced' practices, see Mikhail Bakhtin, *Problems of Dostoevsky's Poetics*, trans. R. W. Rotsel (Ann Arbor: Ardis, 1973), p. 153, and *The Dialogic Imagination*, trans. by Michael Holquist and Caryl Emerson (Austin: University of Texas Press, 1975).

13. See Foucault, *The History of Sexuality* and *Discipline and Punish*.

14. Here three points need to be made. First, as will soon become obvious, on this and subsequent points relating to the modern construct of sovereignty, my analysis leans heavily upon Michel Foucault, *The Order of Things: An Archaeology of the Human Sciences* (New York: Random House, 1973), especially Foucault's treatment of Kant as one who formulates a way of breaking with Classical epistemology, thus to inaugurate a philosophical discourse in which man first appears as the sovereign center of historical meaning.

Second, lest there be any confusion, it is important to observe that Foucault, in his writings, employs the term 'sovereignty' in at least two senses. In the one, he identifies the notion of the 'sovereign' with the king or 'the head of the king,' which in its Classical usage is taken to be the source of law, prohibition, and constraint that works to limit freedoms by acting visibly and often violently upon its subjects. He then goes on to maintain that contemporary social and political theory, in its analyses of power, remains too much beholden to this notion of sovereignty. 'What we need,' he argues, 'is a political philosophy that isn't erected around the problems of law and prohibition. We need to cut off the king's head: in political theory that has still to be done.' (Michel Foucault, 'Truth and Power,' an interview reprinted in Rabinow (ed.), *The Foucault Reader*, p. 63.) In a second usage, however, Foucault understands sovereignty somewhat more generically, as the hegemonic subject who, within a discourse, is taken to be the source and register of truth, meaning, and power in history. Here, sovereignty might refer to the king, and behind the king to God, as it does in Classical epistemology; but it might also refer to man and his capacities for reason, as it does in modern epistemology. And here, sovereignty, as a mode of subjectivity accorded pride of historical place, is regarded by the analyst as a problematic effect to be accounted for in terms of the workings of discursive practices, not as a center of inquiry privileged by the analyst herself. I am using sovereignty in this second sense.

Third, here and throughout the argument to follow I shall continue to refer to 'man' as the modern sovereign, and in doing so I am keenly aware that this is indubitably a sexist locution. I hope that it will be understood that I persist in this locution, not out of any insensitivity, but as a way of sensitizing my analysis to the distinctly *gender-marked* quality of heroic practices in a modern economy of power. Although the point will not be developed here, I would be prepared to argue that the male/female dichotomy, as it recurs in modernist discourse, is derivative of the sovereignty/anarchy opposition on which heroic practices turn. The 'masculine,' on this account, is associated with the historically productive heroic practices that, with their back to an already completed domestic space, aspire to penetrate the anarchic voids of history, thus to assert mastery and render just there the sovereign truths they lack. The 'feminine,' on this same account, is associated with the reproduction of a domain of domesticity whose very existence is dependent upon heroic practices to supply, protect, and guarantee the sovereign truth and meaning of the space it inhabits. This in turn implies what I take to be an important political consequence: just as peace movements are disabled to the extent that they recapitulate the sovereignty/anarchy opposition in their own heroic practices – including their attempts to speak the voice of sovereign 'universal community' of humankind – so also are feminist movements disabled to the extent that they invoke the absolute sovereignty of any idealized 'voice.' The success of both movements may well depend upon putting just this sovereignty/anarchy dichotomy into question. For relevant arguments see Julia

Kristeva, 'Women's Time,' trans Alice Jardine and Harry Blake, *Signs*, 7 (1) (1981), pp. 13–35, and Richard K. Ashley, 'Marginalia: Poststructuralism/International Theory,' paper delivered at the German–American Workshop on International Relations Theory, Bad Homburg, Federal Republic of Germany (31 May–3 June 1987).

15. See Foucault, *The Order of Things*, p. 319.
16. Foucault, *The Order of Things*, pp. 310–316.
17. Hubert L. Dreyfus and Paul Rabinow, *Michel Foucault: Beyond Structuralism and Hermeneutics*, 2nd edn. (Chicago: University of Chicago Press, 1983).
18. Foucault, *The Order of Things*, pp. 14–16.
19. Foucault, *The Order of Things*, p. 339. See also Dreyfus and Rabinow,. *Michel Foucault*, p. 31.
20. Dreyfus and Rabinow, *Michel Foucault*, p. 30.
21. Foucault, *The Order of Things*, p. 310.
22. I am likening a paradigm of sovereignty to the principle that an author, according to Foucault, functions to provide in modern literary discourse. See Michel Foucault, 'What Is an Author?' in Rabinow (ed.), *The Foucault Reader*, pp. 111, 118–119.
23. On the notion of 'conductorless orchestration,' see Pierre Bourdieu, *Outline of a Theory of Practice* (Cambridge: Cambridge University Press, 1977).
24. The functionalist error, in general, is to attribute an independent existence, a pure presence, and an autonomous determinacy to some 'institution' based solely upon the logical inference of what an institution of a social totality must be and do if some problem of social order is reliably to be solved or some requisite of 'system maintenance' is to be performed.
25. On Dewey, see, e.g., Richard Rorty, *Philosophy and the Mirror of Nature* (Princeton: Princeton University Press, 1979).
26. Michel Foucault, *The Use of Pleasure: History of Sexuality Volume Two* (New York: Random House, 1985), pp. 10–11.
27. The terminology is that of Bakhtin, *Problems of Dostoevsky's Poetics*, pp. 102–108.
28. On the construct of hyperrealism, see Umberto Eco, *Travels in Hyperreality* (New York: Harcourt Brace Jovanovich, 1986), esp. Chapter 1; and Jean Baudrillard, *Simulations* (New York: Semiotext (e), 1983).

7 Anarchy is What States Make of it: The Social Construction of Power Politics (1992)*

Alexander Wendt

The debate between realists and liberals has reemerged as an axis of contention in international relations theory.[1] Revolving in the past around competing theories of human nature, the debate is more concerned today with the extent to which state action is influenced by 'structure' (anarchy and the distribution of power) versus 'process' (interaction and learning) and institutions. Does the absence of centralized political authority force states to play competitive power politics? Can international regimes overcome this logic, and under what conditions? What in anarchy is given and immutable, and what is amenable to change?

The debate between 'neorealists' and 'neoliberals' has been based on a shared commitment to 'rationalism.'[2] Like all social theories, rational choice directs us to ask some questions and not others, treating the identities and interests of agents as exogenously given and focusing on how the behavior of agents generates outcomes. As such, rationalism offers a

* *International Organization*, 46 (2) (Spring), pp. 391–425.
This article was negotiated with many individuals. If my records are complete (and apologies if they are not), thanks are due particularly to John Aldrich, Mike Barnett, Lea Brilmayer, David Campbell, Jim Caporaso, Simon Dalby, David Dessler, Bud Duvall, Jean Elshtain, Karyn Ertel, Lloyd Etheridge, Ernst Haas, Martin Hollis, Naeem Inayatullah, Stewart Johnson, Frank Klink, Steve Krasner, Friedrich Kratochwil, David Lumsdaine, M. J. Peterson, Spike Peterson, Thomas Risse-Kappen, John Ruggie, Bruce Russett, Jim Scott, Rogers Smith, David Sylvan, Jan Thomson, Mark Warren, and Jutta Weldes. The article also benefited from presentations and seminars at the American University, the University of Chicago, the University of Massachusetts at Amherst, Syracuse University, the University of Washington at Seattle, the University of California at Los Angeles, and Yale University.

fundamentally behavioral conception of both process and institutions: they change behavior but not identities and interests.[3] In addition to this way of framing research problems, neorealists and neoliberals share generally similar assumptions about agents: states are the dominant actors in the system, and they define security in 'self-interested' terms. Neorealists and neoliberals may disagree about the extent to which states are motivated by relative versus absolute gains, but both groups take the self-interested state as the starting point for theory.

This starting point makes substantive sense for neorealists, since they believe anarchies are necessarily 'self-help' systems, systems in which both central authority and collective security are absent. The self-help corollary to anarchy does enormous work in neorealism, generating the inherently competitive dynamics of the security delemma and collective action problem. Self-help is not seen as an 'institution' and as such occupies a privileged explanatory role *vis-à-vis* process, setting the terms for, and unaffected by, interaction. Since states failing to conform to the logic of self-help will be driven from the system, only simple learning or behavioral adaptation is possible; the complex learning involved in redefinitions of identity and interest is not.[4] Questions about identity- and interest-formation are therefore not important to students of international relations. A rationalist problematique, which reduces process to dynamics of behavioral interaction among exogenously constituted actors, defines the scope of systemic theory.

By adopting such reasoning, liberals concede to neorealists the causal powers of anarchic structure, but they gain the rhetorically powerful argument that process can generate cooperative behavior, even in an exogenously given, self-help system. Some liberals may believe that anarchy does, in fact, constitute states with self-interested identities exogenous to practice. Such 'weak' liberals concede the causal powers of anarchy both rhetorically and substantively and accept rationalism's limited, behavioral conception of the causal powers of institutions. They are realists before liberals (we might call them 'weak realists'), since only if international institutions can change powers and interests do they go beyond the 'limits' of realism.[5]

Yet some liberals want more. When Joseph Nye speaks of 'complex learning,' or Robert Jervis of 'changing conceptions of self and interest,' or Robert Keohane of 'sociological' conceptions of interest, each is asserting an important role for transformations of identity and interest in the liberal research program and, by extension, a potentially much stronger conception of process and institutions in world politics.[6] 'Strong' liberals should be troubled by the dichotomous privileging of structure over process, since transformations of identity and interest through process are transformations of structure. Rationalism has little to offer such an argument,[7] which is in part why, in an important article, Friedrich Kratochwil and John Ruggie argued that its individualist ontology contradicted the intersubjectivist epistemology necessary for regime theory to realize its full promise.[8] Regimes cannot change identities and interests if the latter are taken as given. Because of this rationalist legacy, despite increasingly numerous and rich studies of complex learning in foreign policy, neoliberals lack a systematic theory of how such changes occur and thus must privilege realist insights about structure while advancing their own insights about process.

The irony is that social theories which seek to explain identities and interests do exist. Keohane has called them 'reflectivist;'[9] because I want to emphasize their focus on the social construction of subjectivity and minimize their image problem, following Nicholas Onuf I will call them 'constructivist.'[10] Despite important differences, cognitivists, poststructuralists, standpoint and post-modern feminists, rule theorists, and structurationists share a concern with the basic 'sociological' issue bracketed by rationalists – namely, the issue of identity- and interest-formation. Constructivism's potential contribution to a strong liberalism has been obscured, however, by recent epistemological debates between modernists and post-modernists, in which Science disciplines Dissent for not defining a conventional research program, and Dissent celebrates its liberation from Science.[11] Real issues animate this debate, which also divides constructivists. With respect to the substance of international relations, however, both modern and post-modern constructivists are interested in how knowledgeable practices constitute subjects, which is not far from the strong liberal interest in how institutions transform interests. They share a cognitive, intersubjective conception of process in which identities and interests are endogenous to interaction, rather than a rationalist–behavioral one in which they are exogenous.

My objective in this article is to build a bridge between these two traditions (and, by extension, between the realist–liberal and rationalist – reflectivist debates) by developing a constructivist argument, drawn from structurationist and symbolic interactionist sociology, on behalf of the liberal claim that international institutions can transform state identities and interests.[12] In contrast to the 'economic' theorizing that dominates mainstream systemic international relations scholarship, this involves a 'sociological social psychological' form of systemic theory in which identities and interests are the dependent variable.[13] Whether a 'communitarian liberalism' is still liberalism does not interest me here. What does is that constructivism might contribute significantly to the strong liberal interest in identity- and interest-formation and thereby perhaps itself be enriched with liberal insights about learning and cognition which it has neglected.

My strategy for building this bridge will be to argue against the neorealist claim that self-help is given by anarchic structure exogenously to process. Constructivists have not done a good job of taking the causal powers of anarchy seriously. This is unfortunate, since in the realist view anarchy justifies disinterest in the institutional transformation of identities and interests and thus building systemic theories in exclusively rationalist terms; its putative causal powers must be challenged if process and institutions are not to be subordinated to structure. I argue that self-help and power politics do not follow either logically or causally from anarchy and that if today we find ourselves in a self-help world, this is due to process, not structure. There is no 'logic' of anarchy apart from the practices that create and instantiate one structure of identities and interests rather than another; structure has no existence or causal powers apart from process. Self-help and power politics are institutions, not essential features of anarchy. *Anarchy is what states make of it.*

In the subsequent sections of this article, I critically examine the claims and assumptions of neorealism, develop a positive argument about how self-help and power politics are socially constructed under anarchy, and then explore three ways in which identities and interests are transformed under anarchy: by the institution of sovereignty, by an evolution of cooperation, and by intentional efforts to transform egoistic identities into collective identities.

ANARCHY AND POWER POLITICS

Classical realists such as Thomas Hobbes, Reinhold Niebuhr, and Hans Morgenthau attributed egoism and power politics primarily to human nature, whereas structural realists or neorealists emphasize anarchy. The difference stems in part from different interpretations of anarchy's causal powers. Kenneth Waltz's work is important for both. In *Man, the State, and War*, he defines anarchy as a condition of possibility for or 'permissive' cause of war, arguing that 'wars occur because there is nothing to prevent them.'[14] It is the human nature or domestic politics of predator states, however, that provide the initial impetus or 'efficient' cause of conflict which forces other states to respond in kind.[15] Waltz is not entirely consistent about this, since he slips without justification from the permissive causal claim that in anarchy war is always possible to the active causal claim that 'war may at any moment occur.'[16] But despite Waltz's concluding call for third-image theory, the efficient causes that initialize anarchic systems are from the first and second images. This is reversed in Waltz's *Theory of International Politics*, in which first- and second-image theories are spurned as 'reductionist,' and the logic of anarchy seems by itself to constitute self-help and power politics as necessary features of world politics.[17]

This is unfortunate, since whatever one may think of first- and second-image theories, they have the virtue of implying that practices determine the character of anarchy. In the permissive view, only if human or domestic factors cause *A* to attack *B* will *B* have to defend itself. Anarchies may contain dynamics that lead to competitive power politics, but they also may not, and we can argue about when particular structures of identity and interest will emerge. In neorealism, however, the role of practice in shaping the character of anarchy is substantially reduced, and so there is less about which to argue: self-help and competitive power politics are simply given exogenously by the structure of the state system.

I will not here contest the neorealist description of the contemporary state system as a competitive, self-help world;[18] I will only dispute its explanation. I develop my argument in three stages. First, I disentangle the concepts of self-help and anarchy by showing that self-interested conceptions of security are not a constitutive property of anarchy. Second, I show how self-help and competitive power politics may be produced causally by processes of interaction between states in which anarchy plays only a permissive role. In both of these stages of my argument, I self-consciously bracket the first- and second-image determinants of state identity, not because they are unimportant (they are indeed important), but because like Waltz's objective, mine is to clarify the 'logic' of anarchy. Third, I reintroduce first- and second-image determinants to assess their effects on identity-formation in different kinds of anarchies.

Anarchy, Self-help, and Intersubjective Knowledge

Waltz defines political structures on three dimensions: ordering principles (in this case, anarchy), principles of differentiation (which here drop out), and the distribution of capabilities.[19] By itself, this definition predicts little about state behavior. It does not predict whether two states will be friends or foes, will recognize each other's sovereignty, will have dynastic ties, will be revisionist or status quo powers, and so on. These factors, which are fundamentally intersubjective, affect states' security interests and thus the character of their interaction under anarchy. In an important revision of Waltz's theory, Stephen Walt implies as much when he argues that the 'balance of threats,' rather than the balance of power, determines state action, threats being socially constructed.[20] Put more generally, without assumptions about the structure of identities and interests in the system, Waltz's definition of structure cannot predict the content or dynamics of anarchy. Self-help is one such intersubjective structure and, as such, does the decisive explanatory work in the theory. The question is whether self-help is a logical or contingent feature of anarchy. In this section, I develop the concept of a 'structure of identity and interest' and show that no particular one follows logically from anarchy.

A fundamental principle of constructivist social theory is that people act toward objects, including other actors, on the basis of the meanings that the objects have for them.[21] States act differently toward enemies than they do toward friends because enemies are threatening and friends are not. Anarchy and the distribution of power are insufficient to tell us which is which. US military power has a different significance for Canada than for Cuba, despite their similar 'structural' positions, just as British missiles have a different significance for the United States than do Soviet missiles. The distribution of power may always affect states' calculations, but how it does so depends on the intersubjective understandings and expectations, on the 'distribution of knowledge,' that constitute their conceptions of self and other.[22] If society 'forgets' what a university is, the powers and practices of professor and student cease to exist; if the United States and Soviet Union decide that they are no longer enemies, 'the cold war is over.' It is collective meanings that constitute the structures which organize our actions.

Actors acquire identities – relatively stable, role-specific understandings and expectations about self – by participating in such collective meanings.[23] Identities are inherently relational: 'Identity, with its appropriate attachments of psychological reality, is always identity within a specific, socially constructed world,' Peter Berger argues.[24] Each person has many identities linked to institutional roles, such as brother, son, teacher, and citizen. Similarly, a state may have multiple identities as 'sovereign,' 'leader of the free world,' 'imperial power,' and so on.[25] The commitment to and the salience of particular identities vary, but each identity is an inherently social definition of the actor grounded in the theories which actors collectively hold about themselves and one another and which constitute the structure of the social world.

Identities are the basis of interests. Actors do not have a 'portfolio' of interests that they carry around independent of social context; instead, they define their interests in the process of defining situations.[26] As Nelson Foote puts it: 'Motivation . . . refer[s] to the degree to which a human being, as a participant in the ongoing social process in which he necessarily finds himself, defines a problematic situation as calling for the performance of a particular act, with more or less anticipated consummations and consequences, and thereby his organism releases the energy appropriate to performing it.'[27] Sometimes situations are unprecedented in our experience, and in these cases we have to construct their meaning, and thus our interests, by analogy or invent them *de novo*. More often they have routine qualities in which we assign meanings on the basis of institutionally defined roles. When we say that professors have an 'interest' in teaching, research, or going on leave, we are saying that to function in the role identity of 'professor,' they have to define certain situations as calling for certain actions. This does not mean that they will necessarily do so (expectations and competence do not equal performance), but if they do not, they will not get tenure. The absence or failure of roles makes defining situations and interests more difficult, and identity confusion may result. This seems to be happening today in the United States and the former Soviet Union: without the cold war's mutual attributions of threat and hostility to define their identities, these states seem unsure of what their 'interests' should be.

An institution is a relatively stable set or 'structure' of identities and interests. Such structures are often codified in formal rules and norms, but these have motivational force only in virtue of actors' socialization to and participation in collective knowledge. Institutions are fundamentally cognitive entities that do not exist apart from actors' ideas about how the world works.[28] This does not mean that institutions are not real or objective, that they are 'nothing but' beliefs. As collective knowledge, they are experienced as having an existence 'over and above the individuals who happen to embody them at the moment.'[29] In this way, in-

stitutions come to confront individuals as more or less coercive social facts, but they are still a function of what
actors collectively 'know.' Identities and such collective
cognitions do not exist apart from each other; they are
'mutually constitutive.'[30] On this view, institutionalization
is a process of internalizing new identities and interests,
not something occurring outside them and affecting only
behavior; socialization is a cognitive process, not just a
behavioral one. Conceived in this way, institutions may be
cooperative or conflictual, a point sometimes lost in scholarship on international regimes, which tends to equate institutions with cooperation. There are important differences
between conflictual and cooperative institutions to be sure,
but all relatively stable self-other relations – even those of
'enemies' – are defined intersubjectively.

Self-help is an institution, one of various structures of
identity and interest that may exist under anarchy. Processes
of identity-formation under anarchy are concerned first and
foremost with preservation or 'security' of the self. Concepts of security therefore differ in the extent to which and
the manner in which the self is identified cognitively with
the other,[31] and, I want to suggest, it is upon this cognitive variation that the meaning of anarchy and the distribution of power depends. Let me illustrate with a standard
continuum of security systems.[32]

At one end is the 'competitive' security system, in which
states identify negatively with each other's security so that
ego's gain is seen as alter's loss. Negative identification under
anarchy constitutes systems of 'realist' power politics: risk-
averse actors that infer intentions from capabilities and worry
about relative gains and losses. At the limit – in the
Hobbesian war of all against all – collective action is nearly
impossible in such a system because each actor must constantly fear being stabbed in the back.

In the middle is the 'individualistic' security system, in
which states are indifferent to the relationship between their
own and others' security. This constitutes 'neoliberal' systems: states are still self-regarding about their security but
are concerned primarily with absolute gains rather than
relative gains. One's position in the distribution of power
is less important, and collective action is more possible

(though still subject to free riding because states continue to be 'egoists').

Competitive and individualistic systems are both 'self-help' forms of anarchy in the sense that states do not positively identify the security of self with that of others but instead treat security as the individual responsibility of each. Given the lack of a positive cognitive identification on the basis of which to build security regimes, power politics within such systems will necessarily consist of efforts to manipulate others to satisfy self-regarding interests.

This contrasts with the 'cooperative' security system, in which states identify positively with one another so that the security of each is perceived as the responsibility of all. This is not self-help in any interesting sense, since the 'self' in terms of which interests are defined is the community; national interests are international interests.[33] In practice, of course, the extent to which states' identification with the community varies, from the limited form found in 'concerts' to the full-blown form seen in 'collective security' arrangements.[34] Depending on how well developed the collective self is, it will produce security practices that are in varying degrees altruistic or prosocial. This makes collective action less dependent on the presence of active threats and less prone to free riding.[35] Moreover, it restructures efforts to advance one's objectives, or 'power politics,' in terms of shared norms rather than relative power.[36]

On this view, the tendency in international relations scholarship to view power and institutions as two opposing explanations of foreign policy is therefore misleading, since anarchy and the distribution of power only have meaning for state action in virtue of the understandings and expectations that constitute institutional identities and interests. Self-help is one such institution, constituting one kind of anarchy but not the only kind. Waltz's three-part definition of structure therefore seems underspecified. In order to go from structure to action, we need to add a fourth: the intersubjectively constituted structure of identities and interests in the system.

This has an important implication for the way in which we conceive of states in the state of nature before their first encounter with each other. Because states do not have conceptions of self and other, and thus security interests, apart from or prior to interaction, we assume too much about the state of nature if we concur with Waltz that, in virtue of anarchy, 'international political systems, like economic markets, are formed by the coaction of self-regarding units.'[37] We also assume too much if we argue that, in virtue of anarchy, states in the state of nature necessarily face a 'stag hunt' or 'security dilemma.'[38] These claims presuppose a history of interaction in which actors have acquired 'selfish' identities and interests; before interaction (and still in abstraction from first- and second-image factors) they would have no experience upon which to base such definitions of self and other. To assume otherwise is to attribute to states in the state of nature qualities that they can only possess in society.[39] Self-help is an institution, not a constitutive feature of anarchy.

What, then, *is* a constitutive feature of the state of nature before interaction? Two things are left if we strip away those properties of the self which presuppose interaction with others. The first is the material substrate of agency, including its intrinsic capabilities. For human beings, this is the body; for states, it is an organizational apparatus of governance. In effect, I am suggesting for rhetorical purposes that the raw material out of which members of the state system are constituted is created by domestic society before states enter the constitutive process of international society,[40] although this process implies neither stable territoriality nor sovereignty, which are internationally negotiated terms of individuality (as discussed further below). The second is a desire to preserve this material substrate, to survive. This does not entail 'self-regardingness,' however, since actors do not have a self prior to interaction with an other; how they view the meaning and requirements of this survival therefore depends on the processes by which conceptions of self evolve.

This may all seem very arcane, but there is an important issue at stake: are the foreign policy identities and interests of states exogenous or endogenous to the state system? The former is the answer of an individualistic or undersocialized systemic theory for which rationalism is appropriate; the latter is the answer of a fully socialized systemic theory. Waltz seems to offer the latter and proposes two mechanisms, competition and socialization, by which structure conditions state action.[41] The content of his argument about this conditioning, however, presupposes a self-help system that is not itself a constitutive feature of anarchy. As James Morrow points out, Waltz's two mechanisms condition behavior, not identity and interest.[42] This explains how Waltz can be accused of both 'individualism' and 'structuralism.'[43] He is the former with respect to systemic constitutions of identity and interest, the latter with respect to systemic determinations of behavior.

Anarchy and the Social Construction of Power Politics

If self-help is not a constitutive feature of anarchy, it must emerge causally from processes in which anarchy plays only a permissive role.[44] This reflects a second principle of constructivism: that the meanings in terms of which action is organized arise out of interaction.[45] This being said, however, the situation facing states as they encounter one another for the first time may be such that only self-regarding conceptions of identity can survive; if so, even if these conceptions are socially constructed, neorealists may be right in holding identities and interests constant and thus in privileging one particular meaning of anarchic structure over process. In this case, rationalists would be right to argue for a weak, behavioral conception of the difference that institutions make, and realists would be right to argue that any international institutions which are created will be inherently unstable, since without the power to transform identities and interests they will be 'continuing objects of choice' by exogenously constituted actors constrained only by the transaction costs of behavioral change.[46] Even in a permissive causal role, in other words, anarchy may decisively restrict interaction and therefore restrict viable forms of systemic theory. I address these causal issues first by showing how self-regarding ideas about security might develop and then by examining the conditions under which a key efficient cause – predation – may dispose states in this direction rather than others.

Conceptions of self and interest tend to 'mirror' the practices of significant others over time. This principle of identity-formation is captured by the symbolic interactionist notion of the 'looking-glass self,' which asserts that the self is a reflection of an actor's socialization.

Consider two actors – ego and alter – encountering each other for the first time.[47] Each wants to survive and has certain material capabilities, but neither actor has biological or domestic imperatives for power, glory, or conquest (still bracketed), and there is no history of security or insecurity between the two. What should they do? Realists would probably argue that each should act on the basis of worst-case assumptions about the other's intentions, justifying such an attitude as prudent in view of the possibility of death from making a mistake. Such a possibility always exists, even in civil society; however, society would be impossible if people made decisions purely on the basis of worst-case possibilities. Instead, most decisions are and should be made on the basis of probabilities, and these are produced by interaction, by what actors *do.*

In the beginning is ego's gesture, which may consist, for example, of an advance, a retreat, a brandishing of arms, a laying down of arms, or an attack.[48] For ego, this gesture represents the basis on which it is prepared to respond to alter. This basis is unknown to alter, however, and so it must make an inference or 'attribution' about ego's intentions and, in particular, given that this is anarchy, about whether ego is a threat.[49] The content of this inference will largely depend on two considerations. The first is the gesture's and ego's physical qualities, which are in part contrived by ego and which include the direction of movement, noise, numbers, and immediate consequences of the gesture.[50] The second consideration concerns what alter would intend by such qualities were it to make such a gesture itself. Alter may make an attributional 'error' in its inference about ego's intent, but there is also no reason for it to assume *a priori* – before the gesture – that ego is threatening, since it is only through a process of signaling and interpreting that the costs and probabilities of being wrong can be determined.[51] Social threats are constructed, not natural.

Consider an example. Would we assume, *a priori*, that we

were about to be attacked if we are ever contacted by members of an alien civilization? I think not. We would be highly alert, of course, but whether we placed our military forces on alert or launched an attack would depend on how we interpreted the import of their first gesture for our security – if only to avoid making an immediate enemy out of what may be a dangerous adversary. The possibility of error, in other words, does not force us to act on the assumption that the aliens are threatening: action depends on the probabilities we assign, and these are in key part a function of what the aliens do; prior to their gesture, we have no systemic basis for assigning probabilities. If their first gesture is to appear with a thousand spaceships and destroy New York, we will define the situation as threatening and respond accordingly. But if they appear with one spaceship, saying what seems to be 'we come in peace,' we will feel 'reassured' and will probably respond with a gesture intended to reassure them, even if this gesture is not necessarily interpreted by them as such.[52]

This process of signaling, interpreting, and responding completes a 'social act' and begins the process of creating intersubjective meanings. It advances the same way. The first social act creates expectations on both sides about each other's future behavior: potentially mistaken and certainly tentative, but expectations nonetheless. Based on this tentative knowledge, ego makes a new gesture, again signifying the basis on which it will respond to alter, and again alter responds, adding to the pool of knowledge each has about the other, and so on over time. The mechanism here is reinforcement; interaction rewards actors for holding certain ideas about each other and discourages them from holding others. If repeated long enough, these 'reciprocal typifications' will create relatively stable concepts of self and other regarding the issue at stake in the interaction.[53]

It is through reciprocal interaction, in other words, that we create and instantiate the relatively enduring social structures in terms of which we define our identities and interests. Jeff Coulter sums up the ontological dependence of structure on process this way: 'The parameters of social organization themselves are reproduced on in and through the orientations and practices of members engaged in social interactions over time. . . . Social configurations are not 'objective' like mountains or forests, but neither are they 'subjective' like dreams or flights of speculative fancy. They are, as most social scientists concede at the theoretical level, intersubjective constructions.'[54]

The simple overall model of identity- and interest-formation proposed in Figure 7.1 applies to competitive institutions no less than to cooperative ones. Self-help security systems evolve from cycles of interaction in which each party acts in ways that the other feels are threatening to the self, creating expectations that the other is not to be trusted. Competitive or egoistic identities are caused by such insecurity; if the other is threatening, the self is forced to 'mirror' such behavior in its conception of the self's relationship to that other.[55] Being treated as an object for the gratification of others precludes the positive identification with others necessary for collective security; conversely, being treated

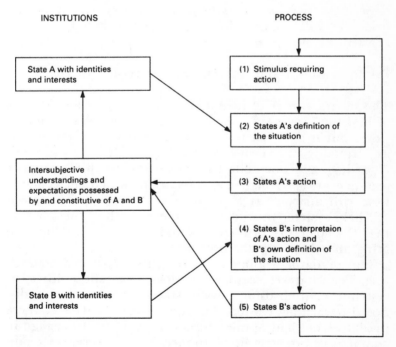

Figure 7.1 The codetermination of institutions and process

by others in ways that are empathic with respect to the security of the self permits such identification.[56]

Competitive systems of interaction are prone to security 'dilemmas,' in which the efforts of actors to enhance their security unilaterally threatens the security of the others, perpetuating distrust and alienation. The forms of identity and interest that constitute such dilemmas, however, are themselves ongoing effects of, not exogenous to, the interaction; identities are produced in and through 'situated activity.'[57] We do not *begin* our relationship with the aliens in a security dilemma; security dilemmas are not given by anarchy or nature. Of course, once institutionalized such a dilemma may be hard to change (I return to this below), but the point remains: identities and interests are constituted by collective meanings that are always in process. As Sheldon Stryker emphasizes, 'The social process is one of constructing and reconstructing self and social relationships.'[58] If states find themselves in a self-help system, this is because their practices made it that way. Changing the practices will change the intersubjective knowledge that constitutes the system.

Predator States and Anarchy as Permissive Cause

The mirror theory of identity-formation is a crude account of how the process of creating identities and interests might work, but it does not tell us why a system of states – such as, arguably, our own – would have ended up with self-regarding and not collective identities. In this section, I examine an efficient cause, predation, which, in conjunction with anarchy as a permissive cause, may generate a self-help system. In so doing, however, I show the key role that the structure of identities and interests plays in mediating anarchy's explanatory role.

The predator argument is straightforward and compelling. For whatever reasons – biology, domestic politics, or systemic victimization – some states may become predisposed toward aggression. The aggressive behavior of these predators or 'bad apples' forces other states to engage in competitive power politics, to meet fire with fire, since failure to do so may degrade or destroy them. One predator will best a hundred pacifists because anarchy provides no guarantees. This argument is powerful in part because it is so weak: rather than making the strong assumption that all states are inherently power-seeking (a purely reductionist theory of power politics), it assumes that just one is power-seeking and that the others have to follow suit because anarchy permits the one to exploit them.

In making this argument, it is important to reiterate that the possibility of predation does not in itself force states to anticipate it *a priori* with competitive power politics of their own. The possibility of predation does not mean that 'war may at any moment occur;' it may in fact be extremely unlikely. Once a predator emerges, however, it may condition identity- and interest-formation in the following manner.

In an anarchy of two, if ego is predatory, alter must either define its security in self-help terms or pay the price. This follows directly from the above argument, in which conceptions of self mirror treatment by the other. In an anarchy of many, however, the effect of predation also depends on the level of collective identity already attained in the system. If predation occurs right after the first encounter in the state of nature, it will force others with whom it comes in contact to defend themselves, first individually and then collectively *if* they come to perceive a common threat. The emergence of such a defensive alliance will be seriously inhibited if the structure of identities and interests has already evolved into a Hobbesian world of maximum insecurity, since potential allies will strongly distrust each other and face intense collective action problems; such insecure allies are also more likely to fall out amongst themselves once the predator is removed. If collective security identity is high, however, the emergence of a predator may do much damage. If the predator attacks any member of the collective, the latter will come to the victim's defense on the principle of 'all for one, one for all,' even if the predator is not presently a threat to other members of the collective. If the predator is not strong enough to withstand the collective, it will be defeated and collective security will obtain. But if it is strong enough, the logic of the two-actor case (now predator and collective) will activate, and balance-of-power politics will reestablish itself.

The timing of the emergence of predation relative to the history of identity-formation in the community is therefore crucial to anarchy's explanatory role as a permissive cause. Predation will always lead victims to defend themselves, but whether defense will be collective or not depends on the history of interaction within the potential collective as much as on the ambitions of the predator. Will the disappearance of the Soviet threat renew old insecurities among the members of the North Atlantic Treaty Organization? Perhaps, but not if they have reasons independent of that threat for identifying their security with one another. Identities and interests are relationship-specific, not intrinsic attributes of a 'portfolio;' states may be competitive in some relationships and solidary in others. 'Mature' anarchies are less likely than 'immature' ones to be reduced by predation to a Hobbesian condition, and maturity, which is a proxy for structures of identity and interest, is a function of process.[59]

The source of predation also matters. If it stems from unit-level causes that are immune to systemic impacts (causes such as human nature or domestic politics taken in isolation), then it functions in a manner analogous to a 'genetic trait' in the constructed world of the state system. Even if successful, this trait does not select for other predators in an evolutionary sense so much as it teaches other states to respond in kind, but since traits cannot be unlearned, the other states will continue competitive behavior until the predator is either destroyed or transformed from within. However, in the more likely event that predation stems at least in part from prior systemic interaction – perhaps as a result of being victimized in the past (one thinks here of Nazi Germany or the Soviet Union) – then it is more a response to a learned identity and, as such, might be transformed by future social interaction in the form of appeasement, reassurances that security needs will be met, systemic effects on domestic politics, and so on. In this case, in other words, there is more hope that process can transform a bad apple into a good one.

The role of predation in generating a self-help system, then, is consistent with a systematic focus on process. Even if the source of predation is entirely exogenous to the system, it is what states *do* that determines the qualities of their interactions under anarchy. In this respect, it is not surprising that it is classical realists rather than structural realists who emphasize this sort of argument. The former's emphasis on unit-level causes of power politics leads more easily to a permissive view of anarchy's explanatory role (and therefore to a processual view of international relations) than does the latter's emphasis on anarchy as a 'structural cause;'[60] neorealists do not need predation because the system is given as self-help.

This raises anew the question of exactly how much and what kind of role human nature and domestic politics play in world politics. The greater and more destructive this role, the more significant predation will be, and the less amenable anarchy will be to formation of collective identities. Classical realists, of course, assumed that human nature was possessed by an inherent lust for power or glory. My argument suggests that assumptions such as this were made for a reason: an unchanging Hobbesian man provides the powerful efficient cause necessary for a relentless pessimism about world politics that anarchic structure alone, or even structure plus intermittent predation, cannot supply. One can be skeptical of such an essentialist assumption, as I am, but it does produce determinate results at the expense of systemic theory. A concern with systemic process over structure suggests that perhaps it is time to revisit the debate over the relative importance of first-, second-, and third-image theories of state identity-formation.[61]

Assuming for now that systemic theories of identity-formation in world politics are worth pursuing, let me conclude by suggesting that the realist–rationalist alliance 'reifies' self-help in the sense of treating it as something separate from the practices by which it is produced and sustained. Peter Berger and Thomas Luckmann define reification as follows: '[It] is the apprehension of the products of human activity *as if* they were something else than human products – such as facts of nature, results of cosmic laws, or manifestations of divine will. Reification implies that man is capable of forgetting his own authorship of the human world, and further, that the dialectic between man, the producer, and his products is lost to consciousness. The reified world is . . . experienced by man as a strange facticity, an *opus alienum* over which he has no control rather than as the *opus proprium* of his own productive activity.'[62] By denying or bracketing states' collective authorship of their identities and interests, in other words, the realist-rationalist alliance denies or brackets the fact that competitive power politics help create the very 'problem of order' they are supposed to solve – that realism is a self-fulfilling prophecy. Far from being exogenously given, the intersubjective knowledge that constitutes competitive identities and interests is constructed every day by processes of 'social will formation.'[63] It is what states have made of themselves.

INSTITUTIONAL TRANSFORMATION OF POWER POLITICS

Let us assume that processes of identity- and interest-formation have created a world in which states do not recognize rights to territory or existence – a war of all against all. In this world, anarchy has a 'realist' meaning for state action: be insecure and concerned with relative power. Anarchy has this meaning only in virtue of collective, insecurity-producing practices, but if those practices are relatively stable, they do constitute a system that may resist change. The fact that worlds of power politics are socially constructed, in other words, does not guarantee they are malleable, for at least two reasons.

The first reason is that once constituted, any social system confronts each of its members as an objective social fact that reinforces certain behaviors and discourages others. Self-help systems, for example, tend to reward competition and punish altruism. The possibility of change depends on whether the exigencies of such competition leave room for actions that deviate from the prescribed script. If they do not, the system will be reproduced and deviant actors will not.[64]

The second reason is that systemic change may also be inhibited by actors' interests in maintaining relatively stable role identities. Such interests are rooted not only in the desire to minimize uncertainty and anxiety, manifested in efforts to confirm existing beliefs about the social world,

but also in the desire to avoid the expected costs of breaking commitments made to others – notably domestic constituencies and foreign allies in the case of states – as part
of past practices. The level of resistance that these commitments induce will depend on the 'salience' of particular role identities to the actor.[65] The United States, for
example, is more likely to resist threats to its identity as
'leader of anti-communist crusades' than to its identity as
'promoter of human rights.' But for almost any role identity, practices and information that challenge it are likely
to create cognitive dissonance and even perceptions of threat,
and these may cause resistance to transformations of the
self and thus to social change.[66]

For both systemic and 'psychological' reasons, then,
intersubjective understandings and expectations may have
a self-perpetuating quality, constituting path-dependencies
that new ideas about self and other must transcend. This
does not change the fact that through practice agents are
continuously producing and reproducing identities and
interests, continuously 'choosing now the preferences [they]
will have later.'[67] But it does mean that choices may not
be experienced with meaningful degrees of freedom. This
could be a constructivist justification for the realist position
that only simple learning is possible in self-help systems.
The realist might concede that such systems are socially
constructed and still argue that after the corresponding
identities and interests have become institutionalized, they
are almost impossible to transform.

In the remainder of this article, I examine three institutional transformations of identity and security interest
through which states might escape a Hobbesian world of
their own making. In so doing, I seek to clarify what it
means to say that 'institutions transform identities and interests,' emphasizing that the key to such transformations
is relatively stable practice.

Sovereignty, Recognition, and Security

In a Hobbesian state of nature, states are individuated by
the domestic processes that constitute them as states and
by their material capacity to deter threats from other states.

In this world, even if free momentarily from the predations of others, state security does not have any basis in social recognition – in intersubjective understandings or norms that a state has a right to its existence, territory, and subjects. Security is a matter of national power, nothing more.

The principle of sovereignty transforms this situation by providing a social basis for the individuality and security of states. Sovereignty is an institution, and so it exists only in virtue of certain intersubjective understandings and expectations; there is no sovereignty without an other. These understandings and expectations not only constitute a particular kind of state – the 'sovereign' state – but also constitute a particular form of community, since identities are relational. The essence of this community is a mutual recognition of one another's right to exercise exclusive political authority within territorial limits. These reciprocal 'permissions'[68] constitute a spatially rather than functionally differentiated world – a world in which fields of practice constitute and are organized around 'domestic' and 'international' spaces rather than around the performance of particular activities.[69] The location of the boundaries between these spaces is of course sometimes contested, war being one practice through which states negotiate the terms of their individuality. But this does not change the fact that it is only in virtue of mutual recognition that states have 'territorial property rights.'[70] This recognition functions as a form of 'social closure' that disempowers nonstate actors and empowers and helps stabilize interaction among states.[71]

Sovereignty norms are now so taken for granted, so natural, that it is easy to overlook the extent to which they are both presupposed by and an ongoing artifact of practice. When states tax 'their' 'citizens' and not others, when they 'protect' their markets against foreign 'imports,' when they kill thousands of Iraqis in one kind of war and then refuse to 'intervene' to kill even one person in another kind, a 'civil' war, and when they fight a global war against a regime that sought to destroy the institution of sovereignty and then give Germany back to the Germans, they are acting against the background of, and thereby reproducing, shared norms about what it means to be a sovereign state. If states stopped acting on those norms, their identity as 'sovereigns' (if not necessarily as 'states') would disappear. The sovereign state is an ongoing accomplishment of practice, not a once-and-for-all creation of norms that somehow exists apart from practice.[72] Thus, saying that 'the institution of sovereignty transforms identities' is shorthand for saying that 'regular practices produce mutually constituting sovereign identities (agents) and their associated institutional norms (structures).' Practice is the core of constructivist resolutions of the agent-structure problem. This ongoing process may not be politically problematic in particular historical contexts and, indeed, once a community of mutual recognition is constituted, its members – even the disadvantaged ones[73] – may have a vested interest in reproducing it. In fact, this is part of what having an identity means. But this identity and institution remain dependent on what actors do: removing those practices will remove their intersubjective conditions of existence.

This may tell us something about how institutions of sovereign states are reproduced through social interaction, but it does not tell us why such a structure of identity and interest would arise in the first place. Two conditions would seem necessary for this to happen: (1) the density and regularity of interactions must be sufficiently high and (2) actors must be dissatisfied with preexisting forms of identity and interaction. Given these conditions, a norm of mutual recognition is relatively undemanding in terms of social trust, having the form of an assurance game in which a player will acknowledge the sovereignty of the others as long as they will in turn acknowledge that player's own sovereignty. Articulating international legal principles such as those embodied in the Peace of Augsburg (1555) and the Peace of Westphalia (1648) may also help by establishing explicit criteria for determining violations of the nascent social consensus.[74] But whether such a consensus holds depends on what states do. If they treat each other as if they were sovereign, then over time they will institutionalize that mode of subjectivity; if they do not, then that mode will not become the norm.

Practices of sovereignty will transform understandings of security and power politics in at least three ways. First, states will come to define their (and our) security in terms

of preserving their 'property rights' over particular territories. We now see this as natural, but the preservation of
territorial frontiers is not, in fact, equivalent to the survival of the state or its people. Indeed, some states would
probably be more secure if they would relinquish certain
territories – the 'Soviet Union' of some minority republics,
'Yugoslavia' of Croatia and Slovenia, Israel of the West Bank,
and so on. The fact that sovereignty practices have historically been oriented toward producing distinct territorial
spaces, in other words, affects states' conceptualizations of
what they must 'secure' to function in that identity, a process
that may help account for the 'hardening' of territorial
boundaries over the centuries.[75]

Second, to the extent that states successfully internalize
sovereignty norms, they will be more respectful toward the
territorial rights of others.[76] This restraint is *not* primarily
because of the costs of violating sovereignty norms, although
when violators do get punished (as in the Gulf War) it
reminds everyone of what these costs can be, but because
part of what it means to be a 'sovereign' state is that one
does not violate the territorial rights of others without 'just
cause.' A clear example of such an institutional effect, con-
vincingly argued by David Strang, is the markedly different
treatment that weak states receive within and outside communities of mutual recognition.[77] What keeps the United
States from conquering the Bahamas, or Nigeria from seiz-
ing Togo, or Australia from occupying Vanuatu? Clearly,
power is not the issue, and in these cases even the cost of
sanctions would probably be negligible. One might argue
that great powers simply have no 'interest' in these con-
quests, and this might be so, but this lack of interest can
only be understood in terms of their recognition of weak
states' sovereignty. I have no interest in exploiting my friends,
not because of the relative costs and benefits of such action but because they are my friends. The absence of recognition, in turn, helps explain the Western states' practices
of territorial conquest, enslavement, and genocide against
Native American and African peoples. It is in *that* world
that only power matters, not the world of today.

Finally, to the extent that their ongoing socialization
teaches states that their sovereignty depends on recogni-

tion by other states, they can afford to rely more on the institutional fabric of international society and less on individual national means – especially military power – to protect their security. The intersubjective understandings embodied in the institution of sovereignty, in other words, may redefine the meaning of others' power for the security of the self. In policy terms, this means that states can be less worried about short-term survival and relative power and can thus shift their resources accordingly. Ironically, it is the great powers, the states with the greatest national means, that may have the hardest time learning this lesson; small powers do not have the luxury of relying on national means and may therefore learn faster that collective recognition is a cornerstone of security.

None of this is to say that power becomes irrelevant in a community of sovereign states. Sometimes states *are* threatened by others that do not recognize their existence or particular territorial claims, that resent the externalities from their economic policies, and so on. But most of the time, these threats are played out within the terms of the sovereignty game. The fates of Napoleon and Hitler show what happens when they are not.

Cooperation Among Egoists and Transformations of Identity

We began this section with a Hobbesian state of nature. Cooperation for joint gain is extremely difficult in this context, since trust is lacking, time horizons are short, and relative power concerns are high. Life is 'nasty, brutish, and short.' Sovereignty transforms this system into a Lockean world of (mostly) mutually recognized property rights and (mostly) egoistic rather than competitive conceptions of security, reducing the fear that what states already have will be seized at any moment by potential collaborators, thereby enabling them to contemplate more direct forms of cooperation. A necessary condition for such cooperation is that outcomes be positively interdependent in the sense that potential gains exists which cannot be realized by unilateral action. States such as Brazil and Botswana may recognize each other's sovereignty, but they need further incentives to engage in joint action. One important source of incentives is the growing 'dynamic density' of interaction among states in a world with new communications technology, nuclear weapons, externalities from industrial development, and so on.[78] Unfortunately, growing dynamic density does not ensure that states will in fact realize joint gains; interdependence also entails vulnerability and the risk of being 'the sucker,' which if exploited will become a source of conflict rather than cooperation.

This is the rationale for the familiar assumptions that egoistic states will often find themselves facing prisoners' dilemma, a game in which the dominant strategy, if played only once, is to defect. As Michael Taylor and Robert Axelrod have shown, however, given iteration and a sufficient shadow of the future, egoists using a tit-for-tat strategy can escape this result and build cooperative institutions.[79] The story they tell about this process on the surface seems quite similar to George Herbert Mead's constructivist analysis of interaction, part of which is also told in terms of 'games.'[80] Cooperation is a gesture indicating ego's willingness to cooperate; if alter defects, ego does likewise, signaling its unwillingness to be exploited; over time and through reciprocal play, each learns to form relatively stable expectations about the other's behavior, and through these, habits of cooperation (or defection) form. Despite similar concerns with communication, learning, and habit-formation, however, there is an important difference between the game-theoretic and constructivist analysis of interaction that bears on how we conceptualize the causal powers of institutions.

In the traditional game-theoretic analysis of cooperation, even an iterated one, the structure of the game – of identities and interests – is exogenous to interaction and, as such, does not change.[81] A 'black box' is put around identity- and interest-formation, and analysis focuses instead on the relationship between expectations and behavior. The norms that evolve from interaction are treated as rules and behavioral regularities which are external to the actors and which resist change because of the transaction costs of creating new ones. The game-theoretic analysis of cooperation among egoists is at base behavioral.

A constructivist analysis of cooperation, in contrast, would concentrate on how the expectations produced by behavior affect identities and interests. The process of creating institutions is one of internalizing new understandings of self and other, of acquiring new role identities, not just of creating external constraints on the behavior of exogenously constituted actors.[82] Even if not intended as such, in other words, the process by which egoists learn to cooperate is at the same time a process of reconstructing their interests in terms of shared commitments to social norms. Over time, this will tend to transform a positive interdependence of *outcomes* into a positive interdependence of *utilities* or collective interest organized around the norms in question. These norms will resist change because they are tied to actors' commitments to their identities and interests, not merely because of transaction costs. A constructivist analysis of 'the cooperation problem,' in other words, is at base cognitive rather than behavioral, since it treats the intersubjective knowledge that defines the structure of identities and interests, of the 'game,' as endogenous to and instantiated by interaction itself.

The debate over the future of collective security in Western Europe may illustrate the significance of this difference. A weak liberal or rationalist analysis would assume that the European states' 'portfolio' of interests has not fundamentally changed and that the emergence of new factors, such as the collapse of the Soviet threat and the rise of Germany, would alter their cost-benefit ratios for pursuing current arrangements, thereby causing existing institutions to break down. The European states formed collaborative institutions for good, exogenously constituted egoistic reasons, and the same reasons may lead them to reject those institutions; the game of European power politics has not changed. A strong liberal or constructivist analysis of this problem would suggest that four decades of cooperation may have transformed a positive interdependence of outcomes into a collective 'European identity' in terms of which states increasingly define their 'self'-interests.[83] Even if egoistic reasons were its starting point, the process of cooperating tends to redefine those reasons by reconstituting identities and interests in terms of new intersubjective understandings and commitments. Changes in the distribution of power during the late twentieth century are undoubtedly a challenge to these new understandings, but it is not as if West European states have some inherent, exogenously given interest in abandoning collective security if the price is right. Their identities and security interests are continuously in process, and if collective identities become 'embedded,' they will be as resistant to change as egoistic ones.[84] Through participation in new forms of social knowledge, in other words, the European states of 1990 might no longer be the states of 1950.

Critical Strategic Theory and Collective Security

The transformation of identity and interest through an 'evolution of cooperation' faces two important constraints. The first is that the process is incremental and slow. Actors' objectives in such a process are typically to realize joint gains within what they take to be a relatively stable context, and they are therefore unlikely to engage in substantial reflection about how to change the parameters of that context (including the structure of identities and interests) and unlikely to pursue policies specifically designed to bring about such changes. Learning to cooperate may change those parameters, but this occurs as an unintended consequence of policies pursued for other reasons rather than as a result of intentional efforts to transcend existing institutions.

A second, more fundamental, constraint is that the evolution of cooperation story presupposes that actors do not identify negatively with one another. Actors must be concerned primarily with absolute gains; to the extent that antipathy and distrust lead them to define their security in relativistic terms, it will be hard to accept the vulnerabilities that attend cooperation.[85] This is important because it is precisely the 'central balance' in the state system that seems to be so often afflicted with such competitive thinking, and realists can therefore argue that the possibility of cooperation within one 'pole' (for example, the West) is parasitic on the dominance of competition between poles (the East–West conflict). Relations between the poles may be amenable to some positive reciprocity in areas such as arms control, but the atmosphere of distrust leaves little room for such cooperation and its transformative consequences.[86] The conditions of negative identification that make an 'evolution of cooperation' most needed work precisely against such a logic.

This seemingly intractable situation may nevertheless be amenable to quite a different logic of transformation, one driven more by self-conscious efforts to change structures of identity and interest than by unintended consequences. Such voluntarism may seem to contradict the spirit of constructivism, since would-be revolutionaries are presumably themselves effects of socialization to structures of identity and interests. How can they think about changing that to which they owe their identity? The possibility lies in the distinction between the social determination of the self and the personal determination of choice, between what Mead called the 'me' and the 'I.'[87] The 'me' is that part of subjectivity which is defined in terms of others; the character and behavioral expectations of a person's role identity as 'professor,' or of the United States as 'leader of the alliance,' for example, are socially constituted. Roles are not played in mechanical fashion according to precise scripts, however, but are 'taken' and adapted in idiosyncratic ways by each actor.[88] Even in the most constrained situations, role performance involves a choice by the actor. The 'I' is the part of subjectivity in which this appropriation and reaction to roles and its corresponding existential freedom lie.

The fact that roles are 'taken' means that, in principle, actors always have a capacity for 'character planning' – for engaging in critical self-reflection and choices designed to bring about changes in their lives.[89] But when or under what conditions can this creative capacity be exercised? Clearly, much of the time it cannot: if actors were constantly reinventing their identities, social order would be impossible, and the relative stability of identities and interests in the real world is indicative of our propensity for habitual rather than creative action. The exceptional, conscious choosing to transform or transcend roles has at least two preconditions. First, there must be a reason to think of oneself in novel terms. This would most likely stem from the presence of new social situations that cannot be managed in terms of preexisting self-conceptions. Second, the expected costs of intentional role change – the sanctions imposed by others with whom one interacted in previous roles – cannot be greater than its rewards.

When these conditions are present, actors can engage in self-reflection and practice specifically designed to transform their identities and interests and thus to 'change the games' in which they are embedded. Such 'critical' strategic theory and practice has not received the attention it merits from students of world politics (another legacy of exogenously given interests perhaps), particularly given that one of the most important phenomena in contemporary world politics, Mikhail Gorbachev's policy of 'New Thinking,' is arguably precisely that.[90] Let me therefore use this policy as an example of how states might transform a competitive security system into a cooperative one, dividing the transformative process into four stages.

The first stage in intentional transformation is the breakdown of consensus about identity commitments. In the Soviet case, identity commitments centered on the Leninist theory of imperialism, with its belief that relations between capitalist and socialist states are inherently conflictual, and on the alliance patterns that this belief engendered. In the 1980s, the consensus within the Soviet Union over the Leninist theory broke down for a variety of reasons, principal among which seem to have been the state's inability to meet the economic–technological–military challenge from the West, the government's decline of political legitimacy at home, and the reassurance from the West that it did not intend to invade the Soviet Union, a reassurance that reduced the external costs of role change.[91] These factors paved the way for a radical leadership transition and for a subsequent 'unfreezing of conflict schemas' concerning relations with the West.[92]

The breakdown of consensus makes possible a second stage of critical examination of old ideas about self and other and, by extension, of the structures of interaction by which the ideas have been sustained. In periods of relatively stable role identities, ideas and structures may become reified and thus treated as things that exist independently of social action. If so, the second stage is one of denaturalization, of identifying the practices that reproduce seemingly inevitable ideas about self and other; to that extent, it is a form of 'critical' rather than 'problem-solving' theory.[93] The result of such a critique should be an identification of new 'possible selves' and aspirations.[94] New Thinking embodies such critical theorizing. Gorbachev wants to free the Soviet Union from the coercive social logic of the cold war and engage the West in far-reaching cooperation. Toward this end, he had rejected the Leninist belief in the inherent conflict of interest between socialist and capitalist states and, perhaps more important, has recognized the crucial role that Soviet aggressive practices played in sustaining that conflict.

Such rethinking paves the way for a third stage of new practice. In most cases, it is not enough to rethink one's own ideas about self and other, since old identities have been sustained by systems of interactions with *other* actors, the practices of which remain a social fact for the transformative agent. In order to change the self, then, it is often necessary to change the identities and interests of the others that help sustain those systems of interactions. The vehicle for inducing such change is one's own practice and, in particular, the practice of 'altercasting' – a technique of interactor control in which ego uses tactics of self-presentation and stage management in an attempt to frame alter's definitions of social situations in ways that create the role which ego desires alter to play.[95] In effect, in altercasting ego tries to induce alter to take on a new identity (and thereby enlist alter in ego's effort to change itself) by treating alter *as if* it already had that identity. The logic of this follows directly from the mirror theory of identity-formation, in which alter's identity is a reflection of ego's practices; change those practices and ego begins to change alter's conception of itself.

What these practices should consist of depends on the logic by which the preexisting identities were sustained. Competitive security systems are sustained by practices that create insecurity and distrust. In this case, transformative practices should attempt to teach other states that one's own state can be trusted and should not be viewed as a threat to their security. The fastest way to do this is to make unilateral initiatives and self-binding commitments of sufficient significance that another state is faced with 'an offer it cannot refuse.'[96] Gorbachev has tried to do this by withdrawing from Afghanistan and Eastern Europe, implementing asymmetric cuts in nuclear and conventional forces, calling for 'defensive defense,' and so on. In addition, he has skillfully cast the West in the role of being morally required to give aid and comfort to the Soviet Union, has emphasized the bonds of common fate between the Soviet Union and the West, and has indicated that further progress in East–West relations is contingent upon the West assuming the identity being projected onto it. These actions are all dimensions of altercasting, the intention of which is to take away the Western 'excuse' for distrusting the Soviet Union, which, in Gorbachev's view, has helped sustain competitive identities in the past.

Yet by themselves such practices cannot transform a competitive security system, since if they are not reciprocated by alter, they will expose ego to a 'sucker' payoff and quickly wither on the vine. In order for critical strategic practice to transform competitive identities, it must be 'rewarded' by alter, which will encourage more such practice by ego, and so on.[97] Over time, this will institutionalize a positive rather than a negative identification between the security of self and other and will thereby provide a firm intersubjective basis for what were initially tentative commitments to new identities and interests.[98]

Notwithstanding today's rhetoric about the end of the cold war, skeptics may still doubt whether Gorbachev (or some future leader) will succeed in building an intersubjective basis for a new Soviet (or Russian) role identity. There are important domestic, bureaucratic, and cognitive – ideological sources of resistance in both East and West to such a change, not the least of which is the shakiness of the democratic forces' domestic position. But if my argument about the role of intersubjective knowledge in creating competitive structures of identity and interest is right, then at least New Thinking shows a greater appreciation – conscious or not – for the deep structure of power politics than we are accustomed to in international relations practice.

CONCLUSION

All theories of international relations are based on social theories of the relationship between agency, process, and social structure. Social theories do not determine the content of our international theorizing, but they do structure the questions we ask about world politics and our approaches to answering those questions. The substantive issue at stake in debates about social theory is what kind of foundation offers the most fruitful set of questions and research strategies for explaining the revolutionary changes that seem to be occurring in the late twentieth century international system. Put simply, what should systemic theories of international relations look like? How should they conceptualize the relationship between structure and process? Should they be based exclusively on 'microeconomic' analogies in which identities and interests are exogenously given by structure and process is reduced to interactions within those parameters? Or should they also be based on 'sociological' and 'social psychological' analogies in which identities and interests and therefore the meaning of structure are endogenous to process? Should a behavioral – individualism or a cognitive – constructivism be the basis for systemic theories of world politics?

This article notwithstanding, this question is ultimately an empirical one in two respects. First, its answer depends in part on how important interaction among states is for the constitution of their identities and interests. On the one hand, it may be that domestic or genetic factors, which I have systematically bracketed, are in fact much more important determinants of states' identities and interests than are systemic factors. To the extent that this is true, the individualism of a rationalist approach and the inherent privileging of structure over process in this approach become more substantively appropriate for systemic theory (if not for first- and second-image theory), since identities and interests are *in fact* largely exogenous to interaction among states. On the other hand, if the bracketed factors are relatively unimportant or if the importance of the international system varies historically (perhaps with the level of dynamic density and interdependence in the system), then such a framework would not be appropriate as an exclusive foundation for general systemic theory.

Second, the answer to the question about what systemic theories should look like also depends on how easily state identities and interests can change as a result of systemic interaction. Even if interaction is initially important in constructing identities and interests, once institutionalized its logic may make transformation extremely difficult. If the meaning of structure for state action changes so slowly that it becomes a de facto parameter within which process takes place, then it may again be substantively appropriate to adopt the rationalist assumption that identities and interests are given (although again, this may vary historically).

We cannot address these empirical issues, however, unless we have a framework for doing systemic research that makes state identity and interest an issue for both theoretical and empirical inquiry. Let me emphasize that this is *not* to say we should never treat identities and interests as given. The framing of problems and research strategies should be question-driven rather than method-driven, and if we are not interested in identity- and interest-formation, we may find the assumptions of a rationalist discourse perfectly reasonable. Nothing in this article, in other words, should be taken as an attack on rationalism *per se*. By the same token, however, we should not let this legitimate analytical stance become a de facto ontological stance with respect to the content of third-image theory, at least not until after we have determined that systematic interaction does not play an important role in processes of state identity- and interest-formation. We should not choose our philosophical anthropologies and social theories prematurely. By arguing that we cannot derive a self-help structure of identity and interest from the principle of anarchy alone – by arguing that anarchy is what states make of it – this article has challenged one important justification for ignoring processes of identity- and interest-formation in world politics. As such, it helps set the stage for inquiry into the empirical issues raised above and thus for a debate about whether communitarian or individualist assumptions are a better foundation for systemic theory.

I have tried to indicate by crude example what such a

research agenda might look like. Its objective should be to assess the causal relationship between practice and inter-action (as independent variable) and the cognitive struc-tures at the level of individual states and of systems of states which constitute identities and interests (as dependent vari-able) – that is, the relationship between what actors *do* and what they *are*. We may have some *a priori* notion that state actors and systemic structures are 'mutually constitut-ive,' but this tells us little in the absence of an understanding of how the mechanics of dyadic, triadic, and *n*-actor inter-action shape and are in turn shaped by 'stocks of knowl-edge' that collectively constitute identities and interests and, more broadly, constitute the structures of international life. Particularly important in this respect is the role of prac-tice in shaping attitudes toward the 'givenness' of these structures. How and why do actors reify social structures, and under what conditions do they denaturalize such reifications?

The state-centrism of this agenda may strike some, par-ticularly postmodernists, as 'depressingly familiar.'[99] The significance of states relative to multinational corporations, new social movements, transnationals, and intergovernmental organizations is clearly declining, and 'postmodern' forms of world politics merit more research attention than they have received. But I also believe, with realists, that in the medium run sovereign states will remain the dominant pol-itical actors in the international system. Any transition to new structures of global political authority and identity – to 'post-international' politics – will be mediated by and path-dependent on the particular institutional resolution of the tension between unity and diversity, or particularism and universality, that is the sovereign state.[100] In such a world there should continue to be a place for theories of anarchic interstate politics, alongside other forms of inter-national theory; to that extent, I am a statist and a realist. I have argued in this article, however, that statism need not be bound by realist ideas about what 'state' must mean. State identities and interests can be collectively transformed within an anarchic context by many factors – individual, domestic, systemic, or transnational – and as such are an important dependent variable. Such a reconstruction of state-centric international theory is necessary if we are to theorize adequately about the emerging forms of transnational political identity that sovereign states will help bring into being. To that extent, I hope that statism, like the state, can be historically progressive.

I have argued that the proponents of strong liberalism and the constructivists can and should join forces in contributing to a process-oriented international theory. Each group has characteristic weaknesses that are complemented by the other's strengths. In part because of the decision to adopt a choice–theoretic approach to theory construction, neoliberals have been unable to translate their work on institution-building and complex learning into a systemic theory that escapes the explanatory priority of realism's concern with structure. Their weakness, in other words, is a lingering unwillingness to transcend, at the level of systemic theory, the individualist assumption that identities and interests are exogenously given. Constructivists bring to this lack of resolution a systematic communitarian ontology in which intersubjective knowledge constitutes identities and interests. For their part, however, constructivists have often devoted too much effort to questions of ontology and constitution and not enough effort to the causal and empirical questions of how identities and interests are produced by practice in anarchic conditions. As a result, they have not taken on board neoliberal insights into learning and social cognition.

An attempt to use a structurationist–symbolic interactionist discourse to bridge the two research traditions, neither of which subscribes to such a discourse, will probably please no one. But in part this is because the two 'sides' have become hung up on differences over the epistemological status of social science. The state of the social sciences and, in particular, of international relations, is such that epistemological prescriptions and conclusions are at best premature. Different questions involve different standards of inference; to reject certain questions because their answers cannot conform to the standards of classical physics is to fall into the trap of method-driven rather than question-driven social science. By the same token, however, giving up the artificial restrictions of logical positivist conceptions of inquiry does not force us to give up on 'Science.' Beyond this, there is little reason to attach so much importance to epistemology. Neither positivism, nor scientific realism, nor poststructuralism tells us about the structure and dynamics of international life. Philosophies of science are not theories of international relations. The good news is that strong liberals and modern and postmodern constructivists are asking broadly similar questions about the substance of international relations that differentiate both groups from the neorealist–rationalist alliance. Strong liberals and constructivists have much to learn from each other if they can come to see this through the smoke and heat of epistemology.

Notes

1. See, for example, Joseph Grieco, 'Anarchy and the Limits of Cooperation: A Realist Critique of the Newest Liberal Institutionalism,' *International Organizations*, 42 (Summer 1988), pp. 485–507; Joseph Nye, 'Neorealism and Neoliberalism,' *World Politics* 40 (January 1988), pp. 235–251; Robert Keohane, 'Neoliberal Institutionalism: A Perspective on World Politics,' in his collection of essays entitled *International Institutions and State Power* (Boulder: Westview Press, 1989), pp. 1–20; John Mearsheimer, 'Back to the Future: Instability in Europe After the Cold War,' *International Security* 13 (Summer 1990), pp. 5–56, along with subsequent published correspondence regarding Mearsheimer's article; and Emerson Niou and Peter Ordershook, 'Realism Versus Neoliberalism: A Formulation,' *American Journal of Political Science* 35 (May 1991), pp. 481–511.

2. See Robert Keohane, 'International Institutions: Two Approaches,' *International Studies Quarterly* 32 (December 1988), pp. 379–96.

3. Behavioral and rationalist models of man and institutions share a common intellectual heritage in the materialist individualism of Hobbes, Locke, and Bentham. On the relationship between the two models, see Jonathan Turner, *A Theory of Social Interaction* (Stanford: Stanford University Press, 1988), pp. 24–31; and George Homans, 'Rational Choice Theory and Behavioral Psychology,' in Craig Calhoun *et al.*, (eds.) *Structures of Power and Constraint* (Cambridge: Cambridge University Press, 1991), pp. 77–89.

4. On neorealist conceptions of learning, see Philip Tetlock, '*Learning in U.S. and Soviet Foreign Policy*,' in George Breslauer and Philip Tetlock (eds.), *Learning in US and Soviet Foreign Policy* (Boulder: Westview Press, 1991), pp. 24–27. On the difference between

behavioral and cognitive learning, see Breslauer and Tetlock (eds.), pp. 20–61; Joseph Nye, 'Nuclear Learning and U.S. – Soviet Security Regimes,' *International Organization* 41 (Summer 1987), pp. 371–402; and Ernst Haas, *When Knowledge Is Power* (Berkeley: University of California Press, 1990), pp. 17–49.

5. See Stephen Krasner, 'Regimes and the Limits of Realism: Regimes as Autonomous Variables,' in Stephen Krasner (ed.), *International Regimes* (Ithaca: Cornell University Press, 1983), pp. 355–368.

6. See Nye, 'Nuclear Learning and US – Soviet Security Regimes'; Robert Jervis, 'Realism, Game Theory, and Cooperation,' *World Politics* 40 (April 1988), pp. 340–44; and Robert Keohane, 'International Liberalism Reconsidered,' in John Dunn (ed.), *The Economic Limits to Modern Politics* (Cambridge: Cambridge University Press, 1990), p. 183.

7. Rationalists have given some attention to the problem of preference-formation, although in so doing they have gone beyond what I understand as the characteristic parameters of rationalism. See, for example, Jon Elster, 'Sour Grapes: Utilitarianism and the Genesis of Wants,' in Amartya Sen and Bernard Williams (eds.), *Utilitarianism and Beyond* (Cambridge: Cambridge University Press, 1982), pp. 219–38; and Michael Cohen and Robert Axelrod, 'Coping with Complexity: The Adaptive Value of Changing Utility,' *American Economic Review* 74 (March 1984), pp. 30–42.

8. Friedrich Kratochwil and John Ruggie, 'International Organization: A State of the Art on an Art of the State,' *International Organization* 40 (Autumn 1986), pp. 753–75.

9. Keohane, 'International Institutions.'

10. See Nicholas Onuf, *World of Our Making* (Columbia: University of South Carolina Press, 1989).

11. On Science, see Keohane, 'International Institutions'; and Robert Keohane, 'International Relations Theory: Contributions of a Feminist Standpoint,' *Millennium* 18 (Summer 1989) pp. 245–53. On Dissent, see R. B. J. Walker, 'History and Structure in the Theory of International Relations,' *Millennium* 18 (Summer 1989), pp. 163–83 (see chapter 12 in this volume); and Richard Ashley and R. B. J. Walker, 'Reading Dissidence/Writing the Discipline: Crisis and the Question of Sovereignty in International Studies,' *International Studies Quarterly* 34 (September 1990), pp. 367–416. For an excellent critical assessment of these debates, see Yosef Lapid, 'The Third Debate: On the Prospects of International Theory in a Post-Positivist Era,' *International Studies Quarterly* 33 (September 1989), pp. 235–54.

12. The fact that I draw on these approaches aligns me with modernist constructivists, even though I also draw freely on the substantive work of postmodernists, especially Richard Ashley and Rob Walker. For a defense of this practice and a discussion of its epistemological basis, see my earlier article, 'The Agent – Structure Problem in International Relations Theory,' *International Organ-*

ization 41 (Summer 1987), pp. 335–70; and Ian Shapiro and Alexander Wendt, 'The Difference That Realism Makes: Social Science and the Politics of Consent,' *Politics and Society*. Among modernist constructivists, my argument is particularly indebted to the published work of Emanuel Adler, Friedrich Kratochwil, and John Ruggie, as well as to an unpublished paper by Naeem Inayatullah and David Levine entitled 'Politics and Economics in Contemporary International Relations Theory,' Syracuse University, Syracuse, N.Y. (1990).

13. See Viktor Gecas, 'Rekindling the Sociological Imagination in Social Psychology,' *Journal for the Theory of Social Behavior* 19 (March 1989), pp. 97–115.

14. Kenneth Waltz, *Man, the State, and War* (New York: Columbia University Press, 1959), p. 232.

15. Waltz, *Man, the State, and War*, pp. 169–70.

16. Waltz, *Man, the State, and War*, p. 232. This point is made by Hidemi Suganami in 'Bringing Order to the Causes of War Debates,' *Millennium* 19 (Spring 1990), p. 34, n. 11.

17. Kenneth Waltz, *Theory of International Politics* (Boston: Addison-Wesley, 1979).

18. The neorealist description is not unproblematic. For a powerful critique, see David Lumsdaine, *Ideals and Interests: The Foreign Aid Regime, 1949–1989* (Princeton: Princeton University Press).

19. Waltz, *Theory of International Politics*, pp. 79–101.

20. Stephen Walt, *The Origins of Alliances* (Ithaca: Cornell University Press, 1987).

21. See, for example, Herbert Blumer, 'The Methodological Position of Symbolic Interactionism,' in his *Symbolic Interactionism: Perspective and Method* (Englewood Cliffs, N.J.: Prentice-Hall, 1969), p. 2. Throughout this article, I assume that a theoretically productive analogy can be made between individuals and states. There are at least two justifications for this anthropomorphism. Rhetorically the analogy is an accepted practice in mainstream international relations discourse, and since this article is an immanent rather than external critique, it should follow the practice. Substantively, states are collectivities of individuals that through their practices constitute each other as 'persons' having interests, fears, and so on. A full theory of state identity- and interest-formation would nevertheless need to draw insights from the social psychology of groups and organizational theory, and for that reason my anthropomorphism is merely suggestive.

22. The phrase 'distribution of knowledge' is Barry Barnes', as discussed in his work *The Nature of Power* (Cambridge: Polity Press, 1988); see also Peter Berger and Thomas Luckmann, *The Social Construction of Reality* (New York: Anchor Books, 1966). The concern of recent international relations scholarship on 'epistemic communities' with the cause-and-effect understandings of the world held by scientists, experts, and policymakers is an important aspect of the role of knowledge in world politics; see Peter Haas,

'Do Regimes Matter? Epistemic Communities and Mediterranean Pollution Control,' *International Organization* 43 (Summer 1989), pp. 377–404; and Ernst Haas, *When Knowledge Is Power*. My constructivist approach would merely add to this an equal emphasis on how such knowledge also constitutes the structures and subjects of social life.

23. For an excellent short statement of how collective meanings constitute identities, see Peter Berger, 'Identity as a Problem in the Sociology of Knowledge,' *European Journal of Sociology*, 7 (1) (1966), pp. 32–40. See also David Morgan and Michael Schwalbe, 'Mind and Self in Society: Linking Social Structure and Social Cognition,' *Social Psychology Quarterly* 53 (June 1990), pp. 148–64. In my discussion, I draw on the following interactionist texts: George Herbert Mead, *Mind, Self, and Society* (Chicago: University of Chicago Press, 1934); Berger and Luckmann, *The Social Construction of Reality*; Sheldon Stryker, *Symbolic Interactionism: A Social Structural Version* (Menlo Park, Calif.: Benjamin/Cummings, 1980); R. S. Perinbanayagam, *Signifying Acts: Structure and Meaning in Everyday Life* (Carbondale: Southern Illinois University Press, 1985); John Hewitt, *Self and Society: A Symbolic Interactionist Social Psychology* (Boston: Allyn & Bacon, 1988); and Turner, *A Theory of Social Interaction*. Despite some differences, much the same points are made by structurationists such as Bhaskar and Giddens. See Roy Bhaskar, *The Possibility of Naturalism* (Atlantic Highlands, N.J.: Humanities Press, 1979); and Anthony Giddens, *Central Problems in Social Theory* (Berkeley: University of California Press, 1979).

24. Berger, 'Identity as a Problem in the Sociology of Knowledge,' p. 111.

25. While not normally cast in such terms, foreign policy scholarship on national role conceptions could be adapted to such identity language. See Kal Holsti, 'National Role Conceptions in the Study of Foreign Policy,' *International Studies Quarterly* 14 (September 1970), pp. 233–309; and Stephen Walker (ed.) *Role Theory and Foreign Policy Analysis* (Durham, N.C.: Duke University Press, 1987). For an important effort to do so, see Stephen Walker, 'Symbolic Interactionism and International Politics: Role Theory's Contribution to International Organization,' in C. Shih and Martha Cottam (eds.), *Contending Dramas: A Cognitive Approach to Post-War International Organizational Processes* (New York: Praeger).

26. On the 'portfolio' conception of interests, see Barry Hindess, *Political Choice and Social Structure* (Aldershot: Edward Elgar, 1989), pp. 2–3. The 'definition of the situation' is a central concept in interactionist theory.

27. Nelson Foote, 'Identification as the Basis for a Theory of Motivation,' *American Sociological Review* 16 (February 1951), p. 15. Such strongly sociological conceptions of interest have been criticized, with some justice, for being 'oversocialized'; see Dennis Wrong, 'The Oversocialized Conception of Man in Modern Sociology,' *American Sociological Review* 26 (April 1961), pp. 183–93. For use-

ful correctives, which focus on the activation of presocial but non-determining human needs within social contexts, see Turner, *A Theory of Social Interaction*, pp. 23–69; and Viktor Gecas, 'The Self-Concept as a Basis for a Theory of Motivation,' in Judith Howard and Peter Callero (eds.), *The Self-Society Dynamic* (Cambridge: Cambridge University Press, 1991), pp. 171–87.

28. In neo-Durkheimian parlance, institutions are 'social representations.' See Serge Moscovici, 'The Phenomenon of Social Representations,' in Rob Farr and Serge Moscovici (eds.), *Social Representations* (Cambridge: Cambridge University Press, 1984), pp. 3–69. See also Barnes, *The Nature of Power*. Note that this is a considerably more socialized cognitivism than that found in much of the recent scholarship on the role of 'ideas' in world politics, which tends to treat ideas as commodities that are held by individuals and intervene between distribution of power and outcomes. For a form of cognitivism closer to my own, see Emanuel Adler, 'Cognitive Evolution: A Dynamic Approach for the Study of International Relations and Their Progress,' in Emanuel Adler and Beverly Crawford (eds.), *Progress in Postwar International Relations* (New York: Columbia University Press, 1991), pp. 43–88.

29. Berger and Luckmann, *The Social Construction of Reality*, p. 58.

30. See Giddens, *Central Problems in Social Theory*; and Alexander Wendt and Raymond Duvall, 'Institutions and International Order,' in Ernst-Otto Czempiel and James Rosenau (eds.), *Global Changes and Theoretical Challenges* (Lexington, MA: Lexington Books, 1989), pp. 51–74.

31. Proponents of choice theory might put this in terms of 'interdependent utilities.' For a useful overview of relevant choice – theoretic discourse, most of which has focused on the specific case of altruism, see Harold Hochman and Shmuel Nitzan, 'Concepts of Extended Preference.' *Journal of Economic Behavior and Organization* 6 (1985), pp. 161–76. The literature on choice theory usually does not link behavior to issues of identity. For an exception, see Amartya Sen, 'Goals, Commitment, and Identity,' *Journal of Law, Economics, and Organization* 1 (Fall 1985), pp. 341–55; and Robert Higgs, 'Identity and Cooperation: A Comment on Sen's Alternative Program,' *Journal of Law, Economics, and Organization* 3 (Spring 1987), pp. 140–42.

32. Security systems might also vary in the extent to which there is a functional differentiation or a hierarchical relationship between patron and client, with the patron playing a hegemonic role within its sphere of influence in defining the security interests of its clients. I do not examine this dimension here; for preliminary discussion, see Alexander Wendt, 'The States System and Global Militarization,' Ph.D. dissertation, University of Minnesota, Minneapolis (1989); and Alexander Wendt and Michael Barnett, 'The International System and Third World-Militarization,' unpublished ms (1991).

33. This amounts to an 'internationalization of the state.' For a

discussion of this subject, see Raymond Duvall and Alexander Wendt, 'The International Capital Regime and the Internationalization of the State,' unpublished ms (1987). See also R. B. J. Walker, 'Sovereignty, Identity, Community: Reflections on the Horizons of Contemporary Political Practice,' in R. B. J. Walker and Saul Mendlovitz (eds.), *Contending Sovereignties* (Boulder: Lynne Rienner, 1990), pp. 159–85.

34. On the spectrum of cooperative security arrangements, see Charles Kupchan and Clifford Kupchan, 'Concerts, Collective Security, and the Future of Europe,' *International Security* 16 (Summer 1991), pp. 114–61; and Richard Smoke, 'A Theory of Mutual Security,' in Richard Smoke and Andrei Kortunov (eds.), *Mutual Security* (New York: St. Martin's Press, 1991), pp. 59–111. These may be usefully set alongside Christopher Jencks' 'Varieties of Altruism,' in Jane Mansbridge (ed.) *Beyond Self-Interest* (Chicago: University of Chicago Press, 1990), pp. 53–67.

35. On the role of collective identity in reducing collective identity in reducing collective action problems, see Bruce Fireman and William Gamson, 'Utilitarian Logic in the Resource Mobilization Perspective,' in Mayer Zald and John McCarthy (eds.), *The Dynamics of Social Movements* (Cambridge, MA: Winthrop, 1979), pp. 8–44; Robyn Dawes *et al.*, 'Cooperation for the Benefit of US – Not Me, or My Conscience,' in Mansbridge (ed.), *Beyond Self-Interest*, pp. 97–110; and Craig Calhoun, 'The Problem of Identity in Collective Action,' in Joan Huber (ed.), *Macro – Micro Linkages in Sociology* (Beverly Hills, Calif.: Sage, 1991), pp. 51–75.

36. See Thomas Risse-Kappen, 'Are Democratic Alliances Special?' unpublished ms, Yale University, New Haven (1991). This line of argument could be expanded usefully in feminist terms. For a useful overview of the relational nature of feminist conceptions of self, see Paula England and Barbara Stanek Kilbourne, 'Feminist Critiques of the Separative Model of Self: Implications for Rational Choice Theory,' *Rationality and Society* 2 (April 1990), pp. 156–71. On feminist conceptualizations of power, see Ann Tickner, 'Hans Morgenthau's Principles of Political Realism: A Feminist Reformulation,' *Millennium* 17 (3) (Winter 1988), pp. 429–40 (see chapter 4 in this volume); and Thomas Wartenberg, 'The Concept of Power in Feminist Theory,' *Praxis International* 8 (October 1988), pp. 301–16.

37. Waltz, *Theory of International Politics*, p. 91.

38. See Waltz, *Man, the State, and War;* and Robert Jervis, 'Cooperation Under the Security Dilemma,' *World Politics* 30 (January 1978), pp. 167–214.

39. My argument here parallels Rousseau's critique of Hobbes. For an excellent critique of realist appropriations of Rousseau, see Michael Williams, 'Rousseau, Realism, and Realpolitik,' *Millennium* 18 (Summer 1989), pp. 188–204. Williams argues that far from being a fundamental starting point in the state of nature, for Rousseau the stag hunt represented a stage in man's fall.

On p. 190, Williams cites Rousseau's description of man prior to leaving the state of nature: 'Man only knows himself; he does not see his own well-being to be identified with or contrary to that of anyone else; he neither hates anything nor loves anything; but limited to no more than physical instinct, he is no one, he is an animal.' For another critique of Hobbes on the state of nature that parallels my constructivist reading of anarchy, see Charles Landesman, 'Reflections on Hobbes: Anarchy and Human Nature,' in Peter Caws (ed.), *The Causes of Quarrel* (Boston: Beacon, 1989), pp. 139–48.

40. Empirically, this suggestion is problematic, since the process of decolonization and the subsequent support of many Third World states by international society point to ways in which even the raw material of 'empirical statehood' is constituted by the society of states. See Robert Jackson and Carl Rosberg, 'Why Africa's Weak States Persist: The Empirical and the Juridical in Statehood,' *World Politics* 35 (October 1982), pp. 1–24.

41. Waltz, *Theory of International Politics*, pp. 74–77.

42. See James Morrow, 'Social Choice and System Structure in World Politics,' *World Politics* 41 (October 1988), p. 89. Waltz's behavioral treatment of socialization may be usefully contrasted with more cognitive approach taken by Ikenberry and the Kupchans in the following articles, G. John Ikenberry and Charles Kupchan, 'Socialization and Hegemonic Power,' *International Organization* 44 (Summer 1989), pp. 283–316; and Kupchan and Kupchan, 'Concerts, Collective Security, and the Future of Europe.' Their approach is close to my own, but they define socialization as an elite strategy to induce value change in others, rather than as a ubiquitous feature of interaction in terms of which all identities and interests get produced and reproduced.

43. Regarding individualism, see Richard Ashley, 'The Poverty of Neorealism,' *International Organization* 38 (Spring 1984), pp. 225–86; Wendt, 'The Agent-Structure Problem in International Relations Theory'; and David Dessler, 'What's at Stake in the Agent-Structure Debate?' *International Organization* 43 (Summer 1989), pp. 441–74. Regarding structuralism, see R. B. J. Walker, 'Realism, Change, and International Political Theory,' *International Studies Quarterly* 31 (March 1987), pp. 65–86; and Martin Hollis and Steven Smith, *Explaining and Understanding International Relations* (Oxford: Clarendon Press, 1989). The behavioralism evident in neorealist theory also explains how neorealists can reconcile their structuralism with the individualism of rational choice theory. On the behavioral – structural character of the latter, see Spiro Latsis, 'Situational Determinism in Economics,' *British Journal for the Philosophy of Science* 23 (August 1972), pp. 207–45.

44. The importance of the distinction between constitutive and causal explanations is not sufficiently appreciated in constructivist discourse. See Wendt, 'The Agent-Structure Problem in International Relations Theory,' pp. 362–65; Wendt, 'The States System and Global Militarization,' pp. 110–13; and Wendt, 'Bridging the

Theory/Meta-Theory Gap in International Relations,' *Review of International Studies* 17 (October 1991), p. 390.

45. See Blumer, 'The Methodological Position of Symbolic Interactionism,' pp. 2–4.

46. See Robert Grafstein, 'Rational Choice: Theory and Institutions,' in Kristen Monroe (ed.) *The Economic Approach to Politics* (New York: Harper Collins, 1991), pp. 263–64. A good example of the promise and limits of transaction cost approaches to institutional analysis is offered by Robert Keohane in his *After Hegemony* (Princeton: Princeton University Press, 1984).

47. This situation is not entirely metaphorical in world politics, since throughout history states have 'discovered' each other, generating an instant anarchy as it were. A systematic empirical study of first contacts would be interesting.

48. Mead's analysis of gestures remains definitive. See Mead's *Mind, Self, and Society*. See also the discussion of the role of signaling in the 'mechanics of interaction' in Turner's *A Theory of Social Interaction*, pp. 74–79 and 92–115.

49. On the role of attribution processes in the interactionist account of identity-formation, see Sheldon Stryker and Avi Gottlieb, 'Attribution Theory and Symbolic Interactionism,' in John Harvey *et al.* (eds.), *New Directions in Attribution Research*, vol. 3 (Hillsdale, N.J.: Lawrence Erlbaum, 1981), pp. 425–58; and Kathleen Crittenden, 'Sociological Aspects of Attribution,' *Annual Review of Sociology*, 9 (1983), pp. 425–46. On attributional processes in international relations, see Shawn Rosenberg and Gary Wolfsfeld, 'International Conflict and the Problem of Attribution,' *Journal of Conflict Resolution* 21 (March 1977), pp. 75–103.

50. On the 'stagecraft' involved in 'presentations of self,' see Erving Goffman, *The Presentation of Self in Everyday Life* (New York: Doubleday, 1959). On the role of appearance in definitions of the situation, see Gregory Stone, 'Appearance and the Self,' in Arnold Rose (ed.), *Human Behavior and Social Processes* (Boston: Houghton Mifflin, 1962), pp. 86–118.

51. This discussion of the role of possibilities and probabilities in threat perception owes much to Stewart Johnson's comments on an earlier draft of my article.

52. On the role of 'reassurance' in threat situations, see Richard Ned Lebow and Janice Gross Stein, 'Beyond Deterrence,' *Journal of Social Issues*, 43 (4) (1987), pp. 5–72.

53. On 'reciprocal typifications,' see Berger and Luckmann, *The Social Construction of Reality*, pp. 54–58.

54. Jeff Coulter, 'Remarks on the Conceptualization of Social Structure,' *Philosophy of the Social Sciences* 12 (March 1982), pp. 42–43.

55. The following articles by Noel Kaplowitz have made an important contribution to such thinking in international relations: 'Psychopolitical Dimensions of International Relations: The Reciprocal Effects of Conflict Strategies,' *International Studies Quarterly* 28 (December 1984), pp. 373–406; and 'National Self-Images,

Perception of Enemies, and Conflict Strategies: Psychopolitical Dimensions of International Relations,' *Political Psychology* 11 (March 1990), pp. 39–82.

56. These arguments are common in theories of narcissism and altruism. See Heinz Kohut, *Self-Psychology and the Humanities* (New York: Norton, 1985); and Martin Hoffmann, 'Empathy, Its Limitations, and Its Role in a Comprehensive Moral Theory,' in William Kurtines and Jacob Gewirtz (eds.) *Morality, Moral Behavior, and Moral Development* (New York: Wiley, 1984), pp. 283–302.

57. See C. Norman Alexander and Mary Glenn Wiley, 'Situated Activity and Identity Formation,' in Morris Rosenberg and Ralph Turner (eds.), *Social Psychology: Sociological Perspectives* (New York: Basic Books, 1981), pp. 269–89.

58. Sheldon Stryker, 'The Vitalization of Symbolic Interactionism,' *Social Psychology Quarterly* 50 (March 1987), p. 93.

59. On the 'maturity' of anarchies, see Barry Buzan, *People, States, and Fear* (Chapel Hill: University of North Carolina Press, 1983).

60. A similar intuition may lie behind Ashley's effort to reappropriate classical realist discourse for critical international relations theory. See Richard Ashley, 'Political Realism and Human Interests,' *International Studies Quarterly*, 38 (June 1981), pp. 204–36.

61. Waltz, has himself helped open up such a debate with his recognition that systematic factors condition but do not determine state actions. See Kenneth Waltz, 'Reflections on *Theory of International Politics*: A Response to My Critics,' in Robert Keohane (ed.) *Neorealism and Its Critics* (New York: Columbia University Press, 1986), pp. 322–45. The growing literature on the observation that 'democracies do not fight each other' is relevant to this question, as are two other studies that break important ground toward a 'reductionist' theory of state identity: William Bloom's *Personal Identity, National Identity and International Relations* (Cambridge: Cambridge University Press, 1990) and Lumsdaine's *Ideals and Interests*.

62. See Berger and Luckmann, *The Social Construction of Reality*, p. 89. See also Douglas Maynard and Thomas Wilson, 'On the Reification of Social Structure,' in Scott McNall and Gary Howe (eds.), *Current Perspectives in Social Theory*, vol. 1 (Greenwich, Conn.: JAI Press, 1980), pp. 287–322.

63. See Richard Ashley, 'Social Will and International Anarchy,' (unpublished essay).

64. See Ralph Turner, 'Role-Taking: Process Versus Conformity,' in Rose, *Human Behavior and Social Processes*, pp. 20–40; and Judith Howard, 'From Changing Selves Toward Changing Society,' in Howard and Callero, *The Self-Society Dynamic*, pp. 209–37.

65. On the relationship between commitment and identity, see Foote, 'Identification as the Basis for a Theory of Motivation'; Howard Becker, 'Notes on the Concept of Commitment,' *American Journal of Sociology* 66 (July 1960), pp. 32–40; and Stryker, *Symbolic Interactionism*. On role salience, see Stryker, *Symbolic Interactionism*.

66. On threats to identity and the types of resistance that they may create, see Glynis Breakwell, *Coping with Threatened Identities* (London: Methuen, 1986); and Terrell Northrup, 'The Dynamic of Identity in Personal and Social Conflict,' in Louis Kreisberg *et al.* (eds.), *Intractable Conflicts and Their Transformation* (Syracuse, N.Y." Syracuse University Press, 1989), pp. 55–82. For a broad overview of resistance to change, see Timur Kuran, 'The Tenacious Past: Theories of Personal and Collective Conservatism,' *Journal of Economic Behavior and Organization* 10 (September 1988), pp. 143–71.

67. James March, 'Bounded Rationality, Ambiguity, and the Engineering of Choice,' *Bell Journal of Economics* 9 (Autumn 1978), p. 600.

68. Haskell Fain, *Normative Politics and the Community of Nations* (Philadelphia: Temple University Press, 1987).

69. This is the intersubjective basis for the principle of functional non-differentiation among states, which 'drops out' of Waltz's definition of structure because the latter has no explicit intersubjective basis. In international relations scholarship, the social production of territorial space has been emphasized primarily by poststructuralists. See, for example, Richard Ashley, 'The Geopolitics of Geopolitical Space: Toward a Critical Social Theory of International Politics,' *Alternatives* 12 (October 1987), pp. 403–34; and Simon Dalby, *Creating the Second Cold War* (London: Pinter, 1990). But the idea of space as both product and constituent of practice is also prominent in structurationist discourse. See Giddens, *Central Problems in Social Theory*; and Derek Gregory and John Urry (eds.), *Social Relations and Spatial Structures* (London: Macmillan, 1985).

70. See John Ruggie, 'Continuity and Transformation in the World Polity: Toward a Neorealist Synthesis,' *World Politics* 35 (January 1983), pp. 261–85. In *Mind, Self, and Society*, p. 161, Mead offers the following argument: 'If we say "this is my property, I shall control it," that affirmation calls out a certain set of responses which must be the same in any community in which property exists. It involves an organized attitude with reference to property which is common to all members of the community. One must have a definite attitude of control of his own property and respect for the property of others. Those attitudes (as organized sets of responses) must be there on the part of all, so that when one says such a thing he calls out in himself the response of the others. That which makes society possible is such common responses.'

71. For a definition and discussion of 'social closure,' see Raymond Murphy, *Social Closure* (Oxford: Clarendon Press, 1988).

72. See Richard Ashley, 'Untying the Sovereign State: A Double Reading of the Anarchy Problematique,' *Millennium* 17 (Summer 1988), pp. 227–62. Those with more modernist sensibilities will find an equality practice-centric view of institutions in Blumer's observation on p. 19 of 'The Methodological Position of Symbolic Interactionism': 'A gratuitous acceptance of the concepts of norms,

values, social rules and the like should not blind the social scientist to the fact that any one of them is subjected by a process of social interaction – a process that is necessary not only for their change but equally well for their retention in a fixed form. It is the social process in group life that creates and upholds the rules, not the rules that create and uphold group life.'

73. See, for example, Mohammed Ayoob, 'The Third World in the System of States: Acute Schizophrenia or Growing Pains?' *International Studies Quarterly* 33 (March 1989), pp. 67–80.

74. See William Coplin, 'International Law and Assumptions About the State System' *World Politics* 17 (July 1965), pp. 615–34.

75. See Anthony Smith, 'States and Homelands: The Social and Geopolitical Implications of National Territory,' *Millennium* 10 (Autumn 1981), pp. 187–202.

76. This assumes that there are no other, competing, principles that organize political space and identity in the international system and coexist with traditional notions of sovereignty; in fact, of course, there are. On 'spheres of influence' and 'informal empires,' see Jan Triska (ed.) *Dominant Powers and Subordinate States* (Durham, N.C.: Duke University Press, 1986); and Ronald Robinson, 'The Excentric Idea of Imperialism, With or Without Empire,' in Wolfgang Mommsen and Jurgen Osterhammel (eds.), *Imperialism and After: Continuities and Discontinuities* (London: Allen & Unwin, 1986), pp. 267–89. On Arab conceptions of sovereignty, see Michael Barnett, 'Sovereignty, Institutions, and Identity: From Pan-Arabism to the Arab State System,' unpublished ms, University of Wisconsin, Madison, 1991.

77. David Strang, 'Anomaly and Commonplace in European Expansion: Realist and Institutional Accounts,' *International Organization* 45 (Spring 1991), pp. 143–62.

78. On 'dynamic density,' see Ruggie, 'Continuity and Transformation in the World Polity'; and Waltz, 'Reflections on *Theory of International Politics*' The role of interdependence in conditioning the speed and depth of social learning is much greater than the attention to which I have paid it. On the consequences of interdependence under anarchy, see Helen Milner, 'The Assumption of Anarchy in International Relations Theory: A Critique,' *Review of International Studies* 17 (January 1991), pp. 67–85.

79. See Michael Taylor, *Anarchy and Cooperation* (New York: Wiley, 1976); and Robert Axelrod, *The Evolution of Cooperation* (New York: Basic Books, 1984).

80. Mead, *Mind, Self, and Society*.

81. Strictly speaking, this is not true, since in iterated games the addition of future benefits to current ones changes the payoff structure of the game at T1, in this case from prisoner's dilemma to an assurance game. This transformation of interest takes place entirely within the actor, however, and as such is not a function of interaction with the other.

82. In fairness to Axelrod, he does point out that internalization of

norms is a real possibility that may increase the resilience of institutions. My point is that this important idea cannot be derived from an approach to theory that takes identities and interests as exogenously given.

83. On 'European identity,' see Barry Buzan *et al.* (eds.), *The European Security Order Recast* (London: Pinter, 1990), pp. 45–63.
84. On 'embeddedness,' see John Ruggie, 'International Regimes, Transactions, and Change: Embedded Liberalism in a Postwar Economic Order,' in Krasner, *International Regimes*, pp. 195–232.
85. See Grieco, 'Anarchy and the Limits of Cooperation.'
86. On the difficulties of creating cooperative security regimes given competitive interests, see Robert Jervis, 'Security Regimes,' in Krasner, *International Regimes*, pp. 173–94; and Charles Lipson, 'International Cooperation in Economic and Security Affairs,' *World Politics* 37 (October 1984), pp. 1–23.
87. See Mead, *Mind, Self, and Society.* For useful discussions of this distinction and its implications for notions of creativity in social systems, see George Cronk, *The Philosophical Anthropology of George Herbert Mead* (New York: Peter Lang, 1987), pp. 36–40; and Howard, 'From Changing Selves Toward Changing Society.'
88. Turner, 'Role-Taking.'
89. On 'character planning,' see Jon Elster, *Sour Grapes: Studies in the Subversion of Rationality* (Cambridge: Cambridge University Press, 1983), p. 117. For other approaches to the problem of self-initiated change, see Harry Frankfurt, 'Freedom of the Will and the Concept of a Person,' *Journal of Philosophy* 68 (January 1971), pp. 5–20; Amartya Sen, 'Rational Fools; A Critique of the Behavioral Foundations of Economic Theory,' *Philosophy and Public Affairs* 6 (Summer 1977), pp. 317–44; and Thomas Schelling, 'The Intimate Contest for Self-Command,' *The Public Interest* 60 (Summer 1980), pp. 94–118.
90. For useful overviews of New Thinking, see Mihkail Gorbachev, *Perestroika; New Thinking for Our Country and the World* (New York: Harper & Row, 1987); Vendulka Kubàlkovà and Albert Cruickshank, *Thinking New About Soviet 'New Thinking'* (Berkeley: Institute of International Studies, 1989); and Allen Lynch, *Gorbachev's International Outlook: Intellectual Origins and Political Consequences* (New York: Institute for East-West Security Studies, 1989). It is not clear to what extent New Thinking is a conscious policy as opposed to an ad hoc policy. The intense theoretical and policy debate within the Soviet Union over New Thinking and the frequently stated idea of taking away the Western 'excuse' for fearing the Soviet Union both suggest the former, but I will remain agnostic here and simply assume that it can be fruitfully interpreted 'as if' it had the form that I describe.
91. For useful overviews of these factors, see Jack Snyder, 'The Gorbachev Revolution: A Waning of Soviet Expansionism?' *World Politics* 12 (Winter 1987–88), pp. 93–121; and Stephen Meyer, 'The Sources and Prospects of Gorbachev's New Political Thinking on

Security,' *International Security* 13 (Fall 1988), pp. 124–63.

92. See Daniel Bar-Tal *et al.*, 'Conflict Termination: An Epistemological Analysis of International Cases,' *Political Psychology* 10 (June 1989), pp. 233–55. For an unrelated but interesting illustration of how changing cognitions in turn make possible organizational change, see Jean Bartunek, 'Changing Interpretive Schemes and Organizational Restructuring: The Example of a Religious Order,' *Administrative Science Quarterly* 29 (September 1984), pp. 355–72.

93. See Robert Cox, 'Social Forces, States and World Orders: Beyond International Relations Theory,' in Keohane, *Neorealism and Its Critics*, pp. 204–55. See also Brian Fay, *Critical Social Science* (Ithaca: Cornell University Press, 1987).

94. Hazel Markus and Paula Nurius, 'Possible Selves,' *American Psychologist* 41 (September 1986), pp. 954–69.

95. See Goffman, *The Presentation of Self in Everyday Life*; Eugene Weinstein and Paul Deutschberger, 'Some Dimensions of Altercasting,' *Sociometry* 26 (December 1963), pp. 454–66; and Walter Earle, 'International Relations and the Psychology of Control: Alternative Control Strategies and Their Consequences,' *Political Psychology* 7 (June 1986), pp. 369–75.

96. See Volker Boge and Peter Wilke, 'Peace Movements and Unilateral Disarmament: Old Concepts in a New Light,' *Arms Control* 7 (September 1986), pp. 156–70; Zeev Maoz and Daniel Felsenthal, 'Self-Binding Commitments, the Inducements of Trust, Social Choice, and the Theory of International Cooperation,' *International Studies Quarterly* 31 (June 1987), pp. 177–200; and V. Sakamoto, 'Unilateral Initiative as an Alternative Strategy,' *World Features*, vol. 24, nos. 1–4, 1987, pp. 107–34.

97. On rewards, see Thomas Milburn and Daniel Christie, 'Rewarding in International Politics,' *Political Psychology* 10 (December 1989), pp. 625–45.

98. The importance of reciprocity in completing the process of structural transformation makes the logic in this stage similar to that in the 'evolution of cooperation.' The difference is one of prerequisites and objective: in the former, ego's tentative redefinition of self enables it to try and change alter by acting 'as if' both were already playing a new game; in the latter, ego acts only on the basis of given interests and prior experience, with transformation emerging only as an unintended consequence.

99. Yale Ferguson and Richard Mansback, 'Between Celebration and Despair: Constructive Suggestions for Future International theory,' *International Studies Quarterly* 35 (December 1991), p. 375.

100. For excellent discussions of this tension, see Walker, 'Sovereignty, Identity, Community;' and R. B. J. Walker, 'Security, Sovereignty, and the Challenge of World Politics,' *Alternatives* 15 (Winter 1990), pp. 3–27. On institutional path dependencies, see Stephen Krasner, 'Sovereignty: An Institutional Perspective,' *Comparative Political Studies* 21 (April 1988), pp. 66–94.

Part III
Discipline and Power

8 The Theory of International Politics, 1919–1969 (1972)*

Hedley Bull

I

By the theory of international politics we may understand the body of general propositions that may be advanced about political relations between states, or more generally about world politics.[1] It includes normative propositions, stating the moral or legal considerations that are held to apply to international politics, as well as positive propositions which define or explain its actual character. It includes comprehensive theories, concerned to describe or to prescribe for international politics as a whole, but also partial theories concerned with some element of it such as war or peace, strategy or diplomacy. It includes theories about international society or the international system, which deal with the interrelatedness of the various units (states; nations; supranational, transnational, and subnational groups' etc.) of which world politics is made up, as well as theories about the units themselves. It includes theories developed in the self-conscious attempt to emulate the methods of the natural sciences, thus rejecting whatever cannot be either logically or mathematically proved or verified by strict, empirical procedures; and it includes theories propounded without a self-denying ordinance of this kind. It embraces theories derived by way of a deliberate simplification of reality, e.g. by the elaboration of deductive models, as well as theories built up by a process of inductive generalization. It includes theories that, at all events in their explicit aim or intention, are not concerned to provide any guide to policy or any

* *The Aberysthyth Papers: International Politics 1919–1969*, Brian Porter (ed.) (London: Oxford University Press), pp. 30–50.

solution to problems of a practical nature, as well as theories that are avowedly 'policy-oriented' or 'praxeological.'

In the preface to his *International Relations*, published in 1922, James Bryce wrote that 'History is the best – indeed the only – guide to a comprehension of the facts as they stand.'[2] If there is a distinctively 'theoretical' approach to the study of international relations, embracing the great variety of sorts of theorizing that have just been mentioned, and uniting theorists on any common platform, it is that which begins with rejection of the view that the subject can be or need be studied in historical terms alone.

To say that the historical approach is not sufficient for the understanding of international relations is not to say that it is not necessary. Championship of a theoretical or systematic study of international relations has sometimes been accompanied by a disparagement of historical training and historical scholarship: it is very noticeable that in some American universities where international relations are taught, historical training has been displaced from curriculae and historical skills have been undervalued in the selection of staff.

Historical understanding is essential in the first place because there are international political situations which have to be seen not merely as cases or illustrations of one or another general proposition but as singular events: there comes a point where, to understand the course of events or to appreciate the moral dilemmas to which it gives rise, we have to know not how international systems undergo transformations but, for example, about how our present international system was affected by the advent of nuclear weapons in 1945; not about the characteristic behavior of small states but about Switzerland; not about the foreign policy role of national leaders but about President de Gaulle; not about how just wars may be distinguished from unjust wars but about the moral choices that confronted the Israeli cabinet in June 1967.[3]

Historical study is essential also because any international political situation is located in time, and to understand it we must know its place in a temporal sequence of events: what the antecedent situations were out of which it grew, what the elements of continuity are that link it with what has gone on before, and what the elements of change are that mark it out as different. The language of theory is a timeless language of definitions and axioms, logical deductions and extrapolations, assertions of causal connections, ascertainments of general law. The exposition or explanation of an historical sequence depends at every point upon an appeal to theory, acknowledged or unacknowledged, but it is not itself the elaboration of a theory.

The historical study of international relations is also essential pedagogically. If we compare the historical with the theoretical study of international relations it is clear that the literature of diplomatic history is still of more evenly high quality, that the standards of the historian's profession are more clearly discernible, his canons of judgment less open to dispute, his territory less encroached upon by the crank or the charlatan, the imparting of his knowledge and techniques more clearly by itself an education.[4]

Finally, historical study is the essential companion of theoretical study itself: not only because history is the laboratory of the social sciences, the source of the material by which general propositions may be verified or falsified, but also because theory itself has a history, and theorists themselves elaborate their ideas with the preoccupations and within the confines or a particular historical situation. An understanding of the historical conditions out of which a theory grows, or to which it is a response, provides vital materials for the criticism of that theory and, for the theorist himself, provides the correction of self-knowledge.

The reason why we must be concerned with the theory as well as the history of the subject is that all discussions of international politics – of the past and the present as well as the future, of what it is as well as of what it should be – in any case proceed upon theoretical assumptions, which we should acknowledge and investigate rather than ignore or leave unchallenged. The enterprise of theoretical investigation is at its minimum one directed towards criticism: towards identifying, formulating, refining, and questioning the general assumptions on which the everyday discussion of international politics proceeds. At its maximum the enterprise is concerned also with theoretical construction: with establishing that certain assumptions are true while others are false, certain arguments valid while others are invalid, and so proceeding to erect a firm structure of knowledge.

The term 'theory of international relations' became fashionable only in the mid-1950s, and then only in the United States: even now the term often provokes puzzlement and incomprehension elsewhere in the world.[5] In the United States the use of the term has signified especially the constructive rather than the merely critical aspect of theoretical inquiry, the hope that a structure of general propositions might be built up that is comprehensive and not merely partial, and that would gain acceptance not merely as a theory but as *the* theory of international relations, a body of knowledge that would minimize disagreement and uncertainty and provide a clear guide to action. Here the term is used in a wider sense to embrace what is merely critical and speculative as well as what is constructive and strictly testable, and to include theorizing that does not form part of some movement for the development of 'a theory of international relations,' as well as that which does.

II

In tracing the course which the theory of international politics has followed since 1919 we shall take account only of those works which have some significant explanatory of analytic content, and shall exclude theoretical ideas or doctrines which are remarkable only because of their place in history or influence upon the course of events. It is not always easy to draw the line, but the ideas of, for example, Rosenberg's *Der Mythus des Zwanzigsten Jahrhunderts* or Nasser's *The Philosophy of the Egyptian Revolution* belong clearly to the latter category.

It is not possible to divide the theoretical works of the last half century into neat categories or schools that are logically exhaustive and exclusive of one another. But it is helpful to recognize three successive waves of theoretical activity: the 'idealist' or progressivist doctrines that predominated in the 1920s and early 1930s, the 'realist' or conservative theories that developed in reaction to them in the late 1930s, and 1940s, and the 'social scientific' theories of the late 1950s and 1960s, whose origin lay in dissatisfaction with the methodologies on which both the earlier kinds of theory were based.

By the 'idealists' we have in mind writers such as Sir Alfred Zimmern, S. H. Bailey, Philip Noel-Baker, and David Mitrany in the United Kingdom, and James T. Shotwell, Pitman Potter, and Parker T. Moon in the United States. The term 'idealist' is not one which they used to describe themselves but was applied to them later by their critics and is in some respects misleading as to what their views actually were. For instance, it is not the case that these writers were specially insistent upon the moral dimension of international relations, still less that they contributed anything important to our understanding of it.

The distinctive characteristics of these writers was their belief in progress: the belief, in particular, that the system of international relations that had given rise to World War I was capable of being transformed into a fundamentally more peaceful and just world order; that under the impact of the awakening of democracy, the growth of 'the international mind,' the development of the League of Nations, the good works of men of peace or the enlightenment spread by their own teachings, it was in fact being transformed; and that their responsibility as students of international relations was to assist this march of progress to overcome the ignorance, the prejudices, the ill will, and the sinister interests that stood in its way.

The belief in progress was inherited from the nineteenth century, but the idea that progress could now be sustained only by radical changes in the system of international relations resulted from the experience of World War I. Some of the ideas for radical change had already been present in pre-war writings about arbitration, international understanding, and the binding effects of world finance and commerce; others developed in the wartime questioning of the old order undertaken in works such as G. Lowes Dickinson's *The European Anarchy* (1916), Leonard Woolf's *International Government* (1916), Jan Smuts' *The League of Nations – A Practical Suggestion* (1918), H. N. Brailsford's *The War of Steel and Gold* (1915) and Arthur Ponsonby's *Democracy and Diplomacy* (1915).[6] None of these works is at all profound, and none is worth reading now except for the light it throws on the preoccupations and presuppositions of its place and time. But in the development of the theory of international relations they have a place for they helped to establish the possibility of questioning established institutions, and they at least raised the question how these institutions (state sovereignty, the balance of power, the old diplomacy, the private manufacture of armaments) functioned in relation to objectives such as peace and international order, even if the answers they gave to this question do not impress us now.

The most polished work of the 'idealist' writers is perhaps Sir Alfred Zimmern's *The League of Nations and the Rule of Law*, and at the basis of all their thinking is the dichotomy expressed in the division of this book into two sections: Part I, 'The Pre-War System;' Parts II and III, 'The Elements of the Covenant' and 'The Working of the League.'[7] On the one hand there was the past, which was not a source of guidance as to the maintenance of order but a series of object lessons, spelt out in the then fashionable studies of 'the causes of war' or 'the international anarchy.' On the other hand there were the present and the future, the possibilities of which were not limited by the test of previous experience but were deducible from the needs of progress.

This was the standpoint from which in the 1920s Philip Noel-Baker studied the problem of disarmament, James T. Shotwell analysed the outlawing of war, and David Davies contended that 'the problem of the twentieth century' was the establishment of an international police force.[8] In the 1930s, in response to the challenge presented to 'the League system' by the revisionist powers, the emphasis changed to the study of collective security and of 'the problem of peaceful change,' but the progressivist premises of these writers remained intact: the only change was that, in their view, the forces of 'power politics,' instead of being distributed among all the nations, were now seen to be concentrated in Germany, Italy, and Japan, and the hopes for the forward march of mankind to rest with the fortunes of Britain and France. Thus in the 1930s what E. H. Carr was to call the utopian doctrine became clearly the special ideology of the satisfied Powers.

The 'idealist' writers were theorists in the sense that they sought not only to present the history and recent development of international relations, but also to raise general questions as to what they were, how they operated, and how they might be influenced so as better to achieve the objectives of peace and order. But their answers to these questions now strike us as superficial. The 'idealists' were not remarkable for their intellectual depth or powers of explanation, only for their intense commitment to a particular vision of what should happen.

In their disparagement of the past they lost sight of a great deal that was already known: in some respects their work represented not an advance but a decline in understanding of international relations, an unlearning of old lessons which a later generation of writers found it necessary to restate. In their assessments of the present and the future they were guided more by their hopes than by the evidence in hand: in their preoccupation with international law, international organization and international society they lost sight of what to later generations of writers became the central focus of the subject, viz. international politics.

In dealing with international morality, which they were inclined to confuse with international law, they contributed only a narrow and uncritical rectitude which exalted the international interest over national interests (but without asking how the former was to be determined), constitutional reform over revolution as the means of transcending the society of sovereign states (but without considering whether states could become the agents of their own extinction), and respect for legality over the need for change (but without facing up to the fact that the international legal system, as they construed it, could not accommodate change). They were men of self-conscious virtue, whose range of human sympathies was slight: they appealed to international morality but had little notion of what it might mean to a Russian Bolshevik, a German nationalist, a Japanese militarist or an Indian anti-imperialist. The quality that shines through all their work is innocence, a disposition to accept the externals of international relations at face value, which in later generations of writers was dislodged by the greater influence upon them of the social sciences.

III

The second main wave of theoretical activity began in the late 1930s and continued throughout the 1940s. The writings of the 'realists,' a name that some of them claimed for themselves, were a reaction against those of the 'idealists,' or rather against wider tendencies in public thinking of which the latter provided an illustration. As against the hopes of the 'idealists' for international cooperation and harmony they drew attention to the reality of conflict and anarchy, which was closer to the surface in the 1930s and 1940s than it had been in the 1920s. As against the belief of the 'idealists' in progress they drew attention to the cyclical or recurrent patterns of international politics. Contrary to the view of the 'idealists' that power politics was a method of conducting international relations that belonged only to the bad old world, they presented power politics as the law of all international life. As against the disparagement of past international experience and the treatment of modern international history as a story merely of anarchy and disorder, the 'realists' sought to rediscover the lessons of the past, to demonstrate the positive functions of state sovereignty, secret diplomacy, the balance of power, and limited war; in some cases they looked to the nineteenth-century international order as a model of relative harmony, and in this sense they were conservatives.

In place of the internationalist rectitude of the 'idealists' in their approach to questions of morals and state practice, the 'realists' sought to reduce the legalistic and moralistic claims of states to a particular form of statement of the national interest (to show, in Schwarzenberger's phrase, that they were 'power politics in disguise'); at the same time they sought to establish the legitimacy of appeals to the national interest (to uphold, in Morgenthau's terms, 'the moral dignity of the national interest').

The 'realists' were participating in a debate in the English-speaking countries, and the starting-point of the 'idealists' was in large measure also their own. The argument for treating the national interest as the principal standard of reference in determining what a country's foreign policy should be is one that assumes that those who appeal instead to principles of law and morality have a case to be answered. These writers all present the case against 'moralism' at least partly in moral terms: the interest of his own nation is what the statesman has a duty to uphold; it is an interest he is better able to define than the interests of other states or of the world at large; the statesman who seeks to defend the national interest is better able to recognize and respect the different interests of other nations than the one who sees himself as custodian of the interests of all mankind. Stated in this way, the defence of the national interest has more in common with the 'idealist' views against which it is directed than with the strict 'Machiavellian' doctrine that anything is justified by reason of state.

Nor did the doctrine of the 'realists' involve a return to the glorification of conflict and war contained in the ideas of Hegelians and Social Darwinists. Raymond Aron has noted that despite the similarity, at certain points, between the ideas of George F. Kennan and those of Heinrich von Treitschke, the latter were propounded in the name of idealism, not realism: 'In crossing the Atlantic, in becoming *power politics*, Treitschke's *Machtpolitik* underwent a chiefly spiritual mutation. It became fact, not value.'[9] Power politics for the American 'realist' was not a moral imperative but an unfortunate state of affairs.

In England the principal works that belong to the second spate of theoretical activity are E. H. Carr's *The Twenty Years' Crisis* (1939); F. A. Voigt's *Unto Caesar* (1939) – a book that deserves to be read more widely than it is now; Georg Schwarzenberg's *Power Politics* (1941) – a massive if somewhat primitive essay in the sociology of international relations; Martin Wight's brief and magnificent *Power Politics* (1945); and Herbert Butterfield's *Christianity, Diplomacy and War* (1953). In some respects Harold Nicolson's *Diplomacy* (1939) belongs to this group, but in general it would be wrong to treat Nicolson as a 'realist.' In the United States the most important works are Nicholas Spykman's *America's Strategy in World Politics* (1942), Reinhold Niebuhr's *The Children of Light and the Children of Darkness* (1945), Hans Morgenthau's *Politics among Nations* (1948), and George F. Kennan's *American Diplomacy* (1952).

It would be wrong to suggest that these writers constituted a 'school' or even that their views overlapped on any except a few central points. The principal source of Carr's ideas, for example, was the Marxist analysis of ideology, as mediated to him through Mannheim's 'sociology of knowledge'; Niebuhr's and Butterfield's ideas had their foundations in Christian pessimism, Spykman's in German geopolitics, Morgenthau's perhaps in Weberian sociology. The target of Carr's attack was 'utopian' liberal internationalism; Voigt's work was chiefly an attack on Communist and Fascist ideology as reflected in the Spanish civil war, and a vindication of English conservative principles of foreign policy; Kennan's target was a form of 'moralism' in foreign policy that is uniquely American. Carr's work was a polemic addressed to 'the urgent task of the day' and disavowed all claims to universal and permanent validity. Morgenthau purported to present a comprehensive theory of all international politics derived from a distillation of its rational elements.

The doctrines of the 'realists' profoundly affected a whole generation of students. Originating in the pre-war world, their influence spanned the period of World War II and also that of the cold war. In the late 1940s and 1950s, when interest in the fundamentals of international relations grew apace as the consequence of America's assumption of world leadership, they had their greatest impact. Their vogue was a cause, as it was also a result, of America's shedding of its innocence of world politics. At a time when the American discussion of international relations was heavily ideological, it appeared to provide a sharp instrument of criticism; when America looked for guidance as to how to conduct herself, it provided a sense of direction; for an American audience in need of a crash course in statecraft, it seemed to offer a convenient crib of European diplomatic wisdom, the more convincing on campus because it was expounded, as often as not, in a thick German accent.

The works of the 'realists' still represent an important starting-point of theoretical understanding of international relations; they may still be compared favourably with a great deal of more recent theoretical writing. The function they served – of deflating the facile optimism and narrow moralism that passed for an advanced attitude to foreign affairs in the English-speaking countries – is one that still requires to be undertaken: the sources of facile optimism and narrow moralism never dry up, and the lessons of the 'realists' have to be learnt afresh by every new generation. But, in terms of the academic study of international relations, the stream of thinking and writing that began with Niebuhr and Carr has long run its course.

Partly this reflects the fact that America has been long enough at the centre of power politics not to feel the need any more of a crash course in the subject: the doctrines of the 'realists' no longer carry with them the sense of revelation they had when expounded by Professor Morgenthau at the University of Chicago in the early post-war period. Partly this reflects the inability of 'realist' writings, within the bounds of their explanation of international life in terms of permanent laws and cyclical patterns, to throw any light on the drastic changes that international politics have evidently undergone in the last quarter of a century: the nuclear revolution, the emergence of a world order that is predominantly non-Western, the march of modernization around the world. Partly also the 'realist' doctrines came to seem less impressive because they were the subject of some very cogent direct criticisms. The laws of international politics to which some 'realists' appealed in such a knowing way appeared on closer examination to rest on tautologies or shifting definitions of terms. The massive investigation of historical cases implied in their Delphic pronouncements about the experience of the past had not always, it seemed, actually been carried out. The extravagant claims made by some of them turned out to rest on assumed authority rather than on evidence or rigorous argument. Indeed, not even the best of the 'realist' writings can be said to have achieved a high standard of theoretical refinement: they were powerful polemical essays – brilliant and provocative in the case of Carr, systematic and comprehensive in the case of Morgenthau, learned and profound in the case of Wight – but the theory they employed was 'soft,' not 'hard.'

IV

The third spate of theoretical activity – that of the late 1950s and 1960s – is more difficult to define. The writers of this period are vastly more numerous than those of the first or the second period, and very much more amorphous. It might be argued that they are so divided among themselves over every aspect of their approach to the subject that nothing is to be gained by considering them together. But this would be a mistake, for they do have a common characteristic, and that is self-consciousness about methodology.

Students of international relations in the period became sensitive as to the under-developed state of theoretical work in their own subject by comparison with that of other branches of the social sciences. In some measure what underlay this sensitivity was the academic inferiority complex that was affecting all the social sciences other than economics, and that was especially evident in political science, of which international relations was by then generally thought to be a branch: as W. T. R. Fox wrote, 'the international relations scholar would feel less inferior if he had a body of propositions as difficult for his colleagues to understand and evaluate as some of theirs are for him.'[10] But underlying it also was the belief or the hope that such a body of propositions might facilitate in international politics the prediction and control that had been achieved in other areas of social life, that our inability so far to achieve such prediction and control resulted not from any inherent impossibility of doing so but from the backward or neglected state of the subject, and that the way to overcome this neglect was to borrow or to adapt the tools that appeared to have yielded results in other disciplines.

Thus students of international relations turned to the natural sciences and the 'harder' social sciences for methodological guidance: to general systems theory, the theory of games, economics, Parsonian sociology, social psychology, cybernetics, communications theory, and simulation. Not only did specialists in international relations seek to inform themselves about these subjects: a considerable number of thinkers trained in one or another of the 'hard' sciences moved into the field of international relations, e.g. Thomas Schelling and Kenneth Boulding from economics, Herman Kahn from engineering physics, Anatol Rapoport from biology, Albert Wohlstetter from mathematical logic.

But it was not only devotees of a strictly 'scientific' approach to international relations that became self-conscious about methodology: practitioners of what came to be called the 'traditionalist' approach to the subject found that they could not ignore the new tendencies, although they did their best to do so for a long time. They had in the end to come to terms with the purportedly 'scientific' methodologies that had found their way into the field, either by showing why they were inapplicable, or by conceding that they had a place. It is noticeable that exponents of a 'traditionalist' approach to international relations writing in this latter period – one thinks, for example, of Raymond Aron and Stanley Hoffmann – display a sensitivity to the methodological standing of their own arguments that marks them off from earlier writers in the same vein.[11]

I do not propose to provide a catalogue of the vast theoretical literature of this period but only to mention a few of the highlights. An early sign of this third spate of activity was the establishment by the Rockefeller Foundation in 1954 of a committee on the theory of international relations that resulted in the publication in 1959 of *Theoretical Aspects of International Relations* edited by W. T. R. Fox. The contributors to this volume, who included Hans Morgenthau and Reinhold Niebuhr, all wrote in the so-called 'traditionalist' vein, and apart from Charles P. Kindleberger's comparison of international political theory with economics, and Kenneth Waltz's call for a union of the study of international relations and political philosophy, methodological questions do not get much of an airing. But this book did serve to place on record the growth of interest in the theory of international politics, and the view of the editor that theory had to be developed if international relations was 'to evolve as a legitimate academic speciality' or was 'to yield results relevant to the major choices which governments and opinion leaders must make in world politics' was one that led naturally to a turning towards the 'harder' sciences.[12]

Morton Kaplan's *System and Process in International Politics* (1957) is a landmark in the emergence of the new fashion, not only because of its path-breaking attempt to deal rigorously with the idea of an international system, but even more because of its heroic originality of intellectual and literary style. By the very esoteric nature of his theme, and the uncompromisingly austere language in which he expounded it, Kaplan flouted the convention that writing about international relations should be directed at the general reader.

Kaplan broke new ground not in viewing international politics as a system, for this had been familiar since the seventeenth century, but in attempting to formulate a rigorous theory about international systems in terms of a more general theory of systems of action. His own theory is not a fully rigorous one, as he acknowledges. The effect of his book, intended or not, is to draw attention to the limitations rather than to the possibilities of a 'systemic' analysis of international politics, to underline the extent to which international politics does not function as a system, and the futility of attempting to predict its future course by reference to its 'systemic' properties. Moreover, while Kaplan's book has helped to make 'system' a vogue word and to secure for it a place in the titles of countless articles and monographs, it cannot be said that it has been followed up by concrete studies that have done any more than convey the illusion that they were building on the foundations he laid. But Kaplan's work has provided an arresting demonstration of what is involved in the attempt to formulate a fully rigorous theory of the international system, and shown up all those who have gone before him as utterly inadequate on this score.

Karl Deutsch's work on national and international political communities, and his attempts to dislodge the concept of power from its central place in the theory of international relations, clearly represent another major point of departure.[13] Whatever one may think of what may be said to be his fetish for measurement, and however much he may be held responsible for initiating a fashion of frenzied and indiscriminate collection of data about international politics, his studies have raised vital questions which previously were left unasked (at least in the context of international relations), as to what it is that holds international political communities together, what determines the 'integration' of disparate groups into a single national or international community or their subsequent 'disintegration,' and what accounts for the fact that in some international relationships the expectation of war has disappeared on both sides, whereas in other international relationships it has not. The central importance of Deutsch's work lies not in the answers that he has sought to provide to these questions, in terms of the flow of communications – not that these answers are unimportant – but in having raised the questions, which since then have necessarily been prominent on the agenda of inquirers into the subject. The view that in the case of international groups such as the English-speaking nations or the Scandinavian nations, within which there appears to be no expectation that conflicts will be resolved by war (the groupings which Deutsch speaks of as 'pluralistic security-communities'), the cohesion and persistence of the grouping are to be explained in terms of 'political community' rather than in terms of the workings of the system of powers, is one pregnant with implications of a general theory of international relations, which Deutsch and others who have ploughed this furrow have perhaps not yet elucidated.[14]

Another highlight of the period has been the thought devoted to United States strategic and arms control policy by such writers as Bernard Brodie, Henry Kissinger, Albert Wohlstetter, Herman Kahn, and Klaus Knorr, to name only a few.[15] The attention of these writers has been focused not upon any comprehensive explanation of world politics or the elements of which it is composed, but upon the policy choices confronting the United States, more especially its choices in military or security policy. All of these writers are, however, theorists, although of very different sorts, for all of them have delved into the theory of international relations in order to illuminate these choices: the notions which they were forced to examine – deterrence, the limitation of war, the stability of the strategic balance, the conditions of arms control, the rationality or non-rationality of nuclear war, the nature of alliance commitments – lie at the heart of the theory of international relations; and what gives distinction to their work is its theoretical content. Moreover, although in their methods they are radically different from one another – Wohlstetter was a pioneer of systems analysis, and derived his conclusions from close quantitative reasoning, Kahn made special use of imaginative 'scenarios' and metaphors, Brodie and Kissinger wrote in the style of reflective or speculative historians – they were all committed, in greater or lesser degree, to the novel enterprise of applying sustained intelligence and expertise to the solution of problems of military policy.

The ideas of this group of writers bear the stamp of their origin in the study of one nation's security interests or requirements, global and comprehensive though that nation's interests are. The whole contemporary study of matters of strategy and arms control, because of the overriding influence upon it of these thinkers, remains to a large extent confined within the framework dictated by this American perspective, and awaits liberation from it. Even if one assumes an American perspective and takes the strategic problem to be essentially 'the problem of national security,' a very great deal of the work that has been done in this field displays a tendency to uncritical acceptance of orthodox assumptions as to what the dimensions of that problem are.

But the contribution of this group of writers has been a major one. Not only do they represent a milestone in the development of thought about strategy and warfare in this century; they have contributed significantly to the wider theory of international relations. What chiefly excited them was the question whether or not, or in what ways, the advent of nuclear weapons brought with it a revolution in international politics and foreign policy, and their achievement is to have thought more deeply about this question than any other group. In recent years there has been an impression that such theoretical work as needs to be done on the implications of nuclear weapons and related technology has now been done. It is true that the creative period in the development of this area of strategic studies was over by the mid-1960s, and that in the years since then, as the danger of nuclear war appears to have receded (and other dangers have come to the fore), such studies have become unfashionable. It seems unlikely, however, that in a subject of such central and lasting importance the last word has been said.

Thomas Schelling, who also belongs to this group of students of strategic policy, stands apart from them inasmuch as in his work it is the theory which is central and the examination of policy alternatives that is incidental. Schelling's ideas about threats of force and the dynamics of bargaining, tacit agreements and restraints, the manipulation of risk and the art of commitments – as expounded in *The Strategy of Conflict* (1966) and *Arms and Influence* (1966) – have not merely profoundly affected thinking about international relations, they have become part of the general intellectual culture of the times. It is not the case, as is sometimes argued, that these ideas are derivable from formal game theory, or that in Schelling's case they have been in fact derived in this way: they represent an imaginative, conceptual exercise in thinking out what the basic ingredients are in certain very general phenomena, and especially in spelling out what is involved in 'rational action' in certain recurrent situations involving the presence of force.

It is this exposition of rational diplomatic and strategic conduct that is the source of the basic ambiguities in Schelling's work. Quite apart from the difficulties of spelling out an adequate conception of what 'rational action' involves, and adhering to it rigidly throughout a lengthy analysis, it is clear that a correct indication of what rational action requires in a variety of strategic situations is not necessarily a guide to how men actually do act, have acted or will act in these situations; yet it does seem that Schelling's extrapolations of 'rational action' are sometimes presented as if they were an account of actual behavior, and they are certainly sometimes interpreted in this way. Moreover, to say that 'rational action' requires, for example, a threat that leaves something to chance, a deliberate maximization of risk, or a strategy of inflicting pain or hurt, is not to say that action of this sort should be taken in given circumstances. But the spelling out of what 'rationality' involves, just as it may be confused with an empirical statement of what strategic behavior actually is, may be confused also with policy recommendation or advice. Although the latter is not the ostensible purpose of these major works of Schelling, it is not always clear that the distinction has been sharply drawn, and it is not always sharply drawn by those who read his writings. The position of a disinterested general theorist of strategic affairs, when he joins in a conversation which is generally taken by those participating in it to be about policy in the making, is a difficult one: disinterested analyses are read as policy recommendations, and have practical effects whether they are intended to or not.

Another notable development has been the emergence of general studies of conflict, which have sought to illuminate war and other forms of international conflict by viewing them as a special case of a general social process. Some of Schelling's work falls under this heading, but so does Kenneth Boulding's *Conflict and Defence* (1962) and Anatol Rapoport's *Fights, Games and Debates* (1960). Studies of the resemblances and differences between international conflict and conflict among primitive groups, and studies of conflict among animals also belong to this genre.[16]

Such studies have helped to bring specialists in international relations into closer touch with sociologists, social psychologists, anthropologists and students of animal behavior. Moreover, by placing 'international relations' in the wider context of human history and evolution they have helped to liberate the study of world politics from the restrictive confines of the modern system of states.

Finally, mention may be made of the development during the last decade of what is called 'peace research.' The studies carried out under this heading overlap with a number of those that have already been mentioned, especially the last. 'Peace research' takes the form of studies which are sometimes wide-ranging and comprehensive, sometimes narrow and partial. It does not logically imply preference for any particular methodology, but it has generally been accompanied by commitment to a 'scientific' theory of the conditions of peace, and the central idea that underlies the movement for 'peace research,' namely that more research specifically oriented towards the establishment of peace will make peace more likely, is one that takes for granted the possibility of progress towards a theory that would facilitate prediction and control in this area.

The defining feature of 'peace research' is not the area of international relations it chooses for study, nor the methods or procedures employed to study it, but a commitment to research which is applied or policy oriented – but applied not, as in the case of the students of strategy just mentioned, to the policy problems faced by governments, but to the enterprise of shifting the world political system as a whole in the direction of universal and permanent peace. In this respect the 'peace research' movement involves a return to the progressivist beliefs and values that marked the 'idealist' phase of the 1920s and early 1930s, and indeed it can be viewed as an attempt to combine the values and commitments of that school with the methodological sophistication that has grown up in recent years.

Advocates of 'peace research' often see themselves as providing an antidote to 'war research,' conceived of as the preoccupation of international relations specialists in the post-war period with the military or strategic problems of governments, for which they wish to substitute a preoccupation with the problem of moving international society as a whole towards a situation in which problems of national strategy do not arise. Yet it is not clear that the study of war and the study of peace are opposite or alternative preoccupations in this way, as peace has in the past always depended on the fulfilment of certain military conditions, and wars arise out of situations of peace; it does not seem desirable to divide and compartmentalize the study of international relations in this way. 'Peace research,' moreover, shares with 'war research' one of the features that has made it most vulnerable to criticism: namely, a commitment to immediate practical ends or results that may endanger the intellectual integrity or scholarly worth of the work undertaken. The substitution of one set of values and priorities for another may not do anything to bring about a restoration of academic integrity if it is the practical rather than the intellectual side of 'peace research' that is to be paramount.

Like some of the studies to which it is intended to provide a response or an antidote, 'peace research' derives from a faith in the power of research to bring about changes of a practical nature that is not accompanied by any very convincing account of how or why these changes will take place. To speak of 'peace research' as an activity that will help promote peace is to raise certain questions. How far is the absence of universal and permanent peace really the

result of lack of knowledge about it? What practical results would flow from an improvement of our understanding of the conditions of peace? To whom would this
information be passed, what action would they be likely to
take as a consequence, and what difference would such action
make? Questions such as these are skated over in glib statements to the effect that if as much money were spent on
studying peace as on studying war, peace might be achieved.
But despite all these difficulties that confront any attempt
to show that 'peace research' represents a viable and coherent intellectual programme, there is no doubt that some
good work has been done under this banner.[17]

In what has been called the third spate of activity, the
theory of international relations became the subject of more
studies than had ever been undertaken before; moreover,
despite the mediocrity of the great bulk of these studies it
is likely that more intellectual talent was applied to the
enterprise than ever before. Within the United States theorists of international relations came to enjoy an unprecedented degree of affluence, prestige, and influence. Outside
the United States theoretical ideas originating within it have
been in the ascendancy, a fact that not only reflects America's dominant political position but also her dominance in
the social sciences.

There are some signs that this third spate of activity,
characterized by methodological self-consciousness and ex-
perimentation, is drawing to a close. The methodological
point has been registered, the experiments shown to have
been fruitful or fruitless as the case may be, and the stage
is set for a return to questions of substance. The search
for a scientific theory that would facilitate prediction and
control of international politics had its origins in a pecu-
liarly American combination of optimism about the solu-
bility of political problems and faith in research as a
problem-solving technique; but the position of the United
States in this area of studies is becoming less dominant. At
the same time, within the United States the social crisis
that has been occasioned by the debate about the Vietnam
War seems likely to bring questions about ends or values
in foreign policy once more to the fore.

While the development of the theory of international relations in the last 50 years has seen these three spates of activity, it would be wrong to suggest that all the theoretical work that has been done falls readily into the categories that have been mentioned. In each of the three periods to which reference has been made there have been individuals who have stood out against (or have been unaware of) the dominant trend, and who may be viewed as being ahead of or behind their times. C. A. W. Manning's inquiry into the presuppositions and consequences of the notion of a society of states spans all three periods and defies classification of any sort: it began in the first period, but was published in full only in the third.[18]

Doctrines having important elements in common with those later expounded by the 'realists' were being put forward during the first or 'idealist' phase by Sir Halford Mackinder in Britain and Karl Haushofer in Germany. During the second or 'realist' phase, the work being done by Quincy Wright and his collaborators at the University of Chicago, which culminated in the publication of *A Study of War* in 1942, anticipated the 'scientific' or 'behaviorist' trends of the third phase; so did the lonely and then unrecognized work of Lewis F. Richardson.[19] During the third phase there have been scholars who, like the members of the British Committee on the Theory of International Politics who contributed to *Diplomatic Investigations* published in 1966, sought to warm the coals of an older tradition of historical and philosophical reflection during the long, dark winter of the 'social scientific' ascendancy.[20]

V

Has 50 years of theoretical investigation of international relations led to any progress? Before we answer this question we should remind ourselves that what began half a century ago was not the study of international relations but merely the recognition of it as an academic subject. The theory of international relations is at least as old as the debates about it recorded in Thucydides' *History of the Peloponnesian War*, and it is arguable that the most important body of systematic theoretical writing on the subject is still that of the classical international lawyers. After reviewing the history of thought about international relations, Martin Wight concluded that 'international theory is marked not only by paucity but also by intellectual and moral poverty.'[21] It is true that if we compare the history of thought about international relations with the mainstream of modern political thought, which is about relations between man and the state, the former is slight and sterile by comparison – although it is not always possible to draw a sharp line between the one and the other. But thought about international relations is still slight and sterile, and if we compare the long record of what took place before 1919 with what has occurred since, the former is a good deal more impressive.

Certainly if it is a profound analysis of the idea of international society we are in search of, it is to Grotius and Vattel that we have to turn rather than to any recent writer. This century has not produced any general delineation of the elements of strategy to compare with Clausewitz, for all his obscurity, nor any treatment of the diplomatic art to set alongside Callières, nor any writing about the morality of war of the depth and subtlety of the Catholic tradition of just war doctrine.

When progress takes place in the 'hard' sciences this signifies that new theories or hypotheses have been put forward that replace the old ones, because logical argument or empirical verification has established them as valid or true. Not only has it in fact been established that the new ideas are superior to the old ones; the scientific community will ultimately reach a consensus to the effect that this is so. It is because of this consensus that, in a 'hard' science, certain questions at least may be regarded as for all practical purposes closed (even though in principle they may be opened up again), and the answers to these questions treated as the foundations upon which future inquirers into the subject may build. As the structure of established knowledge grows, moreover, new and up-to-date expositions of it replace old and out-of-date ones, what is valuable in previous work in the field has been incorporated into the current statement of our knowledge of it, and what is not has been discarded: it is not necessary to study previous work in the field in order to be abreast of what is known about it.

Progress in international relations and comparable subjects is not like this. There may be an outpouring of new or apparently new ideas, but except in peripheral areas of the subject they are not subject to proof or strict confirmation. Sometimes new ideas are put forward that make a real contribution, in that they may be judged to explain some phenomenon more fully or state some problem more clearly, but their superiority to previous ideas cannot be demonstrated in any very conclusive way. Moreover, when such a new contribution is made it is not accompanied by any general consensus to the effect that it is an advance: the questions with which it has dealt remain open in practice as well as in principle, and new inquirers into the same subject, although they may build upon this contribution if they recognize it to be one, will not look upon the matter as finally and exhaustively settled. A textbook which disregards the previous history of thought and controversy in the subject, and which presents a summary of recent work as if this were a comprehensive statement of our present knowledge of the field, incorporating all that was important in what had been done before and rendering it scientifically 'out of date', will convey a quite grotesque impression of the literature of the subject.

In international relations and comparable subjects there often takes place what is actually regression, in the sense that new work appears in which old truths are overlooked or old errors refurbished, or in which problems are analysed without the subtlety and depth that is contained in previous studies. A good deal of contemporary research in international relations constitutes regression of this kind, and a number of features of the academic scene encourage it. The narrow and introspective character of much recent teaching – I mean that which produces students whose intellectual horizons are bounded by the pages of *The Journal of Conflict Resolution* – leads to the duplication of work already done. The premium placed upon novelty or apparent novelty, and especially upon intellectual cuteness and ingenuity, directs attention away from the mastery of established works. The atmosphere of high-pressure salesmanship that has surrounded international studies in recent years is one in which manifestoes must be for ever issued, taxonomies multiplied, research plans designed and broadcast, information feverishly collected, and new findings claimed and prematurely made public. But it tends to dissipate the idea that the subject has a central corpus of ideas, in relation to which any new work must take its bearings. The rhetoric of scientific progress itself, misapplied to a field in which progress of a strictly scientific sort does not take place, has the effect of constricting and obscuring the sort of advance that is possible.

Progress does take place in the theory of international relations, and has taken place in the last 50 years. But in a subject such as this there is an objective which is prior to the achievement of progress, and that is the avoidance of regression by maintaining a tradition of awareness of what the central explanations of international phenomena have been in the past, and what the main positions are that may be taken up in controversies about international conduct; and by attempting to reformulate these ideas in relation to changing circumstances, and to restate them in the changing idiom of the times. If, in addition to this, there is progress, this will sometimes take the form of a sharpening or refinement of previous explanations, a more thorough exploration of old controversies, rather than of the advancement of something fundamentally new; and when it does take the latter form, its claims to superiority over what has gone before, although they may rest on rigorous argument and evidence of a sort, will not be the product of scientific demonstration or test.

In the last half century there cannot be said to have been strictly scientific progress in any area of the theory of international politics; still less has there been developed any satisfactory 'general theory' of the subject as a whole. But progress of a sort has taken place in a number of respects. In the first place there has been a general increase in the sophistication of writings about international relations, a decline of the innocence that marked the ideas of the 1920s, pre-Marxian and pre-Freudian as in large measure they still were. We still encounter writings which, while they display sophistication in the handling of one or another technique for the study of international politics, display innocence about international politics itself. There are reasons for thinking that this kind of innocence is more or less perennial, that the attempt to by-pass or circumvent problems of a political nature is bound to keep cropping up in one form or another. But in general the explanations now provided of international events are deeper and more many-sided than they were 50 years ago. That this is so is partly due to theories that have been advanced within the field of international relations but chiefly to the general advance of the social sciences in this period.

In the second place progress is reflected in an improvement in methodology or at all events in widespread recognition of the need for improvement. That this is so is primarily due to those theorists who have set out to develop a strictly scientific theory of international relations. Their attacks upon the so-called 'traditionalists' have produced an awareness of the intellectually shoddy character of much previous work in the field, and of the need to achieve logical rigour and precision and, where appropriate, to resort to mathematics and to various advanced techniques.

I believe that the attempt to confine the study of international relations within the bounds of what is strictly scientific, in the sense that it entails either logical or mathematical proof or strict empirical procedures of verification, is harmful.[22] It also appears to me that what Morton Kaplan has called 'the new great debate' between the classical and the scientific approaches has gone on long enough: it is a bad sign in a subject that it should be preoccupied with questions of methodology rather than substance. But clearly the debate has introduced an awareness of the methodological problem; and I should not deny that it is the 'scientists' who are responsible for having initiated the debate, even though the position of the purists among them is an untenable one.

The impact of the 'scientific' movement upon the study of international relations may be compared with that of the 'linguistic' movement upon the study of philosophy. In philosophy as in international relations the calm and repose of a customary intellectual pursuit were broken by ruffian intruders from other disciplines, who dismissed all past work in the field as woolly and effete, and proclaimed their brutal new thesis, in this case that the problems to which philosophers had addressed themselves down the ages were no more than verbal puzzles. In this case also the established profession was temporarily knocked off its balance as, under the impact of the initial assault, it contemplated the awful possibility that the intruders might be right. In the case of philosophy also there were a few weak hearts among the old established forces who concluded, prematurely and before any real trial of strength had begun, that they had better accommodate themselves to the new emerging forces, by bowing out gracefully or by seeking to show that the new ideas really represented what they had been trying to say all along. In philosophy, also, after a decade or so in which the issue had seemed in doubt, the revolutionary impulse weakened and the profession returned to its traditional concerns, this having been facilitated by the fact that there had been all along among the old guard certain stout hearts who had been impervious to the pressures of fashion. But although philosophy was not conquered by the 'linguistic' movement it was shaken by the assault and will never be the same again. In the same way, although the 'scientific' movement does not seem likely to reduce international relations to a branch of mathematics or of experimental science, it will have left a permanent mark.

A third kind of progress has taken place which is negative. Certain lines of inquiry have been pursued which have proved failures, but instructive failures. In speaking of failure I do not refer to the putting forward of theories or hypotheses that have been falsified: for the falsification of hypotheses is a normal method of intellectual advance and such theories are not failures. I have in mind rather the case where a whole line of inquiry appears to lead only to a dead end, where one is left with the feeling not merely that no satisfactory theory has been worked out but that none is likely to be through this particular approach.

A good example is Lewis F. Richardson's attempt to develop a mathematical equation that would explain the dynamics of arms races and the conditions under which they lead to war.[23] Not only is it obvious that Richardson's model of the arms race is deficient in a number of ways; it is arguable that no satisfactory general account of arms races is likely to be achieved by the route Richardson chose. But it is clear that a great deal of valuable theorizing has resulted from the study of his example, both about the general features of arms races and about the possibilities and limitations of quantification. Another example of an important and instructive failure is Morton Kaplan's attempt to illuminate the workings of international systems by the elaboration of formal deductive models. Another is the attempt to apply systems analysis to broad problems of choice in defence and foreign policy. Another is Hans Morgenthau's attempt to construct a comprehensive theory of international politics around 'the concept of interest defined in terms of power.' Perhaps the whole attempt to formulate 'a general theory' of international politics has been instructive chiefly because of the thought it has stimulated as to why it has been unsuccessful.

Fourthly, in certain areas we may say that there has been positive progress of a substantive kind. We do not have theories that have been rigorously formulated and adequately tested in any part of the subject. But there are certain subjects about which we can say that a helpful body of theory exists. Terms have been defined, pertinent questions have been asked, previous thought on the subject has been assembled and deployed, plausible hypotheses have been advanced, evidence has been brought to bear, in such a way that our understanding of concrete matters has been greatly assisted. Of any of these subjects it may be said that the inquirer into it does not have to start *de novo*: a body of theoretical writing exists to which he can be directed, and indeed no such inquiry could reasonably begin without some attention being paid to this.

For example, no one could now reasonably study the role of international law in international society without coming to terms with the vast and impressive literature that has accumulated on this subject. No one would be justified in embarking upon an analysis of the place of force in international politics without mastering the literature of contemporary strategic studies. It does not make sense to investigate any problem of disarmament or arms control without paying attention to the theoretical writings of the early 1960s on this subject. The writings of Karl W. Deutsch, Ernst Haas, and Amitai Etzioni on integration in supranational communities command the attention of anyone proposing to think about that subject.[24] A natural starting point for anyone proposing to study the causes of war is the range of considerations deployed by Kenneth Waltz, for anyone wishing to investigate the idea of collective security the analyses provided by Inis L. Claude.[25] And so on.

VI

I do not propose to end this survey by laying down a programme of questions or issues for future investigation. But there is one question, or set of related questions, that deserves mention because it arises naturally from the above exposition.

At first sight the theory of international relations in this century has been overwhelmingly Western, predominantly Anglo–American. It is true that the communist countries and the countries of the Third World, which have done so much to shape the practice of world politics in this century, have produced doctrines characterizing international relations, or moral attitudes towards it, that are distinctive and are central to the history of the times (for example Lenin's analysis of imperialism, Krishna Menon's doctrine of 'permanent aggression,' Lin Piao's notion of the struggle of the world's countryside against its cities). It is true that Gandhi's theories of non-violence and of the relations of means and ends in political activity have a great bearing upon international relations. It is true that Mao has made important and original contributions to strategic theory. But if we focus our attention upon the comprehensive, explanatory theory of how states and other agents in world politics do and should behave in relation to one another, the conclusion to which we are drawn is that in this century such theory has come almost exclusively from the West.

The first question we should ask is whether this conclusion is really correct, or whether a significant body of non-Western theory exists whose importance we have overlooked because of our Western starting-point. But if the conclusion is correct, two further questions suggest themselves. Why has theory of this sort flourished only in the West? Does this reflect simply the unique strength in the West of the tradition of detached investigation of social affairs, or is it also a consequence of a deeper attachment in the West to 'international relations' as a perspective from which to view the politics of the world as a whole? And if the theories that are available are almost exclusively Western in origin and perspective, can they convey an adequate understanding of a world political system that is predominantly non-Western?

Notes

1. Such propositions need not be general in the sense that they assert something about international politics at all times and in all places. They may be general statements which apply only to some particular period ('the nineteenth century international order was stable'), to some particular state or class of states ('Albion is perfidious', 'neighbouring states are natural enemies'), to some particular international institution ('the League is ineffective'), or to some particular condition of international society ('war is inevitable,' 'peace is indivisible'). But a proposition such as 'Germany attacked Belgium on August 4, 1914' falls outside the domain of theory of international politics, although it may raise questions about it. Such a proposition as this is general in the sense that it is divisible into a series of further propositions, but from the perspective of the theory of international politics it is singular not general.
2. James Bryce, *International Relations* (London, 1922), pp. vii–iii.
3. It is true that we investigate singular, including so-called 'unique' events, by seeking to discover to what general classes of event they belong. But an historical inquiry will be focused upon singular events rather than upon what they illustrate; and the point of pursuing it will be to acquire a grasp of, a feeling for, these singular things.
4. Lest this seem too disparaging of 'theoretical' literature of the sort reviewed in this essay, I should add that on the whole I believe it illuminates the subject more than the literature of diplomatic history. But the latter reflects the existence of a highly developed academic discipline and profession, whereas the former does not.
5. I have always disliked the term myself, and were it not for the currency it already has, I should prefer to speak simply of 'the study of international relations,' which is clearly different from the study

of the history of it. In Britain there is a tendency to speak of 'international theory,' but this is quite unsatisfactory, since it is the relations that are international, not the theory.

6. The first edition of Brailsford's work had appeared just before the war (1914).

7. Sir Alfred Zimmern, *The League of Nations and the Rule of Law* (London, 1936).

8. See Philip Noel-Baker, *Disarmament* (London, 1926); James T. Shotwell, *War and Its Renunciation as an Instrument of Policy in the Pact of Paris* (New York, 1929); David Davies, *The Problem of the Twentieth Century* (London, 1930).

9. Raymond Aron, *Peace and War; A Theory of International Relations* (London, 1966), p. 592.

10. W. T. R. Fox, *The American Study of International Relations* (Columbia, South Carolina, 1967), p. 82.

11. See Raymond Aron, *Peace and War*, and Stanley Hoffmann (ed.), *Contemporary Theory in International Relations* (Englewood Cliffs, NJ, 1960) and *The State of War* (London, 1965).

12. W. T. R. Fox (ed.), *Theoretical Aspects of International Relations* (Notre Dame, Indiana, 1959), p. ix.

13. See Karl W. Deutsch, *Nationalism and Social Communication* (New York, 1953); and Karl W. Deutsch (ed.), *Political Community and the North Atlantic Area* (Princeton, 1957).

14. Such a theory does not emerge for me in Deutsch's *The Nerves of Government*, Glencoe, 1965), or his *The Analysis of International Relations* (Englewood Cliffs, NJ, 1968).

15. See e.g. Bernard Brodie, *Strategy in the Missile Age*, (Princeton, 1959); Henry A. Kissinger, *Nuclear Weapons and Foreign Policy* (New York, 1957), *The Necessity for Choice* (New York, 1960), and *The Troubled Partnership*, New York, 1965; Albert Wohlstetter, 'The Delicate Balance of Terror,' *Foreign Affairs* (January 1959); Herman Kahn, *On Thermonuclear War* (Princeton, 1960); Klaus Knorr (ed.), *NATO and American Security* (Princeton, 1959); and Klaus Knorr (ed.), *Limited Strategic War* (Princeton, 1962).

16. For the former see Roger D. Masters, 'World Politics as a Primitive Political System,' *World Politics*, 16 (4) (July 1964). For the latter see Konrad Lorenz, *On Aggression* (New York, 1966) and Robert Ardrey, *The Territorial Imperative* (New York, 1967).

17. See especially *The Journal of Peace Research* (Oslo, 1965 onwards).

18. See C. A. W. Manning, *The Nature of International Society* (London, 1962).

19. Lewis F. Richardson's work of the inter-war period was virtually unknown until it was published posthumously in 1960. See Lewis F. Richardson, *Arms and Insecurity: A Mathematical Study of the Causes of War*, (eds.) (Nicholas Rashevsky and Ernesto Trucco, London, 1960); and *Statistics of Deadly Quarrels*, (eds.) (Quincy Wright and Carl C. Lienau, London, 1960).

20. H. Butterfield and M. Wight, (eds.), *Diplomatic Investigations* (London, 1966).

21. Martin Wight, 'Why is there no International Theory?' in H. Butterfield and M. Wight (eds.), *Diplomatic Investigations*, p. 20; see chapter 2 in this volume.

22. I have argued this in 'International Theory: the Case for a Classical Approach,' in Klaus Knorr and James N. Rosenau (eds.), *Contending Approaches to International Politics* (Princeton, 1969).

23. See Lewis F. Richardson, *Arms and Insecurity*.

24. See Karl W. Deutsch, *Nationalism and Social Communication*; Ernst Haas, *The Uniting of Europe* (Stanford, 1958); Amitai Etzioni, *Political Unification* (New York, 1965).

25. See Kenneth Waltz, *Man, the State and War* (New York, 1959); Inis L. Claude, *Power and International Relations* (New York, 1962).

9 An American Social Science: International Relations (1977)*

Stanley Hoffmann

In the past 30 years, international relations has developed as a largely autonomous part of political science. Even though it has shared many of political science's vicissitudes – battles among various orientations, theories, and methods – it also has a story of its own. What follows is an attempt at neither a complete balance sheet nor a capsule history – merely a set of reflections on the specific accomplishments and frustrations of a particular field of scholarship.[1]

ONLY IN AMERICA

Political science has a much longer history than international relations. The attempt at studying systematically the patterns of conflict and cooperation among mutually alien actors – a shorthand definition of the subject matter – is recent. To be sure, we can all trace our ancestry back to Thucydides, just as political scientists can trace theirs to Aristotle. But Thucydides was a historian. He was, to be sure, a historian of genius, rightly convinced that he was writing for all times because he was using one particular incident to describe a permanent logic of behavior. Yet he was careful to avoid explicit generalizations, 'if . . . then' propositions, and analytic categories or classificatory terms. Modern sociology and political science emancipated themselves from political and social history, political philosophy, and public law in the nineteenth century. International relations did not, even though the kind of social (or asocial) action described by Thucydides never disappeared from a fragmented world, and flourished

* *Daedalus*, 106 (3) (Summer), pp. 41–60.

particularly in the period of the European balance of power.
One can wonder why this was so. After all, here was a realm
in which political philosophy had much less to offer than
it did to those who wondered about the common good in
the domestic order. Except for the vast body of Roman
Catholic literature preoccupied with just war, and not very
relevant to a world of sovereign states, there were only the
recipes of Machiavelli; the marginal comments on the international state of nature in Hobbes', Locke's, and Rousseau's
writings; some pages of Hume; two short and tantalizing
essays of Kant; compressed considerations by Hegel; and
oversimplified fragments by Marx. Even so, the little political philosophy that was available should have been
sufficiently provocative to make students want to look into
the realities. For the philosophers disagreed about the nature
of the international milieu and the ways of making it more
bearable; and they wrote about the difference between a
domestic order stable enough to afford a search for the
ideal state, and an international contest in which order has
to be established first, and which often clashes with any
aspiration to justice. Similarly, the contrast between the
precepts of law and the realities of politics was sufficiently
greater in the international realm than in the domestic realm,
to make one want to shift from the normative to the empirical, if only in order to understand better the plight of
the normative. Without a study of political relations, how
could one understand the fumblings and failures of international law, or the tormented debates on the foundation
of obligation among sovereigns unconstrained by common
values or superior power. And the chaos of data provided
by diplomatic history did not require any less ordering than
the masses of facts turned up by the history of states and
societies.

Why did a social science of international relations nevertheless fail to appear? The answer to the discrepancy may
well be found in that sweeping phenomenon which
Tocqueville identified as the distinctive feature of the modern age: democratization. As domestic societies moved from
their Old Regimes to their modern conditions – parties and
interests competing for the allegiance of large classes of
citizens; the social mobilization of previously dispersed

subjects; the politics of large agglomerations and unified markets; and increasingly universal suffrage; the rise of parliamentary institutions or plebiscitarian techniques; the fall of fixed barriers, whether geographic or social, within nations – the study of flux began in earnest, if only in order to provide concerned observers and insecure official with some clues about regularities and predictions of somewhat less mythical, if also less sweeping nature than those grandiosely strewn around by philosophers of history. With democratization, as Comte had predicted, came the age of positivism (his only mistake was to confuse his own brand of metaphysics, or his grand speculations, with positive science). But international politics remained the sport of kings, or the preserve of cabinets – the last refuge of secrecy, the last domain of largely hereditary castes of diplomats.

Raymond Aron has characterized international relations as the specialized activity of diplomats and soldiers. However, soldiers, to paraphrase Clausewitz, have their own grammar but not their own logic. It is not an accident if armies, having been democratized by the ordeals of the French Revolution and Napoleonic era, found their empirical grammarian in Clausewitz, whereas the still restricted club of statesmen and ambassadors playing with the fate of nations found no logician to account for its activities. Indeed, the historians who dealt with these succeeded only in keeping them beyond the pale of the kind of modern science that was beginning to look at societies, by perpetuating the myth of foreign policy's 'primacy,' isolated from domestic politics. There was, to be sure, one country in which foreign policy was put under domestic checks and balances, knew no career caste, and paid little respect to the rules and rituals of the initiated European happy few: the United States of America. But this country happened to be remarkably uninvolved in the kinds of contests that were the daily fare of other actors. Either it remained aloof, eager merely for continental consolidation and economic growth; or else it expanded, not by conflicts and deals with equals, but by short spurts of solipsistic exuberance at the expense of much weaker neighbors. International relations is the science of the tests and trials of several intertwined actors. Where they were intertwined, no science grew. In the United States before the 1930s, there was no reason for it to grow.

It was only the twentieth century that brought democratization to foreign policy. Diplomatic issues moved from the calculations of the few to the passions of the many, both because more states joined in the game that had been the preserve of a small number of (mainly European) actors and (mainly extra-European) stakes, and above all because within many states parties and interests established links or pushed claims across national borders. And yet, a World War that saw the mobilization and slaughter of millions, marked the demise of the old diplomatic order, and ended as a kind of debate between Wilson and Lenin for the allegiance of mankind, brought forth little 'scientific analysis' of international relations. Indeed, the rude intrusion of grand ideology into this realm gave a new lease of life to utopian thinking, and delayed the advent of social science. Not 'how it is, and why,' but 'how things should be improved, reformed, overhauled,' was the order of the day. Old Liberal normative dreams were being licensed by the League of Nations covenant, while at the same time the young Soviet Union was calling for the abolition of diplomacy itself.

It is against this reassertion of utopia, and particularly against the kind of 'as if' thinking that mistook the savage world of the 1930s for a community, the League for a modern Church, and collective security for a common duty, that E. H. Carr wrote the book which can be treated as the first 'scientific' treatment of modern world politics: *Twenty Years Crisis*[2] – the work of a historian intent on deflating the pretenses of Liberalism, and driven thereby to laying the foundations both of a discipline and of a normative approach, 'realism,' that was to have quite a future. Two paradoxes are worth noting. This historian who was founding a social science, did it in reaction against another historian, whose normative approach Carr deemed illusory – Toynbee, not the philosopher of the *Study of History*, but the idealistic commentator of the *Royal Yearbook of International Affairs*. And Carr, in his eagerness to knock out the illusions of the idealists, not only swallowed some of the 'tough' arguments which the revisionist powers such

as Mussolini's Italy, Hitler's Germany, and the militaristic
Japan had been using against the order of Versailles – arguments aimed at showing that idealism served the interests of the status quo powers – but also 'objectively,' as
Pravda would say, served the cause of appeasement. There
was a triple lesson here: about the springs of empirical
analysis (less a desire to understand for its own sweet sake,
than an itch to refute); about the impossibility, even for
opponents of a normative orientation, to separate the empirical and the normative in their own work; and about
the pitfalls of any normative dogmatism in a realm which
is both a field for objective investigation and a battlefield
between predatory beasts and their prey.

But it was not in England that Carr's pioneering effort
bore fruit. It was in the United States that international
relations became a discipline. Both the circumstances and
the causes deserve some scrutiny. The circumstances were,
obviously, the rise of the United States to world power, a
rise accompanied by two contradictory impulses: renewed
utopianism, as exemplified by the plans for post-war international organization; and a mix of revulsion against, and
guilt about, the peculiar pre-war brew of impotent American idealism (as symbolized by the 'non-recognition' doctrine), escapist isolationism (the neutrality laws), and
participation in appeasement. Two books brought to America
the kind of realism Carr had developed in England. One
was Nicholas Spykman's *America's Strategy in World Politics*,[3]
which was more a treatise in the geopolitical tradition of
Admiral Mahan or Mackinder than a book about the principal characteristics of interstate politics; but it told
Americans that foreign policy is about power, not merely
or even primarily about ideals, and it taught that the struggle
for power was the real name for world politics. The other
book was Hans Morgenthau's *Politics Among Nations*.[4] If our
discipline has any founding father, it is Morganthau. Unlike Carr, he was not a historian by training; he had been
a teacher of international law. Like Carr, he was revolting
against utopian thinking, past and present. But where Carr
had been an ironic and polemical Englishman sparring with
other Englishmen about the nature of diplomacy in the
thirties – a discussion which assumed that readers knew

enough diplomatic history to make pedantic allusions unnecessary – Morgenthau was a refugee from suicidal Europe, with a missionary impulse to teach the new world
power all the lessons it had been able to ignore until then
but could no longer afford to reject. He was but one participant in the 'sea change,' one of the many social scientists whom Hitler had driven to the New World, and who
brought to a country whose social science suffered from
'hyperfactualism' and conformity the leaven of critical perspectives and philosophical concerns.[5] But he was, among
his colleagues, the only one whose interests made him the
founder of a discipline.

Eager to educate the heathen, not merely to joust with
follow literati, Morgenthau quite deliberately couched his
work in the terms of general propositions and grounded
them in history. Steeped in a scholarly tradition that stressed
the difference between social sciences and natural sciences,
he was determined both to erect an empirical science opposed to the utopias of the international lawyer and the
political ideologues, and to affirm the unity of empirical
research and or philosophical inquiry into the right kind
of social order. He wanted to be normative, but to root his
norms in the realities of politics, not in the aspirations of
politicians or in the constructs of lawyers. The model of
interstate relations which Morgenthau proposed, and the
precepts of 'realism' which he presented as the only valid
recipes for foreign policy success as well as for international
moderation, were derived from the views of nineteenth-century and early twentieth-century historians of statecraft (such
as Treitschke, and also Weber). Hence the paradox of introducing to the America of the cold war, and of making
analytically and dogmatically explicit, notions and a 'wisdom' about statecraft that had remained largely implicit
in the age to which they best applied, and whose validity
for the age of nuclear weapons, ideological confrontations,
mass politics, and economic interdependence was at least
open to question.

Be that as it may, Morgenthau's work played a doubly
useful role – one that it may be hard to appreciate fully if
one looks at the scene either from the outside (as does Aron),
or 30 years later, as does the new generation of American

scholars. On the one hand, his very determination to lay
down the law made Morgenthau search for the laws, or
regularities, of state behavior, the types of policies, the chief
configurations of power; by tying his sweeping analyses to
two masts, the concepts of power and the notion of the
national interest, it was boldly positing the existence of a
field of scientific endeavor, separate from history or law.
On the other hand, the very breadth of his brushstrokes,
the ambiguities hidden by his peremptory pronouncements
about power, the subjective uncertainties denied by his
assertion of an objective national interest, and even more
the sleights of hand entailed by his pretense that the best
analytic scheme necessarily yields the only sound normative advice – all of this incited readers to react and, by
reacting, criticizing, correcting, refuting, to build on
Morgenthau's foundations. Those who rejected his blueprint
were led to try other designs. He was both a goad and a
foil. (Indeed, the more one agreed with his approach, the
more one was irritated by his flaws, and eager to differentiate
one's own products.) A less arrogantly dogmatic scholar, a
writer more modest both in his empirical scope and in his
normative assertions, would never have had such an impact on scholarship. Less sweeping, he would not have
imposed the idea that here was a realm with properties of
its own. Less trenchant, he would not have made scholars
burn with the itch to bring him down a peg or two. One
of the many reasons why Raymond Aron's monumental *Peace
and War*[6] – a book far more ambitious in its scope and far
more sophisticated in its analyses than *Politics Among Nations* – incited no comparable reaction from scholarly readers may well have been the greater judiciousness and modesty
of Aron's normative conclusions. Humane skeptics invite nods
and sighs, not sound and fury; and sound and fury are good
for creative scholarship. Moreover, Aron's own scholarship
was overwhelming enough to be discouraging; Morgenthau's
was just shaky enough to inspire improvements.

Still, *Politics Among Nations* would not have played such
a seminal role, if the ground in which the seeds were planted
had not been so receptive. The development of international
relations as a discipline in the United States results from
the convergence of three factors: intellectual predispositions,

political circumstances, and institutional opportunities. The intellectual predispositions are those which account for the formidable explosion of the social sciences in general in the United States, since the end of World War II. There is, first, the profound conviction, in a nation which Ralf Dahrendorf has called the Applied Enlightenment,[7] that all problems can be resolved, that the way to resolve them is to apply the scientific method – assumed to be value free, and to combine empirical investigation, hypothesis formation, and testing – and that the resort to science will yield practical applications that will bring progress. What is specifically American is the scope of these beliefs, or the depth of this faith: they encompass the social world as well as the natural world, and they go beyond the concern for problem-solving (after all, there are trial-and-error, piecemeal ways of solving problems): they entail a conviction that there is, in each area, a kind of masterkey – not merely an intellectual, but an operational paradigm. Without this paradigm, there can be muddling through, but no continuous progress; once one has it, the practical recipes will follow. We are in the presence of a fascinating sort of national ideology: it magnifies and expands eighteenth-century postulates. What has ensured their triumph and their growth is the absence of any counterideology, on the Right or the Left, that challenges this faith either radically (as conservative thought did, in Europe) or by subordinating its validity to a change in the social system. Moreover, on the whole, the national experience of economic development, social integration, and external success has kept reinforcing this set of beliefs.

Second, and as a kind of practical consequence, the very prestige and sophistication of the 'exact sciences' were bound to benefit the social ones as well. The voices of gloom or skepticism that lament the differences between the natural world and the social world have never been very potent in America. Precisely because the social world is one of conflict, precisely because national history had entailed civil and foreign wars, the quest for certainty, the desire to find a sure way of avoiding fiascoes and traumas, was even more burning in the realm of the social sciences. The very contrast between an ideology of progress through the deliberate application of reason to human concerns – an ideology which fuses faith in instrumental reason and faith in moral reason – and a social reality in which the irrational often prevails both in the realm of values and in the choice of means, breeds a kind of inflation of social science establishments and pretensions. At the end of the war, a new dogma appeared. One of the social sciences, economics, was deemed to have met the expectations of the national ideology, and to have become a science on the model of the exact ones; it was celebrated for its contribution to the solution of the age-old problems of scarcity and inequality. This triumph goaded the other social sciences. Political science, the mother or stepmother of international relations, was particularly spurred. It was here that the temptation to emulate economics was greatest. Like economics, political science deals with a universal yet specialized realm of human activity. Its emphasis is not on the origins and effects of culture, nor on the structures of community or of voluntary association, but on the creative and coercive role of a certain kind of power, and on its interplay with social conflict. This also drew it closer to that other science of scarcity, competition, and power, economics, than to discipline like anthropology or sociology, which deal with more diffuse phenomena and which are less obsessed by the solution of pressing problems by means of enlightened central action.

Nations in which this grandiose and activist ideology of science is less overwhelming have also known, after World War II, a considerable expansion of the social sciences. But the United States often served as model and as lever.[8] And political science abroad has usually been more reflective than reformist, more descriptive than therapeutic; although, here and in sociology, foreign social scientists reacted against the traditional intelligentsia of moralists, philosophers, and aesthetes by stressing that knowledge (not old-fashioned wisdom) *was* power (or at least influence), they were not driven by the dream of knowledge *for* power. Moreover, when (inevitably) disillusionment set in, it took often far more drastic forms – identity crises within the professions, violent indictments outside – than in the United States. An ideology on probation cannot afford a fall. An ideology serenely hegemonial reacts to failure in the manner of the work horse in Orwell's *Animal Farm,* or of Avis: 'I will try harder.'

A third predisposition was provided by a transplanted element: the scholars who had immigrated from abroad. They played a huge role in the development of American science in general. This role was particularly important in the social sciences. Here, they provided not merely an additional injection of talent, but talent of a different sort. No social science is more interesting than the questions it asks, and these were scholars whose philosophical training and personal experience moved them to ask far bigger questions than those much of American social science had asked so far, questions about ends, not just about means; about choices, not just about techniques; about social wholes, not just about small towns or units of government. So they often served as conceptualizers, and blended their analytic skills with the research talents of the 'natives.' Moreover, they brought with them a sense of history, an awareness of the diversity of social experiences, that could only stir comparative research and make something more universal of the frequently parochial American social science. In the field of international relations, in addition to Morgenthau, there was a galaxy of foreign-born scholars, all concerned with transcending empiricism: the wise and learned Arnold Wolfers, Klaus Knorr, Karl Deutsch, Ernst Haas, George Liska, and the young Kissinger and Brzezinski, to name only a few. They (and quite especially those among them who had crossed the Atlantic in their childhood or adolescence) wanted to find out the meaning and the causes of the catastrophe that had uprooted them, and perhaps the keys to a better world.

The last two names bring us to politics. And politics mattered. Hans Morgenthau has often written as if truth and power were bound to be enemies (Hannah Arendt has been even more categorical). And yet he shaped his truths so as to guide those in power. The growth of the discipline cannot be separated from the American role in world affairs after 1945. First, by definition (or tautology), political scientists are fascinated with power – either because they want it, at least vicariously, or because they fear it and want to understand the monster, as Judith Shklar has suggested with her usual devastating lucidity.[9] And in the post-war years, what part of power was more interesting than the imperial bit? America the sudden leader of a coalition, the sole economic superpower, the nuclear monopolist, later the nuclear superior, was far more interesting to many students than local politics, or the politics of Congress, or the politics of group pluralism. Almost inevitably, a concern for America's conduct in the world blended with a study of international relations, for the whole world seemed to be the stake of the American–Soviet confrontation. Here was a domain which was both a virgin field for study and the arena of a titanic contest. To study United States foreign policy was to study the international system. To study the international system could not fail to bring one back to the role of the United States. Moreover, the temptation to give advice, to offer courses of action, or to criticize the official ones was made even more irresistible by the spotty character and the *gaffes* of past American behavior in world affairs, by the thinness of the veneer of professionalism in American diplomacy, by the eagerness of officialdom for guidance – America was the one-eyed leading the cripples. Thus, two drives merged, for the benefit of the discipline and to its detriment also, in some ways: the desire to concentrate on what is the most relevant, and the tendency (implicit or explicit) to want to be useful, not only as a scientist, but as an expert citizen whose science can help promote intelligently the embattled values of his country (a motive that was not negligible, among newcomers to America especially). For it was all too easy to assume that the values that underlie scientific research – the respect for truth, freedom of investigation, of discussion, and of publication – were also those for which Washington stood in world affairs.

Second, as I have just said, what the scholars offered, the policy-makers wanted. Indeed, there is a remarkable chronological convergence between their needs and the scholars' performances. Let us oversimplify greatly. What the leaders looked for, once the cold war started, was some intellectual compass which would serve multiple functions: exorcise isolationism, and justify a permanent and global involvement in world affairs; rationalize the accumulation of power, the techniques of intervention, and the methods of containment apparently required by the cold war; explain to a public of idealists why international politics does not leave much leeway for pure good will, and indeed besmirches purity; appease the frustrations of the bellicose by showing why unlimited force or extremism on behalf of liberty was no virtue; and reassure a nation eager for ultimate accommodation, about the possibility of both avoiding war and achieving its ideals. 'Realism,' however critical of specific policies, however (and thus self-contradictorily) diverse in its recommendations, precisely provided what was necessary. Indeed, there was always a sufficient margin of disagreement between its suggestions and actual policies, and also between its many champions, to prevent it from being nothing but a rationalization of cold war policies. And yet the first wave of writings – those of Morgenthau, Wolfers, ur-Kissinger, Kennan. Osgood, Walt Rostow, or McGeorge Bundy – gave both the new intellectual enterprise and the new diplomacy the general foundations they needed. The second wave – roughly, from 1957 to the mid-1960s – turned strategy in the nuclear age into a dominant field within the discipline. This coincided with the preoccupation of officialdom to replace the reassuring but implausible simplicities of massive retaliation with a doctrine that would be more sophisticated; but it also reflected the conviction that force, in a mixture of nuclear deterrence and conventional (or subconventional) limited uses, remained both the most important aspect of power and a major American asset. Here again, in the literature, the attempt at finding principles for any 'strategy of conflict' in a nuclear world is inseparable from the tendency to devise a strategy for America, at a time when both sides had weapons of mass destruction, and when there were serious problems of alliance management, guerrilla wars, or 'wars of national liberation.' A third wave is quite recent: I refer to the growing literature on the politics of international economic relations. It coincides with what could be called the post-Vietnam aversion for force, and with the surge of economic issues to the top of the diplomatic agenda, caused by a combination of factors: the degradation of the Bretton Woods system, the increasing importance of economic growth and social welfare in the domestic politics of advanced societies, the resurgence of aggressive or protectionist impulses in order to limit the bad effects or to maximize the gains from interdependence, the revolt of the Third World. Once more, the priorities of research and those of policy-making blend.

The political preeminence of the United States is the factor I would stress most in explaining why the discipline has fared so badly, by comparison, in the rest of the world (I leave aside countries like the Soviet Union and China, in which it would be hard to speak of free social science scholarship!). Insofar as it deals primarily with the contemporary world, it seems to require the convergence of a scholarly community capable of looking, so to speak, at global phenomena (i.e. of going beyond the study of the nation's foreign policy, or of the interstate politics of an area) and of a political establishment concerned with world affairs; each one then strengthens the other. When the political elites are obsessed only with what is happening to their country, because it lacks the power to shape what is happening elsewhere, or because this lack of power has bred habits of dependence on another state (such as the United States), or because (as in the case of Japan and West Germany) there are severe constraints on the global use of the nation's power, the chances are that the scholars will not have the motivation or receive the impulse necessary to turn individual efforts into a genuine scientific enterprise, and will either turn to other fields with more solid traditions and outlets (such as, say, electoral behavior in France and Britain) or merely reflect, more or less slavishly, and with some delays, American fashions; or else there will be often brilliant individual contributions, but unconnected and unsupported: a Hedley Bull in Australia (and England), a Pierre Hassner in France, to name just these two, do not make a discipline. Even in England and France, which have become nuclear powers, strategic studies have been to a very large extent the preserve of a few intellectual military men, concerned either with reconciling national policy with the predominant doctrines of deterrence, or with challenging these. But the predominant doctrines have remained American, as if even in the more abstract efforts at theorizing about a weapon that has transformed world politics, it mattered if one was the citizen or host of a country with a worldwide writ. Scholars do not like to think about their intellectual dependence on the status of their country, and on the ambitions of its political elite; it disturbs their sense of belonging to a cosmopolitan, free-floating community of science. Even the sociology of knowledge, which has often looked at the debts of scholars to their countries, has been singularly coy about this particular kind of bond. And yet, the link exists. And it is sometimes reinforced by institutional arrangements.

In the case of the United States, there have been three institutional factors that have acted as multipliers of political connection – factors which have not existed, and certainly not simultaneously, elsewhere. One is the most direct and visible tie between the scholarly world and the world of power: the 'in-and-outer' system of government, which puts academics and researchers not merely in the corridors but also in the kitchens of power. Actually, it may be wise to distinguish two phases. In the late 1940s and 1950s, those kitchens remained the preserves of the old establishment: a mix of career civil servants, businessmen, and lawyers. They had to cope with the whole world, with a persistent enemy, with the travails of economic reconstruction and the turmoil of nuclear deterrence. They needed both data and ideas, and they turned to the universities. This was the age of the academic as consultant (officially or not), and this was the period in which much research got funded by those departments that had the biggest resources (Defense more than State). The year 1960 was a turning point. Academics became proconsuls and joined the old boys; often they tried to prove that they could cook spicier dishes and stir pots more vigorously than their colleagues. If one had some doubts about 'policy scientists,' these could only be doubled by the spectacle of scientific policy-makers. Be that as it may, the Washington connection turned an intellectual interchange into a professional one. In countries with a tight separation between the career of bureaucracy or politics and the academic *métier*, such exchanges are limited to occasional formal occasions – seminars or colloquia – and frequent *diners en ville*; but the former tend to be sterile, and the latter hover between witty debates on current affairs, and small talk.

A second institutional factor of great importance is the

role of what I have elsewhere called the relays between the
kitchens of power and the academic salons. The most important of these dumbwaiters is the network of foundations
that fed international relations research after the war, and
whose role is essential if one wants to understand exactly
why the three waves of scholarship coincided so aptly with
the consecutive concerns of the statesmen. A combination
of intellectual encouragement to 'frontiers of knowledge'
and civic desire to be of service, the sociological peculiarities
of boards of directors composed, to a large extent, of former
academics and former officials, the happy accident of vast
financial resources that kept growing until the end of the
1960s, all this made of the foundations a golden half-way
house between Washington and academia. Wasps served in
the CIA – pardon, the institution – as well as State; ex-
State officials served in the foundations; and even those
professors who had some reservations about serving in the
government, had no objection to applying to the foundations. It was a seamless pluralism. These precious relays
exist virtually nowhere else.

The third institutional opportunity was provided by the
universities themselves. They had two immense virtues. They
were flexible; because of their own variety, which ensured
both competition and specialization, and also because of
the almost complete absence of the straitjackets of public
regulations, quasi-feudal traditions, financial dependence,
and intellectual routine which have so often paralyzed the
universities of postwar Europe. The latter got caught in
the contradiction between their own past – a combination
of vocational training and general education for the elites
– and the sudden demands of mass higher education; they
could vacillate from confusion to collapse, but the one thing
they could rarely do was to innovate. The other virtue of
American universities resulted in part from the fact that
mass higher education was already a *fait accompli*: they had
large departments of political science, which could serve
as the matrices of the discipline of International Relations.
In France until the late 1960s, in Britain until the spread
of the new universities, international relations remained the
handmaid of law, or the laughingstock of historians; and
when political science departments began to mushroom, the

other reasons for the development of the discipline in America were still missing. Only in America could a creative sociologist write about the university as the most characteristic institution of the post-industrial age, the laboratory of its discoveries.[10] In other countries, universities are rarely the arenas of research; and when they are, the research funded by public institutions concentrates on issues of public policy which are rarely international – partly for the political reason I have mentioned above, partly because the existence of a career foreign service with its own training programs perpetuates the tendency to look at international relations as if it were still traditional diplomacy. Civil servants obliged to deal with radically new tasks such as urbanization, the management of banks and industries, or housing sometimes think they can learn from the social sciences. Civil servants who deal with so 'traditional' a task as national security and diplomacy do not always realize that the same old labels are stuck on bottles whose shapes as well as their content are new. And when diplomats discover that they too have to cope with the new, technical issues of technology, science, and economics, it is to 'domestic' specialists of these subjects that they turn – if they turn at all.

EVEN IN AMERICA

If one looks at the field 30 years after the beginning of the 'realist' revolution, can one point to any great breakthroughs? The remarks which follow are, of course, thoroughly subjective, and undoubtedly jaundiced. I am more struck by the dead ends than by the breakthroughs; by the particular, often brilliant, occasionally elegant, but generally non-additive contributions to specific parts of the field, than by its overall development; by the contradictions that have rent its community of scholars, than by its harmony. The specific contributions have been well analyzed in a 1975 volume of the *Handbook of Political Science*,[11] and I shall not repeat what is said there. If I had to single out three significant 'advances,' I would list the concept of the international system, an attempt to do for international relations what the concept of a political regime does for 'domestic' political science: it is a way of ordering data, a construct for describing both the way in which the parts relate, and the way in which patterns of interaction change. It emerged from the first period I have described above, and continues to be of importance. Next, I would mention the way in which the literature on deterrence has analyzed and codified 'rules of the game' which have been accepted as such by American statesmen, and which have served as the intellectual foundation of the search for tacit as well as explicit interstate restraints: MAD ('Mutual Assured Destruction') and arms control are the two controversial but influential offsprings of the doomsday science. Third, there is the current attempt to study the political roots, the originality, and the effects of economic interdependence, particularly in order to establish whether it shatters the 'realist' paradigm, which sees international relations as marked by the predominance of conflict among state actors. And yet, if I were asked to assign three books from the discipline to a recluse on a desert island, I would have to confess a double embarrassment: for I would select one that is more than 2000 years old – Thucydides' *Peloponnesian War*, and as for the two contemporary ones, Kenneth Waltz's *Man, the State and War*[12] is a work in the tradition of political philosophy, and Aron's *Peace and War* is a work in the grand tradition of historical sociology, which dismisses many of the scientific pretenses of the post-war American scholars, and emanates from the genius of a French disciple of Montesquieu, Clausewitz, and Weber. All three works avoid jargon; the two contemporary ones carry their erudition lightly: the sweat of toil is missing. How more unscientific can you get?

Let us return to the ideology I alluded to earlier. There was the hope of turning a field of inquiry into a science, and the hope that this science would be useful. Both quests have turned out to be frustrating. The desire to proceed scientifically, which has been manifest in all the social sciences, has run into three particular snags here. First, there was (and there remains) the problem of theory. I have discussed elsewhere at some length the difficulties scholars have encountered when they tried to formulate laws accounting for the behavior of states, and theories that would explain those laws and allow for prediction. A more recent analysis, by Kenneth Waltz, comes to an interesting conclusions: if theory is to mean here what it does in physics, then the only 'theory' of international relations is that of the balance of power, and it is unfortunately insufficient to help us understand the field! The other so-called general theories are not more than grand conceptualizations, using 'confused, vague and fluctuating definitions of variables.'[13] This may well be the case; Waltz seems to blame the theorists, rather than asking whether the fiasco does not result from the very nature of the field. Can there *be* a theory of undetermined behavior which is what 'diplomatic-strategic action,' to use Aron's terms, amounts to?

Aron has, in my opinion, demonstrated why a theory of undetermined behavior cannot consist of a set of propositions explaining general laws that make prediction possible, and can do little more than define basic concepts, analyze basic configurations, sketch out the permanent features of a constant logic or behavior, in other words make the field intelligible.[14] It is therefore not surprising if many of the theories dissected, or vivisected, by Waltz are, as he puts it, reductionist, such as the theories of imperialism, which are what he had called in his earlier book 'second image' theories (they find the causes of interstate relations in what happens *within* the units); or else, the theories he dismisses were all produced during the first phase – the neophytish (or fetish) stage – of post-war research: the search for the scientific equivalent of the philosopher's stone has been far less ardent in the past 20 years. Waltz's own attempt at laying the groundwork for theory is conceptually so rigorous as to leave out much of the reality he wants to account for. I agree with him that a theory explaining reality must be removed from it and cannot be arrived at by mere induction; but if it is so removed that what it 'explains' has little relation to what occurs, what is the use? One finds some of the same problems in all political science; but Waltz is right in stating that international relations suffers from a peculiar 'absence of common sense clues:' the key variables are far clearer in domestic political systems, whereas here 'the subject is created, and recreated, by those who work on it.'[15] Still, here as in the rest of political science, it is the fascination with economics that has led scholars to pursue the chimera of the masterkey. They have believed that the study of a purposive activity aimed at a bewildering variety of ends, political actions, could be treated like the study of instrumental action, economic behavior. They have tried in vain to make the concept of power play the same role as money in economics. And they have acted as if the mere production of partial theories unrelated to a grand theory was tantamount to failure.

A 'science' without a theory may still be a science with a paradigm; and, until recently, the paradigm has been that of permanent conflict among state actors – the realist paradigm. However, in the absence of a theory, a second question has been hard to answer: what is it that should be explained? The field has both suffered and benefited from a triple fragmentation – benefited, insofar as much ingenious research has been brought to each fragment, yet suffered because the pieces of the puzzle do not fit. First, there has been (and still is) the so-called level of analysis problem. Should we be primarily concerned with the international system, that is, the interactions among the units? Or should we concentrate our efforts on the units themselves? There are two conflicting hypotheses behind these strategies. One postulates that the system has, so to speak, some sort of life of its own, even if some of the actors obviously have a greater role than others in shaping and changing the rules of interaction. The other approach postulates that the actors themselves are the strategic level for understanding what goes on among them. One says, in effect: Grasp the patterns of interaction, and you will understand why the actors behaves as they do; the other one says: Look at the actors' moves, and you will comprehend the outcomes. Students of the international system and students of foreign-policy making have never really blended their research. My own conclusion is that of a writer who has worked both sides of the street: I am dissatisfied with each, but I admit that it is hard to be on both at once. The study of the international system provides one with a fine framework, but no more – precisely because the system may well put constraints on and provide opportunities for the actors, but does not 'dictate' their behavior; and the study of the actors tells you, inevitably, more about the actors than about the interactions. But what used to be called linkage theory (before linkage became a Kissinger-inspired technique), that is, propositions about the bonds between foreign policy and international politics, has remained in the frozen stage of static taxonomies.

Second, there has also been fragmentation at each level of analysis. One could say, not so flippantly, that each student of international systems has hugged his own version of what that abstract scheme 'is.' Aron's is not Richard Rosecrance's, which is not Morton Kaplan's. Moreover, each one has tended to look at the post-war international system in a different way (one again, in the absence of a single theory, it is not easy to determine authoritatively the dynamics of a particular system that still unfolds under one's eyes). A dozen years ago, scholars acted as if they were competing for a prize to the best discourse on the subject: are we in a bipolar system? Waltz, Liska, Kissinger, and many others (including me) took part, but since there was no Academy, there was no prize. In recent years, the new contest is about 'Persistence or Demise of the Realist Paradigm?': is the state-centered concept of international politics, with its focus on the diplomatic-strategic chessboard and its obsession with the use of force, still relevant to the age of interdependence? Aron, Joseph Nye and Robert Keohane, Edward Morse, Bull, and many others (including myself) are busy evaluating. As before, I suspect that the verdict will be history's, and that like the long-awaited Orator in Ionesco's *Chairs*, it will speak in incomprehensible gibberish. At the other level of analysis, we have accumulated masses of studies of concrete foreign policies, and moved from the period of Chinese boxes – the decision-making theories of the 1950s – to the age of the 'bureaucratic politics' model. The former provided endless items for laundry lists; the other one draws attention to the kitchen where the meal is being cooked, but forgets to tell us that what matters is whether the chefs cook what they want or what they are ordered to prepare, and assumes all too readily that what they do is determined by their particular assignment in the kitchen, rather than by what they have learned outside, or their personal quirks.

Third, there has been functional fragmentation as well.

If there is, or can be, no satisfactory general theory, if the 'overarching concepts' are excessively loose-fitting clothes, why not try greater rigor on a smaller scale? At the systemic level, we have thus witnessed such clusters of research as work on regional integration (where, for once, the theoretical ingenuity of scholars has far out-reached the practical, 'real-life' accomplishments of statesmen), modern theories of imperialism, arms race models and measurements of wars, recent studies of transnational relations and international economics. At the foreign policy level (although it tries to straddle both) the main cluster has been that of strategic literature; and there is a growing literature on decision-making in the United States. Unfortunately, each cluster has tended to foster its own jargon and this kind of fragmentation has had other effects, which will be discussed below.

Finally, the quest for science has led to a heated and largely futile battle of methodologies, in answer to a third question: Whatever it is we want to study how should we do it? Actually, it is a double battle. On the one hand, there is the debate between those 'traditionalists' who, precisely because of the resistance the field itself opposes to rigorous theoretical formulations, extol the virtues of an approach that would remain as close to historical scholarship and to the concerns of political philosophy as possible (this is the position taken by Hedley Bull), and all those who, whatever their own brand of theorizing, believe that there can be a political science of international relations – if not in the form of a single theory, at least in that of systematic conceptualizations, classifications, hypotheses, etc. – a science which can be guided in its questions by the interrogations of past philosophers, yet finds reliance on philosophical discourse and diplomatic intuition both insufficient and somewhat alien to the enterprise of empirical analysis. There is little likelihood that this debate will ever come to a conclusion – especially because neither side is totally consistent, and each one tends to oversimplify what it actually does. On the other hand, here as in other branches of political science, there is the battle of the literates versus the numerates; or, if you prefer, the debate about the proper place and contributions of quantitative methods and mathematical models. The fact that the practitioners of the latter tend to hug the word science, and to put beyond the pale of science all those who, while equally concerned with moving 'from the unique to the general' and with considering 'classes of events and types of entities,' believe that these cannot be reduced to numbers or that science does not consist in 'accumulating coefficients of correlation... without asking which theories lead one to expect what kind of a connection among which variables'[16] – this fact has made for rather strained relations among scholars of different methodological persuasions. In domestic political science, behaviorists and old-fashioned scholars have found coexistence easier, because their respective approaches fit separate parts of the field – electoral behavior or the behavior of legislative bodies lends itself to mathematical treatment. In international affairs, such a functional division of labor is much harder to apply. As a result, the prophets of quantitative methodologies dismiss as mere hunches based on 'insight' (a word they often use as if it were an insult) the elaborate ruminations of their opponents, and these in turn ridicule the costly calculations that tell one nothing about causes or lump together different types of the same phenomenon (say, wars), and the endless correlations among variables lifted from their context, that all too often conclude that... no conclusive evidence can be derived from them: endless nonanswers to trivial questions.

If there is little agreement as to what constitutes a science, and little enthusiasm for the state of the science of international relations, what about the other great expectation, that of usefulness? I am struck by one apparent contradiction. The champions of a science of international affairs have, on the whole, declared their independence from philosophy and their allegiance to objective empiricism. And yet, most of them have wanted to draw consequences for the real world from their research: the greater the drive to predict (or the tendency to equate science, not just with intelligibility but with control and prediction), the greater the inclination to play the role of the wise adviser – or of the engineer. It is in the nature of human affairs, and of the social sciences.

But in this specific realm, there are some very peculiar problems. The first could be called: advice to whom? Many scholars, especially those whose level of analysis is systemic, implicitly write as if they were addressing themselves to a world government, or as if they aimed at reaching those who wish to transcend the traditional logic of national self-righteousness and state calculations (the same can be said, even more strongly, of theorists of regional or functional integration; they tend to distribute recipes for going beyond the nation-state). Unfortunately, the chair of World State-craft is empty, and change comes (if at all) through the operations of state agents. And so, scholars of this kind oscillate from condemnation of state practices that make for conflict, or retard integration, or promote injustice, to advice to state agents on how to transcend the limits of the game which it is however these agents' role and duty to perpetuate, or advice to international secretariats and sub-national bureaus on the best strategy for undercutting and turning the resistance of national statecraft. These are all perfect guarantees of unhappy consciousness for the scholars.

Other scholars, especially among those whose level of analysis is national decision-making, see themselves as efficient Machiavellians – they are advising the Prince on how best to manage his power and on how best to promote the national interest. This is particularly the case of the strategists, the group which contains the highest proportion of researchers turned consultants and policy-makers. 'Systemic' writers who are fully aware of the differences between an international system and a community of mankind, that is, the 'realists,' do their best to make advice to the only Prince who still matters – the national statesman, bound to enhance the interests of his state – coincide with their views of the interests of the whole. They advocate 'enlightened' concepts of the national interest, or 'world order' policies that would somewhat reconcile the needs of the part and of the whole. But this is a difficult exercise. The logical thrust of 'realism' is the promotion of the national interest, that is, not unhappy global consciousness but happy national celebration. 'Realists' who become aware of the perils of realism in a world of nuclear interconnection and economic interdependence – writers like Morgenthau, or myself – suffer from the addition of two causes of unhappiness: that which afflicts all 'systemic' writers in search of a radically new order, and that which comes from knowing only too well that utopianism does not work.

Thus, basically, in their relations which the real world, the scholars are torn between irrelevance and absorption. Many do not like irrelevance, and want even the most esoteric or abstract research to be of use. The oscillation I have described above is what they want to escape from, and yet they do not want to be absorbed by that machine for self-righteousness, the service of the Prince. But their only excuse is the populist dream – the romantic hope that 'the people' can be aroused and led to force the elites that control the levers of action, either out of power altogether or to change their ways. Much of peace research, once it got tired of advocating for the solution of world conflicts the discrete techniques used for accommodation in domestic affairs, has been traveling down that route. It is one on which scholarship risks finding both irrelevance and absorption, for the policies advocated here do inspire both those intelligentsias that want to displace certain elites in developing countries, and those established elites that are eager to boost national power against foreign dominance. Yet if the former come to power, and if the latter follow the advice of 'dependencia' theorists, the result is not likely to be a world of peace and justice, but a world of revolutions, and new conflicts, and new inequities.

As for the scholars who want to avoid esoterica or romanticism and who set their sights on Washington, they, in turn, run into problems. There are two reasons why the Washingtonian temptation is so strong. There is the simple fact that international politics remains the politics of states: whether or not, in the abstract, the actor is the shaper of or is shaped by the system, in reality there is no doubt that the United States remains the most potent player. And there is the fact that a science of contemporary politics needs data, and that in this realm, whereas much is public – in the records of international organizations, speeches, published state documents – a great deal remains either classified or accessible only to insiders: the specific reasons for a decision, the way in which it was reached, the bargains that led to a common stand, the meanderings of a negotiation, the circumstances of a breakdown. Far more than domestic political science, international relations is an insider's game, even for scholars concerned with the systemic level.

But a first problem lies in the fact that gathering information from and about the most potent actor, creates an irresistible urge to nudge the players: the closer the Washingtonian connection, the greater the temptation of letting oneself be absorbed. Second, outsider advice always suffers from oversimplification. When it comes to tactical suggestions, the insiders, who control not only all the facts but also the links connecting separate realms of policy, have the advantage. This increases the scholar's urge to get in closer. Third, once one starts rolling down the slope from research-with-practical-effects, to practical-advocacy-derived-from-research, the tendency to slight the research and to slant the advocacy for reasons either of personal career or of political or bureaucratic opportunity, will become insidious. Which means that the author may still be highly useful as an intelligent and skilled decision-maker – but not as a scholar. Either his science will be of little use, or else, in his attempt to apply a particular pet theory or dogma, he may well become a public danger. This does not mean that the experience of policy-making is fateful to the scholar, that the greatest hope for the science would lie in blowing up the bridge that leads across the moat into the citadel of power. A scholar-turned-statesman can, if his science is wise and his tactics flexible, find ways of applying it soundly; and he can later draw on his experience for improving his scholarly analytical work. But it is a delicate exercise which few have performed well.

BECAUSE OF AMERICA

The problems I have examined have arisen mainly in America, because the profession of international relations specialists happens to be so preponderantly American. Insofar as it flourishes elsewhere, the same difficulties appear: they result from the nature of the field. But because of the American predominance, the discipline has also taken some additional traits which are essentially American, and less in evidence in those other countries where the field is now becoming an object of serious study.

The most striking is the quest for certainty.[17] It explains the rage for premature theoretical formulation, the desire to calculate the incalculable (not merely power but status), the crusade to replace discussions of motives with such more objective data as word counts and vote counts, the crowding of strategic research (here, the ends are given, and it becomes a quest for the means). International relations should be the science of uncertainty, of the limits of action, of the ways in which states try to manage but never quite succeed in eliminating their own insecurity. There has, instead, been a drive to eliminate from the discipline all that exists in the field itself – hence a quest for precision that turns out false or misleading. Hence also two important and related gaps. One is the study of statecraft as an art. With very few exceptions (such as *A World Restored*) it has been left to historians. (One could say much of the same about domestic political science.) The other is the study of perceptions and misperceptions, the subjective yet essential side of international politics. Robert Jervis' work is beginning to fill that gap, but it is not certain that his example will be widely followed.[18] Almost by essence, the study of diplomatic statecraft and of perceptions refuses to lend itself to mathematical formulations, or to a small number of significant generalizations (one may generalize, but the result is likely to be trivial). Taxonomies and case studies do not quench the thirst to predict and to advocate.

A second feature, intimately tied to the discipline's principal residence rather than to its nature, is the preponderance of studies dealing with the present. Historians continue to examine past diplomatic history in their way. Political scientists concerned with international affairs have concentrated on the politics of the post-war era; and when they have turned to the past, it has all too often been either in highly summary, I would say almost 'college outline' fashion, or in the way long ago denounced by Barrington Moore, Jr., which consists in feeding data detached from their context into computers. This is a very serious weakness. It leads not only to the neglect of a wealth of past experiences – those of earlier imperial systems, of systems of interstate relations outside Europe, of foreign policy-making in domestic policies far different from the contemporary ones – but also to a real deficiency in our understanding of the international system of the present. Because we have an inadequate basis for comparison, we are tempted to exaggerate either continuity with a past that we know badly, or the radical originality of the present, depending on whether we are more struck by the features we deem permanent, or with those we do not believe existed before. And yet a more rigorous examination of the past might reveal that what we sense as new really is not, and that some of the 'traditional' features are far more complex than we think.

There are many reasons for this flaw. One is the fear of 'falling back into history' – the fear that if we study the past in depth, we may indeed find generalizations difficult and categorization either endless or pointless; and we may lose the thread of 'science.' A related reason is the fact that American political scientists do not receive sufficient training either in history or in foreign languages, indispensable for work on past relations among states. A third reason is to be found in the very circumstances of the discipline's birth and development. In a way, the key question has not been, 'What should we know?' It has been 'What should we do?' – about the Russians, the Chinese, the bomb, the oil producers. We have tried to know as much as we needed in order to know how to act – and rarely more: a motivation that we find in other parts of political science (the study of political development, for instance), where some disillusionment has set in. But we can say to ourselves that there are no shortcuts to political development, that the United States cannot build nations for others and that we should go back to the foundations, that is, to an understanding of the others' past. We are unable to say to ourselves that we must stop having a diplomacy, and impose a moratorium on our advising drive until we have found out more about the past of diplomatic–strategic behavior. And the interest which, quite naturally, the government and, less wisely but understandably the foundations have shown in supporting research that deals with the present (or extrapolates it into the future, or scrutinizes the near future so as to discern what would be sound action in the present) has kept the scholars' attention riveted on the contemporary scene.

The stress on the present and the heavily American orientation have combined to leave in the dark, at least relatively, several important issues – issues whose study is essential to a determination of the dynamics of international politics. One is the relation of domestic politics (and not merely bureaucratic politics) to international affairs – we need to examine in far greater detail the way in which the goals of states have originated, not (or not only) from the geopolitical position of the actors, but from the play of domestic political forces and economic interests; or the way in which statesmen, even when they seemed to act primarily for the world stage, nevertheless also wanted their moves abroad to reach certain objectives within; or the way in which external issues have shaped domestic alignments and affected internal battles. The desire to distinguish the discipline of international relations from the rest of political science is partly responsible for this gap; scholars who study a given political system do not usually pay all that much attention to foreign policy, and the specialists of international politics simply do not know enough about foreign political systems. The only country for which the bond between domestic and external behavior has been examined in some depth is, not so surprisingly, the United States. Here again, an assessment of the originality of the present – with its visible merging of domestic and foreign policy concerns, especially in the realm of international economic affairs – requires a much deeper understanding of the past relations between domestic politics and foreign policy. We may discover that the realist paradigm, which stresses the primacy of foreign policy, has to be seriously amended, not only for the present but for the past.

Another zone of relative darkness is the functioning of the international hierarchy, or, if you prefer, the nature of the relations between the weak and the strong. There has been (especially in the strategic literature) a glaring focus on bipolarity, accompanied by the presumption that moves to undermine it (such as nuclear proliferation) would be calamitous (it may not be a coincidence if the French have, on the whole, taken a very different line). Much of the study of power in international affairs has been remarkably Athenian, if one may refer to the famous Melian dialogue in Thucydides (the strong do what they can, the weak what they must). How the strong have often dealt with the weak in ways far more oblique, or less successful than the simple notion of a high correlation between might and achievements would suggest; how and under what conditions the weak have been able to offset their inferiority – these are issues which, until OPEC came along, had not been at the center of research and for which, again, far more historical work ought to be undertaken.

What was supposed to be a celebration of creativity seems to have degenerated into a series of complaints. We have found here an acute form of a general problem that afflicts social science – the tension between the need for so-called basic research, which asks the more general and penetrating questions that derive from the nature of the activity under study, and the desire of those who, in the real world, support, demand, or orient the research, for quick answers to pressing issues. And if the desire often seems more compelling than the need, it is because of the scholars' own tendency to succumb to the Comtian temptation of social engineering. This temptation is enhanced by the opportunities the United States provides to scholar-kings (or advisers to the Prince), or else by the anxiety which scholars, however 'objective' they try to be, cannot help but feel about a world threatened with destruction and chaos by the very logic of traditional interstate behavior.

Born and raised in America, the discipline of international relations is, so to speak, too close to the fire. It needs triple distance: it should move away from the contemporary, toward the past; from the perspective of a superpower (and a highly conservative one), toward that of the weak and the revolutionary – away from the impossible quest for stability; from the glide into policy science, back to the steep ascent toward the peaks which the questions raised by traditional political philosophy represent. This would also be a way of putting the fragments into which the discipline explodes, if not together, at least in perspective. But where, in the social sciences, are the scientific priorities the decisive ones? Without the possibilities that exist in this country, the discipline might well have avoided being stunted, only by avoiding being born. The French say that if one does not have what one would like, one must be content with what one has got. Resigned, perhaps. But content? A state of dissatisfaction is a goad to research. Scholars in international relations have two good reasons to be dissatisfied: the state of the world, the state of their discipline. If only those two reasons always converged!

Notes

1. For an earlier discussion, see my *Contemporary Theory in International Relations* (Englewood Cliffs, NJ: Prentice-Hall, 1960); and my *The State of War* (New York: Praeger, 1965), chs. 1 and 2.
2. E. H. Carr, *The Twenty Years' Crisis* (London: Macmillan, 1939).
3. Nicholas Spykman, *America's Strategy in World Politics* (New York: Harcourt, Brace, 1942).
4. Hans Morgenthau, *Politics Among Nations* (New York: Knopf, 1948).
5. Cf. H. Stuart Hughes, *The Sea Change* (New York: Knopf, 1975).
6. Raymond Aron, *Peace and War* (Paris: Calmann-Lévy 1962; New York: Doubleday, 1966).
7. Ralf Dahrendorf, *Die angewandte Aufklärung* (Munich: Piper, 1963).
8. See the forthcoming Ph.D. thesis (Harvard University, Department of History) of Diana Pinto, who deals with postwar sociology in Italy and France.
9. Judith Shklar, in an introduction to the field of political science written for Harvard freshmen.
10. Cf. Daniel Bell, *The Coming of Post-Industrial Society* (New York: Basic Books, 1973).
11. *Handbook of Political Science*, vol. 8, *International Politics*, Fred I. Greenstein and Nelson W. Polsby (eds.) (Reading, MA: Addison-Wesley, 1975).
12. Kenneth Waltz, *Man, the State and War* (New York: Columbia University Press, 1959).
13. *Handbook of Political Science*, vol. 8, *International Politics*, ch. 1, p. 14.
14. See my *The State of War*, ch. 2.
15. *Handbook of Political Science*, vol. 8, *International Politics*, p. 8.
16. *Handbook of Political Science*, vol. 8, *International Politics*, p. 12.
17. On this point, see also Albert O. Hirschman, 'The Search for Paradigms as a Hindrance to Understanding,' *World Politics* (April 1970), pp. 329–343.
18. See Robert Jervis, *Perception and Misperception in International Politics* (Princeton: Princeton University Press, 1976).

10 The Dialectics of World Order: Notes for a Future Archeologist of International *Savoir Faire* (1984)*

Hayward Alker and
Thomas Biersteker

Generated by an intent to write an internationally useful text on the theory and practice of world politics in the twentieth century, this paper represents a preliminary attempt to review and make sense of that field.[1] Our focus will be on the contending world order concepts, designs or doctrines embodied within the recent history of globally oriented *political practices*, as well as the evaluative criticisms, alternative explorations and *theoretical rationalizations* occasioned by such practices. The search for order in and beyond contemporary world politics has repeatedly transcended or redefined the boundaries of the political. Hence International Relations, rather than its major subdiscipline World Politics, is the most generally relevant academic field for studying contending world orders.

One way of describing this paper is from the vantage point of some future Foucaultean archeologist of world knowledge concerned with how the different tribes on our planet came to understand each other and the world they all inhabited in the 20th century of the Christian era.[2] A future global archeologist would not be misled by the apparent unity of book titles or mathematical symbols dis-

* *International Studies Quarterly*, 28(2)(June), pp. 121–142.

coverable in the writings of 20th-century international relations scholars. He or she would know that the linguistically unified hieroglyphics found in the different temples of ancient Egypt represented earthly conflicts among immortal gods, and therefore would suspect the same primitive phenomenon of top deities with different names, symbols and powers to reappear in different temples of another archaic civilization several millenia later.[3] This scholar would be suspicious of the diffusion of mathematical symbols and specialized terminologies. An archeologist would want to know further what were the real differences in world understanding associated with the different approaches or traditions of scholarship. He or she would want to know also if there were any common or convergent themes underlying the contending perspectives and their scholarly accomplishments.

Our approach to knowledge cumulation is, in this sense, archeological. It might more accurately be called 'modern' or 'synthetic' dialectics. Its concerns follow first the dialectical heuristic to look deeply within the realm of being for contradictions in the essence of things. Hence we look within particular pieces of research for the most important knowledge producing and conserving entities – here conceived of as research disciplines, traditions, approaches, paradigms or programs – and study the principal contradictions within and among them. If historians of natural science are correct that intimate, often reciprocal and sometimes constitutive connections exist between the historical context of such research and the research activities themselves, these connections should be all the more obvious when the object of study is the world historical context itself. Hence we expect such disciplines to be doubly conflicted: both by their subject matter and by the divergent socio-political contexts of their development.

Once fundamental oppositions have been identified, we try to look for knowledge interests, conceptual orientations, problematiques, themes, generalizations or theories unifying opposed knowledge-cumulating perspectives. Thus we are also searching for synthesis, order amongst chaos, the unity of opposites that interpenetrate and sometimes turn into each other.[4]

THE GLOBAL 'INTERDISCIPLINE' OF INTERNATIONAL RELATIONS

Would our archeologist be able to find some kind of intellectual order in a field which is attempting to comprehend a century characterized by as much disorder as our own? The 20th century has been a 'century of total war' among totalizing states; it is a century which has seen the emergence of anti-capitalist, radical, and often Marxist–Leninist regimes which now govern perhaps one-third of humankind in the name of laboring classes; it is an anti-colonial century which has seen a global 'revolt against the West'. Partly because of these divisions, no single research approach has managed to gain world-wide acceptance in, or impose a globally shared intellectual interpretation on, this century of disorder. Different theoretical approaches have emerged to comprehend and amend this disorder, but they have been sharply divided by region, time, political orientation and epistemology.

Traditional approaches concerned with analyzing and preventing conflicts in the great power core of the international system dominated discussion in the United States and Europe during the inter-war years and in the immediate aftermath of World War II. Dialectical approaches concerned with challenging the existing world order emerged in postrevolutionary Russian and Chinese scholarship, and can also be found in much of the work coming out of Latin America during the 1960s and 1970s. For several decades, behavioral-scientific approaches concerned with explaining and managing a complex world order have predominated in the United States, the hegemonial world power of the 1950s and 1960s.

Although a single research approach may be readily identified as prominent or dominant within a given time and a given national setting, it is never entirely alone. In the United States, much of our theoretical discussion since World War II has centered on the utility of traditional versus behavioral approaches, but dialectical alternatives have also been visibly present, at least since the war in Vietnam. Similarly, although dialectical approaches clearly dominate in the Soviet Union and its allied states (and American behavioralism has been dismissed as 'bourgeois social science'), both traditionally trained diplomat-professors and behaviorally trained mathematical modelers and survey researchers can also be found there.[5] In the scholarly environments of contemporary Latin America, Africa and Western Europe, multiple variants of these approaches are not only the subject of wide debate, they more or less openly contend for hegemony.

Thus, when asked whether the great disorders of the century have destroyed the coherence of international relations as a discipline, a recently reinvigorated Cold Warrior might be tempted to say that now 'disruptive Marxists' are everywhere, not just 90 or 9000 miles away. But a moment's reflection on the tendencies just reviewed suggests that behavioralists are also sweeping the globe. And, despite the hope of some modern behavioralists that traditional approaches would die out with the coming to maturity of new generations of graduate students, this has not happened either. Within the limits imposed by differences in circumstance, profession and epistemological orientation, both communication and cumulative criticism of scholarly ideas have been at least occasionally possible. Hence it appears paradoxically that *multiple* disciplines of international relations have been created, diffused and have indeed thrived in the 20th century.

THE GLOBAL INTERDISCIPLINE: A SYNTHETIC PERSPECTIVE

In light of our preference for an integrative dialectical approach, what sense can we make of the paradoxical multiplicity of seemingly self-renewing research traditions of international relations in the 20th century? Borrowing a term from Dougherty and Pfaltzgraff,[6] we propose treating International Relations as an 'interdiscipline' constituted at least as much by its principled differences in research approaches, teaching and practice as by its communalities.

It is useful, therefore, to begin to conceptualize the field by constructing a dialectical triad that incorporates oppositions among the dominant and recurring traditional,

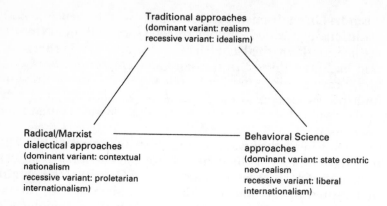

Figure 10.1 The interdiscipline of international relations in the 1980s

dialectical, and behavioral-scientific approaches which we think summarize most of the main bodies of international relations scholarship around the globe. Although the approaches of Figure 10.1 may properly be viewed as contradictory toward each other,[7] it would be a fundamental misconstrual of reality or of our intent to treat them as mutually exclusive. *As illustrated by our previous remarks about disciplinary alternatives, it is the sharing, the interpenetration and the principled opposition of these often antagonistic approaches in the First, Second and remaining 'Worlds' that truly constitute the global interdiscipline of International Relations.*

Let us elaborate more systematically on the characteristic features of these polar approaches, as well as the major, discipline-defining debates within and between them. Each approach generates paradigm-like research programs and evaluates results according to its own evaluative criteria. Each claims to be theoretical and scientific, but not always in the same ways. Each reflects certain values rooted in concrete historical and political contexts. Each approach also contains both dominant and recessive variants (often several of the latter), and each of the approaches can be defined in terms both of its internal and its external scholarly controversies.

In the 1930s and 1940s writers like Arnold Toynbee, E. H. Carr, Quincy Wright and Hans Morgenthau all offered modernized, 'scientific' versions of traditional historical and legal approaches to international relations. But these new traditionalists were not all agreed on what constituted their science. The major discipline-defining debate within these newer *traditional approaches*, both in the English-speaking world and elsewhere, has been between 'realists' like Carr and Morgenthau and those like Toynbee and Wright they choose to call 'idealists' or 'utopians'. The new realists were occupied with power politics, a preoccupation given great credibility by the desperate politics of World War II. Their dominance of scholarly discussions in the immediate post-war era was based, at least in part, on the failure of the League of Nations' collective security system; it was heightened by the beginning of the Cold War. Earlier the disastrous costs of World War I had similarly discredited, for many Wilsonian idealists, the secretive power balancing diplomacy of the previous era. In Figure 10.1 these debates are put in a larger context of anti-traditionalist alternatives, involving not only the behavioral descendent of 'idealism', liberal internationalism, but also the 'utopian' proletarian internationalism of certain dialectical approaches.

Traditionally, realists have valued prudence, respected the sovereignty of great powers and been concerned with maintaining world order for one or several of them, while their 'communitarian' opponents (to suggest a less pejorative label) have sought legal, religious, societal, historical or other communitarian bases for international government of some kind. For traditionalists, international practice has been seen as more of a practical art than a natural science. Indeed all traditionalists highly value the study of diplomatic history, but realists are more likely than communitarians to find in such history evidence for timeless descriptive and prescriptive laws linking power, survival and national interests. For realists, world order alternatives are defined principally in terms of power configurations rather than the fundamental legal principles of a social order.[8] The exemplary work within this tradition for our generation is Morgenthau's *Politics Among Nations*. Raymond Aron, Hedley Bull, Martin Wight and Henry Kissinger would usually be considered 'traditional realists,' while scholars like Inis Claude and Richard Falk would be somewhat closer to early 'idealist' concerns with international law, order, and organization.

Dialectical approaches dominate analyses in the Soviet Union and China and have been important in many other parts of the world as well. Typically, dialectical theorists have valued emancipation, favored structural or revolutionary change, and have fundamentally challenged the legitimacy of the existing world order. The priority of practice over 'mere' theory fits in this tradition with the high degree of attention given to the reflections on practice of leading Marxist–Leninist practitioners.

It is worth recalling that both Marx and Lenin attacked the traditional realist and idealist writers of their time, claiming to be proposing and attempting to realize in practice a more fundamentally humane and scientifically supported socioeconomic and political order. The same kinds of criticisms are made against newer 'traditional' approaches. Thus Marxian dialectics clearly preceded the behavioral scientific challenge to older forms of traditional international relations: and it should be thought of as antithetical to many newer traditional approaches as well. Hence a separate axis of contention (Traditional vs. Radical/Marxist Dialectics) is necessary in Figure 10.1. Corresponding to the traditional realist's charge that Marxist thought is 'utopian' would be the modern radical/dialectical indictment of both traditional realism and idealism that imperialistic capitalism is inherently war-prone, that non-revolutionary system reforms are futile, that class biases have distorted the objective content and practical significance of both realist and idealist inquiry.

But it would be a serious oversimplification to see the dialectical approach as exclusively Marxist (neither was Marx the only Left Hegelian nor is Hegel the only source of modern dialectical thought). And it is also not correct to treat Marxism–Leninism as an entirely homogeneous theoretical school. Among the principal contradictions of discipline-defining debates within the dialectical tradition are those between the proletarian internationalism of Marx, Lenin, Trotsky and Che Guevara and the sometimes more conservative, contextually oriented nationalists (Stalin as an advocate of socialism in one country, Mao most of the time, and many contemporary dependency theorists). Figure 10.1 expresses our judgment that the world orientation of the more conservative nationalist practices of the Soviet Union and China (and even Cuba at the moment) dominate the internationalism more evident in West European and North American scholarly Marxism. Conceptually, dialectical theorists have typically contrasted actual (dominant, imposed) structures of world order with emergent alternatives that may or must supersede them. These alternative orders have been defined as much in terms of their socio-economic bases (which inform, sustain and limit more narrowly 'political' actions) as in terms of their overall power configurations and dynamics.

Just as the English radical Hobson used many Marxist arguments in his attacks on British imperialism and also attacked 'positivist' social science[9] discussed by Siegelman in his introduction to the 1962 edition of Hobson's *Imperialism*), we are aware that radical peace researchers like Galtung[10] and ourselves are currently using non-Marxist dialectical approaches. We consider the motivations for such efforts to include the desire to convey scientific recognition to the best works in the modern dialectical tradition, to avoid the pitfalls of Marxist reductionism and Leninist orthodoxy, to gain greater self-understanding than is possible with naturalistic or positivistic models of social inquiry modeled on physics, to improve communication, to explicate influential but implicit epistemological and normative differences, and to focus debate across polar opposite modern scientific disciplines.

Behavioral science approaches may be either more inclusively or exclusively characterized; we prefer a more inclusive conception. Whether behavioralists focus on the international perspectives or behavior of individuals or institutions, all in our view share a commitment to some form of value neutral analytic empiricism as a philosophy of science, as exemplified in the data-making and hypothesis-testing procedures of contemporary polimetric practice. More generally, there is an emulative admiration of the mathematical and logical practices assumed to characterize the natural sciences, including the search for objective, timeless, universal laws. Also characteristic of behavioralism as we see it is a kind of positivistic or even technocratic scientific self-understanding close to what Hoffmann has described, following Dahrendorf, as

> [the] Applied Enlightenment, [especially in America] that all problems can be resolved, that the way to resolve them is to apply the scientific method – assumed to be value free, and to combine empirical investigation, hypothesis formation, and testing – and that the resort to science will yield practical applications that will bring progress.[11]

Due both to the perceived importance of science and technology in the Allies' victory in World War II, the discredited, 'unrealistic' role of much idealist thinking by that time and the prior successes of pragmatic empiricism in American social science, behavioral approaches have gradually become hegemonic since the post-war period, especially in the United States. Thus they have come into their prime much later than Marxist–Leninist dialectics; nonetheless they too typically define themselves primarily by distinguishing themselves from traditionalist approaches. Deutsch supports this view, describing the behaviorally oriented 'third and fourth waves' of international relations research as coming after earlier preoccupations with diplomatic history and power politics, international law and international organization.[12]

Reflecting certain of their acknowledged ancestors, many of the more optimistic American behavioral scientists of the 1950s and 1960s showed signs of idealistic reformism. More globally conceived, values such as 'liberal' internationalism or a belief in international 'coexistence' do indeed complement the naturalistic commitment of the exemplary behavioralist to logical-empirical 'rigor' and, sometimes, a rather unreflective version of scientific 'objectivity'. But like their traditional predecessors, behavioralists have also often been realistically and conservatively concerned with managing world order from a hegemonial power perspective. Unlike most traditionalists, the 'modern' manager usually relies more strongly on scientific and technical expertise.

Almost all behavioral scientists have cut their teeth on the confused, 'unscientific' nature of traditional thinking about the balance of power; many others have also been taught about the 'unscientific' quality of Marxist scholarship (Lenin's *Imperialism*, Adorno *et al.*'s *The Authoritarian Personality*, and crude economic reductionism in explaining US behavior in Vietnam are favorite targets). It is of particular significance, then, that more recent debates between behavioral scientists and dependency theorists have not *started* with the assumption that the latter are unscientific scholars; such conclusions have often followed from those not seriously trained in dialectical epistemologies.[13]

The major discipline-defining debates within the behavioral scientific tradition have at least on the surface appeared to be methodological, involving levels of analysis (state-centric neo-realists can currently be distinguished from the more multi-level perspectives of American liberal internationalists), modes of inference (the relative merits of induction, deduction and heuristic abduction) and methods of analysis (gaming vs. decision-making analysis, world modeling, etc.). Although multi-level order concepts of a liberal-internationalist sort dominated American scholarly innovation briefly during the 1970s (as exemplified by Keohane and Nye's *Power and Interdependence*), state-centered neo-realists (exemplified by Waltz's *Theory of International Politics*) have, we believe, resumed dominance within the American branches of the behavioral tradition since the late 1970s.

Figure 10.2 visually represents a few of the more significant external controversies and disciplinary defining debates that have taken place among traditional, dialectical and behavioral scientific approaches. In no case have we exhaustively delineated even all the major 'rounds' in these confrontations, but it is our belief that each of the third paths indicated does represent an improvement in important respects over the earlier 'salvos' in the same direction. Some of the particular reasons for this belief will be given in the rest of this paper, which Figure 10.2 helps to preview. As we shall see in the section which follows, however, such exchanges and the traditions from which they emerge are not treated as equally legitimate or worthy of attention in all parts of the globe, including the United States.

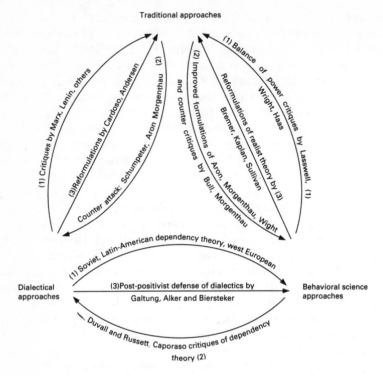

Figure 10.2   Some interdisciplinary arguments across the IR triad

THE AMERICAN INTERDISCIPLINE OF INTERNATIONAL RELATIONS

If our future archeologist were to commence digging in the United States – whether in Berkeley, Cambridge, Rochester, or New Haven – the old texts or reading lists unearthed in one university center would give a rather different impression from the others from one decade to the next. As we have already indicated, however, digging up university library reserves would yield recognizable variants of each of the major research traditions discussed above, a phenomenon that transcends the lack of agreement by American scholars on specific readings.

We believe that a more careful examination of the

archeological evidence would reveal a rather striking additional tendency: *most 'leading' American instructors of courses on theories of international relations were exceedingly parochial.* This was true even during the enlightened era of the early 1980s. Not only were the bulk of the readings on their syllabuses written by other American scholars, but those readings were also derived almost exclusively from a single one of the three major research approaches identified in Figure 10.1 – behavioral science. This means that the questions asked, the values assumed, the issues addressed, and the debates considered (the multiple problematiques of Figure 10.2) have been nearly all addressed from within the narrow confines of a single epistemological tradition.[14]

In an era when many scientifically trained behavioralists have recently declared their adherence to 'neo-realism,' it would not be surprising to us if many or most recent American international relations courses have mentioned the debates between traditional realists and liberal behavioral scientists, or assigned works discussing them. More disappointing would be the systematic neglect in these courses of the *ongoing* debates either of these schools has had with Marxist writers on imperialism, the nation-state, dependency or the capitalist world system. We believe that most American general theory courses do not do justice to the world-wide variety of substantively and politically significant approaches to international relations identified above.[15]

A Behavioral Test of American Parochialism

The primary source material for our present testing of this argument is an archeologist's gold mine: Kornberg's recent compilation[16] of 'Innovative Reading Lists from Leading Political Scientists' on the topic of *Theories of International Relations*, together with several of the standard or popular textbooks – Waltz, Morgenthau, Kaplan, Rosenau, Dougherty and Pfaltzgraff – repeatedly cited in that collection. Almost characteristically, Kornberg omits the highly accurate descriptor *'American'* from his title.[17]

If we employ the methods and evaluation criteria of behavioral science to examine the distribution of reading list items on the syllabuses in the Kornberg collection, we have a crude but useful indication of the extent of the parochialism that exists in the contemporary teaching of international relations (including world politics) in the United States. We have drawn our sample extensively, but not entirely, from Kornberg's compilation. Graduate level, general theory courses were selected in preference to undergraduate or specialized courses on topics like international organization, international political economy, or American foreign and military policy, most of which would belong in another Kornberg compilation. Only one course list per 'leading political scientist' was examined, selected on the basis of its breadth (the broader, the better), level of students (graduate-level courses were preferred), and numbers of citations (the greater the N, the better). Thus we examined the reading lists of Alker (p. 3), Falk (p. 13), Gilpin (p. 16), Haas (p. 20), Holsti (p. 63), Jervis (p. 77), Keohane (p. 87), Krasner (p. 95), Krasner and Stein (p. 98), Lipson (p. 107), Mandelbaum (p. 111), Quester (p. 118), Russett (p. 130), Starr (p. 145), and Waltz (p. 160).

We also included the Yale Graduate Examination List (p. 165), the only such list in the Kornberg collection, and Biersteker's joint graduate-undergraduate theory course taught at Yale.[18] Including both of these helps give a more accurate picture of the range and contrast in offerings at a single institution, Yale (the Krasner and Krasner–Stein lists provide comparable coverage for UCLA). Our expectation of parochialism is one that takes into account the reality of multiple course offerings in most graduate departments; it refers as well to field requirements and structures of support and selection for students and faculty, and to the presence or absence of uncoerced, reasoned confrontations among the alternative approaches described here. Misleading course labels are not the most serious problems we have in mind.

This sample is not entirely representative of the way international relations is taught in the United States. Traditional approaches are probably under-represented, since the sample is derived largely from major research and graduate training institutions. Except for the absence of any offerings from some major American universities of multiple offerings from most of the others, the sample does appear to be representative of these institutions, where a generation of teacher-scholars in their 40s seems especially prominent.

All required items on these 17 reading lists were coded into one of the ten categories listed in Table 10.1. Although many items could be classified in more than one category, the decision to assign a single classification was based on an assessment of the central concern or logic of the work, an examination of its placement within the structure of the course, and/or a consideration of the central focus of the relevant pages assigned. Several courses were independently coded, with initial coder agreement in the 83–90% range. All difficult items were discussed and either recategorized or classified as 'D' in Table 10.1, i.e. as 'Ambiguous,' 'Hard to Classify,' or 'Not Codable.' Despite these coding rules, the characterization of interpenetrating traditions in Figures 10.1 and 10.2 should not be forgotten. Each of these three major approaches can be found in the others. Thus dialectical perspectives have informed traditional, historical approaches (A3), realism has re-emerged in contemporary behavioralism (B1), and internationalism is present in some dialectical approaches (C1).

When all of the required items on all of these 17 reading lists are coded and arbitrarily assigned an equal weight, our vision of the rather parochial character of American international relations teaching is corroborated. Of the 826 items assigned on these 17 lists, 792 can be coded as traditional, behavioral, or dialectical. Of that number, 553 (70%) are in the behavioral tradition, and the overwhelming majority of those items (357 of 553, or 72%) can be described as neo-realist. Slightly more than 20% (or 164) of the items assigned are from traditional approaches. Again, the overwhelming number of traditional citations (134 of 164, or 82%) are from the dominant realist variant of the approach. Only 75 of the 792 items assigned, or less than 10%, are from a dialectical tradition. And many of those (43%) are non-Marxist. If we were to exclude our own reading lists from these computations, both of which make deliberate efforts to assign items employing a dialectical mode of analysis and which contain surprisingly few overlapping items, an even more parochial and narrow picture of American international relations would emerge.

Table 10.1 Coding scheme for classification of syllabus items

Approach	Helpful distinctions and emphases	Exemplary work
A. Traditional approaches		
1. Realism*	State-centric; power politics; balance of power; conflictual relations; diplomatic history	Morgenthau, *Politics Among Nations*
2. Idealism⁻	International law; international organization and cooperation; normative, prescriptive tone	Falk, *A Study of Future Worlds*
3. Dialectical	Use of dialectical perspective to understand a specific historical period where the period (and not method) is the central focus	Barraclough, *An Introduction to Contemporary History*
B. Behavioral approaches		
1. Neo-realism	Develop and test general theories of war and conflict; state-centric	Waltz, *Theory of International Politics*
2. Liberal-internationalism	Interdependence; integration; regimes; non-military aspects of IR; multiple actors; emphasize cooperation and common interests	Keohane and Nye, *Power and Interdependence*
3. Radical transnationalism	Test radical critiques of liberal or realist theories; study imperialism, dominance, dependency	Choucri and North, *Nations in Conflict*

C. Dialectical approaches		
1. Contextual nationalism	Recent Marxist theories sensitive to local context; dependency; the 'Monthly Review – school'	Cardoso and Faletto, *Dependency and Development in Latin America*
2. Proletarian internationalism	Classical Marxist approach to imperialism and revolution; the 'New Left Review school'	Lenin, *Imperialism*
3. Non-Marxist dialectics	Does not use dialectical materialism, but employs a dialectical approach; emphasizes internal conflict and internal sources of change; focuses on multiple interpretations of reality; also cross-paradigm syntheses	Galtung, *The True Worlds*
D. Other	Excluded because hard to classify, ambiguous or not codable	

* The first variant within each tradition (A1, B1, C1) is the one we expect to find dominant in US syllabuses from the 1980s.

⁻ The first and second variants (A1 and A2, B1 and B2, C1 and C2) define the principal contradiction within each tradition.

Aggregate results provide useful summaries of interesting phenomena but inevitably lose much interesting information. A more revealing picture is obtained when individual reading lists are separately coded. Thus, Falk's codable, assigned syllabus items are remarkably traditional (59%) and dialectical (29%), at the expense of very little behavioral coverage (12%). The internationalizing experience of the World Order Models Project is evident. By contrast, Starr's readings are 7% traditional, 92% behavioral, and 1% dialectical. Similar percentages can be calculated for each course.

In the interests of a comprehensive visual summary of these data, we have constructed an equilateral triangle (Figure 10.3) in which each course syllabus can be positioned on the basis of these percentages. Each vertex represents an entirely parochial course list, with 100% of its items from a single tradition and 0% attention to the other two major approaches. Each actual course becomes a point whose projections on the three axes of Figure 10.3 indicate its percent traditional, percent behavioral and percent dialectical coverage. Thus, for example, Falk's course described above is located by a point which defines the intersections of three lines: one drawn perpendicular to the traditional axis (vertical in Figure 10.3) 59% of the way from the base line at point F to point A, a second line drawn perpendicular to the behavioral axis 12% from point D to point B, and a third line drawn perpendicular to the dialectical axis 29% of the way from point E to point C. Since Figure 10.3 is an equilateral triangle and all the percentages add up to 100%, any two lines actually determine the course point.

Consequent to our earlier stated beliefs concerning the pervasiveness and the potential of each of these approaches, at least when appropriately confronted, we have not taken sides in choosing this operationalization of 'parochialism.' Fortunately there are no courses that are entirely parochial, although those analysed from Starr, Russett, plus Krasner and Stein are noticeably close to being so.[19]

A completely non-parochial course, one with one-third traditional, one-third behavioral, and one-third dialectical reading list items would be found by the true archeological

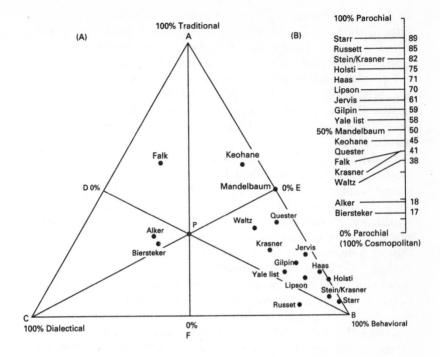

Figure 10.3   The distribution of American international
relations theory courses in the global interdiscipline

mystic located deep inside our pyramid, where its axes *AF*,
BD and *CE* intersect. This is the *point P, the point of complete cosmopolitanism, or perfect pluralism.* As the distances
from this point make clear – they are vertically summarized on the right of Figure 10.3 – we practice what we
preach. Our own courses, whose reading lists only partially
overlap, come out much more cosmopolitan than our peers'.
Some distance away in a more parochial direction we find
Waltz, Krasner and Falk to be only moderately cosmopolitan.

Figure 10.3 suggests a good deal about the nature, the
direction, and the magnitude of the parochialism present
in the current teaching of international relations in the United
States. First, there is an obvious clustering of courses predominantly behavioral in orientation (located in the quad-
rilateral *PFBE*). 13 of the 17 courses examined are located

in this area. Second, if there is any consideration of another approach it is likely to be citation of traditional works. Thus with the exception of Russett (who interestingly requires more dialectical than traditional readings), all of the predominantly behavioral lists deviate only slightly from a single one of the three previously identified axes of debate – that of pitting traditionalism vs. behavioral science, as exemplified in the famous exchange between Bull and Kaplan.[20]

It should now be more evident that little serious attention is paid to scholarship from a dialectical tradition in most American teaching of international relations. But is this necessarily a bad thing? Why should a pluralism of traditions be preferred, why even try to approximate 'arbitrary' quotas on the number of items cited in a course syllabus? Behavioralists and traditionalists prefer the poles they belong to; Marxists have readily available putdowns of 'eclecticism'. We think a more theoretically cosmopolitan approach, one which gives serious consideration to each of the major competing traditions, is essential. There are large parts of the world where, in some form, each of these traditions is the dominant form of analysis and self-understanding practiced by serious international scholars. As we have already argued, their oppositions and interpenetrations make up both the substance and the promise of a truly global 'interdiscipline' of international relations.

AN IMPORTANT CASE: WALTZ'S THEORY TEXT

Let us get more concrete and consider some of the consequences of not giving serious consideration to competing traditions. We have chosen to examine in some detail the most widely cited general theory of international relations text on the 17 lists we analyzed: Waltz's *Theory of International Politics*.[21] Waltz's text not only reflects the behavioral parochialism observed in the American international relations syllabuses already examined, but it also reveals the consequences of that parochialism: specifically, an inability to contribute to interdisciplinary knowledge cumulation across dialectical and behavioral approaches.

Waltz's course list received a moderate cosmopolitan score of 62% in Figure 10.3. But his reading assignments more equally treat traditional (37%) and behavioral (53%) writers than they do dialectical writers (only 10%). The same, rather abbreviated treatment, with little attention to the development and internal structure of the radical dialectical tradition occurs in his text.

Waltz's approach is clearly neo-realistic behavioralism, as we have described it: His conception of theory building and hypothesis testing is largely logical empiricist. A search for 'value free' timeless laws is proposed with Olympian detachment. As we shall see below, Waltz finds Marxist arguments deficient in these terms, but the underlying epistemology and ontology of social change is really the issue.

Waltz's main treatment of the dialectical tradition comes in his second, preliminary chapter on 'reductionist theories'. Claiming he can largely ignore more recent work on theories of economic imperialism because the earlier work of Hobson-Lenin is the 'best', i.e. the 'most elegant and powerful' theory of its kind, Waltz treats Hobson and Lenin as 'highly similar and largely compatible.' Only much later in the chapter is there a fairly cursory treatment of several other modern dialectical writers (Baran, Wallerstein, Galtung, Sweezy, and Magdoff among them), who are dismissed for defensively redefining imperialism in order to try to save the 'Hobson–Lenin' theory.

Waltz fails to recognize the existence of dialectical knowledge-cumulating traditions, as well as their involvement in the learning that has taken place across the poles of Figure 10.1. Globally important past achievements and interdisciplinary cumulative prospects are ignored, at least as far as dialectical approaches are concerned. For example, functional differentiations among units, i.e. economic roles in a global political economy (a major area of Marxist research) can be ignored, we are told by Waltz, because states try to be economically self-sufficient.

Moreover, contrary to Waltz's view, Lenin is not the best theorist of imperialism. Writing within the Marxist tradition, Emmanuel[22] and Cardoso[23] have clearly improved on some of Lenin's arguments concerning net capital flows to and from colonial and neo-colonial territories. Were Waltz more knowledgeable, he could have noted that sophisticated Marxists like Gramsci[24], Cardoso and Faletto[25], and Anderson[26] have accepted as valid some version of the criticisms by Schumpeter[27] about an anachronistic presence of feudal/absolutist elements in the war machinery of 20th-century power. There is genuine cross-tradition knowledge cumulation here, but Waltz makes no mention of it. Perhaps also as a consequence of his joining together Hobson and Lenin, Waltz makes very little mention of the essential, stage-defining role of the qualitative change from competitive industrial capitalism to monopolistic finance capital, a key dialectical conception explicitly and cumulatively borrowed by Lenin from Hilferding[28], and dependent for its force on Marx's even earlier theoretical arguments about the inherent tendencies towards the concentration of capital.

Waltz's concatenation of Hobson and Lenin confuses fundamental differences in approaches as well as different philosophies of social science. Hobson emphasizes the priority of underconsumption as a cause of imperialism (its 'economic taproot'), while Lenin stresses the concentrating effects of export-oriented finance capital. As a liberal reformer, Hobson saw the possibility of a peaceful change in imperialism, thought of only as a social policy; Lenin saw imperialism as an inherently war prone multi-level system, a stage in the transformative development of the world capitalist system. Waltz misses how Lenin creatively, i.e. cumulatively, integrated Hobson's *descriptions* into his own dialectical, essentialist *definitions* of a transitional stage in the world capitalist system.

When it comes to testing Lenin's ideas empirically, Waltz is epistemologically blinded to the real issues in knowledge cumulation they present. Hence, his negative conclusions concerning Lenin's work and the tradition it is used to exemplify are suspect. Waltz repeatedly lectures his readers (including any possible devotees of Lenin or Hobson) that imperialism is 'at least as old as recorded history', essentially 'the imperialism of great power'.[29] So from his Newtonian perspective he has little interest in conceptualizations (like Darwin's, Hegel's or Lenin's) more directly facilitative of fundamental, i.e. structural, change. His response to Lenin's clearly motivated attempt to mobilize and use popular distaste toward *contemporary* imperialism is to belittle the argument 'that the 'new imperialism' was different from the old because of [the current mode of production, finance] capitalism. That there were some differences is of course true, but *theoretically trivial*'.[30]

These matters are far from trivial if one is trying to change the course of history by striking at its exploitative essence. And they are not trivial issues academically, because they separate traditional realism from modern political economy perspectives. Charging Lenin with state-attribute explanatory reductionism (falsely treating capitalism as merely an inner attribute of states) and then treating as trivial the introduction of a non-reductionistic generative, systemic structural concept – a transitional mode of production – produces only a sham victory. Since Waltz goes on to suggest the standard anti-Marxist realist view that 'the organization of the powers of technology on a national scale' and unequal industrial modernization are the true causes of this imperialism,[31] he should know better than to call a statement of the central issues involved 'trivial.' Reductionistically failing to mention even the possibility that different modes of production *might* have important structural effects also reveals a characteristic misreading by behavioralists of dialectical writings about essences and internal relations.[32]

Since Lenin goes to considerable effort to identify the essential features of imperialism, e.g. the emergence of finance capital, the increased export of capital, the formation of capitalist monopolies, sharing the world among them, and *the territorial division and redivision of the world among the greatest capitalist powers*, he is clearly not treating capitalism reductionistically, merely as an internal national attribute. Nor is the new imperialism a national *policy* unilaterally and uniquely caused by the export of surplus capital. Yet Waltz falsely accuses him (or the 'Hobson–Lenin theory') of making these mistakes.

Moreover, Lenin's text admits some version of the realists' argument and gives a response to it that Waltz ignores:

Relations of this kind ['protectorates,' 'commercial advantages, preferential imports of goods, and . . . of capital . . ., etc.'] *have always existed between big and little states.*

But during the period of capitalist imperialism they become a general system, they form part of the process of 'dividing the world;' they become a link in the chain of operations of world finance capital.[33]

Interdisciplinary cumulation fails when Waltz ignores this and other subsumptive, non-reductionistic, constructive critiques by earlier dialectical systems theorists of the realist view.

Lenin's search for the right meld of 'essential' or 'characteristic' features of a particular phase of capitalism clearly assumes the existence of changing, generative essences within social and political relationships, which we ought to try more concretely to define, admitting that all such definitions can only relatively or conditionally catch 'all the concatenations of a phenomenon in its complete development'.[34] If Waltz were to acknowledge at the beginning of his critical discussion that dialectical perspectives frequently and reasonably regard changing empirical relationships like capital flows as *phenomenal* manifestations of contradictory systemic *essences*, he would be logically forced to resolve a number of ontologically complex methodological issues as well as debatable presuppositions of the behavioral approach *before* proceeding to relevant criticisms and empirical tests of Lenin's work and the alternative research programs or paradigms it has inspired.

Finally, the importance of political orientation, intended audience, and practical context for Lenin's time-specific arguments must be noted, since it suggests different standards of scientific assessment, or at least different priorities as to their importance, can be found in the major approaches to international scholarship. Lenin was primarily seeking to develop and convey practical understanding, not merely disinterested scientific 'generalizations.' He was writing from exile in Switzerland for both disaffected activists and the popular classes, with one eye on the censors – a reason for his use of respectable 'bourgeois' writers like Hobson that his detractors rarely mention – and another on his competition in the Socialist movement, in particular Kautsky, another scholarly Marxist, a leading theoretician of the Second International.

Given the avowed intent to popularize certain key Marxist–Leninist ideas – in particular to motivate and mobilize popular understanding of World War I in terms of bloody intra-class conflict rather than inter-national conflict – should not the main criteria for judging the truth of Lenin's account refer to the positively or negatively evaluated '*possible*,' within particular contexts, not just the '*probable*' (in Wright's or Waltz's language)?[35] How successful, *relative to other political writers*, was Lenin in conveying to exploited and discontented Russians (his primary but not exclusively intended audience) the politically significant essence of (or revolutionary opportunity presented by) the great war?

We conclude, therefore, that Waltz has failed to judge theories of imperialism adequately. Not only does he fail to apply his own criteria and use 'the definition of terms found in the theory under test',[36] but he has also ignored the larger issues of epistemology and context-specific practical theorizing that are at the core of the behavioral-dialectical dialogue in the emergent interdiscipline of international relations.

SOME GUIDELINES FOR FUTURE WORK

The dialectical tradition stresses the paradoxical claim of the unity of opposites. Above, we have argued for the unity of the interdiscipline of international relations in terms of its inter-penetrating, but opposed approaches to knowledge cumulation, and in terms of the partly realized potential that exists for generating knowledge through genuine interdisciplinary debates. In terms of this interdisciplinary ideal, we indicated the extent of parochialism in the teaching of international relations in the United States and some of the consequences that parochialism has had for theory description and theory development. Let us conclude, therefore, by trying to summarize the conclusions of our historical, conceptual and critical analyses in more positive terms. These guidelines should not be carelessly detached from the context of their invocation.

1. Surely we have emphasized by our table, figures and illustrative arguments that *at least three alternative approaches to International Relations theorizing (traditional, behavioral and dialectical) should be taken seriously*. Although we could have given our own criticisms of the Marxian dialectical approach, it appeared more appropriate at this juncture to argue that *both* recent dialectical *and* behavioral approaches to international relations derive from *modern social scientific research traditions*. This statement suggests five important comments. First, it presupposes that *any* research approach or tradition is at best arguably legitimate, the subject of serious critiques. Second, any approach or tradition can be subject to cheap put-downs or sham victories ('bourgeois science' or 'reductionist theory') by the cavalier projection of concepts and standards of evaluation a theory was not designed originally to meet. Third, there are genuine insights to be gained from any of the major traditions which are hard to appreciate until their vantage points and learned achievements are better understood. Fourth, neither modern dialectical nor behavioral approaches should be content with the positivist canons of inquiry regularly attributed to Russellian logic, conventional statistical procedures or the physical sciences. And finally, even if and when there are marked differences in scholarly openness to debates among these traditions, no research context is or can be totally free of relevant *and* biasing influences on truth seeking. Much, therefore, can be learned from attempts to achieve free, rational agreement among scholars from such different traditions. This leads directly to our second guideline.

2. Even if sometimes fortuitous, *real scientific universalism must be a skilled human achievement*. It is not the unreflective presupposition of liberal behavioral research. Across the major political, economic and cultural divisions of the present day nothing appears to come easily. The standard of partial convergence across approaches, paradigms, or research programs carefully built up from genuine cross-paradigm communalities is a slow and arduous one to apply. But given the essentially contested status of both the theory and practice of world politics,

we think it an important road toward greater truth. Much of the best empirical and theoretical work in international relations has come as a result of genuine cross-paradigmatic fertilization, leavened by changing international realities.

For example, one of the most widely shared consequences of behavioral and radical critiques of classical (or mathematically reformulated) power-balancing theory is the recognition that rapid technological development, total ideologies, and the highly mobilized mass politics of the twentieth century militate against traditional power balancing state behavior, especially the rule against eliminating major actors. For those not familiar with the pioneering behavioralist discussions by Lasswell[37] and Wright[38] written before World War II, the atomic bombing of Japan and the dismemberment of Germany should have revealed the obsolescence of the classic realist theory. In various ways Morgenthau, Herz and Hoffmann have accepted these arguments from their behavioral critics and others. Hence, cumulative learning of the sort indicated in Figure 10.2 has occurred.

Similarly, consider the Schumpeter versus Lenin 'debate' on imperialism. Properly understood, this ongoing exchange of views conveys a number of important insights about the changing role of the modern state, as well as important cautions about the ways in which serious international relations research programs can start from very different core conceptions of imperialism. We can cite additional positive accomplishments recognizable in these terms without repeating the other examples provided in Figure 10.2. Discussions of levels of analysis problems by Waltz and Singer in the behavioral tradition parallel clarifications of similar ideas developed by Marxian writers on the structural determinants of stability and transformation in domestic and international systems.[39] Finally, significant gains in knowledge are attributable to a research program on lateral pressure theory[40] designed to mediate across realist, communitarian and Marxist conceptions of imperialism.

3. We have argued for an increase in *international savoir faire*, the ability rationally and persuasively to navigate

one's scientific investigations across and through a variety of paradigmatic contexts. Learning from the heavy use and abuse of behavioral research in the Vietnam era, American behavioralists should move to context-wise stage of political self-understanding, if they have not already done so. And as a result of the dependency debates, they should have the sophistication to recognize that epistemological orientations really differ among serious theorists, and are not reducible to self-serving apologetics. To ignore such differences, or judge one's own context as the only situation capable of sustaining scientific work is both self-serving and self-defeating in the long run. It ignores the dialectical interpenetration of the opposed poles of Figure 10.1. Moreover, *major ongoing research approaches in international relations can be more fully understood as composed from the transformative intersection of general political orientations and different cumulation-oriented epistemologies.*

We believe it is not only possible but illuminating to try to systematize certain elements of the international savoir faire that we have frequently found lacking in American international relations research. We propose to treat each of the nine positions identified originally as our coding scheme in Table 10.1 as characteristically dominated (1) by dynamically defined radical/Marxist, liberal internationalist or conservative political orientations, which are (2) selectively combined with modern dialectical, analytical-empirical or traditional (primarily historical) epistemological perspectives. Defined in terms of such a transformative intersection [symbolized by a circled ampersand], Figure 10.4 suggests two principal sources for each of these nine positions.

Like other of its critics from the right or left, we have repeatedly suggested that behavioral international relations studies in the 1960s and early 1970s were on the whole best understood as attempting to combine liberal internationalist values and a naturalistic philosophy of science. The very evident coincidence of conservative and traditional realist perspectives in many older State Department careerists (identified as approach A1 in Table 10.1) suggests another resonance of political orientation

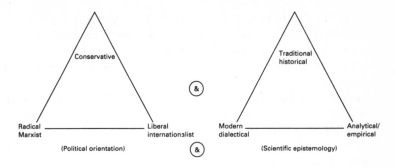

Figure 10.4   A generative basis for the nine approaches of
Table 10.1

and scientific epistemology, a resonance which should
not be confused, however, with the recent rise of behavioral neo-realism (identified as B1 in Table 10.1). Nor
should the possibility of dialectical conservatism (represented by contextual nationalists, C2 in Table 10.1)
be excluded. Radical modes of both traditional and
behavioral scholarship have also been visible (identified
as A3 and B3 respectively). Reflecting on the synthetic
pluralism or cosmopolitan internationalism of our own
concerns, one might view this article as the product of
a dialectical epistemology and a liberal internationalist
orientation (C3 in Table 10.1).

The relationships between political orientation and scientific epistemology implied by Figure 10.4 are not supposed
to be timeless, unchanging truths. Our examination of
American international relations syllabuses – in particular
the current prominence of writings by Waltz, Morgenthau
and Kaplan – suggests that the dominant orientation may
be changing. Specifically, the realist (or neo-realist) perspective appears to have replaced the liberal internationalist political orientation (symbolized by Keohane and
Nye's popular study) we believe earlier to have been
dominant. The broadly logical positivist, analytical-empirical or 'logical empiricist' philosophy of science[41] of
most American behavioralist scholars has not changed,
however, although less exclusively positivistic perspectives, like that of Dougherty and Pfaltzgraff can be seen.

This change can be dynamically interpreted as the result of a shift toward more conservative political orientations and a renewed interest in alternative epistemologies. Like shifts in the Soviet Union during the Khrushchev and Brezhnev eras, this change is clearly linked to its domestic (in this case American) political context. Where has the main impetus for research on 'global interdependence' gone? Waltz gives many arguments against this conception, but it has largely disappeared for the conservative political reason that such thinking does not fit the more aggressively capitalist rhetoric and practice of the Reagan era. Real knowledge cumulation in our contemporary environment requires an international *savoir faire* that incorporates a broader and deeper kind of political and epistemological self-consciousness.

4. Our international explorations and historical reflections reinforce what many historical sociologists of knowledge would suggest: the importance of specifying and clarifying the value bases, driving interests, historical backgrounds, generative and interpretive meaning scripts, purposes, audiences and domains of intended application for any theorist being seriously reviewed. Lasswell[42] would say that it is appropriate to make a multi-valued configurative analysis of each theorist's concrete situation. To put it differently, *develop, use and teach the importance of contextual sensitivity in cumulation-oriented theoretical work.* This injunction is not to be taken as a denial of all universalistic goals; rather it is a mandate to find unifying principles of action within different contexts.

There are a variety of social and intellectual interests found in and around the research situation of the serious international relations scholar. Our brief discussion of the historical and national context of alternative approaches to international relations theorizing suggests the deep connections between the social and political contexts of particular theoretical enterprises and the kind of work actually done. Two global superpowers both able to destroy each other, but likely to self-destruct in the same process, are likely to have scholars especially interested in 'global interdependence' or 'peaceful coexistence.' Anti-colonial revolutionaries in relatively undeveloped countries are driven by other practical imperatives. Successful scholars from the most highly penetrated peripheries of world power contests, as well as those identifying with especially diverse multinational constituencies, need to demonstrate appropriate contextual sensitivities.

But is not the implication of this realization that future theory building should be much more context-sensitive in the statement of its main arguments? Waltz's highly abstract discussions of the age-old 'imperialism of great power' and of bipolar and multipolar international systems, whose stability is seen in terms of decades or centuries, ignore the contexts in which both his and rival theoretical explanations have emerged. The 20th century without Fascism, Soviet Socialism, Maoism and US hegemonial Liberalism is conceptualized at such a high level of abstraction that we are in danger of having thrown out the essential political-economic features of contemporary world history. The impulse to grand theorizing with timeless and universal concepts (and the reductionism that invariably accompanies it) must be corrected by a greater degree of contextual self-awareness on the part of those making such efforts.

5. *Our last guideline is a call for greater dialectical sensitivity concerning one's own research situation, combined with humility and openness in theory development.* We should begin by recognizing that being at the center of the Anglo – American world is not a sufficient condition for good theorizing – it may even be a positive hindrance in the discussion of central 20th-century phenomena such as imperialism and dependency. We have found the best approximation to genuine debates among traditional, behavioral and dialectical approaches to occur more often in or across the highly penetrated and contested arenas of the globe, such as Allende's Chile, a divided Berlin, or Beirut. But we would also agree that some of the most insightful writers we have seen in Kornberg's compilation of course lists are American scholars who have richly benefitted from serious emersions in alternative, competing perspectives on world affairs.

This means our call for the dialectical virtues of humility and openness need not necessarily be in vain. These virtues are especially relevant, and of demonstrated value, for citizens of a declining world power. Neither the reactionary realism of the New Right here and abroad, nor the hegemonial nostalgia of behavioral liberals with their interest in international regimes are adequate. Being open and humble allows for adaptive development, not reactive stagnation.

Notes

1. An earlier version of this paper was given at the Annual Meeting of the American Political Science Association, Denver, September, 1982. It is part of a larger project which we share with Ijaz Gilani and Takashi Inoguchi. The research assistance of Paul Huth and Susumu Yamakage is gratefully acknowledged, as well as insights suggested by many commentators and anonymous reviewers of earlier drafts.
2. M. Foucault, *The Order of Things: An Archeology of the Human Sciences* (New York: Pantheon, 1970); *Power/Knowledge: Selected Interviews, Other Writings, 1972–1977* (New York: Pantheon, 1980); *The Archeology of Knowledge* (New York: Pantheon, 1982).
3. Beyond this brief characterization of synthetic dialectics and that of the other dialectical approaches in Table 10.1 below, we refer the reader to Alker (1981 and 1982) for a more extensive, but not definitive treatment of 'logical positivism', 'dialectical hermeneutics,' 'analytical empiricism,' 'logical empiricism, and the related terms that will be used throughout this paper without further explanation.
4. As Budge (1969) wrote some time ago '[a] prolonged study of the religious and mythological texts of ancient Egypt has convinced me of the futility of attempting to reconcile the conflicting beliefs and to harmonize the contradictory statements which are found in them. ... The cult of Osiris, the dead man deified ... were ... of African origin; ... [t]he Followers of Horus, who brought a [more ethereal] solar religion with them into Egypt from the East, never succeeded in dislodging Osiris from his exalted position...' See Also van de Walle (1969: 30ff).
5. S. Brucan, *The Dialectics of World Politics* (New York: Free Press, 1978); Kubálková and A. A. Cruickshank, *Marxism-Leninism and Theory of International Relations.* (London: Routledge and Kegan Paul, 1980); Soviet Political Sciences Association, *Political Sciences Research Methodology*, Problems of the Contemporary World, No. 102. Moscow: 'Social Sciences Today' Editorial Board, USSR Academy of Science, (1982).

6. J. F. Dougherty and R. L. Pfaltzgraff, *Contending Theories of International Relations: A Comprehensive Survey*, 2nd edn (New York: Harper & Row, 1981). On p. 568 they cite Dror's (1969) use of the term. Wright (1955) earlier treated International Relations as a multidisciplinary field.

7. Basically, social contradictions involve social practices with inconsistent organizing principles. An excellent introduction to the dialectical use of the concept of contradictions in an international (and dometic) political context is Mao Tse-Tung (1964). Four additional useful analytical treatments of this concept of contradiction are Rescher (1977), Elster (1978), Giddens (1980), and Wright (1978), as applied by McGowan and Walker (1981). We recognize it as one of the main points of this critical, yet constructive, literature that social contradictions are not the same as logical contradictions (which they may often involve) or social conflicts (which they often engender).

8. A clear exception to the generalizations about realists' definitions of world order alternatives principally in terms of power configurations in Wight (1977). We also find Kaplan's early work on systems theory (1957) and the current work of behavioral neorealists working on regimes not to be guilty of this oversimplification.

9. J. Hobson, *Free Thought in the Social Sciences*, (1926), as discussed by Siegelman in his introduction to the 1962 edition of Hobson's *Imperialism*).

10. J. Galtung, *Methodology and Ideology, Papers on Methodology, Vol. I* (Copenhagen: Christian Ejlers, 1977); *The True Worlds* (New York: Free Press, 1980).

11. S. Hoffmann, 'An American Social Science. International Relations,' *Daedalus* 106: 41–60 1977, p. 45; R. K. Ashley, 'World Modeling and Its Politics'. *International Organization* 37 (1983), pp. 495–535.

12. K. W. Deutsch, *The Analysis of International Relations* (Englewood Cliffs, NJ: Prentice-Hall, 1968).

13. See Caporaso (1974), Duvall and Russett (1976), and Cardoso (1977) for an early exchange. In the perspective of the present article, our current judgment of the debate is that paradigm-like near incommensurabilities are a major stumbling block for most of those trained only in behavioral methodology and logical-empiricist epistemology. See Biersteker (1978) for an early attempt to recognize and deal with the incommensurability problem, and further discussions of these issues in Alker (forthcoming).

14. Although our argument about the parochialism of American international relations theory teaching owes something to Hoffmann's frequently insightful discussions (1977), it differs in several important respects. First, he has an earlier and more dismal view of international relations abroad (especially the dialectical tradition). Secondly, Hoffmann details ways in which the 'sea change' (migration) of a generation of European scholars, like himself, has leavened 'the frequently parochial American social science' (Hoffmann, 1977: 47). While we agree, we see many of those historically well informed

scholars as now or soon retiring from the scene. Thirdly, we applaud his characterization of the Applied Enlightenment quoted above, but we ask that Marxian optimism in this regard also be given its due, and that the basically conservative orientation of much American neo-realism since the 1970s also be acknowledged.

15. It is probably true that more attention is paid to dialectical scholarship in international political economy courses, and therefore in the curriculum as a whole. However, even in those courses it has been our frequent discovery that most of the attention is focused on debates within the behavioral tradition (on regimes or between interdependence and neo-mercantilism) rather than on theoretical developments within neo-Marxist scholarship or ongoing debates between dialectical and behavioral writers.

16. A. Kornberg, (ed.) *Political Science Reading Lists and Course Outlines, Vol. 5: Theories of International Relations* (Durham: Eno River Press, 1981).

17. In the course lists we selected from the Kornberg collection, Waltz's was the most widely used general theory book. Citation frequencies in this set of lists are:

General works	Specialized works
Waltz, *Theory of International Politics* (5)	Keohane and Nye, *Power and Interdependence* (9)
Kaplan, *System and Process in International Politics* (4)	Waltz, *Man, the State and War* (5)
Morgenthau, *Politics Among Nations* (4)	Jervis, *Perception and Misperception in International Politics* (4)
Rosenau, *International Politics and Foreign Policy* (4)	Hartz, *The Liberal Tradition in America* (3)
Dougherty and Pfaltzgraff, *Contending Theories of International Relations* (3)	Snyder and Diesing, *Conflict, Among Nations* (3)
Holsti, *International Politics* (2)	
Aron, *Peace and War* (2)	

18. Biersteker was asked to submit this syllabus for the Kornberg collection.

19. This independently arrived at result thus partially confirms Krippendorf's concluding observation in his recent review (1982) of Russett and Starr's *World Politics: The Menu For Choice*. Krippendorf assails ' . . . the pragmatic provincialism of so many of our American colleagues in the realm of ideas,' which is perhaps a 'corollary of . . . the arrogance of power'. We find Russett's distinction between *disciplinary* parochialism and *paradigmatic* parochialism (in a recent personal communication) quite helpful. See also Russett and Starr (1982). Although we see Russett and Starr as evidencing all three of the variants of the behavioral approach noted in Table 10.1, they do so with a common analytical-empirical epistemology. This allows them to be exceptionally inter-disciplinary in the multiple levels of analysis they address, while at the same time avoiding the

epistemological dimensions of controversy at the center of the global interdiscipline.

20. H. Bull, 'International Theory, The Case for a Classical Approach.' *World Politics* 21 (1966), pp. 361–377; M. Kaplan, 'The New Great Debate: Traditionalism vs. Science in International Relations.' *World Politics* XIX: 1–20 (1966); Sullivan's work summarized in Alker and Bock, 'Propositions about International Relations,' in James Robinson (ed.), *Political Science Annual* Vol. 2, Indianapolis: Bobbs-Merrill, (1972) and S. Bremer 'Machiavelli in Machina: Or Politics among Hexagons,' in K. W. Deutsch, B. Fritsch, H. Jaguaribe and A. Markovits (eds.) *Problems of World Modeling* (Cambridge: Ballinger, 1977); and, from the traditional side, Wights's excellent books.

21. Recall the frequency distribution of general theory texts in note 9.

22. A. Emmanuel, *Unequal Exchange* (New York: Monthly Review Press, 1972).

23. F. H. Cardoso, 'Imperialism and Dependency in Latin America,' in Frank Bonilla and Robert Girling (eds.) *Structures of Dependency* (Stanford: Institute of Political Studies, Stanford University, 1973); 'The Consumption of Dependency Theory in the United States', *Latin American Research Review* 12: 7–24, 1977.

24. A. Gramsci, *Selections from the Prison Notebooks.* Edited by Quintin Hoare and Nowell Smith (1971) (New York: International Publishers, 1935).

25. F. H. Cardoso and E. Faletto, *Dependency and Development in Latin America* (Berkeley: University of California Press, 1978).

26. P. Anderson, *Lineages of the Absolutist State* (London: New Left Books, 1974).

27. J. Schumpeter, *Imperialism and Social Classes,* translated by Heinz Norden 1955 (New York: Meridian Books, 1927).

28. R. Hilferding, *Finance Capital.* Translated by T. Bottomore (1981) (London: Routledge and Kegan Paul, 1910).

29. K. N. Waltz, *Theory of International Politics* (Reading, Mass. Addison-Wesley, 1979), pp. 25, 26.

30. K. N. Waltz, *Man, The State, and War.* (New York: Columbia University Press, 1954), p. 25n.

31. K. N. Waltz, *Man, The State, and War* (New York: Columbia University Press, 1954), p. 25.

32. B. Ollman, *Alienation: Marx's Concept of Man in Capitalist Society.* (New York: Cambridge University Press, 1971).

33. V. I. Lenin, *Imperialism* (Moscow: Progress Publishers (1939), 1916), p. 86.

34. Good discussions of this style of defining things are found in Copi (1982).

35. Wright (1955) distinguishes formulative truths (scientists' probabilities) from incitive truths (practitioner's possibilities). He also asserts as goals for international relations convincing and correct evaluative truths, and historically descriptive informative truths. Although they clearly need scholarly reworking, such distinctions

have the merit of delimiting a much broader disciplinary conception than a positivistic focus on explanation and prediction as the only goals for science.

36. K. N. Waltz, *Theory of International Politics* (Reading, Mass. Addison-Wesley, 1979), p. 13.

37. H. D. Lasswell, *World Politics and Personal Insecurity*, reprinted in H. D. Lasswell, C. E. Merriam and T. V. Smith, *A Study of Power* (Glencoe: Free Press (1950), 1934).

38. Q. Wright, *A Study of War* (Chicago: Chicago University Press, 1942).

39. Excellent syntheses of some of these points may be found in Ruggie (1981) and McGowan and Walker (1981).

40. N. Choucri and R. C. North, *Nations in Conflict* (San Francisco: W. H. Freeman, 1975); R. K. Ashley, *The Political Economy of War and Peace* (London: Frances Pinter, 1980).

41. H. R. Alker, Jr., 'Logic, Dialectics and Politics: Some Recent Controversies,' in H. R. Alker, Jr., (ed.), *Dialectical Logics for the Political Sciences*, Poznan Studies in the Philosophy of the Sciences and the Humanities, vol. 7 (Amsterdam: Rodopi, 1982).

42. H. D. Lasswell, *World Politics and Personal Insecurity*, reprinted in H. D. Lasswell, C. E. Merriam and T. V. Smith, *A Study of Power* (Glencoe: Free Press (1950), 1934).

Part IV
Reason and History

11 International Institutions: Two Approaches (1988)*

Robert Keohane

Contemporary world politics is a matter of wealth and poverty, life and death. The members of this Association have chosen to study it because it is so important to our lives and those of other – not because it is either aesthetically attractive or amenable to successful theory-formulation and testing. Indeed, we would be foolish if we studied world politics in search of beauty or lasting truth. Beauty is absent because much that we observe is horrible, and many of the issues that we study involve dilemmas whose contemplation no sane person would find pleasing. Deterministic laws elude us, since we are studying the purposive behavior of relatively small numbers of actors engaged in strategic bargaining. In situations involving strategic bargaining, even formal theories, with highly restrictive assumptions, fail to specify which of many possible equilibrium outcomes will emerge.[1] This suggests that no general theory of international politics may be feasible. It makes sense to seek to develop cumulative verifiable knowledge, but we must understand that we can aspire only to formulate conditional, context-specific generalizations rather than to discover universal laws, and that our understanding of world politics will always be incomplete.

* *International Studies Quarterly*, 32(4) (December), pp. 379–396.

Author's note: This essay was written while the author was a fellow at the Center for Advanced Study in the Behavioral Sciences, 1987–88. I am grateful for financial support to the Social Science Research Council Foreign Policy Program and to National Science Foundation grant #BNS-8700864 to the Center. My colleagues in the institutional theory seminar at the Center provided inspiration, advice, and literature references; and helpful comments on earlier drafts were received from James A. Caporaso, Glenn Carroll, Lawrence Finkelstein, Ernst B. Haas, Peter J. Katzenstein, Nannerl O. Keohane, John Kingdon, Stephen D. Krasner, Douglass C. North, Claus Offe, John Gerard Ruggie, Barry Weingast, and two editors of *International Studies Quarterly*, Richard K. Ashley and Patrick McGowan.

The ways in which members of this Association study international relations are profoundly affected by their values. Most of us are children of the Enlightenment, insofar as we believe that human life can be improved through human action guided by knowledge. We therefore seek knowledge in order to improve the quality of human action. Many of us, myself included, begin with a commitment to promote human progress, defined in terms of the welfare, liberty, and security of individuals, with special attention to principles of justice.[2] With this commitment in mind, we seek to analyze how the legal concept of state sovereignty and the practical fact of substantial state autonomy coexist with the realities of strategic and economic interdependence.

These value commitments help to account for the topic of this essay: the study of international institutions. I focus on institutions because I share K.J. Holsti's desire to 'open intellectual doors to peer in on international collaboration, cooperation, and welfare'.[3] To understand the conditions under which international cooperation can take place, it is necessary to understand how international institutions operate and the conditions under which they come into being. This is not to say that international institutions always facilitate cooperation on a global basis: on the contrary, a variety of international institutions, including most obviously military alliances, are designed as means for prevailing in military and political conflict. Conversely, instances of cooperation can take place with only minimal institutional structures to support them. But all efforts at international cooperation take place within an institutional context of some kind, which may or may not facilitate cooperative endeavors. To understand cooperation and discord better, we need to investigate the sources and nature of international institutions, and how institutional change takes place.

'Cooperation' is a contested term. As I use it, it is sharply distinguished from both harmony and discord. When harmony prevails, actors' policies *automatically* facilitate the attainment of others' goals. When there is discord, actors' policies hinder the realization of others' goals, and are not adjusted to make them more compatible. In both harmony and discord, neither actor has an incentive to change his or her behavior. Cooperation, however, 'requires that the actions of separate individuals or organizations – which are not in pre-existent harmony – be brought into conformity with one another through a process of policy coordination'.[4] This means that when cooperation takes place, each party changes his or her behavior *contingent on* changes in the other's behavior. We can evaluate the impact of cooperation by measuring the difference between the actual outcome and the situation that would have obtained in the absence of coordination: that is, the myopic self-enforcing equilibrium of the game. Genuine cooperation improves the rewards of both players.

International cooperation does not necessarily depend on altruism, idealism, personal honor, common purposes, internalized norms, or a shared belief in a set of values embedded in a culture. At various times and places any of these features of human motivation may indeed play an important role in processes on international cooperation; but cooperation can be understood without reference to any of them. This is not surprising, since international cooperation is not necessarily benign from an ethical standpoint. Rich countries can devise joint actions to extract resources from poor ones, predatory governments can form aggressive alliances, and privileged industries can induce their governments to protect them against competition from more efficient producers abroad. The analysis of international cooperation should not be confused with its celebration. As Hedley Bull said about order, "while order in world politics is something valuable, ... it should not be taken to be a commanding value, and to show that a particular institution or course of action is conducive of order is not to have established a presumption that that institution is desirable or that that course of action should be carried out'.[5]

Cooperation is in a dialectical relationship with discord, and they must be understood together. Thus to understand cooperation, one must also understand the frequent absence of, or failure of, cooperation, so incessantly stressed by realist writers. But our awareness of cooperation's fragility does not require us to accept dogmatic forms of realism, which see international relations as inherently doomed to persistent zero-sum conflict and warfare. As Stanley Hoffmann has put it, realism 'does not, and cannot, prove that one is doomed to repeat the past and that there is no middle ground, however narrow, between the limited and fragile moderation of the past and the impossible abolition of the game'.[6]

Realist and neorealist theories are avowedly rationalistic, accepting what Herbert Simon has referred to as a 'substantive' conception of rationality, characterizing 'behavior that can be adjudged objectively to be optimally adapted to the situation'.[7] But adopting the assumption of substantive rationality does not commit the analyst to gloomy deterministic conclusions about the inevitability of warfare. On the contrary, rationalistic theory can be used to explore the conditions under which cooperation takes place, and it seeks to explain why international institutions are constructed by states.[8]

That rationalistic theory can lead to many different conclusions in international relations reflects a wider indeterminacy of the rationality principle as such. As Simon has argued, the principle of substantive rationality generates hypotheses about actual human behavior only when it is combined with auxiliary assumptions about the structure of utility functions and the formation of expectations. Furthermore, rationality is always contextual, so a great deal depends on the situation posited at the beginning of the analysis. Considerable variation in outcomes is therefore consistent with the assumption of substantive rationality. When limitations on the cognitive capacities of decision-makers are also taken into account – as in the concept of bounded rationality – the range of possible variation expands even further.

Even though the assumption of substantive rationality does not compel a particular set of conclusions about the nature or evolution of international institutions, it has been used in fruitful ways to explain behavior, including institutionalized behavior, in international relations. Its adherents are often highly self-conscious about their analytical perspective, and they have been highly successful in gaining legitimacy for their arguments.

Traditionally counterposed to rationalistic theory is the sociological approach to the study of institutions, which stresses the role of impersonal social forces as well as the impact of cultural practices, norms, and values that are not derived from calculations of interests.[9] Yet the sociological approach has recently been in some disarray, at least in international relations: its adherents have neither the coherence nor the self-confidence of the rationalists. Rather than try in this essay to discuss this diffuse set of views about international relations, I will focus on the work of several scholars with a distinctive and similar point of view who have recently directly challenged the predominant rationalistic analysis of international politics. These authors, of whom the best-known include Hayward Alker, Richard Ashley, Friedrich Kratochwil, and John Ruggie, emphasize the importance of the 'intersubjective meanings' of international institutional activity.[10] In their view, understanding how people think about institutional norms and rules, and the discourse they engage in, is as important in evaluating the significance of these norms as measuring the behavior that changes in response to their invocation.

These writers emphasize that individuals, local organizations, and even states develop within the context of more encompassing institutions. Institutions do not merely reflect the preferences and power of the units constituting them; the institutions themselves shape those preferences and that power. Institutions are therefore *constitutive* of actors as well as vice versa. It is therefore not sufficient in this view to treat the preferences of individuals as given exogenously: they are affected by institutional arrangements, by prevailing norms, and by historically contingent discourse among people seeking to pursue their purposes and solve their self-defined problems.

In order to emphasize the importance of this perspective, and to focus a dialogue with rationalistic theory, I will treat the writers on world politics who have stressed these themes as members of a school of thought. I recognize, of course, that regarding them as members of a group or school obscures the many differences of view among them, and the substantial evolution that has taken place in the thought of each of them. Yet to make my point, I will even give them a label. In choosing such a label, it would be fair to refer to them as 'interpretive' scholars, since they all emphasize the importance of historical and textual interpretation and the limitations of scientific models in studying world politics. But other approaches, such as strongly materialist historical-sociological approaches indebted to Marxism, or political-theoretical arguments emphasizing classical political philosophy or international law, also have a right to be considered interpretive. I have therefore coined a phrase for these writers, calling them 'reflective,' since all of them emphasize the importance of human reflection for the nature of institutions and ultimately for the character of world politics.

My chief argument in this essay is that students of international institutions should direct their attention to the relative merits of two approaches, the rationalistic and the reflective. Until we understand the strengths and weaknesses of each, we will be unable to design research strategies that are sufficiently multifaceted to encompass our subject-matter, and our empirical work will suffer accordingly.

The next section of this essay will define what I mean by 'institutions,' and introduce some distinctions that I hope will help us to understand international institutions better. Defining institutions entails drawing a distinction between specific institutions and the underlying practices within which they are embedded, of which the most fundamental in world politics are those associated with the concept of sovereignty. I will then attempt to evaluate the strengths and weaknesses of the rationalistic approach, taking into account the criticisms put forward by scholars who emphasize how actors are constituted by institutions and how subjective self-awareness of actors, and the ideas at their disposal, shape their activities. Throughout the essay I will emphasize the critical importance, for the further advance of knowledge, of undertaking empirical research, guided by these theoretical ideas. It will not be fruitful, in my view, indefinitely to conduct a debate at the purely theoretical level, much less simply to argue about epistemological and ontological issues in the abstract. Such an argument would take us away from the study of our subject matter, world politics, toward what would probably become an intellectually derivative and programmatically diversionary philosophical discussion.

INTERNATIONAL INSTITUTIONS: DEFINITIONS AND DISTINCTIONS

'Institution' is an even fuzzier concept than cooperation. Institutions are often discussed without being defined at all, or after having been defined only casually. Yet it sometimes seems, as a sociologist lamented half a century ago, that 'the only idea common to all usages of the term 'institution' is that of some sort of establishment of relative permanence of a distinctly social sort'.[11] In the international relations literature, this vagueness persists. We speak of the United Nations and the World Bank (part of the 'United Nations System'), IBM and Exxon, as institutions; but we also consider 'the international monetary regime' and 'the international trade regime' to be institutions. Hedley Bull refers to 'the balance of power, international law, the diplomatic mechanism, the managerial system of the great powers, and war' as 'the institutions of international society'.[12] John Ruggie discusses 'the institutional framework of sovereignty',[13] and Stephen Krasner writes about 'the particular institutional structures of sovereignty'.[14]

It may help in sorting out some of these troubling confusions to point out that 'institution' may refer to a *general pattern or categorization* of activity or to a *particular* human-constructed arrangement, formally or informally organized. Examples of institutions as general patterns include Bull's 'institutions of international society,' as well as such varied patterns of behavior as marriage and religion, sovereign statehood, diplomacy, and neutrality. Sometimes norms such as that of reciprocity, which can apply to a variety of situations, are referred to as institutions. When we speak of patterns or categorizations of activity as institutions, the particular instances are often not regarded themselves as institutions: we do not speak of the marriage of the Duke and Duchess of Windsor, international negotiations over the status of the Panama Canal, or the neutrality of Sweden in World War II as institutions. What these general patterns of activity have in common with specific institutions is that they both meet the criteria for a broad definition of institutions: both involve persistent and connected sets of rules (formal or informal) that prescribe behavioral roles, constrain activity, and shape expectations.

Specific institutions, such as the French state, the Roman Catholic church, the international non-proliferation regime, or the General Agreement on Tariffs and Trade, are discrete entities, identifiable in space and time. Specific institutions may be exemplars of general patterns of activity – the United Nations exemplifies multilateral diplomacy; the French state, sovereign statehood; the Roman Catholic church, organized religion. But unlike general patterns of activity, specific institutions have unique life-histories, which depend on the decisions of particular individuals.

General patterns of 'institutionalized' activity are more heterogeneous. Some of these institutions are only sets of entities, with each member of the set being an institution. Bull's institution of international law, for instance, can be seen as including a variety of institutions codified in legal form. In this sense, all formal international regimes are parts of international law, as are formal bilateral treaties and conventions. Likewise, the institution of religion includes a variety of quite different specific institutions, including the Roman Catholic church, Islam, and Congregationalism. Other general patterns of activity can be seen as norms that are applicable to a wide variety of situations, such as the norm of reciprocity.[15]

It is difficult to work analytically with the broad ordinary-language definition of institutions with which I have started, since it includes such a variety of different entities and activities. In the rest of this essay, therefore, I will focus on institutions that can be identified as related complexes of rules and norms, identifiable in space and time. This conception of the scope of my analytical enterprise deliberately omits institutions that are merely categories of activity, as well as general norms that can be attached to any of a number of rule-complexes. It allows me to focus on *specific institutions* and on *practices*. As explained below, it is the mark of a practice that the behavior of those engaged in it can be corrected by an appeal to its own rules. This means that practices are deeply embedded – highly institutionalized in the sociological sense of being taken for granted by participants as social facts that are not to be challenged although their implications for behavior can be explicated.

Specific institutions can be defined in terms of their rules. Douglass North[16] defines institutions as 'rules, enforcement characteristics of rules, and norms of behavior that structure repeated human interaction.' Institutions can be seen as 'frozen decisions,' or 'history encoded into rules'[17]. These rules may be informal or implicit rather than codified: in fact, some very strong institutions, such as the British constitution, rely principally on unwritten rules. To be institutionalized in the sense in which I will use the term, the rules must be durable, and must prescribe behavioral roles for actors, besides constraining activity and shaping expectations. That is, institutions differentiate among actors according to the roles that they are expected to perform, and institutions can be identified by asking whether patterns of behavior are indeed differentiated by role. When we ask whether X is an institution, we ask whether we can identify persistent sets of rules that constrain activity, shape expectations, and prescribe roles. In international relations, some of these institutions are formal organizations, with prescribed hierarchies and the capacity for purposive action. Others, such as the international regimes for money and trade, are complexes of rules and organizations, the core elements of which have been negotiated and explicitly agreed upon by states.[18]

This definition of specific institutions incorporates what John Rawls has called the 'summary view' of rules, in which 'rules are pictured as summaries of past decisions,' which allow the observer to predict future behavior.[19] Rules such as these can be changed by participants on utilitarian grounds without engaging in self-contradictory behavior. This definition is useful as far as it goes, but it does not capture what Rawls calls 'the practice conception' of rules. A practice in the sense used by Rawls is analogous to a game such as baseball or chess: 'It is the mark of a practice that being taught how to engage in it involves being instructed in the rules that define it, and that appeal is made to those rules to correct the behavior of those engaged in it. Those engaged in a practice recognize the rules as defining it.[20] Were the rules of a practice to change, so would the fundamental nature of the activity in question.

Someone engaged in a practice has to explain her action by showing that it is in accord with the practice. Otherwise, the behavior itself is self-contradictory. As Oran Young points out, 'It just does not make sense for a chess player to refuse to accept the concept of checkmate, for a speaker of English to assert that it makes no difference whether subjects and predicates agree, or for an actor in the existing international society to disregard the rules regarding the nationality of citizens.' In international relations, the 'menu of available practices' is limited: 'a "new" state, for example, has little choice but to join the basic institutional arrangements of the states system'.[21]

The concept of a practice is particularly applicable to certain general patterns of activity such as sovereignty and multilateral diplomacy. Their rules, many of which are not codified, define what it means to be sovereign or to engage in multilateral diplomacy.[22] Like the rules of chess and the grammar of the English language, respect for state sovereignty and multilateral diplomacy are taken for granted by most of those who participate in them. When fundamental practices are violated, as in the seizure of the American Embassy in Teheran in 1979, disapproval is virtually universal. This is not surprising, because such practices are based on what Hans J. Morgenthau referred to as 'the permanent interests of states to put their normal relations on a stable basis by providing for predictable and enforceable conduct with respect to these relations'.[23]

Rawl's distinction helps us to see the specific institutions of world politics, with their challengeable rules, as embedded in more fundamental practices. Just as the actors in world politics are constrained by existing institutions, so are institutions, and prospects for institutional change, constrained by the practices taken for granted by their members. For each set of entities that we investigate, we can identify institutionalized constraints at a more fundamental and enduring level.

Consider, for instance, the practice of sovereign statehood, which has been fundamental to world politics for over three hundred years. At its core is the principle of sovereignty:

that the state 'is subject to no other state and has full and exclusive powers within its jurisdiction without prejudice to the limits set by applicable law' (*Wimbledon* case, Permanent Court of International Justice, series A, no. 1, 1923; cited in Hoffmann).[24] Sovereignty is thus a relatively precise legal concept: a question of law, not of fact, of authority, not sheer power. As a legal concept, the principle of sovereignty should not be confused with the empirical claim that a given state in fact makes its decisions autonomously. Sovereignty refers to a legal status, a property of an organized entity in world politics. It does not imply that the sovereign entity possesses de facto independence, although as a political matter, the fact that an entity is sovereign can be expected to have implications for its power and its autonomy.[25]

Sovereign statehood is a practice in Rawls' sense because it contains a set of rules that define it and that can be used to correct states' behavior. These rules are fundamental to the conduct of modern international relations. Extraterritorial jurisdiction for embassies is such a central rule, implied by the modern conception of sovereignty: immunity from ordinary criminal prosecution for a state's accredited diplomats is a corollary of this principle. More generally, as Martin Wight has argued, the norm of reciprocity is implied by that of sovereignty, and respect for reciprocity is therefore part of the practice of sovereign statehood: 'It would be impossible to have a society of sovereign states unless each state, while claiming sovereignty for itself, recognized that every other state had the right to claim and enjoy its own sovereignty as well. This reciprocity was inherent in the Western conception of sovereignty'.[26]

Treating sovereign statehood as a practice does not imply that the process of recognizing entities as sovereign is automatic: on the contrary, states follow political convenience as well as law in deciding which entities to regard as sovereign. But once an entity has been generally accepted by states as sovereign, certain rights and responsibilities are entailed. Furthermore, acceptance of the principle of sovereignty creates well-defined roles. Only sovereign states or entities such as international organizations created by states can make treaties and enforce them on subjects within their jurisdictions, declare and wage wars recognized by international law, and join international organizations that are part of the United Nations System.

Definitions are not interesting in themselves, but they may be more or less clear, and lead to identification of more or less tractable problems. I have begun with a broad definition of institutions as persistent and connected sets of rules that prescribe behavioral roles, constrain activity, and shape expectations. I have focused my attention, however, on specific institutions and practices. Specific institutions can be defined in the first instance in terms of rules; but we must recognize that specific institutions are embedded in practices. In modern world politics, the most important practice is that of sovereignty. To understand institutions and international change in world politics, it is necessary to understand not only how specific institutions are formulated, change, and die, but how their evolution is affected by the practice of sovereignty.

THE RATIONALISTIC STUDY OF INTERNATIONAL INSTITUTIONS

Rationalistic research on international institutions focuses almost entirely on specific institutions. It emphasizes international regimes and formal international organizations. Since this research program is rooted in exchange theory, it assumes scarcity and competition as well as rationality on the part of the actors. It therefore begins with the premise that if there were no potential gains from agreements to be captured in world politics – that is, if no agreements among actors could be mutually beneficial – there would be no need for specific international institutions. But there are evidently considerable benefits to be secured from mutual agreement – as evidenced for millennia by trade agreements, rules of war, and peace treaties, and for the last century by international organizations. Conversely, if cooperation were easy – that is, if all mutually beneficial bargains could be made without cost – there would be no need for institutions to facilitate cooperation. yet such an assumption would be equally as false as the assumption that no potential gains from agreements exist. It is the combination of the potential *value* of agreements and the *difficulty* of making them that renders international regimes significant. In order to cooperate in world politics on more than a sporadic basis, human beings have to use institutions.

Rationalistic theories of institutions view institutions as affecting patterns of costs. Specifically, institutions reduce certain forms of uncertainty and alter transaction costs: that is, the 'costs of specifying and enforcing the contracts that underlie exchange'.[27] Even in the absence of hierarchical authority, institutions provide information (through monitoring) and stabilize expectations. They may also make decentralized enforcement feasible, for example by creating conditions under which reciprocity can operate.[28] At any point in time, transaction costs are to a substantial degree the result of the institutional context. Dynamically, the relationship between these institutionally affected transaction costs and the formation of new institutions will, according to the theory, be curvilinear. If transaction costs are negligible, it will not be necessary to create new institutions to facilitate mutually beneficial exchange; if transaction costs are extremely high, it will not be feasible to build institutions – which may even be unimaginable.

In world politics, sovereignty and state autonomy mean that transaction costs are never negligible, since it is always difficult to communicate, to monitor performance, and especially to enforce compliance with rules. Therefore, according to this theory, one should expect international institutions to appear whenever the costs of communication, monitoring, and enforcement are relatively low compared to the benefits to be derived from political exchange. Institutions should persist as long as, but only so long as, their members have incentives to maintain them. But the effects of these institutions will not be politically neutral: they can be expected to confer advantages on those to whom their rules grant access and share in political authority; and insofar as the transaction costs of making agreements outside of an established institution are high, governments disadvantaged within an institution will find themselves at a disadvantage in the issue area as a whole. More generally, the rules of any institution will reflect the relative power positions of its actual and potential members, which constrain the feasible bargaining space and affect transaction costs.[29]

These transaction-cost arguments have been applied in qualitative terms to international relations. As anticipated by the theory, effective international regimes include arrangements to share information and to monitor compliance, according to standards established by the regime; and they adapt to shifts in capabilities among their members.[30] Furthermore, the access rules of different international regimes affect the success of governments in the related issue areas.[31] As a general descriptive model, therefore, this approach seems to do quite well: international regimes work as we expect them to.

However, the rationalistic theory has not been used to explain why international institutions exist in some issue areas rather than in others. Nor has this theory been employed systematically to account for the creation or demise of such institutions. Yet the theory implies hypotheses about these questions: hypotheses that could be submitted to systematic, even quantitative, examination. For instance, this theory predicts that the incidence of specific international institutions should be related to the ratio of benefits anticipated from exchange to the transaction costs of establishing the institutions necessary to facilitate the negotiation, monitoring, and enforcement costs of agreements specifying the terms of exchange. It also predicts that in the absence of anticipated gains from agreements, specific institutions will not be created, and that most specific institutions in world politics will in fact perform the function of reducing transaction costs. Since the theory acknowledges the significance of sunk costs in perpetuating extant institutions, and since its advocates recognize that organizational processes modify the pure dictates of rationality,[32] its predictions about the demise of specific institutions are less clear.

The rationalistic theory could also help us develop a theory of compliance or non-compliance with commitments.[33] For international regimes to be effective, their injunctions must be obeyed; yet sovereignty precludes hierarchical enforcement. The game-theoretic literature suggests that reputation may provide a strong incentive for compliance.[34] But we do not know how strong the reputational basis for enforcement of agreements is in world politics, since we have not done the necessary empirical work. What Oliver Williamson calls 'opportunism' is still possible: reputations can be differentiated among partners and violations of agreements can often be concealed. Historically, it is not entirely clear to what extent governments that renege on their commitments are in fact punished for such actions. Indeed, governments that have defaulted on their debts have, it appears, not been punished via higher interest rates in subsequent periods for their defections.[35]

Rationalistic theory can often help us understand the direction of change in world politics, if not always its precise extent or the form that it takes. For instance, there are good reasons to believe that a diffusion of power away from a hegemonic state, which sponsored extant international regimes, will create pressures on these regimes and weaken their rules – even though it is dubious that hegemony is either a necessary or a sufficient condition for the maintenance of a pattern of order in international relations.[36] That is, if we are able to specify the characteristics of a given institutional situation, rationalistic theory may help us anticipate the path that change will take. As Alexander Wendt points out, rationalistic theory has 'proved useful in generating insights into the emergence of and reproduction of social institutions as the unintended consequences of strategic interactions'.[37]

Yet even on its own terms, rationalistic theory encounters some inherent limitations. The so-called Folk Theorem of game theory states that for a class of games that includes 2×2 repeated Prisoner's Dilemma, there are many feasible equilibria above the maximin points of both players.[38] We cannot predict which one will emerge without knowing more about the structure of a situation – that is, about the prior institutional context in which the situation is embedded. This means that the conclusions of formal models of cooperation are often highly dependent on the assumptions with which the investigations begin – that they are context-dependent. To be sure, once we understand the context, it may be possible to model strategies used by players to devise equilibrium-inducing institutions.[39] The literatures on bureaucratic politics and agency theory complicate matters further by suggesting that the organizational 'actor' will not necessarily act as 'its' interests specify, if people within it have different interests.[40] Thus even on its own terms rationalistic theory seems to leave open the issue of what kinds of institutions will develop, to whose benefit, and how effective they will be.

Even within the confines of the rationalistic research program, therefore, formal theory alone is unlikely to yield answers to our explanatory puzzles. Rationalistic theory is good at posing questions and suggesting lines of inquiry, but it does not furnish us with answers.[41] Creative uses of simulation, as in Robert Axelrod's work are helpful;[42] but most of all we need more empirical research, guided by theory. Such research could begin to delineate the specific conditions under which cooperation takes place. It should seek to map out patterns of interests, information flows and barriers, and anticipated long-term relationships in order to understand more specifically under what conditions cooperation will or will not take place. Brent Sutton and Mark Zacher have illustrated the value of such research in their recent analysis of the international shipping regime.[43] They explore in depth six issue-areas within shipping, on the basis of a hypothesis that cooperation will be greatest where market imperfections and failures, hence possibilities for global welfare gains, exist. Unfortunately, there has so far been relatively little of this type of work done; but I hope and expect that we will see more during the next few years.[44]

Rationalistic theory also needs to extend its vision back into history. To do so in a sophisticated way entails a departure from the equilibrium models emphasized by neoclassical economic theory. It requires intellectual contortions to view the evolution of institutions over time as the product of a deterministic equilibrium logic in which rational adaptation to the environment plays the key role. Institutional development is affected by particular leaders and by exogenous shocks – chance events from the perspective of a systemic theory. Theories of 'path-dependence' in economics demonstrate that under specified conditions, accumulated random variations can lead an institution into a state that could have been predicted in advance.[45] From a technological standpoint, path-dependence occurs under conditions of increasing rather than decreasing returns – resulting for instance from positive externalities that give established networks advantages over their competitors, from learning effects, and from the convergence of expectations around an established standard. Examples include the development of the typewriter keyboard, competition between different railroad gauges or between Betamax and VHS types of video recorders, and between gasoline and steam-powered cars. Viewed from a more strictly institutional perspective, path-dependence can be a result of sunk costs. Arthur Stinchcombe[46] points out that if 'sunk costs make a traditional pattern of action cheaper, and if new patterns are not enough more profitable to justify throwing away the resource, the sunk costs tend to preserve a pattern of action from one year to the next.'

Surely the General Agreement on Tariffs and Trade (GATT), the International Monetary Fund (IMF) and the United Nations are not optimally efficient, and they would not be invented in their present forms today; but they persist. In some cases, this may be a matter of sunk costs making it rational to continue involvement with an old institution. Sometimes the increasing returns pointed to by path-dependence theorists may account for this persistence. Or considerations of power and status may be more important than the functions performed by the institutions. In politics, where institutional innovators may be punished, existing institutions may have an additional advantage. Even in Congress, 'it is risky to try to change institutional arrangements in a manner adverse to the interests of those currently in control.'[47] At the very least, theories of path-dependence demonstrate once again that history not only matters, but that historical investigation is consistent with a rationalistic research program.

REFLECTIVE APPROACHES

Scholars imbued with a sociological perspective on institutions emphasize that institutions are often not created consciously by human beings but rather emerge slowly through a less deliberative process, and that they are frequently taken for granted by the people who are affected by them. In this view the assumption of utility maximization often does not tell us much about the origins of institutions; and it also does not take us very far in understanding the variations in institutional arrangements in different cultures and political systems. Ronald Dore, for instance, suggests that Oliver Williamson's attempt to construct 'timeless generalizations' perhaps 'merely reflects the tendency of American economists to write as if all the world were America. Or perhaps [Williamson] does not have much evidence about America either, and just assumes that 'Man' is a hard-nosed short-run profit maximizer suspicious of everyone he deals with'.[48]

Values, norms and practices vary across cultures, and such variations will affect the efficacy of institutional arrangements. This point can be put into the language of rationalistic theory: institutions that are consistent with culturally accepted practices are likely to entail lower transaction costs than those that conflict with those practices. But such a statement merely begs the question of where the practices, or the preferences that they reflect, came from in the first place. The most ambitious form of rationalistic theory, which takes fundamental preferences as uniform and constant, is contradicted by cultural variation if preferences are meaningfully operationalized. The more modest form of this theory, which treats variations in preferences as exogenous, thereby avoids seeking to explain them.

Similar problems arise with explanations of changes in institutions over time. Rationalistic theories of specific institutions can be applied historically, as we have seen. Each set of institutions to be explained is viewed within an institutional as well as material context: prior institutions create incentives and constraints that affect the emergence or evolution of later ones. Change is then explained by changes in opportunity costs at the margin, as a result of environmental changes.

Such an approach has been highly revealing, as the literature on institutional change in economics demonstrates.[49] However, these rationalistic theories of specific institutions have to be contextualized before they are empirically useful: that is, they must be put into a prior framework of institutions and practices. Only with this prior knowledge of the situation at one point in time to guide us, can we use this theory effectively to improve our knowledge of what is likely to happen next. We can then work our way back through the various levels of analysis – explaining actor behavior by reference to institutional constraints and opportunities, explaining specific institutions by reference to prior institutions, explaining those institutions by reference to fundamental practices. Up to a point, rationalistic theory can pursue its analysis backwards in time; and it can only gain by becoming more historically sensitive. But as Field[50] pointed out and as North[51] has recognized in the field of economic history, at some point one must embed the analysis in institutions that are not plausibly viewed as the product of human calculation and bargaining. And ultimately, the analysis has to come to grips with the structures of social interaction that 'constitute or empower those agents in the first place'.[52]

International institutions are not created *de novo* any more than are economic institutions. On the contrary, they emerge from prior institutionalized contexts, the most fundamental of which cannot be explained as if they were contracts among rational individuals maximizing some utility function. These fundamental practices seem to reflect historically distinctive combinations of material circumstances, social patterns of thought, and individual initiative – combinations which reflect 'conjunctures' rather than deterministic outcomes,[53] and which are themselves shaped over time by path-dependent processes. Rationalistic theory can help to illuminate these practices, but it cannot stand alone. Despite the ambitions of some of its enthusiasts, it has little prospect of becoming a comprehensive deductive explanation of international institutions.

Quite apart from this limitation, the writers whom I have labeled 'reflective' have emphasized that rationalistic theories of institutions contain no *endogenous* dynamic. Individual and social reflection leading to changes in preferences or in views of causality – what Hayward Alker refers to as *historicity*[54] and what Ernst Haas discusses under the rubric of *learning*[55] – is ignored. That is, preferences are assumed to be fixed. But this assumption of fixed preferences seems to preclude understanding of some major changes in human institutions. For example, as Douglass North points out, 'the demise of slavery, one of the landmarks in the history of freedom, is simply not explicable in an interest group model'.[56] Nor, in the view of Robert Cox, is American hegemony explicable simply in power terms: on the contrary, it implies a 'coherent conjunction or fit between a configuration of material power, a prevalent collective image of world order (including certain norms) and a set of institutions which administer the order with a certain semblance of universality'.[57]

From this perspective, rationalistic theories seem only to deal with one dimension of multidimensional reality: they are incomplete, since they ignore changes taking place in consciousness. They do not enable us to understand how interests change as a result of changes in belief systems. They obscure rather than illuminate the sources of states' policy preferences. The result, according to Richard Ashley, has been a fundamentally unhistorical approach to world politics, which has reified contemporary political arrangements by denying 'history as process' and 'the historical significance of practice.'[58]

Some analysts in the reflective camp have sought to correct this lack of attention to historicity and learning. In analyzing Prisoner's Dilemma, Alker[59] emphasizes not merely the structure of payoff matrices but the sequential patterns of learning taking place between actors over the courses of a sequence of games. And Ruggie[60] has argued that only by understanding how individuals think about their world can we understand changes in how the world is organized – for instance, the shift from medieval to modern international politics. Socially influenced patterns of learning are crucial as Karl Deutsch and Ernst Haas – the teachers, respectively, of Alker and Ruggie – have always emphasized.

Reflective critics of the rationalistic research program have emphasized the inadequacies of rationalism in analyzing the fundamental practice of sovereign statehood, which has been instituted not by agreement but as a result of the elaboration over time of the principle of sovereignty. Sovereignty seems to be *prior* to the kinds of calculations on which rationalistic theory focuses: governments' strategies assume the principle of sovereignty, and the practice of sovereign statehood, as givens. Indeed, according to some critics of rationalistic thinking, sovereignty is of even more far-reaching significance, since it defines the very nature of the actors in world politics. Ruggie conceptualizes sovereignty as a 'form of legitimation' that 'differentiates units in terms of juridically mutually exclusive and morally self-entailed domains.' Like private property rights, it divides space in terms of exclusive rights, and establishes patterns of social relationships among the resulting 'possessive individualists,' whose character as agents is fundamentally shaped by sovereignty itself.[61]

Ruggie's critical analysis of sovereignty calls our attention once again to the significance of practices such as sovereign statehood for our understanding of the specific institutions of world politics. The international monetary or non-proliferation regimes of the 1980s, for example, can be understood only against the background of the constraints and opportunities provided by the practice of sovereign statehood. We are reminded again of the partial nature of rationalistic theory and the need to contextualize it if we are to derive meaningful insights from its analytical techniques.

The criticisms of rationalistic theory, both from within the framework of its assumptions and outside of them, are extensive and telling. The assumption of equilibrium is often misleading, and can lead to mechanical or contorted analysis. Rationalistic theory accounts better for shifts in the strength of institutions than in the values that they serve to promote. Cultural variations create anomalies for the theory. It does not take into account the impact of social processes of reflection or learning on the preferences of individuals or on the organizations that they direct. Finally, rationalistic theory has had little to say about the origins and evolution of practices, and it has often overlooked the impact of such practices as sovereignty on the specific institutions that it studies.[62]

Yet the critics have by no means demolished the rationalistic research program on institutions, although taking their argument seriously requires us to doubt the legitimacy of rationalism's intellectual hegemony. To show that rationalistic theory cannot account for changes in preferences because it has omitted important potential explanatory factors is important, but it is not devastating, since no social science theory is complete. Limiting the number of variables that a theory considers can increase both its explanatory content and its capacity to concentrate the scholarly mind. Indeed, the rationalistic program is heuristically so powerful precisely because it does not easily accept accounts based on post hoc observation of values or ideology: regarding states as rational actors with specified utility functions forces the analyst to look below the surface for interests that provide incentives to behave in apparently anomalous ways. In quite a short time, research stimulated by rationalistic theory has posed new questions and proposed new hypotheses about why governments create and join international regimes, and the conditions under which these institutions wax or wane. A research program with such a record of accomplishment, and a considerable number of interesting but still untested hypotheses about reasons for persistence, change, and compliance, cannot be readily dismissed.

Indeed, the greatest weakness of the reflective school lies not in deficiencies in their critical arguments but in the lack of a clear reflective research program that could be employed by students of world politics. Waltzian neo-realism has such a research program; so does neo-liberal institutionalism, which has focused on the evolution and impact of international regimes. Until the reflective scholars or others sympathetic to their arguments have delineated such a research program and shown in particular studies that it can illuminate important issues in world politics, they will remain on the margins of the field, largely invisible to the preponderance of empirical researchers, most of whom explicitly accept one or another version of rationalistic premises. Such invisibility would be a shame, since the reflective perspective has much to contribute.

As formulated to date, both rationalistic and what I have called reflective approaches share a common blind spot: neither pays sufficient attention to domestic politics. It is all too obvious that domestic politics is neglected by much game-theoretic strategic analysis and by structural explanations of international regime change. However, this deficiency is not inherent in the nature of rationalistic analysis: it is quite possible to use game theory heuristically to analyze the 'two-level games' linking domestic and international politics, as Robert Putnam[63] has done. At one level reflective theory questions, in its discussion of sovereignty, the existence of a clear boundary between domestic and international politics. But at another level it critiques the reification of the state in neo-realist theory and contemporary practice, and should therefore be driven to an analysis of how such reification has taken place historically and how it is reproduced within the confines of the domestic-international dichotomy. Such an analysis could lead to a fruitful reexamination of shifts in preferences that emerge from complex interactions between the operation of international institutions and the processes of domestic politics. Both Kenneth Waltz's 'second image' – the impact of domestic politics on international relations – and Peter Gourevitch's 'second image reversed' need to be taken account of, in their different ways, by the rationalist and reflective approaches.[64]

CONCLUSION

I believe that international institutions are worth studying because they are pervasive and important in world politics and because their operation and evolution are difficult to understand. But I also urge attention to them on normative grounds. International institutions have the *potential* to facilitate cooperation, and without international cooperation, I believe that the prospects for our species would be very poor indeed. Cooperation is not always benign; but without cooperation, we will be lost. Without institutions there will be little cooperation. And without a knowledge of how institutions work – and what makes them work well – there are likely to be fewer, and worse, institutions than if such knowledge is widespread.

A major challenge for students of international relations is to obtain such knowledge of institutions, through theory and the application of theory to practice, but especially through empirical research. Neither pure rationalistic theory nor pure criticism is likely to provide such knowledge. We should demand that advocates of both rationalistic and reflective theory create genuine research programs: not dogmatic assertions of epistemological or ontological superiority, but ways of discovering new facts and developing insightful interpretations of international institutions.

Both rationalistic and reflective approaches need further work if they are to become well-developed research programs. Rationalistic theories of institutions need to be historically contextualized: we need to see specific institutions as embedded in practices that are not entirely explicable through rationalistic analysis. And the many hypotheses generated by rationalistic theory need to be tested empirically. Reflective approaches are less well specified as theories: their advocates have been more adept at pointing out what is omitted in rationalistic theory than in developing theories of their own with a *priori* content. Supporters of this research program need to develop testable theories, and to be explicit about their scope. Are these theories confined to practices or do they also illuminate the operations of specific institutions? Above all, students of world politics who are sympathetic to this position need to carry out systematic empirical investigations, guided by their ideas. Without such detailed studies, it will be impossible to evaluate their research program.

Eventually, we may hope for a synthesis between the rationalistic and reflective approaches – a synthesis that will help us to understand both practices and specific institutions and the relationships between them. Such a synthesis, however, will not emerge full-blown, like Athena from the head of Zeus. On the contrary, it will require constructive competition and dialogue between these two research programs – and the theoretically informed investigation of facts. Thus equipped with our new knowledge, we can intervene more persuasively in the policy process, by drawing connections between institutional choices and those practices of cooperation that will be essential to human survival, and progress, in the twenty-first century.

Notes

1. Kreps, D. M. (1984) 'Corporate Culture and Economic Theory,' Manuscript. Stanford, Calif.: Graduate School of Business, Stanford University, p. 16.
2. Rawls, J. (1971) *A Theory of Justice*, Cambridge, Mass: Harvard University Press; Haas, E. B. (1986) 'Progress and International Relations', Berkeley: Institute of International Studies, manuscript.
3. Holsti, K. J. (1986) 'The Horsemen of the Apocalypse: At the Gate, Detoured or Retreating?', *International Studies Quarterly* 30, 355–72.
4. Keohane, R. (1984) *After Hegemony: Cooperation and Discord in the World Political Economy*, Princeton: Princeton University Press.
5. Bull, H. (1977) *The Anarchical Society*, New York: Columbia University Press, p. 98.
6. Hoffmann, S. (1987) 'Hans Morgenthau: The Limits and Influence of "Realism"', in *Janus and Minerva: Essays in the Theory and Practice of International Politics*, edited by S. Hoffmann, pp. 70–81. Boulder: Westview, p. 74.
7. Simon, H. A. (1985) 'Human Nature in Politics: The Dialogue of Psychology with Political Science,' *American Political Science Review* 79:293–304.
8. Axelrod, R. (1984) *The Evolution of Cooperation*, New York: Basic Books. Keohane, R. O. (1984) *After Hegemony: Cooperation and Discord in the World Political Economy*, Princeton: Princeton University Press; Oye, K. A. ed. (1986) *Cooperation under Anarchy*. Princeton: Princeton University Press.
9. Barry, B. (1970) *Sociologists, Economists and Democracy*, London: Macmillan; Gilpin, R. (1981) *War and Change in World Politics*, New York: Cambridge University Press.
10. Kratochwil, F. and J. G. Ruggie. (1986) 'International Organization: A State of the Art on an Art of the State,' *International Organization* 40, 753–76, p. 765.
11. Hughes, E. C. (1936) 'The Ecological Aspect of Institutions,' *American Sociological Review* 1, 180–86, quoted in Zucker, L. G. (1977) 'The Role of Institutionalization in Cultural Persistence' *American Sociological Review* 42, p. 726.
12. Bull, *The Anarchical Society*, p. 74. Bull also declares that 'states themselves are the principle institutions of the society of states' (p. 71), which implies that he subscribed to the view, discussed above, that the international institution of sovereignty is prior to the state.
13. Ruggie, J. G. (1986) 'Continuity and Transformation in the World Polity: Toward a Neorealist Synthesis,' in *Neorealism and Its Critics*, edited by R. O. Keohane, pp. 131–57 (New York: Columbia University Press, p. 147.
14. Krasner, S. D. (1987) 'Sovereignty: An Institutional Perspective.' Manuscript. Stanford, Calif.: Center for Advanced Study in the Behavioral Sciences, October.
15. Keohane, R. O. (1986) 'Reciprocity in International Relations,' *International Organization* 40, 1–27.

16. North, D. C. (1987) 'Institutions and Economic Growth: An Historical Introduction.' Paper prepared for the Conference on Knowledge and Institutional Change sponsored by the University of Minnesota, Minneapolis, November, p. 6.

17. March, J. and J. Olson (1984) 'The New Institutionalism; Organizational Factors in Political Life,' *American Political Science Review* 79, p. 741.

18. *International regimes* are specific institutions involving states and/or transnational actors, which apply to particular issues in international relations. This is similar to the definition given by Krasner (*International Regimes*, Ithaca: Cornell University Press, 1983), but makes it clearer that regimes are institutions, taking advantage of the definition of institutions given above. *Formal international organizations* are purposive institutions with explicit rules, specific assignments of roles to individuals and groups, and the capacity for action. Unlike international regimes, international organizations can engage in goal-directed activities such as raising and spending money, promulgating policies, and making discretionary choices.

19. Rawls, J. (1955) 'Two Concepts of Rules,' *Philosophical Review* 64, p. 19; Rawls, J. (1971) *A Theory of Justice*, Cambridge, Mass.: Harvard University Press.

20. Rawls, 'Two Concepts,' p. 24. Young defines institutions in terms of practices: 'Social institutions are recognized practices consisting of easily identifiable roles, coupled with collections of rules or conventions governing relations among the occupants of these roles' (p. 107). This is quite an acceptable definition, although it does not emphasize the distinctions among different types of 'institutions' that I wish to make.

21. Young, O. R. (1986) 'International Regimes: Toward A New Theory of Institutions,' *World Politics* 39, p. 120.

22. These practices have evolved over the course of decades or centuries and can therefore be considered in Young's terminology to be *spontaneous* order: 'the product of the action of many men but . . . not the result of human design' (Young, O. R. (1983) 'Regime Dynamics: The Rise and Fall of International Regimes,' in *International Regimes*, edited by S. D. Krasner, pp. 93–114, Ithaca: Cornell University Press quoting Hayek, F. A. (1973) *Rules and Order*. Vol. 1 of *Law, Legislation and Liberty*. Chicago: University of Chicago Press), p. 98.

23. Morgenthau, H. J. (1940) 'Positivism, Functionalism and International Law,' *American Journal of International Law* 34, p. 279. Morgenthau's language is remarkably close to the language of transaction costs employed by rationalistic theorists discussed in the next section.

24. Hoffmann, 'Hans Morgenthau,' pp. 172–173.

25. McIlwain (*Constitutionalism and the Changing World*. New York: Macmillan; and Cambridge: Cambridge University Press, 1939) is particularly good on this point; see also James (*Sovereign Statehood*. London: Allen and Unwin, 1986). Waltz confuses this issue by stat-

ing that 'to say that a state is sovereign means that it decides for itself how it will cope with its internal and external problems, including whether or not to seek assistance from others and in so doing to limit its freedom by making commitments to them' (Waltz, *Theory of International Politics*, Reading, Mass.: Addison-Wesley 1979, p. 96).

26. Wight, M. (1977) *Systems of States*, edited with an introduction by H. Bull. Leicester: Leicester University Press, p. 135.

27. North, D. C. (1984) 'Government and the Cost of Exchange in History,' *Journal of Economic History* 44, p. 256.

28. North, D. C. (1981) *Structure and Change in Economic History*. New York: W. W. Norton; Williamson, O. E. (1981) 'The Modern Corporation: Origins, Evolution, Attributes,' *Journal of Economic Literature* 19, pp. 1537–68; Williamson, O. E. (1985) *The Economic Institutions of Capitalism*, New York: Free Press; Keohane, *After Hegemony*; Moe, T. M. (1987) 'Interests, Institutions and Positive Theory: The Politics of the NLRB,' *Studies in American Political Development* 2, pp. 236–99.

29. The assertion that hegemony is necessary for institutionalized cooperation, and the less extreme view that hegemony facilitates cooperation, can both be interpreted within this framework as declaring transaction costs to be lower when a hegemon exists than when power resources are more fragmented.

30. Finlayson, J. A. and M. W. Zacher (1983) 'The Gatt and the Regulation of Trade Barriers: Regime Dynamics and Functions,' in *International Regimes*, edited by S. D. Krasner, pp. 273–315, Ithaca: Cornell University Press; Keohane, *After Hegemony*, Chapter 10; Aggarwal, V. K., *Liberal Protectionism: The International Politics of Organized Textile Trade*. Berkeley: University of California Press, 1985; Lipson, C. (1986) 'Banker's Dilemmas: Private Cooperation in Rescheduling Sovereign Debts,' in *Cooperation under Anarchy*, edited by K. Oye, pp. 200–25. Princeton: Princeton University Press; Haggard, S. and B. A. Simmons. (1987) 'Theories of International Regimes,' *International Organization* 41, pp. 491–517.

31. Krasner, S. D. (1985) *Structural Conflict: The Third World against Global Liberalism*, Berkeley: University of California Press.

32. Keohane, *After Hegemony*. Chapter 7.

33. For a pioneering exploration of these issues, see Young (1979).

34. Kreps, D. and R. Wilson (1982) 'Reputation and Imperfect Information,' *Journal of Economic Theory* 27, pp. 253–79.

35. Eichengreen, B. (1987) 'Till Debt Do Us Part: The U.S. Capital Market and Foreign Lending, 1920–1955,' Cambridge: NBER Working Paper no. 2394 (October); Lindert, P. H. and P. J. Morton (1987) 'How Sovereign Debt Has Worked,' University of California, Davis, Institute of Governmental Affairs, Research Program in Applied Macroeconomics and Macro Policy, Working Paper series no. 45, August.

36. Keohane, *After Hegemony*.

37. Wendt, A. E. (1987) 'The Agent–Structure Problem in International Relations Theory,' *International Organization* 41, p. 368.

38. Kreps, D. M. (1984) Corporate Culture and Economic Theory. Manuscript, Stanford, Calif.: Graduate School of Business, Stanford University, p. 16.

39. Shepsle, K. (1986) 'Institutional Equilibrium and Equilibrium Institutions,' in *Political Science: The Science of Politics*, edited by H. F. Weisberg, pp. 51–81, New York: Agathon Press.

40. Moe, T. M. (1984) 'The New Economics of Organization,' *American Journal of Political Science* 28:739–77; Arrow, K. J. (1985) 'The Economics of Agency,' in *Principals and Agents: The Structure of Business*, J. W. Pratt and R. J. Zeckhauser (eds.) pp. 37–51, Boston: Harvard Business School Press.

41. The theoretical indeterminacy of rationalistic theory suggests that in international relations, as in the economics of institutions, 'theory is now outstripping empirical research to an excessive extent' (Matthews, 1986, p. 917).

42. Axelrod, R. (1984) *The Evolution of Cooperation*; Axelrod, R. (1986) 'An Evolutionary Approach to Norms,' *American Political Science Review* 80, pp. 1095–1111.

43. Sutton, B. A. and M. W. Zacher (1987) 'The Calculus and Conditions of International Collaboration: Evolution of the International Shipping Regime,' prepared for delivery at the Annual Meeting of the American Political Science Association, Chicago, September.

44. Some work by sociologists, although not applied to international relations, seems relevant here since it focuses on the role played by professional and personal networks in facilitating social cooperation. See Dore R. (1983) 'Goodwill and the Spirit of Market Capitalism,' *British Journal of Sociology* 34, pp. 459–82, Granovetter, M. (1985) 'Economic Action and Social Structure: The Problem of Embeddedness,' *American Journal of Sociology* 91, pp. 481–510, and Powell, W. W. (1987) 'Hybrid Organizational Arrangements: New Form or Transitional Development?' California Management Review 30, pp. 67–87.

45. David, P. A. (1985) 'Clio and the Economics of QWERTY,' *American Economic Review Proceedings* 75, pp. 332–37; Arthur, W. B., Y. M. Ermoliev and Y. M. Kaniovski (1987) 'Path-Dependent Processes and the Emergence of Macro-Structure,' *European Journal of Operational Research*, 30:294–303; March and Olson, 'The New Constitutionalism,' p. 745.

46. Stinchcombe, A. L. (1968) *Constructing Social Theories*, New York: Harcourt, Brace and World.

47. Shepsle, 'Institutional Equilibrium,' p. 69.

48. Dore, 'Goodwill,' p. 469.

49. North, 'Government and the Cost of Exchange.'

50. Field, A. J. (1981) 'The Problem with Neoclassical Institutional Economics: A Critique with Special Reference to the North/Thomas model of pre-1500 Europe,' *Explorations in Economic History* 18:174–98.

51. North, 'Government and the Cost of Exchange.'

52. Wendt, 'The Agent–Structure Problem,' p. 369.

53. Hirschman, A. D. (1970) 'The Search for Paradigms as a Hin-

drance to Understanding,' *World Politics* 22(3), pp. 329–43.

54. Alker, H. R. Jr. (1986) 'The Presumption of Anarchy in World Politics,' draft manuscript, Department of Political Science, MIT, August.

55. Haas, E. B. (1987) 'Adaptation and Learning in International Organizations,' Manuscript. Berkeley: Institute of International Studies.

56. North, 'Institutions and Economic Growth,' p. 12.

57. Cox, R. W. (1986) 'Social Forces, States and World Orders: Beyond International Relations Theory,' in *Neorealism and Its Critics*, edited by R. O. Keohane, pp. 204–55, New York: Columbia University Press, p. 223.

58. Ashley, R. K. (1986) 'The Poverty of Neorealism,' in *Neorealism and Its Critics*, edited by R. O. Keohane, New York: Columbia University Press, p. 290; see also Alker, 'The Presumption of Anarchy'; Kratochwil, F. (1986) 'Of Systems, Boundaries and Territoriality: An Inquiry into the Formation of the State System,' *World Politics* 39, pp. 27–52.

59. Alker, H. R. Jr. (1985) 'From Quantity to Quality: A New Research Program on Resolving Sequential Prisoner's Dilemmas', paper delivered at the August meeting of the American Political Science Association.

60. Ruggie, 'Continuity and Transformation.'

61. Ruggie, 'Continuity and Transformation,' p. 144–147.

62. This does not mean, however, that rationalistic theory is incapable of contributing to our understanding of the evolution of practices. As Wendt argues, 'there is no *a priori* reason why we cannot extend the logic of [rationalistic] analysis of generative structures' (Wendt, 'The Agent–Structure Problem.' p. 368). In note to the author, Barry Weingast has illustrated this point by sketching a functional, transaction-cost argument for the existence of sovereignty, as a set of relatively unambiguous conventions, known to all players and not revisable *ex post*, which facilitate coordination and signaling.

63. Putnam, R. D. (1988) 'Diplomacy and Domestic Politics; The Logic of Two-Level Games,' *International Organization* 42, pp. 427–60.

64. Recently major work has been done on links between domestic and international politics, by scholars trained in comparative politics. Unlike the critics of rationalistic theory discussed above, however, these writers emphasize international structure, material interests, and state organization as well as the role of ideas and social patterns of learning. Also unlike the critics of rationalist international relations theory, these writers have engaged in extensive and detailed empirical research. See Zysman, J. *Governments, Markets and Growth* (Ithaca: Cornell University Press, 1983), Katzenstein, P. J. *Small States in World Markets* (Ithaca: Cornell University Press, 1985), Gourevitch, P. A. 'The Second Image Reversed: International Sources of Domestic Politics' *International Organization* 32, pp. 881–912, (1978); *Politics in Hard Times* (Ithaca: Cornell University Press, 1986), and Alt, J. A. 'Crude Politics: Oil and the Political Economy of Unemployment in Britain and Norway, 1970–85,' *British Journal of Political Science* 17, pp. 149–99.

12 History and Structure in the Theory of International Relations (1989)*

R.B.J. Walker

The explanation of social and political life is a notoriously contentious enterprise, and the Anglo – American discipline of international relations is no exception to the general rule. As with so many other disciplines that have been shaped by the broader ambitions of post-war social science, controversy has occurred largely on the terrain of epistemology. All too often, the more far-reaching epistemological problems, posed by those who seek to understand what is involved in making knowledge claims about social and political processes, have been pushed aside in favor of more restricted concerns about method and research techniques. Narrowing the range of potential dispute in this manner has undoubtedly enhanced an appearance of professional solidarity. But it has also obscured many of the more troublesome and, in my view, more important fractures visible to anyone now canvassing contemporary debates about the general nature and possibility of social and political enquiry.

In this article I want to draw attention to some of these fractures and to indicate their significance for current discussions of appropriate research strategies in the analysis of world politics.[1] To begin with, I distinguish between different philosophical contexts in which appropriate research strategies may be judged. Here I reflect on a recent assessment of these strategies offered by Robert Keohane,

* *Millennium: Journal of International Studies*, 18(2) (Summer), pp. 163–183. This paper was written under the auspices of the Center of International Studies, Princeton University.

308

who judges them primarily according to epistemological and methodological criteria. I then explore some of the broader ontological, ethical and ideological dilemmas that are at stake in the literature that Keohane discusses. I am especially concerned with the tension between the atemporal structuralism that informs current social scientific approaches – especially the theory of international regimes and structural realism – and approaches that give priority to historical interpretation.

While my primary intention is simply to insist on the significance of themes that are played down in Keohane's analysis rather than to pursue them in any detail, I also argue in favor of three broad conclusions. First, priority should be given to history and thus to approaches that stress interpretation, practice and the critique of reification. Second, differences among approaches to world politics must be addressed at the level of basic ontological assumptions: the possibility of empirical research strategies is a significant but decidedly secondary matter. Third, the contemporary analysis of world politics poses fundamental questions of political theory – questions that remain interesting and provocative despite socio-scientific attempts to reduce them to problems of utilitarian calculation and empirical testing.

BEYOND HEGEMONY, BEFORE EPISTEMOLOGY

In a recent text, first delivered as a presidential address to the International Studies Association in 1988, Robert Keohane offered what is in some respects a generous assessment of the different perspectives currently used to exam-ine developing patterns of inter-state co-operation.[2] Distinguishing between his own 'rationalistic' orientation and positions that he identifies as the 'reflective' approach, Keohane is relatively sympathetic to the contributions of those who have criticized the rationalists for their reliance on ahistorical utilitarian presuppositions adapted from liberal microeconomics and public choice theory. Moreover, his claims for the explanatory power of the rationalist or utilitarian position are relatively modest. The text as a whole is written as an invitation to a more constructive dialogue between what are characterized as potentially complementary schools of thought.

Nevertheless, the central argument of the text is bold and blunt: the reflective school have 'failed to develop a coherent research program of their own' – coherent, that is, in the sense that it bears comparison with the paradigmatic research programme exemplified by the structuralist models of Kenneth Waltz or the utilitarian categories that constitute the theory of international regimes. An encouraging opening towards a positive assessment of the plurality of theoretical perspectives is quickly closed off by the preference given to a highly specific and philosophically contested account of what a proper research programme should look like.

It is not difficult to find evidence of the continuing influence of similar claims that scholarly controversies should be resolved on the preferred terrain of empirical method. These claims have been especially tenacious in international relations, although even here they have begun to seem outdated. One of the significant achievements of the debates about social scientific explanation in the 1960s and 1970s is a much greater awareness of the controversial character of what social science is or should be. Invocations of the logic of explanation in the physical sciences have become relatively rare, not least because our understanding of what is involved in even the most precise sciences is sharply contested. The general lesson that seems to have been drawn is not that empirical social science is impossible or undesirable, but that its achievements and possibilities ought to be placed in a more modest perspective.

This lesson is reflected in Keohane's emphasis on the context-specific character of generalizations, as well as in the emphasis on model-building in the work of the utilitarian rationalists more generally. The hope, of course, is that the models offered for empirical testing can transcend their origins as analogical or metaphorical speculation. Whether the utilitarian images that have been deployed recently to explain inter-state cooperation are successful in this respect will undoubtedly remain contentious. Some students of world politics will continue to be fascinated by the social, political, ideological and philosophical conditions under which a liberal utilitarian account of human action can aspire to hegemony – particularly in a discipline that continues to have more success in raising interesting questions than in providing plausible answers.

Meanwhile, those concerned with what it means to study social and political life have turned away from the largely discredited positivistic accounts of scientific explanation to a much broader arena of philosophical debate. In this arena, the explorations of literary theorists are treated at least as seriously as pre-Kuhnian dogmas about cumulative scientific knowledge. Some scholars have been impressed by the vitality of interpretive or hermeneutic procedures, especially where the old Cartesian assumption that language can be separated from the world in which it participates is resisted. Some have become immersed in controversies generated by the revival of political economy, controversies in which it has been relatively difficult to erase fundamental philosophical and ideological differences through the claims of universal methods. Others have been drawn into forms of critical theory associated with, for example, the Frankfurt School or post-structuralism and thus into long-standing controversies about modernity and late/counter/post-modernity. Whatever one makes of such trends, they undoubtedly reflect a different intellectual atmosphere than prevailed when the discipline of international relations became institutionalized as a major branch of social science some three decades ago.[3] Keohane is clearly aware of these developments. But in affirming a more social scientific account of what a proper research agenda should look like, he minimizes much of their significance and complexity.

Keohane groups together a very broad range of perspectives as exemplars of the reflective approach. They include the broad sociological influences on the work of John Ruggie, Hayward Alker's explorations of dialectical logics, Friedrich Kratochwil's concern with analytic philosophies of action and post-modernist sensitivities that have guided Richard Ashley's critical commentaries on the modernist impulses affirmed by the utilitarians. If we add all those who have resisted the charms of social scientific theories of international relations by drawing on neo-Marxist forms of political economy, theories of ideology and discourse, or critical and interpretive forms of political thought, the ranks of the reflective school could be made to swell still further. If we then consider the potential range of ontological, ethical and ideological commitments that are likely to be held by such a diverse group of scholars, Keohane's hope for some kind of convergence with the insights of utilitarian rationalism seems exaggerated.

In this sense, much of Keohane's discussion is reminiscent of the quite misleading exchange in the 1960s between 'scientific' and 'traditionalist' approaches to international relations. Keohane's judgment reflects epistemological preoccupations, and is reinforced through an undiminished confidence in the promises of modern social science. However, as with the earlier exchange, many of the crucial differences between the utilitarian rationalists and the historically inclined reflective school extend to prior and even more contentious problems, many of which have long been assumed to challenge the claims of modern social science.

In the earlier exchange, debate was preoccupied with contrasting accounts of scientific explanation, and with how the more historical and even philosophical concerns of the traditionalists might be updated through the judicious application of appropriate method.[4] Yet in initiating the debate, Hedley Bull offered a critique of the pretensions of scientific method that rested less on claims about knowledge as such than on arguments about the very nature of world politics. Scientific method was inappropriate, he argued, because of what world politics is. He was especially concerned with the dangers of the 'domestic analogy', that is, the transfer of philosophical and theoretical premises derived from the analysis of political community within states to the analysis of relations among states. After all, from the classical Greek accounts of life in the *polis* to more recent accounts of the persistence of the state as the dominant expression of political power, inter-state relations have been treated as quite fundamentally different from political life within states, both in essential character and potential.

Unfortunately, Bull's underlying concerns about whether inter-state relations or world politics are in principle any different from politics within states were quickly translated into more limited epistemological questions about how analysis should be conducted. While initiated on the ground of an ontological dualism – between statist community and the society of states, or in the unfortunately more common rendition, community and anarchy – debate quickly turned to the claims of an epistemological monism. Consequently, where Bull articulated a traditional claim that relations between states are distinctive enough to justify a separate discipline and different research strategies (not to mention an account of the relation between knowledge and power, or truth and violence, that would seem scandalous in the context of theories of political life within states), social scientific approaches have affirmed a fundamental continuity. Hence the possibility, so eagerly grasped by those searching for empirically testable models, of transferring assumptions, metaphors, research strategies and accounts of rational actions from one context to the other.

Nevertheless, Bull's concerns cannot be made to disappear quite so easily. It may now be common to speak of 'interdependence', to analyze international regimes, or to enquire about the pontentials of international organization, but few would argue that we have moved from a world of statist communities to a global community. The early modern European account of political life as the establishment of relatively autonomous political communities coexisting in territorial space has yet to be superseded by a coherent account of a common planetary identity or a cosmopolitan human community. The epistemological claim to a universally applicable scientific method thus coexists quite uneasily with the contrary claim, articulated variously in ontological, ethical and ideological forms, that human life is fragmented. Similar problems have beset students of comparative politics or anthropology, where they have generated considerable controversy. In international relations, they have captured the attention of a few critical theorists and defenders of the more traditional approaches represented by Bull, but for the most part they have gone unnoticed, obscured by the achievements of what can now plausibly pass for the social scientific orthodoxy.

Keohane's more recent discussion poses similar difficulties. Many of the differences among the positions he examines arise far more from disagreements about what it is that scholars think they are studying than from disagreements about how to study it. The latter depend in large part upon the former. To attempt to turn all theoretical disputes into differences over method and epistemology is to presume that we have acceptable answers to questions about the kind of world that we are trying to know. This is a rather large presumption, as Keohane only partly acknowledges. Moreover, even if Keohane's distinction proves useful at some level, it is not altogether clear why the methodological prescriptions of the utilitarian rationalists should be treated as the successful orthodoxy on whose terms the contributions of the reflective school should be judged. It might be argued, for example, that there are very strong continuities between the work of the reflective theorists – Kratochwil and Ashley especially, though quite distinctively – and the work of Bull and others who begin their work by attempting to come to terms with the historically constituted distinction between politics within and among statist communities.[5] Keohane's polarity might then be reversed by suggesting that utilitarian rationalism merely adds some interesting analytic models and a distinctive vocabulary to traditions of considerable standing and achievement. Claims about what constitutes orthodoxy in this respect can vary considerably depending on the cultural and temporal horizons of the claimant.

In any case, the appropriate context in which to situate Keohane's discussion is less the controversy about social science than the even earlier 'great debate' between realists and idealists. While it is against the obvious limitations of that debate that the promises of social science were articulated in the first place, the categories through which that debate was constituted have remained very influential. In fact, far from being merely one of a series of debates that have characterized the history of the discipline, the distinction between political realism and political idealism has provided the context within which other disputes about appropriate method or the priority of state-centered accounts of world politics could occur at all.[6] Framed within this distinction, 'metaphysics,' 'ethics' and 'ideology' have become the names for roles in an old and obviously decrepit manichean theatre. Tamed in this way, it is hardly surprising that they have been marginalized in favor of the louder and seemingly more up-to-date claims of social science. Nevertheless, as Keohane moves closer and closer to the primary themes that distinguish utilitarian rationalists from the historically inclined reflective school, the echoes of this older debate become clearer.

To draw attention to the connection between current controversies and the older debate is certainly not to suggest that the categories of either realist or idealist can now offer much useful guidance. As roles in a manichean theatre, these terms have served primarily to close off serious discussion in a manner that has helped to insulate the discipline of international debate ever since. Rather, the categories of realist and idealist, as they were deployed in these debates – and as they have since come to provide convenient labels and systems of classification – should be understood as the primary forms in which the basic assumptions governing the study of world politics have been left to congeal, requiring little further exploration. As such, they provide a starting point, and a point at which awkward questions may be deferred. Within their stylized horizons it is possible to honor all those who, for some reason, are revered as contributors to the distilled wisdom of tradition. Thucydides, Marchiavelli, Hobbes, Rousseau and the rest may then commune with more modern masters like E. H. Carr, Hans J. Morgenthau and their even more modern disciples.

Much of the literature that Keohane seeks to judge as contributions to empirical social science can also be understood as attempts to re-engage with the philosophical and theoretical dilemmas that we packed away when the realist-idealist dichotomy was constructed as the appropriate arena in which orderly, unthreatening dispute could be permitted to occur. Unpacking these categories, it is possible to reformulate questions about, for example, the relationship between claims to legitimate political community within states and the legitimacy of violence in relations between political communities; or the relative claims of people as human beings and people as citizens; or the tensions between universalist and pluralist ethical claims; or the relation between power and knowledge as this has been mediated by the claims of state sovereignty.

Questions like these have come to be treated largely as the preserve of those toiling in the vineyards of social and political theory. They raise the awkward philosophical themes designated as ontology, ethics, ideology or even the relation between theory and practice. These are themes that most scholars in the discipline of international relations have been loath to confront, except on terms permitted by the discipline's great debates. These are also themes that are at play in the differing perspectives canvassed by Keohane. To enquire into patterns of interdependence or dependence, or the emergence of international regimes and institutions, is to work both within and against inherited accounts of the possibility of political community. These inherent problems in these accounts, I believe, are systematically obscured by ahistorical utilitarianism and the categories of realist and idealist alike.

The assumption that informs the alternative reading of contemporary perspectives on world politics to be sketched here, therefore, is that the central task now confronting students of world politics is not the refinement of utilitarian calculation or social scientific method, but a renewed engagement with questions in relation to which the categories of realist and idealist constitute only a great refusal. These categories fix historically contingent answers to questions about the nature and location of political community. Such questions are necessarily re-opened by any attempt to understand what terms like international regime, or international institution, or interdependence and dependence – and especially *world* politics – can possibly mean.

Keohane rightly emphasizes the significance of historical interpretation for all those who have challenged the structuralist tendencies of the utilitarian rationalists, and it is this theme that I want to explore. One way of reframing an account of current debates about approaches to world politics is to emphasize how contrasting perspectives have tended to give priority to either history and time, on the one hand, or structure and space on the other. The tendency to privilege either history or structure rests upon historically constituted philosophical options. To emphasize one or the other is to generate distinctive theoretical puzzles.

These options and puzzles explain part of what is at stake in the opposition between realism and idealism. They also underlie many of the claims made on behalf of, as well as the criticisms voiced against, social scientific forms of structural realism and regime theory. Moreover, the categories through which the priority given either to history or to structure is sustained are themselves the product of distinctive historical conditions. They now tend to freeze or reify complex philosophical questions into a permanent problem: either an eternal debate between realists and idealists or a progressive struggle to establish a properly empirical social science against the recalcitrant metaphysicians, ideologists, historicists, hermeneuticists or critical theorists. Neither of these legacies seems likely to advance our understanding of the transformative character of contemporary world politics very far.

In this article's introductory and schematic exploration of the tension between history and structure in the analysis of world politics, I want to suggest that it provides a clearer indication of what is at stake in current debates than is derived from fixing the discussion on the terrain of epistemology or method. Beginning with history, I move on to structure before returning to problems raised by Keohane's delineation of the options before us.

HISTORY, STRUCTURE AND REIFICATION

Once upon a time, as the story goes, the world was not as it is now. Precisely what it was like is not clear. Accounts vary, depending on when and where 'once upon a time' is supposed to have occurred. Records and memories are notoriously deceptive, and require careful coding and interpretation. The skills of the story-teller may be judged mainly by the expectations of the audience, but even so, the story remains evocative. It tells of feudal modes of production, hierarchical arrangements of power and authority, and medieval forms of life and consciousness. The story can be told in many different versions. The version that concerns me here might be called 'Life before International Relations.'

The telling of this story is often short and snappy, a preface to an equally concise denouement: feudalism gives way to capitalism, more modern forms of life and consciousness emerge, and political community gradually coheres around the sovereign claims of the state. This story in turn has a sequel, full of plots etched deeply in the contemporary imagination. This sequel has come in two quite distinctive, but mutually interdependent variations.

One, especially favored by those who refer to their stories as histories of social and political thought, impresses us with accounts of the progressive emancipation of statist political communities and the emergence of modern conceptions of freedom, justice and rationality. Another, favored by an apparently more hard-bitten breed who refer to their scripts as theories of international relations, depresses us with tragic tales of violence, intrigue and the triumph of might over right. In both versions, however, the story of how the world that was not as it is now recedes into the background, and we are gripped instead by more topical tales of the world as it has become.

References to accounts of medieval life or the complex transformations of early modern Europe as mere stories may seem flippant given the massive and erudite literature that has advanced our understanding of these phases of human experience. Nevertheless, this literature is not invoked very often in the contemporary analysis of world politics. Significant exceptions to this rule are not difficult to find, but, for the most part, influential strategies of analysis have been framed against a generalized story about when, where and how inter-state politics emerged as an appropriate object for scholarly reflection. In this sense, the well-known stories continue to exercise a powerful hold over categories of analysis and methodological strategies. Implicated in these stories are at least four groups of puzzles, which regularly enter discussions of what the analysis of world politics ought to involve.

One set of puzzles arises from the rather sharp disjunction between the comfortable rhythms in which the best known stories about the early modern period have been reiterated and the untidy, even recalcitrant, evidence that enters into the deeply contested accounts offered by contemporary historians. While old distinctions between ancients and moderns remain deeply entrenched in popular accounts of our origins, the role of these distinctions in legitimizing modernity against the presumed darkness that came before is transparent. While the grand narratives of Marx and Weber continue to offer crucial insight into the forces responsible for the emergence of capitalism, modernity and the state, linear projections and monocausal theories have been sharply qualified by the details of multiple transitions. While we may remain impressed by the rapidity and scale of the socio-economic innovations of the sixteenth and seventeenth centuries or the spectacular intellectual achievements of the Renaissance, it is increasingly clear that the transformations of the early modern period grew out of complex, mutually reinforcing processes that had already been underway for a considerable period. Continuities have come to seem at least as important as ruptures.[7]

In short, the simple story of life before international relations has become quite implausible. Yet while often prepared to admit the inadequacy of the conventional stories, theorists of international relations are easily drawn into an affirmation of them as a convenient myth of origins. By identifying when inter-state relations began, and providing a sharp contrast with what came before, these stories offer a powerful account of what inter-state politics must be, given what it has always been since the presumed beginning.

Without such a myth of origins, of course, a number of rather basic questions from the philosophy of history begin to assert themselves. To what extent does our interpretation of contemporary inter-state politics depend on particular readings of macro-history? To what extent might these readings be challenged by, say, anthropologists, or by macro-historians who are more reluctant to place early modern European experiences at the centre of their analysis? To what extent are these readings caught up in unacknowledged assumptions about progress, or evolution, or eternal return? To what extent is our understanding of the possibilities of contemporary transformations constrained by our assumptions about the historical processes that have made us what we are now? Threatened by the implications of

questions like these, a retreat to a clear point of origin
from which contemporary trajectories may be delineated
and continuities generalized can seem very comforting.
Nevertheless, it has rarely escaped the notice of the more
astute political commentators that the capacity to construct
a myth of origins carries enormous political advantage.

Similar questions are at play in a second set of puzzles
that regularly beset analysts of world politics, which arise
from competing accounts of the most appropriate point at
which to identify the origin of the modern states-system.
Once we move away from the most caricatured accounts of
life before and after the rise of the state, the variety of
presumed points of origin can be quite striking. Two options have been especially popular. One is to focus on the
emergence of the state as a distinctive and relatively autonomous form of political community in late fifteenth century Europe. Another is to stress the period in which claims
of state sovereignty became formalized and codified in international law. Here the Treaty of Westphalia of 1648 serves
as a crucial demarcation between an era still dominated by
competing claims to religious universalism and hierarchical authority and an era of secular competition and cooperation among autonomous political communities. But
there are also analysts who would direct our attention to
earlier periods. They may want to push accounts of relatively autonomous state authority back further into the feudal
era, or more usually, point to analogies between early modern
Europe and the states systems of antiquity. Others prefer
to focus on later dates on the grounds that, for example,
only in the eighteenth century does the states-system generate recognizably modern procedures and 'rules of the game',
or that only later still do we discover a system of relations
between properly national states. Taking things to rather
absurd extremes, it is even possible to derive the impression
from some textbooks that inter-state politics is the invention of the twentieth century.

This elastic identification of points of origin again raises
serious questions about what an analysis of world politics
ought to involve. To examine the literature on the emergence and development of the states system is to be impressed by the transformative quality of both the state and

the character of relations between states. States can then appear to us as historically constituted and always subject to change. In this context, such distinctions as those among the absolutist state, the nation-state, the welfare state and the national-security state become very interesting. For example, the Canadian state is likely to be a significantly different phenomenon 10 years after the advent of the 'free trade' agreement with the United States than it is now. And yet this historicity of states is at odds with a contrary sense that whatever their historical transformations, states and states systems exhibit certain regularities across time. Scholars do claim to be able to make plausible analogies between, for example, the struggles of Athens and Sparta and our own epoch. Canadian spokesmen on defence policy will continue to justify their proposed procurements in the name of Canadian sovereignty.

In this way, the perspectives of history begin to give way to those of structure. In some accounts, definitions are offered of a sort of permanent essence: the inter-state system is in principle always anarchical, for example, or the state is always a maximizer of power, status or its own welfare. Sometimes it takes the form of comparative analysis of various structural configurations: the differences between multipolar and bipolar systems, for example, or of systems with and without a dominant actor. In either case, the historicity of states and state systems recedes into the background, and world politics begins to be portrayed as a permanent game, which can appear to have followed more or less the same rules for time immemorial.

This sense of permanence, or at least repetition, is particularly attractive to scholars who seek to develop an explanatory science of the politics of states-systems. Problems from the philosophy of history are difficult to negotiate. The historicity of states systems leads to contentious constructions of historical sociology or political economy. Discontinuity and historical transformation have long been viewed as threats to the accumulation of objective knowledge. One cannot step into the same river twice, say some. We have only managed to interpret the world while the point is to change it, say others. Against temporal flux, contingency, idiosyncrasy and revolutionary praxis, the identification of structural form offers an alluring possibility of a universalizing objectivity.

This leads directly to a third set of puzzles, arising from claims that there is indeed a firm body of knowledge about the character of inter-state politics enshrined in the 'great tradition' of international theory. The account of tradition may take a number of distinct forms. Three versions have been particularly influential: the permanent debate between realism and idealism; the repetitious monologue spoken by those who have been conscripted into the army of realists; and – the most interesting version – the account of tradition of international relations theory as a negation of a presumed tradition of political theory.[8] In all three cases, anachronistic interpretive procedures have served to obscure another version of the contradiction between history and structure. Thucydides, Machiavelli, Hobbes, Rousseau and the rest are presented as unproblematic figures, often in disguises that make them unrecognizable to anyone who examines the textual evidence we have of them. That each of these figures is open to sharply differing interpretations has mattered little. In place of a history of political thought is offered an ahistorical repetition in which the struggles of these thinkers to make sense of the historical transformations in which they were caught are erased in favor of assertions that they all articulate essential truths about the same unchanging and usually tragic reality: the eternal game of relations between states.

Following from this, a fourth set of puzzles arises from the historically constituted character not only of the state and the states system, but also of the categories in which we seek to understand the dynamics of contemporary world politics. This is perhaps the most disconcerting puzzle of all. It is tempting to minimize the significance of the historical experiences through which crucial concepts and ways of speaking have been formed. The longing for timeless categories has exercised a profound influence on many of those we associate with rationalism in the more philosophical sense of this term. Yet it is possible to trace the history of the terms 'state,' 'sovereignty,' 'individual,' 'culture,' 'security' and many of the other terms now taken for granted. In doing so, it is possible to discover how they emerged in response to specific historical conjunctions and contradictions. Accounts of history as a sharp break between life before international relations and life since international relations detract attention from the historically specific meanings embodied in concepts and categories that can so easily appear to transcend historical contingency. The categories and concepts we have learnt to use with such facility, almost without thinking, come to appear natural and inevitable. Their contested history is soon forgotten.

STRUCTURES, MEANINGS AND PRACTICES

Once the story has been written, and has solidified into received accounts of origins, traditions and analytical concepts, attention may turn to the architecture of structures. Grand structures having emerged, it is possible to enquire into their modes of operation, their mechanisms and determinations, their forms and their functions, their regularities and repetitions. Some of the most familiar and enduring analysis of world politics has been facilitated by a certain forgetting of history.

In its more extreme forms, structuralist analysis tends towards universalism. It is associated historically with attempts to identify the universal principles of reason, myth or language – the deep structures that inform the spatial variety and temporal variability on the surface of things. In practice, however, structuralist analysis is itself subject to considerable variation, partly with respect to the number of structural patterns that may be identified, and partly with respect to the way that structural patterns always seem to mutate into processes of historical transformation under critical inspection.

It is in this context, for example, that Thomas Hobbes can be identified as a paradigmatic thinker. Because individuals are autonomous and equal under conditions of scarcity, Hobbes suggested, they necessarily find themselves in a position of perpetual insecurity. Each individual's struggle to enhance his or her own security increases everyone else's sense of insecurity. Hence the imagery of both the 'state of nature' and the 'security dilemma'. On the other

hand (and contrary to the usual direct translation of the
fictive state of nature into an account of the security dilemma between states) Hobbes argued that precisely because states are both unequal and much less vulnerable
than individuals, they have significantly different structural
relationships among themselves than individuals have. Among
individuals, Hobbes argued, structural relations of insecurity
demand a superior sovereign power for an ordered polity
to be constituted. Hence the powerful resolution of the
relation between sovereign individuals and sovereign states
through a contract that is both freely entered into and yet
necessitated by structural conditions. Among states, by contrast, structural conditions of inequality suggest other ordering principles in what is nevertheless a 'state of war',
although Hobbes himself was not much concerned to identify
these principles.

It could be argued, of course, that in contemporary world
politics, both the proliferation of nuclear weapons and the
legal principle of sovereign equality have begun to make
Hobbes' account of relations between individuals a more
instructive guide to the dynamics of inter-state relations than
Hobbes himself suggested. For the most part, however,
despite continuing references to Hobbes as a theorist of
international anarchy, most accounts of world politics presume that states are not equal. Conflict there may be, insecurity certainly, but structuralist accounts of world politics
are just as likely to show that insecurity arises from patterns of hegemony, hierarchy and penetration as from autonomy and equality.

Among the most important structural forms in world politics
primacy has commonly been given to the balance of power,
especially by those who identify the subject of world politics specifically as relations among states. The familiar themes
of different distributions of power and the presence or absence
of great or hegemonic powers lead directly to a concern
with, for example, the nature of alliances or the transformations induced by the deployment of weapons of mass destruction and the regularized rituals of nuclear deterrence. When
patterns of hegemony begin to seem especially significant,
attention may turn to the difficulty of distinguishing the
dynamics of states systems from those of empires.

Those who situate the dynamics of inter-state relations within a broader account of international or global political economy see different primary structuring principles in world politics. Here the range of perspectives is striking. Much of the literature on international regimes is classified under this rubric. But the liberal categories of economic analysis deployed by this literature set it apart from more explicitly mercantilist or Marxist traditions that also inform contemporary political economy, especially outside the ideological confines of the United States. Some, like Robert Gilpin, seek to combine liberal economic categories with a more mercantilist or 'realist' account of the state, especially in the context of contemporary disruptions and transformations in international trade and finance. Some, like Immanuel Wallerstein, echo Adam Smith in stressing the determining nature of a global division of labor and a world market, minimizing the autonomous role of the state while highlighting the relations between centre and periphery in a world system. Others, like Robert Cox and Stephen Gill begin – in my view more helpfully – with a concern for the global structuring of relations of production, and thus emphasize the transformation of state practices in response to the contemporary global reorganization of production currently in progress.[9]

To canvass the range of structuralist accounts of world politics in this way is to become aware of the diversity of philosophical, theoretical and ideological assumptions that can be embraced under the heading of structuralism. In this sense, Keohane's category of rationalists is just as much in need of differentiation as his fusion of reflective approaches. But equally striking is the difficulty of distinguishing between structuralist and historical analysis.

Keohane recommends a greater openness to the reflective approach partly because it would complement the ahistoricism of the rationalists. But once we move away from the explicitly utilitarian models of regime theory, it is clear that accounts of the character of historical change are already built into many of the structural approaches to world politics. These accounts may not be entirely convincing, falling back, for example, on notions of changes as alterations in the distribution of power in a system that remains essentially the same, or on accounts of history as either a sequence of repetitive cycles or a linear road from darkness to light. Nevertheless it is probably fair to say that few students of world politics would argue that structuralist analysis can be divorced from a concern with history and change. There is a 'plain common sense' view that both perspectives are necessary. Some might argue, for example, that purely structural analyses of balances of power are intrinsically interesting, and that formal modeling or ahistorical ascriptions of utilitarian behavior to states are entirely justified, as long as a complementary historical perspective is also encouraged. Even so, both the superficial tolerance of 'plain common sense' and the division of academic labor can obscure some of the characteristic difficulties structuralist analysts have in explaining the historical political practices through which structural forms have been constructed.

Again it is helpful to reflect upon the supposedly paradigmatic quality of Hobbes' thinking for the analysis of world politics. Hobbes built upon a fairly radical reworking of philosophical categories within the broad context of the scientific cosmologies associated with the early modern period. He was impressed, for example, with the unchanging character of reason, the spatial regularities of Euclidean geometry and the possibility of grounding social explanation in a firm foundation of precise definitions. Unlike Machiavelli before or Rousseau after, he paid little attention to history, at least not in the passages for which he has become a realist icon. Instead we find a classic expression of life before and life after the social contract, a shrinking of historical time and human practice to an ahistorical moment of utilitarian calculation informed by reason and fear.

Again, it is possible to identify a range of difficult questions that have beset those who have followed Hobbes in assigning overriding importance to structural form. Even if we try to avoid questions about whether structures can be said to exist, it is still necessary to engage in complex philosophical interrogations that converge on the question of defining a structure. Many of these arise from the contemporary emphasis on relationality rather than substance.

Understood as part of a broader challenge to Newtonian metaphysics, contemporary structural analysis conflicts with popular accounts of the world as an accumulation of things. Some people may kick tables to affirm the material solidity of the 'real world,' but the demonstration is unlikely to be convincing to anyone familiar with categories of contemporary physics.

With a stress on relationality come questions about how one understands the distinction between the parts of structure and the 'emergent properties' that arise because the whole is greater than the sum of its parts. Hence the dilemma, especially familiar in sociological theory, of whether social explanation should begin with an account of 'society' or with the behavior of 'individuals.' Hence also some of the central dilemmas of the theory of international relations: the delineations of distinctions between individual, state and states-system in the so-called 'levels of analysis' typology, for example, or controversies about whether the state-system should be considered to have an autonomous logic of its own or to be part in a broader system of global political economy. The concept of causality also becomes problematic in this context, especially given that most popular accounts of causality are still informed by images of billiard balls colliding in a Newtonian universe. With causality come questions about determinism, particularly whether structural forms should be understood as constraining or enabling.

In pursuing questions like these, however, questions about the relationship between structure and history are never far away. Thus contemporary structuralism does not exhibit the same attachment to timeless universals as the earlier forms of axiomatic rationalism. On the contrary, as it has been used by anthropologists and theorists of language, structuralism has become more preoccupied with understanding the rules of transformation than with identifying patterns of continuity. More crucially, as a broad philosophical and theoretical movement, associated with the work of Claude Levi-Strauss and Louis Althusser, for example, structuralism mutated rather rapidly into what has become known as post-structuralism. And one of the central insights of post-structuralism, explored especially by theorists of language from Fernand de Saussure to Jacques Derrida, has been that structural patterns are constituted through historical processes of differentiation. The emphasis on relationality is pursued in a temporal direction with the well-known result that post-structuralist analysis has come to be indicted for all the sins previously associated with those who insisted on the historicity of human existence. The indictment is issued in the name of objectivity and universal standards, although it is the historically constituted nature of the capacity to issue the indictment in the first place that post-structuralism has sought to challenge.

As if this is not enough, questions about whether structures do, in fact, exist will not go away. They are especially important for attempts to construct a theory of international regimes. The very term regime, like similar uses of the term governance, attempts to capture phenomena that seem to have a status somewhere between a concrete institution and a more or less invisible field of forces generated by structural determinations. The term international organization is also problematic in this respect, caught as it is between accounts of specific institutional arrangements like the United Nations and incohate attempts to forge an analysis of processes that are neither inter-state relations as conventionally understood nor precursors of some kind of world state.[10]

Interrogations like these lead into some of the most difficult conceptual terrain in contemporary social and political theory. They ought to give pause to anyone attempting to confine discussion of contrasting perspectives on world politics to questions about epistemology and method. Even those who adhere most rigorously to an empiricist conception of research discover that they have to struggle with interrogations of this kind. Kenneth Waltz's accounts of systemic explanation and the level-of-analysis typology or Robert Gilpin's attempt to reconcile modernist social science with an essentially historicist account of a classical tradition of theories of international relations, clearly, involve taking positions on these questions. Their positions may or may not be satisfactory, but their work has to be judged at least partially in terms of how far their more empirical work is both shaped and constrained by their prior ontological commitments.[11]

A second set of questions follows directly from such considerations, for in practice answers to these more philosophical problems are often articulated in the form of metaphors, analogies and models derived from other areas of human experience. Metaphors, analogies and models are a crucial aspect of theory formation, even in the more rigorous sciences. They assist in conceptual clarification and the development of systems of classification. It may well be that much of what we understand to be scientific analysis has been articulated against the dangers of false analogy or the slippages in meaning that are intrinsic to metaphorical reasoning; that is, against the very possibilities that are often celebrated in the realms of literature and art. But again, the conventional distinction between the sciences and humanities obscures more than it reveals. In the analysis of social and political life especially, textual strategies and literary devices are a characteristic part of even the most formalized modeling.

Two sub-themes are especially important here. One concerns the tendency to draw analogies between relatively simple structures in order to explain ones that are more complex. The role of images taken from Newtonian mechanics or Darwinian biology is relatively familiar and has generated long standing debate about the reductionist character of much functionalist explanation in sociology.[12] In the analysis of world politics, the concept of a balance of power itself rests on an analogy, and leads to questions about whether the notion of equilibrium it implies is sufficiently nuanced to encompass the dynamics of great power diplomacy or the dialectics of nuclear deterrence. Similarly, many of the ideas articulated under the rubric of social choice theory or utilitarian accounts of instrumental rationality have a reductionist quality. In part this derives from the assumption that social processes can be explained in terms of the behavior of individuals, as if individuals somehow exist prior to society. A second sub-theme concerns the circulation of the metaphors and analogies used to analyze world politics within a broader cultural and political economy. Social and political explanation constantly draws on and collides with the imagery, prejudices and ways of speaking of the society being explained. The meanings of such terms as 'security', 'equilibrium' or 'nuclear umbrella' are mediated by complex cultural codes of which strategic analysts are themselves only partly aware.[13]

This leads directly to a third group of questions, which focus on the relationship between structures and human consciousness or practice. Some of the most intense debates about structural analysis in modern social and political theory have occurred on this terrain, not least because structuralism has seemed to imply the erasure of human subjectivity. In the context of world politics, versions of this problem have occurred in debates about whether a balance of power should be understood as an automatic mechanism to which statesmen simply respond, or whether it should be regarded as a practice or policy that statesmen have developed on the basis of long historical experience.

Something similar is involved in the different accounts of international co-operation and regime formation. In an extreme utilitarian approach, for example, human action is explained in terms of the rules of efficient conduct, rules that have a certain structural necessity. It is in this context that 'normative' behavior is interpreted as following the prudential rules of utility maximization. This is clearly not the only available account of human action, or of what normative behavior involves. Even Max Weber, whose account of instrumental rationality is often invoked by utilitarian analysts, tended to see modernity not as a simple embrace of instrumental rationality, but as an intensifying clash between the meaningless rules of efficient action and a struggle to give meaning to life in a disenchanted world. And those who begin their account of human action in an analysis of, for example, labor or language are unlikely to be persuaded by the limited claims of utilitarian efficiency. To begin with the constitutive character of labor or language is to challenge the fundamental premises on which a utilitarian account of social and political life is grounded. There is nothing very novel about this. It merely serves as a reminder that the distance between Keohane's categories covers some deeply rooted, complex differences among those who seek to understand social and political life.

To make matters worse, it is possible to raise a still further group of questions about our prevailing understanding of terms like structure and history, and how it is informed by historically constituted concepts of space and time. Here metaphysics enters with a vengeance. Questions about ethics and ideology cannot be far behind. For some, of course, this would be enough to bring on a bad case of positivist vertigo. But in a discipline in which the reflections of Machiavelli, Kant and St. Augustine have not been entirely obliterated by the myth of a tradition, this should come as no surprise.

FROM INTERNATIONAL RELATIONS TO WORLD POLITICS

While introducing his analysis of the relative merits of the rationalistic and reflective approaches, Keohane affirmed his commitment to a socio-scientific analysis of world politics by explicitly marginalizing the themes I have tried to sketch here. In his view, he said, it

> will not be fruitful . . . indefinitely to conduct a debate at the purely theoretical level, much less to argue about epistemological and ontological issues in the abstract. Such an argument would only take us away from the study of our subject matter, world politics, towards what would probably become an intellectually derivative and programmatically diversionary philosophical discussion.[14]

The problem, however, is that Keohane's discussion is full of ontological and epistemological claims that are left abstract; his account of an empirical research programme is dependent upon ontological (as well as ethical and ideological) commitments; and in marginalizing problems that have long been central to (non-empiricist) philosophies of social science, he diverts attention from the serious philosophical and political problems that are at stake in even postulating world politics as subject matter. This is not, I should re-emphasize, to underestimate the importance of serious empirical research, merely to suggest that there is rather more involved in postulating concepts like interdependence, regimes, or international institutions than the formulation of an empirical research programme. As neo-

Kantian philosophies of science have insisted time and time again, the appropriate conceptualization of the problem already prefigures the solution. It is not a matter of arguing about ontological and epistemological issues in the abstract. Philosophical commitments are already embedded in concepts like state or state system, typologies like the level-of-analysis distinction and utilitarian accounts of rational action. The ideology-laden distinction between social science and socio-political theory, between empirical and normative forms of enquiry, simply cannot be sustained, no matter how much it may have legitimated disciplinary divisions and claims to professional expertise.

To advance concepts like interdependence or international regime is already to admit the significance of historical transformation. But to begin with history is to encounter problems that are usually encountered under the heading of the philosophy of history. Given the difficulty of some of these problems, it is perhaps not entirely surprising that they are so often marginalized and resolved in favor of ahistorical accounts of continuity and structural form. This has even happened to the interpretation of such a central figure as Machiavelli who is invoked, perhaps more than anyone else, as the prototypical theorist of international relations. Despite the prime place he occupies in the myth of a tradition, his concern with the relationship between the force of circumstance (*fortuna*) and the possibility of *virtu* in a political community is rarely taken seriously in this context. Machiavelli's *questions*, in fact, are hardly discussed at all. Hobbes has been much easier to assimilate for, with Hobbes, temporal questions are subordinated to historically specific accounts of structural form. For all his reputation as the devil incarnate, Machiavelli's thought has been reified and tamed. Yet Machiavelli's questions about the relationship between time or history (an era of accelerating transformations) and the possibility of new forms of political community are arguably much closer to what is involved in speaking about interdependence, or regimes or world politics, than are Hobbesian-style structuralist models.[15]

Similarly, many of the older realists were deeply preoccupied with questions about the philosophy of history. Many explicitly invoked an Augustinian contrast between time and eternity to explain the tragic condition of life on earth. Others responded to the relativistic implications of a loss of faith in the grand vision of historical progress. To read older realists like Carr, Morgenthau, Herz or Niebuhr is to be struck by the intensity of their philosophical and even theological concerns with time and history. As such, their writings stand in the sharpest possible contrast with those of contemporary structural or neo-realists. Unfortunately, however, their concern with history was rarely serious enough. It usually amounted to little more than the negation of Christian views of eternity or Enlightenment views of progress, a negation understood to be especially appropriate for a realm – inter-state relations – that was itself understood as the negation of that political community in which perfectability on earth was at least approachable – the state.

A sensitivity to history and time is always in danger of being undermined through reification. This is the essential complaint brought against the utilitarian approach by those who are identified with reflection. Historical practices are analyzed as ahistorical structures. Conscious human practices are erased in favor of structural determinations. But problems of temporality rarely disappear entirely. Attempts have even made to analyze temporal process in terms of structural patterns. The flux of time has been portrayed as teleological or dialectical necessity. The history of human consciousness has been portrayed in relation to the generative structure of grammar. The logic of scientific explanation has been extended from the sciences of inert matter to encompass patterns of probability in historical practices. But such strategies have always encountered powerful opposition. The historicity of human experience remains deeply problematic.

These are not simply abstract considerations, to be deferred as somehow merely theoretical or philosophical. They are at play in the concrete practices of intellectual life. Claims about a point of origin, a tradition or an essentially timeless form known as the state have had an enormous impact on what world politics is assumed to be, and thus on what it means to participate in or offer a legitimate account of world politics. Questions about the relationship between reified structures and conscious human practices are at the heart of the dominant ideological forces of modern political life, though these forces resolve the questions in distinctive ways.

These remarks do not imply that empirical research is unimportant, nor that structuralist analysis has nothing to offer. Still less do they suggest that the questions pursued by the utilitarian rationalists are trivial. On the contrary, questions about processes of inter-state co-operation and discord; the emergence of new patterns of interdependence and dependence; the appropriate conceptualization of regimes or institutions; the globalization of production, distribution and exchange or the changing character of state formation in response to economic and technological transformations, functional problems and political struggles are obviously crucial. Contemporary world politics is, as Keohane rightly emphasizes, 'a matter of wealth and poverty, life and death.' Indeed, these questions should be understood in relation to the possibility of thinking about political life at all in the late twentieth century. They put in doubt the political categories that assume, with both Machiavelli and Hobbes, a fundamental distinction between political life within states and political life between states – the distinction that is constitutive of the discipline of international relations as we now know it. The questions are undoubtedly crucial, but the inherited categories of international relations theory do not necessarily offer the sharpest articulation of what they involve.

Structuralist analysis is also important, but so too are the persistent problems that structuralist analysis brings with it. Kenneth Waltz has to wrestle with the relative merits of systemic and reductionist forms of explanation, choosing – contentiously – to resolve competing metaphysical claims through a reifying typology of the individual, the state and states system as the essential components of the 'real world.' Others try to reconcile conflicting accounts of the primary structure as either the states system or a more inclusive global political economy. In both cases, it is possible to see powerful tensions between the claims of structure and those of history.

These tensions have characterized much of contemporary

intellectual life. They have been a familiar theme even within North American social science. Attempts to employ functional explanation or cybernetic and systems analysis, for example, have quickly attracted the charge of conservatism on the grounds that mechanistic and biological models systematically downplay the significance of human consciousness and political struggle. In a broader context, existential or phenomenological humanism was once challenged by the structuralism of Claude Levi-Strauss or Louis Althusser; which were then challenged in turn both by reassertions of humanism and, more iconoclastically, by the non-humanist historicism of the post-structuralists and postmodernists. In the background, of course, lie all those complex yet stylized codings in which Hegel's universal history challenges Kant's universal reason, or Aristotelian teleology follows Plato's geometrically inspired account of unchanging forms. In contemporary social and political theory, the tension between structure and history remains especially acute in ongoing debates about the relative significance of structure and action (and thus of explanation and interpretation) and about the status of modernity. It is no accident, therefore, that claims about the promise of a social scientific approach to world politics should be challenged by positions that draw from the interpretive and critical techniques of hermeneutics and deconstruction.

It seems reasonable to expect that the need for accounts of world politics that are somehow both structuralist and historically informed will continue to be urged. Keohane's hope for an eventual synthesis of utilitarian and reflective approaches can be read in this way. So can several other major theoretical perspectives that are for some reason excluded from Keohane's discussion: the society of states perspective associated with Hedley Bull, for example, or forms of political economy that seek to extend Marx's account of capital as an historically structured and always transformative force. It is certainly likely that greater attention will in future be given to understanding the historical interplay between the structuring of the states system and the structuring of global relations of production, distribution and exchange. But again, the limitations of traditions that give priority to either politics or economics draw attention less to the problems of a particular academic discipline than to tendencies that inform the most influential currents of social and political theory in general.

Yet if it is reasonable to argue the necessity of both structuralist and historical sensitivities, then it is also necessary to insist that empirical social science holds no monopoly on what this might bring. It might bring about a greater concern for the reifying practices that have been so powerful in accounts of a tradition of international relations theory, or in the more extreme presumption that a state is a state is a state. It might force open serious philosophical questions that have been closed off by the categories of realist and idealist, or by the pretence that neo-realism or structural realism is just an updated account of eternal realist principles. It might focus greater attention on the principle of state sovereignty as the crucial practice through which questions about human community are fixed within a spatial dimension that is sharply at odds with the historically constituted claims of the state. It might even focus attention on the deeply rooted categories through which we pretend to know what space and time are.

All of the above serves to identify the analysis of world politics with a much broader account of social and political enquiry than is usual in the specific discipline of international relations. If questions about interdependence, dependence, regimes and institutions are taken seriously – that is as possibly putting into question the early modern European accounts of what political community can be, given the passing of life before international relations – then it is not clear that such explorations are any less significant than, in need of subsumption into or just a prelude to a utilitarian and empirical social science. Vague and obscure hypotheses about the existence of something called world politics involve a claim to historical and structural transformation that throws historically derived concepts and disciplinary divisions into rather serious doubt. The difficulty of analyzing political life at this historical juncture remains more impressive than the achievements of theories of international relations. It is this difficulty, not the extravagant presumptions of modernist social science, that demands our immediate attention.

Notes

1. In this paper, I refer to international relations as an academic discipline; to world politics as an array of political processes that extend beyond the territoriality and competence of single political communities and affect large proportions of humanity; and to inter-state relations or the politics of states-systems as the narrower array of practices constituted through interactions between states. All these terms are highly problematic in ways that serve to underline the significance of questions about the character and location of political community in the late twentieth century. International relations, for example, reifies a specific historical convergence between state and nation; references to states systems tend to encourage a conflation of accounts of the state as a territorial space and as governmental apparatus; while world politics is used to refer to global political processes that largely escape prevailing analytical categories. The horizons of our language in this respect reflect the limits of traditions of political analysis that depend on a distinction between community within states and non-community (relations, anarchy, war) between them. For brief elaborations of this argument – which forms the subtext of the present paper – see R. B. J. Walker, *State Sovereignty, Global Civilisation and the Rearticulation of Political Space* (Princeton: Center of International Studies, Princeton University, World Order Studies Program, Occasional Paper, 8, 1988) and R. B. J. Walker, 'Ethics, Modernity and the Theory of International Relations,' paper presented at the Conference on New Directions in International Relations: Implications for Australia, Australian National University (Canberra, 15–17 February 1989).

2. Robert O. Keohane, 'International Institutions: Two Approaches,' *International Studies Quarterly* 32 (4) (December 1988), pp. 379–396 (see chapter 11 in this volume). See also Robert O. Keohane (ed.), *Neorealism and its Critics* (New York: Columbia University Press, 1986).

3. Typical discussions include Richard J. Bernstein, *The Restructuring of Social and Political Theory* (Philadelphia: University of Pennsylvania Press, 1976); Brian Fay, *Critical Social Science* (Cambridge: Polity Press, 1987); John G. Gunnell, *Between Philosophy and Politics: The Alienation of Political Theory* (Amherst: University of Massachusetts Press, 1986); and William E. Connolly, *Political Theory and Modernity* (Oxford: Basil Blackwell, 1988).

4. The main papers from this debate were collected in Klaus Knorr and James N. Rosenau (eds.), *Contending Approaches to International Politics* (Princeton: Princeton University Press, 1969).

5. Hedley Bull, *The Anarchical Society* (London: Macmillan, 1977). Cf., Friedrich N. Kratochwil, *Rules, Norms and Decisions* (Cambridge: Cambridge University Press, 1989); Richard K. Ashley, 'Living on Border Lines: Man, Post-Structuralism and War,' in James Der Derian and Michael Shapiro (eds.), *International/Intertextual Relations: The Boundaries of Knowledge and Practice in World Politics* (Lexington:

Lexington Books, 1989); Richard K. Ashley, 'The Geopolitics of Geopolitical Space', *Alternatives*, 12 (October 1987); and Richard K. Ashley, 'Untying the Sovereign State: A Double Reading of the Anarchy Problematique,' *Millennium* 17 (2), (Summer 1988).

6. The most instructive formulations of the realist – idealist distinction remain E. H. Carr, *The Twenty Years Crisis, 1919–1939*, 2nd edn (London: Macmillan, 1946); and Hans J. Morgenthau, *Scientific Man Vs. Power Politics* (Chicago: University of Chicago Press, 1946). They are especially instructive when read not as founding texts of the theory of international relations but as belated formulations of dilemmas associated with early twentieth-century German historicism as these dilemmas were mediated through the work of Karl Mannheim and Max Weber. See, e.g., Stephen P. Turner and Regis A. Factor, *Max Weber and the Dispute over Reason and Value* (London: Routledge & Kegan Paul, 1984).

7. See, e.g., the relatively accessible discussions in R. J. Holton, *The Transition from Feudalism to Capitalism* (London: Macmillan, 1985) and Michael Mann, *The Sources of Social Power*, vol. 1 (Cambridge: Cambridge University Press, 1986).

8. It is the most interesting, I have argued elsewhere, because it clarifies the connection between the contemporary usages of categories like realist and idealist and the early modern spatio-temporal resolution of questions about the possibility of political community offered by the principle of state-sovereignty, a resolution that is also constitutive of international relations as a field of enquiry. See. R. B. J. Walker, '*The Prince* and the Pauper. Tradition, Modernity and Practice in the Theory of International Relations' in Der Derian and Shapiro (eds.), *International/Intertextual Relations*.

9. Robert Gilpin, *The Political Economy of International Relations* (Princeton: Princeton University Press, 1987); Immanuel Wallerstein, 'The Rise and Future Demise of the World Capitalist System: Concepts of Comparative Analysis,' *Comparative Studies in Society and History* 16 (4), (September 1974); Robert W. Cox, *Production, Power and World Order: Social Forces in the Making of History* (New York: Columbia University Press, 1987); and Stephen Gill and David Law, *The Global Political Economy: Perspectives, Problems and Policies* (Baltimore: John Hopkins University Press, 1988).

10. See the important analysis in Friedrich Kratochwil and John Gerald Ruggie, 'International Organizations: A State of the Art on an Art of the State,' *International Organization* 40 (4) (Autumn, 1986).

11. For a more extended discussion are R. B. J. Walker 'Realism, Chance and International Political Theory,' *International Studies Quarterly*, 31 (1) (March 1987); and 'The Territorial State and the Theme of Gulliver,' *International Journal*, 39 (Summer 1984).

12. In international relations the adequacy of these images become especially important in the literature on systems analysis. For a helpful discussion see Richard Little, 'Three Approaches to the International System: Some Ontological and Epistemological Considerations,' *British Journal of International Studies* 3 (1), (October 1977).

13. On this theme see especially Der Derian and Shapiro (eds.), *International/Intertextual Relations*, and Michael Shapiro, *The Politics of Representation* (Madison: University of Wisconsin Press, 1988).
14. Keohane, 'International Institutions.'
15. For an argument to this effect see Walker '*The Prince* and The Pauper.'

13 Feminist Themes and International Relations (1991)

Jean Bethke Elshtain

I am a political theory interloper in the world of international relations. I studied international relations with Kenneth Waltz – the post-*Man, the State and War* Waltz and pre-*Theory* of International Politics Waltz. At the time, it must be said, I was not particularly concerned with the 'man' portion of the title of Waltz's splendidly lucid volume. I was, instead, taken with his conceptual schema which I found enormously helpful in sorting out the world of *feminist* theory. I returned to my dissertation recently as I thought of the influence of Waltz on my own theoretical work and I discovered an utterly Waltzian formulation in my introduction. It goes like this: '*Women and Politics: A Theoretical Analysis* is a critique of much current Feminist analysis because I have found that the solutions proposed to solve the problems of women in contemporary society often bear no logical relation to the arena pin-pointed as the source of the problem in the first place.'[1] And in the dissertation's final chapter, 'Tactics, Strategies, Ends and Means: foci for change and their implications,' I insisted:

> Solutions to the problem of women run the gamut from what R. D. Laing has termed the individual pirouette of change and repentance to take-over of the machinery of the state. The questions involved in examining the political strategies of the women's movement and their foreseeable consequences are many. The analyst must relate proposals for change back to the causes assigned as the source of women's dilemma. There should be a logical relation between the image of what precisely is wrong, and where, and the prescriptions put forth to alter the situation and implement desirable change. As Kenneth

340

N. Waltz puts it: 'Is the image adequate, or has the analyst simply seized upon the most spectacular cause or
the one he thinks most susceptible to manipulation and
ignored other causes of equal or greater importance?'
Corollary questions suggested by Waltz include whether
or not the final proposals can be implemented and how
attempts to implement them will affect other goals.

I will relate these questions back to the four foci most
commonly pinpointed as the source or sources of the problem of women in contemporary society, namely (a) woman
herself or man himself, hence human nature, (b) the
relations between women and men, (c) various subsystems
intermediary between the individual and macro-level structures, and (d) the macro-system itself or economic and
political structures. In exploring the ways Feminists have
looked at the problem, I will attempt to determine whether
their proposals for change bear a logical relation to the
arena cited as the chief source of the problem. It is obvious that one's proposals for what is necessary to give
women equality will differ depending upon whether one
locates the trouble in capitalist society, the family, or
male chauvinism.'[2]

I went on to blast the individualist fallacy; to criticize
analyses that began – and ended – with the *folie à deux* of
male–female relations; to suggest that one cannot locate 'the
problem' exclusively in families (then, and sometimes even
now, a feminist *bête noir*); and to insist that some sort of
structural analysis was most promising. Now, notice if you
will, that where Waltz's structural analysis pitches itself to
the level of inter-state relations and the presumption of an
anarchic sphere within which those relations occur, with
no final arbiter to disputes between and among states save
a resort to self-help on the part of states, my structural
approach ended, more or less, at the boundaries of states.
When I talked about system, I was referring to the 'domestic' political arena: whether a state is collectivist, authoritarian, capitalist, democratic, constitutional and the like.

I concluded that women's oppression or inequality was
overdetermined, that cause and consequence, the political
and the personal, percolated in and through the social system

in toto; thus 'any image for change frozen at a level of complexity beneath the systemic is perforce inadequate . . . Sexism, like war in Kenneth N. Waltz's analysis, exists because there is nothing to stop it. The oppression of women serves needs on the systemic level.'[3]

That was then; this is now. As Bob Dylan once sang, 'I was so much older then/I'm younger than that now.' This is a generational way of saying: I'm far less confident of my own solutions and resolutions than I was at the tender age of 30. But let me also add that I don't find my dissertation-level analysis all that bad – it at least gestured towards a complexity that fell out of all-too-many feminist theories and, it must be said, international relations arguments as well. I have in mind particularly the game theoretical approaches to which I was subjected in Waltz's course. I found them befuddling and still do – a version of reductionism, economism, that sacrifices authentic explanatory power, which must be historical and cultural as well as *political* in a 'thick sense', by contrast to the cold comfort of a twentieth-century version of Occam's famous razor.

Let me begin 'where I am at now' with an awkward metaphor: no doubt not the most robust way to start things off but so be it. How does one carve up the universe of feminist discourse and the study of international relations? I think of it as a rougher beast than I did 20 years ago, perhaps not sloughing towards Bethlehem but to a far less certain destination. Taking the measure of this creature is tricky unless one begins to hack off bits here and there in order to serve up the scholarly repast neat, as it were. I prefer to stay with the image of a somewhat disconcerting, rough and ready entity which ongoingly eludes our capacity to capture, tame, define and ultimately serve it up tidily.

It all depends on the nature of the beast one is serving up. There are many creatures with many names inhabiting the universe of international relations and feminism: realism, neo-realism, world systems theory, neo-liberal institutionalism, dependency theory, game theory, rational choice theory, structuralism, neo-structuralism, and, now post-structuralism. Similarly, feminism defies premature attempts at closure. There are the political–theoretical versions: radical, Marxist, liberal, psychoanalytic feminisms and there are more abstract conceptual visions or versions including a feminist variant on structuralism, world systems theory, feminist standpoint theory (which often comes to the same thing) as well as feminist post-modern theories.[4] Some feminist theories are universalist in claim and aim; others eschew such universalistic aspirations, a repudiation coupled frequently with the vehement insistence that to reach for the universal is by definition to do damage to the culturally specific, to illegitimately seek to appropriate and to tame 'the Other' most often cast as the post-colonial Other, the third world victim, the silenced denizen of a realm of suppressed knowledges and the like. For most feminist IR scholars, I dare say, *all* pre-feminist international relations theory is suspect if not hopeless altogether because of its systematic 'gender bias.'[5]

My way of working will be rather different. The exploration of 'bias' seems to me not the most fruitful way to go, for a number of reasons. First, it suggests a tacit commitment to an emotivist account in which that which is called good depends upon one's biases, thus: a bias has infused previous studies of international relations. That bias is one that excludes women from whatever perspective, inquiry, or conclusion is at hand. Putting gender in corrects the bias, presumably. But matters are far more complex than that, in ways I cannot here explore.[6] Second, the claim of 'bias' tends to generate a 'counter-bias' in which gender becomes all-determinative, the key to any and all questions and problems, functioning rather like 'class' in classical Marxist discourse.

Absolutizing gender is a temptation to be resisted. All scholars find the prospect of a privileged epistemic ground seductive. Those laboring in the vineyard of feminist theory are no exception. The problem of 'point of view' is central to debates within and between feminist thinkers. Let me offer several examples drawn from anthropology but applicable to the matter at hand. Assessing the contention of a group of feminist anthropologists that, as members of a 'universal category,' they are 'somehow . . . free from bias,' Marilyn Strathern notes the self-confirming nature of their claims. The argument is that one validates one's anthropological study by taking up, and speaking from, the 'women's point of view,' under the presumption that a woman has a 'specific, non-replicable insight' into any given culture that is unavailable to a male researcher.

The self-consciously female–feminist point of view, the argument goes, is not subject to the charges of bias that can, indeed must, be leveled against a male point of view. Moreover, an identity is said to exist between 'the author and subject of study,' a 'naturally grounded' congruity. (Unkindly, one might call this the collapse into empathy.) The result is a position of privilege that enables the feminist anthropologist to dismiss male knowledge claims or interpretations. It also lets her derail challenges from female anthropologists who disagree on the ground that 'some' women who have experienced western patriarchy but fail to 'see' through the double-consciousness that their femaleness–feminism affords them are instead double-blinded. Similarly, Judith Shapiro questions the claim that a double standard in anthropology is legitimate for assessing 'male bias' on the one hand and a privileged female 'double consciousness' on the other.[7]

An alternative approach – critical, interpretive, theoretically modest, prepared to keep an appropriate distance between the subject matter of one's inquiry and one's own world and identity, open-ended yet willing to embrace strong possibilities for knowledge and for adjudicating between stronger and weaker perspectives and explanatory frameworks – attempts to keep alive debates rather than to move to definitive closure. Hermeneutical dilemmas cannot be evaded. Though knowledge and understanding may, in some interesting ways, be embodied – and this might help to explain why men and women, at least some of the time and to culturally specific ends and purposes, experience the world in different ways – no embodied being, male or female, has access to 'the whole' or anything like 'the totality.' One is free, therefore, to explore differences without presuming the superiority of a gendered narrative that closes out contesting interpretations. Not being hobbled in advance by the conceptual claims of gender as prison, the critic is open to the intimations and possibilities of gender as prism. This paper, then, should be taken as an invitation to an engagement, one already underway, between and among those who see themselves primarily as feminist scholars, those who identify themselves first and foremost as political theorists, and, finally, those laboring in the vineyard of international relations scholarship.

One final preliminary point must be made. It is perhaps a banal point but it surfaces again and again. Those of us who are looking at constructions of gender and international relations are not primarily lobbying for an increase in the number of women in the ranks of international relations scholars or as heads of states. Of course one can hope this happens as a matter of simple equity. Rather, we are pondering what difference it might make to the study of international relations if representations of gender were centrally and routinely included rather than being peripheral, a sideshow, to the extent they appear at all. By 'gender representations' I do not have in mind the much debated notion that were women to gain control over states, wars would be resorted to less frequently and less relentlessly. For now, let me indicate that I recognize that women as leaders and women as mothers and women as workers have sustained and supported the wars of their states in far greater numbers than women in any capacity have acted in opposition to wars and militarism and nationalistic excess.

What, then, are the issues or what might emerge as issues if one believes, as I do, that representations of gender have been essential to theorizing about the study of politics, including international relations, even in their 'absence'? My assumption is that tending to the inclusion of feminist themes – and none of those I will take up are narrowly or *exclusively* feminist – may contribute to all our thinking about the world of women, men, the state, and war.

First, texts as contested terrain. Contesting the discursive terrain is not unique to feminism but has become part and parcel of many contemporary challenges to what is called 'discursive practices' and the power these exert to frame our study of international politics. For example, in an earlier study I argued that contemporary versions of realism or neo-realism in their most robust incarnations not only offer up the bracing promise than one can spring politics free from the constraints of ethical limits, but that realism itself is constructed through a particular reading of a canonized set of texts – Thucydides, Machiavelli, Hobbes, Clausewitz, and others drawn in as apologists for *raison d'état*. The contemporary realist locates himself inside a well-honed tradition, exuding the confidence of one whose narrative long ago won the war.[8] But many of the texts central to the construction of realism and neo-realism are far more problematic than standard readings would indicate. For example, in his interesting piece, 'Thucydides and Neorealism,' Daniel Garst presents a 'sharply different' interpretation of Thucydides' *The Peloponnesian War* than that which appears in the work of Kenneth Waltz, Roger Gilpin and Robert Keohane. One of the most telling points made by Garst is that the generalizations Thucydides offers should not be taken as causal laws of politics but, instead, correspond to what Peter Winch (following the later Wittgenstein) calls 'ruled-governed behavior.' To understand *The Peloponnesian War*, one must unravel its complex rhetorical universe and culture of argument which consists of the 'discourse, the conventions of argument and action' by which the Greek city-states 'maintain and regulate their relations with one another' – Garst here cites Martin Wight.[9] Thucydides does not begin by talking about the distribution of power in a system, or the behavior of states, but about forms of political knowledge and identity that propel states into particular relations with one another *given* their historic 'habits, customs, and political institutions' and the activities and forms of power that flow from, or are contingent upon, well-defined and accepted social conventions and institutions.[10] Garst goes on to draw out the implications for contemporary neo-realist theory of his alternative reading by indicating that his approach undermines the views of political power that prevail in realist and neo-realist argument. And he moves at that point to distinctions between force, strength, violence and power indebted to Hannah Arendt.

What this effort to create a counter-tradition by reading texts against the grain offers is a gambit that may help to prise open received arenas of discourse to critical scrutiny. Such alternative readings are not just the endless play of intertextualities with which post-modernists are saddled or saddle themselves but, rather, a fundamental challenge. For to the extent that alternative readings of founding works come to prevail, modes of discourse that depend upon ongoingly re-encoded readings will be altered, as will the presumptions, meanings, even predictions they have been drawn upon to help generate, for example, the presumption that if we just isolate a few 'laws' and get some parameters straight, we can move to predict events. As Alan Ryan, in a review essay in *The Times Literary Supplement*, put it recently: 'It is absurd . . . to demand what the social sciences can't deliver. They can at best illuminate what *has* happened, not predict what will; describe the politician's opportunities, not tell him how to act.'[11]

It seems appropriate to note at this juncture that going back over classical texts is a controversial enterprise in the world of feminism and international relations, with some questioning the exercise as yet another attempt to 'defeat the master with his own weapons,' or something like that. But, as a political theorist, I work ongoingly with texts from the past and what makes many of these works great is that one can return to them again and again without exhausting what they have to say. Moreover, it surely matters whether, for example, Machiavelli belongs within a school which assumes that laws of behavior can be adumbrated by contrast to the alternative, namely, that rules for action can be explored. This is a big difference. Jane Jaquette argues that Machiavelli, far from being a constructor of causal laws, invented dialogue, deployed mythical modes of understanding, and was attuned to 'contradiction, association, metaphor, and multiple, often antithetical points of view.' Hence Machiavelli offers up an 'effective alternative to positivism,' with his cyclical vision of historic temporality, his ironic sensibility, and his awareness of the agonistic dimensions of political action. Jaquette, by the way, urges feminists to consider Machiavelli's approach as instructive, the world of phronesis or 'practical reason' by contrast to abstracted and universally categorical ways of thinking.[12] Criticisms of foundational texts is one feature of a more general attempt to prise open received arenas of discourse to critical scrutiny. Once one does this, contests about meaning open up that were previously eclipsed.

In my approach to Machiavelli, I argue that his understanding of politics, political power, and so on, revolves around

a particular sort of split in which women are separated
from what Joan Scott calls the 'high politics' of wars and
states.[13] I refer, of course, to the way in which he celebrates
virtu, a particular manly virtue as well as collective armed
esprit, by contrast to soft Christian inefficacy in the tough
world of men and states. Following on the heels of this
observation, I have since gone on to argue that, despite
Machiavelli's insistence on the exclusion of women from the
many arts of war and politics as a defining public activity,
he nevertheless analogizes from private to public rather
insistently in his work. He breaches the divide he has himself set up with implications that, for the most part, are
ignored, or were until feminist scholars began to point certain things out. Arguing from simile rooted in classical
precedent (images of the bitch goddess Fortuna who must
be mastered by the bold prince and bent to his will draws
upon Nemesis, for example), Machiavelli also mines, indeed
presumes, a distinction between form and matter (*forma* and
materia) in which the male principle gives shape to what
would otherwise be a formless mass. The prince's relationship to his people is akin to that of form to matter as
masculinized and feminized representations. There is, then,
a conceptual barrier between private and public in the
Machiavellian world that is paradoxically breached with his
free-flow analogizing between public and private imperatives where bringing feminized disorder to heel is concerned.
Preventing disorder is the overriding *raison être*.

Second, the politics of identity. Much contemporary feminist theorizing can be understood as coming to grips with
the construction of gendered identities; indeed, this has been
a near obsession with feminist theorizing from the early
1970s to the present moment. I have attempted to deal with
this question variously. For example, in *Women and War*, I
argue that war has been productive of identities, that it
calls men and women forth as civic subjects of a particular kind or kinds. Collective, historically constructed and
ongoingly reinscribed exemplars come into play when we
consider war and war-making in the West. Thus war entices
us in part (or so I claim) because we continue to locate
ourselves inside its prototypical emblems and identities –
the just war fighter, the heroine of the home front, the
country united and the like.

Men have fought as avatars of the nation-state's sanctioned violence; women have worked and wept and sometimes protested within the frame of practices that turn them out, militant Spartan Mother and pacifist protestor alike, as collective 'others' to the male warrior. These have served as the underpinnings for decision and action nonetheless real for being, if you will, symbolic, or, perhaps better put, represented symbolically. The 'Just Warrior' and the 'Beautiful Soul,' as I tag them, tropes on the social identities of men and women, do not denote what men and women really are in an essentialist sense but function, or have functioned in the past, to secure women's location as non-combatants and men's as soldiers. These paradigmatic linkages overshadow other voices and stories – of bellicose women, pacific males, or cruelty incompatible with just war fighting, of martial fervor at odds, or so we choose to believe, with maternalism in women and so on. The point is that the imagery of war, the collective identities called forth by war, do capture features of what men and women have actually become or are capable of becoming. We are dealing with identities, remember, not easily sloughed off external garments.

Why mention this in a discussion of feminist approaches to international relations? For this reason: to speak of identities in a rich socio-culture or collective sense is to transgress the classical 'levels of analysis' or 'three images' model deeded to us by Waltz, among others. You know the story: the individual (especially 'psychological characteristics' or presumably universal motivations); the state; the anarchic international arena itself, compromise three levels of explanation and causation: you must opt for one. The politics of identity, by contrast, compels one to move in and through these various levels as one looks at the ways in which individual, group, and national identities are constructed and the ways in which gender figures and moves in and through each category as a historically transformed and transforming 'reality.'

Let me give a hint of what is at stake here. In my discussion of just war theorizing in *Women and War*, I argued that, rather than obedience or disobedience to an abstract set of stipulative requirements, in times of war what really makes the difference in how a nation-state, as a collective identity, 'behaves' is the structure of that nation's history and experience – its strategic culture, if you will. The latter is by far more salient in assessing how 'decision-makers' act than finely honed deontological argumentation or theoretical assumptions about international anarchy and the pursuit of self-interest narrowly defined.

This makes contact with my first theme: we must look at the repertoire of possibilities available in particular societies at particular points in time. What dominates the political rhetoric? How do the citizens of *this* society compared to other societies construe themselves 'domestically' and in their relations with others? And how, then, does *this* collective identity have determinative force when it comes to relations between one state and another? For example: the strong claims often made on American international action – by contrast to claims made on others – are couched frequently in the language of human rights and the particular responsibility the United States has for upholding a normative vision of decent political relationships.

As well, looking at criss-crossing identities which transgress levels of analysis puts one in a critical relation to assumptions of the role of sovereign states as preposited ontological entities whose identity is given by stipulated definitions of what states 'are' and how they must act given what they are. Taking up identity politics means one *cannot* presume that all states work to maximize or secure their own power (with 'power' understood in an unproblematic way either as capabilities or as force one can bring to bear and so on). It opens up challenges to the notion of 'sovereignty' as the presumed motor that moves the system, conceptually, and in the realm of 'behavior.'

When we talk about those modes of argumentation that have prevailed in the academic study of international relations we are talking about sets of assumptions that add up to a predetermined 'identity' for states *qua* states as well as for men and women and the parts they play in the great story of war and politics. Identity theory makes these central categories and assumptions less secure and helps us to rethink what 'we are going', indeed, to rethink *how* to rethink how we have been thinking.

Third, challenging the state. What I have in mind here is

not the notion that were the state to melt away or fall under the repeated hammer blows of our critical assaults we would all be better off. I doubt that, actually. Rather, I am building on the question of a politics of identities: that which is taken for granted must be scrutinized, including the presumed identity of the state. I have in mind the assumption that the state is a unitary rational actor, a view which builds upon the analogy of a similar view of the individual as a rational, autonomous, independent actor propelling himself forward unless checked by counter-pressure of some sort – an unlikely fusion of Kantian and Hobbesian imperatives. An enormous body of feminist work challenges this view of the ideal moral agent as disembodied, ageless, sexless, transcendent of historic particularity. I will not rehearse those arguments here. My point for our purposes is to suggest that the presumed givenness of the rational actor as a wholly autonomous agent got joined to a species of utilitarianism to deed us that pastiche-person assumed by much political science. In international relations dominated, by a view of utility maximization, the person is the collectivized rational actor, the state.

Feminist questions concerning this particular representation of the state come at us from many directions and perspectives. Suffice it to say that seeing the state as a problem rather than a pregiven starting point is an ineluctable outgrowth of feminist concerns. And, of course, there is no single 'answer' once this view of the state is challenged. Marxist feminists will come up with a very different understanding of the state than pacifist feminists or post-modern feminists. Questioning given views of the state is not an end in itself, clearly, but an incitement to further thought which touches, finally, on political obligation and action itself.

I have approached this matter through the prism of sovereignty, arguing that the grand, classical account of sovereignty is parasitic upon metaphysical constructions of the deity as an absolute, sovereign, omnipotent and omniscient law giver. The law as command tradition fed into and helped to constitute sovereignty in the West. There is precious little constraint in the worlds of Bodin and Hobbes on the sovereignty of the absolute *dominus* over a bounded earthly territory, a vast domestic space requiring a final, absolute point of determination in order to maintain and sustain itself. Sovereign absolutism holds that sovereignty is indivisible, inalienable. Sovereignty over time shifts from King to State and this state 'can no more alienate its sovereignty than a man can alienate his will and remain a man.'[14] Rousseau himself protects sovereignty in this way through his postulation of the inalienability of the general will. The state and sovereignty are united. Each sovereign country is free to regulate its own domestic affairs without outside interference. The state is an independent, territorial monopoly of political power. We all know this story.

But how secure is it? Is it really the case that the modern body politic would grind to a halt if the assumption that there was a final and absolute authority within it were softened? Is not sovereignty constrained in all sorts of ways the classical theory represses – whether through the presumptions in medieval Christendom that there can be no unitary conception of sovereignty for all earthly rule is subject to divine judgment and higher law, or in the post-Reformation West that there are entities which may exert rival claims on us – for example, the Church. Are not domestic spaces themselves various and often at odds, scarcely decoctable to points of unitary harmony? And is not the international arena itself a society – in Hedley Bull's term – comprised of many actors, not just or only states? The possessiveness and exclusiveness of the classical concept of sovereignty deeded to us by elaborate legalistic justifications for earlier political formations, is open to challenge from many directions, then. The feminist direction points to a multiplicity of 'powers' and loyalties, moving away from the unitariness of sovereign willing, required, in the classical account, to stave off cacophony and chaos. Feminist concern with this matter is traceable, in part, to analogies drawn historically between the power of an absolute *dominus* in the household and the power of the absolute King or Parliament in the polity. The two got analogized and within the family, as within the commonwealth, the view prevailed that final authority must be singular. The face of the sovereign was distinctly masculinized.

To those who insist that final authority within a political region and, as well, the sovereignty of instrumental reason must reign supreme, one modulated feminist response might be to defend the notion of territorial political entities but to argue that they need not be sovereign in the classical sense – absolute power as dominion, laying down the law in a unitary way, and the like. Could not the notion of a homeland and of sovereignty as a limited concept come to prevail? Like the franchise, to press a different analogy, sovereignty offers political standing and enables people to defend the integrity of particular ways of life – not their inviolability but their integrity. Can one de-sovereignize political entities even as one continues to endorse a notion of political independence that recognizes and promotes forms of interdependence? What is at stake is an anti-monistic defense of particularism that ongoingly subjects that particularism to forms of judgment that limit it in actual operation: no doubt an uneasy fusion of universal and historically particular and specific possibilities.

One final point: I have argued previously that received notions of sovereignty incorporated in their absolutist heart of hearts a demand for blood-sacrifice: *pro patria mori*. This sacrificial demand got encoded into modern identities, male and female, with the triumph – the very bloody triumph – of the modern nation-state. In moving to a post-sovereign politics, might one not shift the focus of political loyalty and identity from *sacrifice* to *responsibility*? If the claims of sovereignty are chastened; the demands lowered and challenged; the will-to-sacrifice supplanted by a more skeptical, critical sense of political identity, one can then envisage a politics open to all sorts of diverse pressures – both foreign and domestic.

I am thinking here, for example, of the Mothers of the Plaza de Mayo, the Mothers of the Disappeared, in Argentina who challenged the absolutist claims of a military authoritarian state with an ethical–politics grounded in human rights. Human rights is an international discourse, sometimes the only way people have to fight state terror. But when they do so they are 'not alone,' to speak, because an entire international movement links up with them.

This opens upon the vista of the idea of its nation, stripped of some of the pretentions of sovereignty, as a genuinely non-aggressive and non-exclusive site, and suggests a plea for cultural *self*-determination comfortable with insistence upon the possibility of co-existence. As Isaiah Berlin has argued, the plurality of cultures is irreducible and that plurality is best recognized in and through institutions that create and protect independence. 'Once pluralism of ways of life is accepted, and there can be mutual esteem between different uncombinable outlooks, it is difficult to suppose than all this can be flattened out – *gleichgeschaltet* – by some huge, crushing jackboot.'[15] And such entities, open to plurality, offer political space within which questions of gender and other forms of inequality can be debated. Until people have some guarantee of communal or community safety and order, however, these issues will be on the backburner. This is a recognition not as widely shared among feminist thinkers as it should be.

Four, rethinking power. Feminist thinkers who have challenged neorealist assumptions as well as the ahistoric abstractions of game theory, formal modeling, and so on, compel us to re-examine our key concepts, including power. For if politics is about power what is power about? The hardline answer is domination, control, compulsion, bringing force to bear to best advantage. One can see power in operation, both posit and test it, because you can assess it 'behavioralistically,' by contrasting the moves of one entity compared to another. This very mechanical definition of power once reigned in American political science, reducing to the formula: *X* has power over *Y* if he can get *Y* to do something *Y* would not otherwise do – with endless variations on this theme.

Of course, nearly everyone is more sophisticated than this formula allows. But the reductive 'mechanicalness' of many views of power continue to haunt the projects of those devoted to prediction. Interestingly, the tradition of Western political thought challenges the notion of power as the compulsion of one unitary actor or agent on another – a challenge rarely taken up by international relations scholars. It – this tradition – offers multiple understandings of power, its meaning, its range of application, its legitimate and illegitimate uses, its relation to authority, justice and political order.

Let me just note that something interesting happens if

one recalls two Latin terms for power: *potestas* and *potentia*. The former denotes control, supremacy, dominion; the latter is power understood as might or ability, efficacy, potency, especially 'unofficial' and possibly threatening anarchy and disorder. Fascinatingly, these contrasting usages demarcate roughly the boundaries of gendered representations of power historically. Men have been the official wielders of institutional power and dominion; women the unofficial (hence potentially uncontrollable) repositories of 'non-political' power. *Potentia* may conjure up the threatening, occupying a boundary that touches on the uncanny, the 'outside,' the potentially disordered, calling to mind St Augustine's quip that the Romans should have erected a statue to the goddess Aliena, the threatening outsider who must be conquered, because she had served them so well.

Potestas has taken the form of highly institutionalized, centralized entities – including states – with their sovereign power layered over older understandings, as I suggested above. Much more needs to be said in order to unravel the thread that seems to run through the tangle of historic and ethnographic evidence picturing formal male power being balanced or even undermined by informal female power, at some times; at others, formal power (*potestas*) eclipses and even seeks to eradicate unorganized power.[16] The point, once again, is that power as a unitary concept 'rests on – contains – repressed or negated material, and so is unstable, not unified.'[17]

Such an exploration would help one to make sense of the irony of women's participations in struggle for statehood. Such struggles involve a collective identity as a people and a search for the means to protect and to defend that identity. But, once statehood is secured, women tend to be absent in the counsels of state. A historic reconstruction of the drive toward state systems, focusing on their elimination of competing forms of social organization and power, is surely a pre-eminent and important enterprise for feminist scholars. What is at work here is the possibility of opening up political space and 'complexifying' identity by pushing back the sway of *potestas* in favor of modes of social organization less dominated by fear of those multiple sources of power and action which exists both domestically and internationally. These forces should be nurtured not swamped. For in process of centralization and codification of hierarchies, women have tended to get lost, to be excluded. There seems to be something about moves toward centralization and codification – the triumph of *potestas* – that relegates women to particular sites which are *essential* to the social order which has emerged but are seen as marginal to it. This, surely, would admit of empirical adjudication – case studies of the sort anthropologists have already undertaken about who wins and who loses when things change.

One other point on this point: many feminist and 'nontraditional' male scholars draw upon Hannah Arendt, noting her attempt to rescue politics from war by separating violence from power. I have been one of these, noting that by 'conflating the crude instrumentalism of violence with power, defined by Arendt as the human ability to act in concert and to begin anew, we guarantee further loss of space within which authentic empowerment is possible. In this way violence nullifies power and stymies political being.'[18] Arendt's argument is provocative, as is her insistent use of the metaphor of natality to characterize new and fragile political beginnings. But Arendt is by no means unproblematic, not so much because she was disinterested in feminism as a genre – that, after all, is her prerogative – but because, when it comes to relations between states, she opts for the Hobbesian view of a war of all against all. We have wars because 'there is no alternative to victory' in conflicts between states.[19] To be sure, she goes on to decry the sovereignty of the state as the source of this Hobbesian rule, but that is as far as she goes, despite the fact that she declares the 'identification of freedom with sovereignty' to be 'perhaps the most pernicious and dangerous consequence of the political equation of freedom and free will.' She further adds that the 'famous sovereignty of political bodies has always been an illusion, which, moreover, can be maintained only by instruments of violence, that is, with essentially nonpolitical means.'[20] This is a terribly untheorized feature of Arendt's political thought. Simply reincorporating it as a preferred alternative to older notions of dominion does not push us very far towards believable theoretical and political alternatives. One common theme in feminist analyses is to endorse a vision of power as a form of 'connection' and 'care' by contrast to harsher images. But connection may as easily breed conflict as anything else. And care may turn maternalistic as well as paternalistic.

Finally, the relation between feminism, the politics of peace, and international relations. All sorts of studies of 'conflict management' preceded the feminist resurgency in international relations. There is a vast literature available on this theme. I have in mind something else, namely, the concept of peace which dominates much feminist reflection as an alternative to war or 'the war system' or it is sometimes called.

I have argued that one version of peace politics is ontologically suspicious for it never appears without its violent *doppelgänger*, war, lurking in the shadows. Peace is inside, not outside a frame with war in the most powerful and utopian expressions of its desirability and realizability. War is threatening disorder; peace is healing order. War is human aggressivity – male primarily if not exclusively; peace is human benevolence – female primarily if not exclusively. These assumptions are among the most dubious outgrowths of 'genderizing identities' and any feminism worth its salt must challenge them.

As I have previously argued, women's stake in sorting this out is great. If peace requires various endorsements that project a world of ongoing equilibrium, harmony and perfect order, it makes enormous good sense for women – especially feminists – to eschew its blandishments. For *this* peace traffics in Manichean constructions that have long relied upon particular visions of the 'feminine.' This has not yet happened in a persistent way, for those feminists who most dominate debates about war and peace have tended to be ideologists who simply invert the older ontological ledger, rankings and evaluations, calling for a free flow from a benevolent, feminized and transformed, private and domestic world to a peaceful, because feminized and transformed, public world. This watery feminized universalism finds many spokeswomen contrasting masculinism, patriarchy, violence, and disorder with feminism, matriarchy, non-violence and harmonious order. There are those who insist that feminism

sees power only in its 'healthy form' as a 'holistic understanding' which 'leads naturally to the cooperative and
nurturing behavior necessary for harmonious existence.' This
creates the character I call the Beautiful Soul and gives
her a feminist gloss. Such is the irony of total inversions
which wind up endorsing, even requiring, that which they
would oppose. Until such absolutist constructions are challenged in the name of a critical and ironic feminism, peace
remains a problem.[21]

I have proposed the following thought experiment at conferences and symposia: suppose the current war/state system were somehow to pass: what forms of conflict would
occur? What alternative conceptualizations of struggle do
we imagine? Is there a specifically feminist way to conceptualize politics as an agonistic activity which avoids the
deadliness of older construals? I am not really so sure about
this. But I do know that if one is going to call for an 'end'
to states, one must come up with plausible alternative ways
of organizing political space. One cannot posit coherently
a world totally at odds with the world we know, altogether
different, hence fanciful, hence not serious in the best sense.
Perhaps, as Michael Howard suggests, a world without states
would be a more, not less, violent world – a universal
Lebanonization. Historically and currently, feminism has
driven towards utopianism in many of its most widely known
incarnations. But this, as 'peace politics,' winds up empty
as explanatory theory and naive as politics.

No single standpoint or perspective gives us transparent
pictures of reality. Many perspectives and ways of seeing
expand the horizons of our discourse and make more supple
our thinking. Even as women struggle against their
demonization or its mirror image, their exaltation into airy,
angelic innocents (with the irony of some feminists bur-
nishing this vision to their own purposes), so it is important to clarify that in criticizing received approaches and
various practitioners, including statesmen, diplomatists and
even war-fighters, one is not judging the 'wicked' masculinity that good feminism will one day best. The most robust
feminist project – in its relation to international relations –
is one that embraces an attitude of constraint and moderation
even as those pressing this project challenge dominant pre-

sumptions. For a final feminist theme, if we are to endorse politics and open up power plays, is the vital importance of debate itself as a political and conceptual imperative of the first rank.

Notes

1. Jean Bethke Elshtain, *Women and Politics: A Theoretical Analysis*, University Microfilms, 1973, p. 5.
2. *Women and Politics*, pp. 346–347.
3. *Women and Politics*, p. 316.
4. For an interesting sorting out of the field of feminist discourse and international relations see Christine Sylvester, 'The Emperors' Theories and Transformations: Looking at the Field Through Feminist Lenses,' in Dennis Pirages and Christine Sylvester (eds.), *Transformations in the Global Political Economy* (London: Macmillan, 1988). I would cavil somewhat with my own placement securely in the 'feminist post-modernism' category by Sylvester but this is not a point worth belaboring. See also Spike Peterson's 'Introduction' to her edited volume (Boulder: Westview Press, 1992) *Gendered States*. R. B. J. Walker, 'On the Discourses of Sovereignty: Gender and Critique in the Theory of International Relations,' in the Peterson volume, sees the value of feminist theory in a difficult and rather ascetic way: it can help us to answer questions about who we are given the 'fragility of historically constituted certainties;' hence a 'more active intersection between feminism and international relations' is called for.
5. See, for example, the discussion by Rebecca Grant, 'The Sources of bias in international relations theory,' in R. Grant and K. Newland (eds.), *Gender and International Relations* (Bloomington and Indianapolis: Indiana University Press, 1991), pp. 8–26.
6. See Jean Bethke Elshtain, 'Methodological Sophistication and Conceptual Confusion: A Critique of Mainstream Political Science,' in Julia A. Sherman and Evelyn Torton Beck (eds.), *The Prism of Sex* (Madison: University of Wisconsin Press, 1979), pp. 229–252.
7. This paragraph and the following paragraph are drawn from my essay, 'Feminist Political Rhetoric and Women's Studies,' in John S. Nelson, Allan Megill, and Donald N. McCloskey, *The Rhetoric of the Human Sciences. Language and Argument in Scholarship and Public Affairs* (Madison: University of Wisconsin Press, 1987), pp. 319–340. See also Marilyn Stratherrn, 'Culture in a Netbag: The Manufacture of a Subdiscipline in Anthropology,' *Man*, 16, 1981, pp. 665–688; and Judith Shapiro, 'Anthropology and the Study of Gender,' in Langland and Gove, *A Feminist Perspective in the Academy: The Difference it Makes* (Chicago: University of Chicago Press, 1981), pp. 110–29.
8. Jean Bethke Elshtain, 'Realism, Just War and Feminism in a Nuclear

Age,' *Political Theory*, 13 (1) (February 1985), pp. 39–57.

9. Daniel Garst, 'Thucydides and Neorealism,' *International Studies Quarterly*, 33 (1) (March 1989), pp. 3–28 at p. 7. See also James H. Nolt, 'Social Order and War; Thucydides, Aristotle, and the Critique of Modern Realism,' unpublished ms. presented at the Annual Meeting of the American Political Science Association (1989).

10. Garst, 'Thucydides', p. 11.

11. Alan Ryan, 'A society of nations?', *Times Literary Supplement* (March 22, 1991), p. 506.

12. Jane Jaquette, 'Machiavelli,' unpublished ms., pp. 2, 4, 5.

13. Joan Scott, *Gender and the Politics of History* (New York: Columbia University Press, 1988), pp. 7, 48–49.

14. Charles Merrian, *History of Sovereignty Since Rousseau: Studies in History, Economics and Public Law*, vol. XII, no. 4 (New York: Columbia University Press, 1900), p. 33.

15. Isaiah Berlin, 'Two Concepts of Nationalism: An Interview with Isaiah Berlin,' *New York Review of Books* (November 21, 1991), pp. 19–23.

16. I am relying here on the work of a number of cultural anthropologists. All are cited in my essay, 'The Power and Powerlessness of Women,' in *Power Trips and Other Journeys* (Madison: University of Wisconsin Press, 1990).

17. Scott, *Gender and the Politics of History*, p. 7.

18. Elshtain, 'Realism, Just War and Feminism,' p. 39.

19. Hannah Arendt, *On Violence* (New York: NBJ, 1969), p. 6.

20. Hannah Arendt, *Between Past and Future* (Baltimore: Penguin Books, 1968), p. 164.

21. Here I draw upon my essay, 'The Problem with Peace,' *Millennium*, 17(3) (Winter 1988), pp. 441–451.

Part V
Reinvestigations

14 A Reinterpretation of Realism: Genealogy, Semiology Dromology

James Der Derian

> Things are going to slide in all directions
> Won't be nothing
> Nothing you can measure anymore.
>
> Leonard Cohen, 'The Future', 1992

SYNCHRONICITIES

In periods of accelerated global change, when patterns are elusive and predictions difficult, one is more likely to accept conterminous events as signs of what is to come in international relations. One such moment of seeming synchronicity happened while I was attending a conference on 'Comprehending Sovereignty' – the day the bomb went off in the parking garage of the World Trade Center. It began with the news coverage in the morning interrupted by an advertisement for an NBC special to be aired that night, 'Terror Hits Home', followed by the scheduled Dean Witter ad in which the narrator intoned – as a helicopter shot of the two towers of the Trade Center rotated in the background – 'Our business is to protect our investors.' Unlike the procedures following an airplane crash, the producers of network television did not seem to have a contingency plan to yank sensitive ads after a terrorist attack on American soil. The day proceeded in an oddly normal way. No one in the course of the presentations brought up this highly symbolic, highly successful breaching of US sovereign territory. The night ended auspiciously: preparing to leave from the backdoor of my host's early Federalist home, I inadvertently leaned up against the control panel of his security system, setting it off. No one knew the access code, so a circuit breaker was thrown to stop the sirens. I left before the police arrived.

The signs, as I read them, is that the attenuations and articulations of sovereignty have became so complexly linked that the official as well as theoretical response has been to condemn rather than comprehend any new challenge to it. To be sure, it is a tragedy that six people were killed in the bomb blast; and it is likely that home security systems stop break-ins. But how are we to gauge the level of response to those deaths and security alarms against the 'normal' homicides and crimes that visit New York City every day? While it is still fresh, reconsider the immediate aftermath and after-images of the incident. On the first day, Governor Mario Cuomo set the stage: 'The damage looks like a bomb; it smells like a bomb; it's probably a bomb.' He went on to declare that 'normalcy' cannot return 'to this safest and greatest city and state and nation in the world until the culprits are caught.'[1] Considering that this statement came at the end of a week in which six residents of the Bronx were lined up and shot through the back of the head, and a seventh, in a related incident was shot outside a Bronx courthouse, one must ask, what constitutes 'normalcy'? The answer: abnormalized events such as this one.

If we are mesmerized by the violence or blink from the horror of terrorism, we are likely to miss the significance of the aftermath, when the calculus of the state, force-multiplied by the media and the fear of the body politic, drops like a stone through the web of its own sovereignty myth. Woven from strands of words, tropes, and concepts with sticky meanings, it is a flimsy construction but one nonetheless which can entrap the critically unwary. Constant discursive repairs must be made to this web of meaning, for it is under daily assault by a range of external and internal forces, material and immaterial challenges. The list is long and by now familiar: accelerating economic flows, viral epidemics, acid rain and acid-wash jeans, ICBMs and BCCIs, Sony, Krupps, and Time-Warner, TRW, IBM, and CNN. But these challenges effect only low-order maintenance repairs to sovereignty, like selective tariff-borders and protectionist rhetoric. These sovereignty effects simultaneously provide the illusion of protection and immune the citizen from the costs that might attend such protection. It takes a brick falling through the web, a rented Ryder van full of K-Mart explosives, to reveal the highly tenuous and increasingly ambiguous nature of sovereignty. Again, Cuomo provides good testimony. The day after the blast he declares that: 'No foreign people or force has ever done this to us. Until now, we were invulnerable'.[2] A cover story of *Newsweek* mixes metaphors of illness, religion, and evil to powerful effect:

> 'The explosion shook more than the building; it rattled the smug illusion that Americans were immune, somehow, to the plague of terrorism that torments so many countries.[3]

With barely concealed *schadenfreuden*, the foreign press played the chord of vulnerability. Some upped the fear ante by throwing in intertextual references to even greater apocalypses. '"Invulnerable" US is rocked by a strike at its heart' was the headline of the London *Sunday Times*, followed by the lead, 'Geordie Grieg reports on a nightmare New Yorkers had previously seen only in the movies.':

> He began the day as a clerk working for the Dean Witter brokerage on the 74th floor of the World Trade Centre in New York and ended it as an extra in a real-life sequel to Towering Inferno . . . The threat of terrorism may now introduce to the city the nervous tedium of security that Londoners and others know so well. But it also appears to thrust New York importantly into the midst of the world's many tribalisms.[4]

And the experts were quick to speculate on foreign sources to this type of terrorism. News weeklies carried a list of the usual suspects, ranging from Quadafi and Escobar to Serbian nationalists and Iranian fundamentalists. In a rare Deleuzian moment, the *New York Times* explained why we are especially vulnerable to a particular kind of people who by nature are prone to terrorism – and all the more difficult to find and punish for it:

'One search is leading to another', said one ranking investigator. 'But these are nomadic people. While it may lie in the culture, they bounce from place to place. All different people sleep there and stop there, stay a short time, then leave.'[5]

By the end of the week terrorist experts were dusting off their data banks and adding to the chorus. Rivaling the tabloids in pure sensationalism, the *New York Times* weighed in with an editorial by Mark Edington, who is evidently an expert in-training at the Fletcher School of Law and Diplomacy. Signaling his preference for hyperbole over analysis, hysteria over history, he goes for the metaphorical power of synecdoche in his essay 'Suddenly, America is a World Trade Centre.'[6]

> If the attack against World Trade Center proves anything, it is that our offices, factories, transportation and communication networks and infrastructures are relatively vulnerable to a skilled terrorists [*sic*] so long as they can get a foot in the door . . . The new world disorder means we'll be a bigger target . . . Among the rewards for our attempts to provide the leadership needed in a fragmented, crisis-prone world will be as yet unimagined terrorists and other assorted sociopaths determined to settle scores with us.

Obviously alarmed and taking no commercial chances, the producers of the new Schwarzenegger film, 'The Last Action Hero,' disarmed the 75-foot-high balloon of the star that straddled the Armed Forces Recruitment Center in Times Square, by replacing two sticks of dynamite in his left hand with a lawman's badge.

It would be nice if all events with sovereignty effects deconstructed themselves so readily as the World Trade Center. But they don't. Events come wrapped in representations, bundled in ideology, edited by the media, warped by official stories.[7]

For instance, the massacre at El Mozote of 700 peasants by the Salvadoran military, rendered a non-event by Jean Kirkpatrick, Alexander Haig, and Thomas Enders, among others, is only subject to reinterpretation 10 years later under a new regime of power and truth. More is needed: new historical challenges to sovereignty require new theoretical approaches. As a first step, this essay targets the representational power of realism which has coded and continues to code the world-historical events from which sovereignty is constructed. With Nietzsche as my guide – and Virilio as occasional drop in – I present three critical approaches for understanding realism: genealogy, semiology and dromology. Some might try (and I wish them godspeed) to map an uncertain future with these approaches. Here I can only introduce them as post-realist sign posts for understanding late modernity.

AGAINST TRADITION

First, to reinterpret realism is to step backward, look wider, and dig deeper, not to excavate some reality that has been lost or lurks beneath the surface of things, but to lay bare persistent myths of a reality that can be transcribed by a school of thought and yet still claims to speak for itself. As I have argued in previous cases, a *genealogy* is the most appropriate way to begin such a task.[8] A genealogy calls into question the representation of immaculate origins, essential identities, and deep structures of realism, revealing the metaphorical and mythical beginnings of a uniform realism while producing through interpretation several realisms that never 'figure' in the IR official story. What Bertolt Brecht said of the study of realism in literature equally applies to our own field of inquiry: 'Realism is an issue not only for literature: it is a major political, philosophical and practical issue and must be handled and explained as such – as a matter of general human interest.[9]

Second, a *semiology* is needed, in the sense of a study of realism as a symptom of a more general condition of late modernity, in which an old order is dying and a new one not yet constituted. To the ear of the other, this might have the sound of a marxian dialectic, a linguistic structuralism, or even a metaphysical eschatology. In intent if not in fact a semiology is an *anti*-metaphysical, pragmatic investigation of realism's reliance on an archaic sign-system in which words mirror objects and theory is independent of the reality it represents. The subsidiary purpose is to show how this para-philosophical conceit has disabled realism's power to interpret as well as to manage the current disorder of things.[10]

A semiology, then, provides a method for a study of the interdependent mix of power, meaning and morality that makes up realism. In *The Twilight of the Idols*, Nietzsche exposes this link with a harsh clarity:

> To this extent moral judgment is never to be taken literally: as such it never contains anything but nonsense. But as *semeiotics* it remains of incalculable value: it reveals, to the informed man at least, the most precious realities of cultures and inner worlds which did not *know* enough to 'understand' themselves. Morality is merely 'sign' language, merely symptomatology: one must already know *what* it is about to derive profit from it.'[11]

He is equally blunt about the potentially radical effects of a semiological inquiry: 'I fear we are not getting rid of God because we still believe in grammar.'[12] His fear applies as well to this critical investigation: disturbing the apodictic link between a positivist theory of realism and a correspondence philosophy of language, it cannot be construed as merely an academic exercise – which perhaps is one more reason why the IR academy has kept semiology at a distance.[13] The dual imperative of securing the state and IR theory from anything more than threatening than incremental change has placed a premium on 'traditional' approaches. A semiology disturbs this naturalized order, not out of a faddish desire for innovation or a heroic vanguardism, but out of a suspicion that there are high moral costs attached to the kinds of inertial systems of thought that become institutionalized in high politics and higher learning.[14] William Connolly seizes on this troubling of complacency by Nietzsche:

> The dogmatic assertion of will to power carries within it the corollary assertion that there is an element of resistance and recalcitrance in every human formation. And the Nietzschean presumption of resistance exposes in other theories implicit assumptions about a world susceptible to human mastery or a world designed to respond to human

yearnings for harmonious community. It calls both of these projections into question together rather than allowing thinkers to incline automatically toward the first whenever the second is doubted and then to incline toward the second whenever the first is doubted. In this way it takes thought off its automatic pilot.[15]

Third, a *dromology* of realism is required, in Paul Virilio's sense of a study of the science or logic of speed, because the representational principle of correspondence described above which underpins realism has itself increasingly become undermined by the ascendency of temporality over spatiality in world politics.[16] Elsewhere I have identified this as the '(s)pace problematic' of IR, where the displacement of geopolitics by chronopolitics makes a nation-state security founded on the stasis of a fixed identity and impermeable territory increasingly difficult to maintain.[17] In turn, the multifarious effects of speed compound the need for a semiology of realism: the instantaneity of communication, the ubiquity of the image, the flow of capital, the videographic speed of war have made reality ever more a transitory, technologically contingent phenomenon.[18]

In a world in which speed is not just the measure but the end of progress, tendencies and flows, arrivals and departures, all forms of movement come to govern and devalue both the immobile object and objectivity itself. *Real estate*, in the dual sense of transparent and immovable property, loses out to *irreal representations* which are infinitely transferable. In short, the dromocratic machine colonizes reality and its 'reflective' mediation, realism. With a casual hyperbole Virilio freeze-frames this imperialism of movement:

> It's clear that we are currently in a period of substitutions. One generation of reality is in the process of substituting itself for another and is still uncertain about how to represent itself. And we have to understand that it is very much connected to real-time images. It's not a problem of the configuration or the semiotics of the image, but a problem of the temporality of the image.[19]

In the current age of speed, surveillance, and simulation, genealogy, semiology and dromology provide new deconstructive tools *and* antidiplomatic strategies to reinterpret realism.[20] This essay, then, is doubly prodomal, a sign of both the heightened anxiety and trammeled hope that appear when the mirror of an old order cracks and we must remember, reimagine, and if possible, reconstruct a new image of our self-identity.

THE SCHOOL(YARD) OF REALISM: GET REAL, GO FIGURE

How do genealogy, semiology, and dromology differ from past efforts to interpret realism? First, they offer new perspectives on realism in a period of rapid change. The failure of realism to anticipate or to explain the end of the Cold War, and its willingness in gravelly baritones to rationalize the violence that ensued in Nagorno-Karabakh, Bosnia, Somalia and elsewhere, can be studied as signs of how the very inability of realism to represent and decelerate change *necessitates* the rationalization and ethical cleansing of violence. This is not a reiteration of the question whether realism reflects or belatedly rationalizes the harsh realities of an anarchical system. Nor is it a rehash of the realist–idealist debate of the 1930s. To be sure, some similarities – most explicitly in the Balkans and no less so in the Baltic – do cry out for a comparative appraisal of what states and international institutions must do to manage the post-Cold War better than the inter-war period. But first an intellectual effort is needed to demythologize the antimonies of realism that have from its beginnings constituted and so confounded International Relations.[21]

The three approaches that make up a critical pluralism continue the refiguring of realism begun by Richard Ashley, Hayward Alker, Rob Walker, Nicholas Rengger, Frederich Kratochwil, Nicholas Onuf, Alexander Wendt, Francis Beer, Robert Hariman, and a new generation of IR thinkers.[22] This school, if it could be called such, differs from previous ones because it interprets realism as an ongoing discursive struggle that cuts across the traditional theory–practice, idealist–realist, and other synchronic and scholastic antinomies of world politics. It gives notice of how realism in its universalist philosophical form and particularist state application has figuratively *and* literally helped to constitute the discordant world it purports to describe.[23] In other words, the scholars of this school do not seek to repudiate realism: they seek instead to dismantle a variety of epistemic privileges by which one form of realism dominates contesting forms.[24]

A critical, pluralist approach to realism should not, however, be mistaken as one more policing action, to substitute a new disciplinary gaze for realism's para-philosophical guise. There is nothing to be gained by positing some 'new,' purer form of realism in opposition to older, corrupted ones. My aim, as perverse and colonial as it may sound, is to deconstruct realism in order to save it. This is an attempt to open up the hermeneutic circle, to enlarge the interpretive community, to break out of the prison-house of a reductive vocabulary that has so attenuated the ethico–political dimension of realism. The intent is to flood the protected marketplace of IR theory with a multiplicity of realisms, devalue its proprietary origins, and in the process break its traditional dependency upon an evil, utopian, or merely irrational other to maintain a pure identity. We might just then be able to reinterpret the value of realism in a period of rapid systemic change.

As I have said, others have already begun to pursue this line of inquiry. But at this point it would be a mistake to call the refiguring of realism a debate between uniform schools of thought. Within the schools, there have been impressive intellectual contributions which have reinvigorated IR theory. However, between them it has been more of a scrap in the schoolyard, with slogans instead of theory filling the air. As I see it, there is a 'get real' crowd on one side and the 'go figure' on the other. Nonetheless, for the sake of exposition it might be useful to pretend that these two groups exist as, or at least have the potential to become inter-discursive communities.

On the one hand (sometimes ready to curl into the fist), the 'get real' group first domesticates an internal order and constructs an anarchical external one with stories of the recurrence and repetition of struggles for power, enjoining us, in circular fashion, to prepare for the worst if we do not maintain a realist perspectives and a global engagement.

Recent statements from two out-of-work arch-realists reinscribe the discursive boundaries of the traditional antinomy of order and anarchy through a favored tactic of historical analogy. The first is from the National Security Advisor to former President George Bush, Brent Scowcroft:

> The last time the world was in a roughly analogous situation was in 1919. At that time, there were no great, global threats apparent to American interests . . . Though we couldn't see where the threat was coming from in 1919, the US nourished the seeds of World War II by disengaging.[25]

The other is from Zbigniew Brzezinski, who held the same office in the Carter administration:

> In some respects the post-Cold War situation in the Far East is reminiscent of Europe prior to World War I. In light of that, continued American involvement in the Far East remains a necessary stabilizing factor.[26]

How this world-view has been reproduced and legitimized in think-tanks, mid-level foreign policy and intelligence bureaucracies, centers for international studies, and international financial and corporate institutions has been ably chronicled.[27] What needs to be studied *now* is how and why the academic technicians of realism are able less and less to resort to a resistant history or a fragmenting commonsense to make their prescriptions. Facing accelerating new world disorders, their preferred rapid-response philosophy has increasingly become the hyperrealist simulation. In this technical manner realism is reproduced by other means in IR, ranging from game and rational choice theory to the computer simulation of worst-case scenarios and the serialization of war game after-action reviews.

On the other hand (often with pen as sword), the figuration crowd advocates a more reflective, rhetorically-conscious attitude towards a rapidly shifting, highly ambiguous, heavily mediated international politics. They challenge the axiomatic, positivist conception of the real that assumes an object for every name, the authority of every referent. They disabuse the realist use of historical analogy to domesticate contingency, citing not just new, non-analogous configurations of power but also new modes of representing them, such as simulations, CNN, faxes, camcorders, and the like. They understand realism as a powerful, performative script which now more than ever must be reinterpreted and refigured for a changed world.

How the script is figuratively conceived, how it uses and is used by literary tropes, historical analogues, technical reproduction, and spectacular staging, is considered to be as 'real' and important a factor as any 'literal' or 'material' reality. For the figurative realist, 'theory' and 'story' rejoin in their common Greek and Indo-European root, *weid*: a 'vision' that gives us knowledge of the world. In every script a stage is set, actors cast, and a vision inscribed. Whether an audience will come to the show depends on much more than a particular script's ability to copy reality. The verisimilitude which empowers realism depends upon a dramatic and rhetorical bag of tricks that are socially and performatively produced.[28] Hence, our understanding of the power of realism requires an equally if not excessively performative *de-scription* of its current figurations, in the sense of a critical distancing from present vocabularies and canonistic readings that might engender not just a new perspective but open up the possibility for a variety of new realisms.

THE MEANING OF BEGINNINGS, THE NAMING OF NAMES

Where might a genealogy begin? First, by de-familiarizing the most familiar beginnings.

'What do we mean by realism?' The question triggers a mix of familiar phrases, like 'states,' 'struggle for power,' human nature,' 'international anarchy,' 'balance of power,' 'security dilemma.' Sometimes for pedigree, German words like *Realpolitik* or its American malapropism 'geopolitics' are thrown in, along with a representative quote or two from Thucydides, Hobbes, or Machiavelli. Sometimes explicitly but more often implicitly, onto–theological foundations for realism are presented as natural laws, as in the Augustinian dogma that evil is real and pervasive, or its

Benthamite secularization that all humans are reducible to self-optimizing units. And finally, to add veridical power to the common epistemic model is the Rankean fiat – often cross-dressed by the neo-realists as a scientific truth – that a realist depicts things as they really are, rather than as an idealist might wish them to be, or worse, a textualist might interpret them into being. Thus credentialed, authors can get down to the business of defending their particular realism as the arch-method for the field.

But what happens – as seems to be the case to this observer – when the 'we' fragments, 'realism' takes on prefixes and goes plural, the meaning of meaning itself is up for grabs? A stop-gap solution is to supplement the definitional gambit with a facile gesture. The IR theorist, mindful of a creeping pluralism, will note the 'essentially contested' nature of realism – duly backed up with a footnote to W. B. Gallie or W. E. Connolly – and then get down to business as usual, that is, using realism as the best language to reflect a self-same phenomenon. This amounts to an intellectual plea of *nolo contendere*: in exchange for not contesting the charge that the meaning of realism is contestable, the IR 'perp' gets off easy, to then turn around and commit worse epistemological crimes. In honor of the most notorious benefactor of *nolo contendere* in recent American legal history, we might call this the 'Spiro-ette effect' in International Relations.

This is only one of many rhetorical moves that shore up the identity of an epistemic realism based on difference.[29] What form might an alternative script take? The first act would have to go to the medieval nominalists, for they, not the idealists, were the first to present the philosophical antinomies which gave rise to a realist school of thought. Medieval scholar Friedrich Heer sets the apocalyptic scene for the arrival of nominalism in the beginning of the fourteenth century:

> Stagnation, the shock to Christendom, national antagonisms, social arrogance and exclusiveness all found their reflection in the intellectual and spiritual life of the time. This was the period when nominalism triumphantly invaded the universities and theology, a victory for those who would sharply distinguish faith from knowl-

edge, spirit from matter, God from man, and the natural from the supernatural; this philosophy, like mysticism, was expressive of the doubts and despair which troubled the age. Both nominalism and mysticism were attempt at building inner kingdoms of the mind and soul whilst outside the peoples of Europe remained locked in a state of permanent civil war.[30]

William of Ockham (1300–1349), one of many thinkers nominated for the dubious title of 'father of modern thought,' is most closely identified with the origins of nominalism – to such an extent that it often went by the name of 'Ockhamism.' A Franciscan who attacked the stupidity of the Inquisitors, the avarice of the theology professors, and the lust for power of the Pope – and spent some time in papal custody for his good work – matched his radical theological views with a highly individualist philosophy. Writing against the dominant Thomist doctrine that words stood for universals which reflected the order of the cosmos, Ockham put forward the 'relativist' thesis that universal or abstract terms were conveniences of language, existing in name only. There were no universal meanings authorized by God, only temporal understandings reached through dialogue and agreed upon by a plurality. Hence, there is no absolute guarantee, as claimed by the realists, that there is a physical reality that corresponds to particular terms. From this reinterpretation of language some drew radical conclusions: much of the Bible was a fictional naming-game, and although God probably did exist, he had become a very remote 'other' who no longer had much to do with human affairs. According to Heer, Ockham was 'excommunicated in 1328, conquered Paris with his nominalism about 1340, and from there it spread to the German universities.'[31]

Can one not detect in this doctrine of the late Middle Ages an echo of a representational battle going on in the late Modern Ages? The 'death of the author,' 'logocentrism,' 'undecidability,' 'indeterminacy' – the bellwether words of postmodernism – all have the tintinnabulation of a latter-day nominalism in them. This problematical relationship of words to objects is certainly front-and-center in the seminal encounter of idealism and realism in IR. In *The Twenty Years' Crisis* E. H. Carr locates the weakness of the League of Nation idealists in their slippery use of language. He approvingly quotes Bertrand Russell – 'Metaphysicians, like savages are apt to imagine a magical connexion between words and things' – to lead his attack on the 'metaphysicians of Geneva' who 'found it difficult to believe that an accumulation of ingenious texts prohibiting war was not a barrier against war itself.'[32]

The injunction that words mean what they say and say what they mean is the core principle of realism – and its greatest evasion of the *aporia*, or road to nowhere that IR theory, often with the best intentions, posts with authoritative signs of where we have been (realism) or where we are heading (idealism). To be sure, profound thinkers like Martin Wight have questioned the ability of international theory, absent a sovereign authority, to chart a collective destination for world politics. But the question must be extended, to ask whether we can, absent a Leviathan of language, legislate the universal meaning necessary for single theory of realism. As long as there was a commonly accepted diplomatic culture and a 'natural' hegemony or balance of power, the question does not impinge on the practice of world politics. But when power and culture fragments and diffuses, and change itself accelerates, there is more dissonance than harmony in realism. To paraphrase Frederick the Great: discourse without power is like an orchestra without a score. Or in the trope that opened this essay – without a hegemonic script, realism begins to resemble an absurdist play.

HETEROREALISM

Better, some might think, an absurdist play than a three-ring circus. This would seem to be the view of those feeling buffeted by the winds of change who would seek to close the disciplinary shutters against new intellectual challenges. The illiberal attitude of neoliberal institutionalism towards postmodernist feminism, and the insecurity of security studies towards poststructuralism fit the bill.[33] I do not wish to rehearse this (so far) non-debate. I note it only as part of a necessary academic exercise, in the hope that a discursive space can be opened and maintained for the start of a dialogue that would make these defensive reactions – including, of course, this one – unnecessary. Instead, I wish to re-introduce the antinomies and prototypes of realism that never seem to 'figure' in the reductive identity of realism in IR. This just might help us to construct a form of 'heterorealism' that can imagine, constitute, and help to manage many new world orders.

If nominalism represents the first act of the lost script of realism, then it is the literary and artistic creeds of realism that make up the second and third. It might seem ironic that realism as a school of thought should be resurrected in the eighteenth century in the fictional form of the novel. It was also expedient: Britain's censorial Licensing Act of 1737 encouraged the intellectual talents of the day to turn to the novel as a relatively safe conduit for social satire. Writers like Daniel Defoe and Henry Fielding were described as 'realists' because of their detailed depiction of everyday life, the drawing of characters from the lower classes and outlaw fringe, and the use of an easy and familiar language. For the modern purist who consider the 'docudrama' an affront to truth and good taste, a reading of Defoe's *Journal of the Plague Years* (1722), or Fielding's *Tom Jones* (1749) is suggested. Both are considerably more 'realistic,' that is, superior in verisimilitude, than the 'factual' accounts of the day (such as Samuel Pepys' account of the 1665 London plague). The same was thought by Marx and Engels of the greatest literary realist, Honoré de Balzac, who considered himself a scientific historian first and a novelist second.[34] And in his influential *Studies in European Realism*, the marxist scholar Georg Lukács lauds Balzac's 'profound comprehension of the contradictorily progressive character of capitalist development' and, then, after noting that 'the great realist of France found worthy heirs only in Russia,' claims that 'It is not by chance that Lenin . . . formulated the Marxist view of the principles of true realism in connection with Tolstoy.'[35]

In painting a similar battle was being played out, with realism once again defined by a dominating antinomy. The

first salvo, 'The Realist Manifesto,' written by the painter
Gustave Courbet against the classicist affectations of the
Salon, self-consciously eschews eloquence and rhetorical
flourishes for a spare and neutral style that is meant, one
can surmise, to convey authenticity and – realism:

> The title of Realist was thrust upon me just as the title
> of Romantic was imposed upon the men of 1830. Titles
> have never given a true idea of things: it were otherwise,
> the works would be unnecessary.
>
> I have studied, outside of any system and without preju-
> dice, the art of the ancients and the art of the moderns.
> I no more wanted to imitate the one than to copy the
> other, nor, furthermore, was it my intention to attain the
> trivial goal of *art for art's sake*. No! I simply wanted to
> draw forth from a complete acquaintance with tradition
> the reasoned and independent consciousness of my own
> individuality.
>
> To know in order to be able to create, that was my
> idea . . . in short, to create living art – this is my goal.[36]

As a school of thought and movement of painting, realism
was once again born from its critics. The best appreciation
of this birth that I have located is the strange mix of respect, confusion, and ridicule that fills the letter of the
French writer Champfleury to George Sand. A lengthy ex-
cerpt is warranted, both for its seminal remarks and the
lessons it holds for a later debate in IR between neorealism
and its critics:

> If I write you this letter, Madame, it is because of the
> lively curiosity, full of good faith, that you have shown
> for a doctrine which takes shape from day to day and
> which has its representatives in all the arts. A hyper-
> romantic German musician, Mr. Wagner, whose works are
> unknown in Paris, has received extraordinary maltreat-
> ment in the musical journals, by M. Fetis who accuses
> the new composer of being tainted with *Realism*. All those
> who put forward new aspirations are called *Realists*. We
> shall surely see realistic doctors, realistic chemists, real-
> istic manufacturers, realistic historians. M. Courbet is a
> realist; I am a realist: since the critics say so, I let them

say it. But, to my great shame, I confess that I have never studied the code containing the laws according to which the first comer is allowed to produce realistic works.

The name horrifies me by its pedantic ending; I am afraid of schools as of the cholera and my greatest joy is to encounter clear-cut personalities. That is why, in my opinion, M. Courbet is a new man.

With ten intelligent people, one could get to the bottom of the question of *Realism*, with this mob of ignorant people, envious, powerless, critical, all one gets is words. I will not define *Realism* for you, Madame: I do not know where it comes from, and where it goes, what it is.[37]

What is the point of this historical sprint through the various beginnings of realism? First, realism, which presents itself as a superior representation of reality, has displayed a wide range of rhetorical and figurative styles, cultural values and philosophical tendencies. Whether it was used to refer to a doctrine of the material world, to 'things as they really are,' or as artistic or literary movement, the variations and interpretations of realism have been conditioned by the tradition against which a particular form of realism emerges. For instance, in France the realist novel was heavily materialist, evolving from the anti-romantic, sociological forms of Balzac and the Goncourt brothers, to the deterministic, practically Darwinistic naturalism of Zola. In England, realism missed the naturalist turn, preferring to explore a moral landscape rather than document a mechanistic universe, as best exemplified in the work of Charles Dickens and George Eliot. A similar range of differences can also be traced in the variety of paintings, from Gustave Courbet to Chuck Close, which have been categorized under the rubric of 'realist.'

What generalizations can we make of this richer if checkered history of realism, in its passage from counter-hegemonic force to a dominant discourse? Different forms emerge from the struggle against nominalism in the late medieval ages; against capitalism and romanticism in the nineteenth century; and against idealism in the twentieth. Judging from the diversity and complexity of its historical opposition, it seems absurd to try to attach a fixed identity to realism, as has been the tendency in IR. This is a lesson learned early by one of the greatest students of realism, Martin Wight – a lesson seemingly lost on many of the neo-realists who followed:

> Statesmen act under various pressures, and appeal with varying degrees of sincerity to various principles. It is for those who study international relations to judge their actions, which means judging the validity of their ethical principles. This is not a process of scientific analysis; it is more akin to literary criticism.[38]

Unless, of course, the very function of realism is to reappear when uncertainty rises, when the link between referent and object becomes too attenuated, when the mirror of nature cracks: that is, in times like our own, when a less accessible and more unstable reality shows its face. We need, then, to consider the paradox that the power of 'realism' lies not in its immanence but in its distance from reality, from the realities of contingency, ambiguity, and indeterminacy that realism tries to keep at bay. This is why I believe we should turn to the doctor of reality, Nietzsche, to understand the power of persistence of realism in irreal times.

THE NEED FOR A NIETZSCHEAN READING OF REALISM

I suggest Nietzsche for this purpose, both because his genealogical approach is a powerful investigatory tool, and because no one has more deeply charted the figurative and literal power of realism. Not, of course, the realism *per se* of IR, but the primordial form of natural, fundamental, or rational realism underlying it, that which holds there is a physical world independent of its perception or representation. In *The Wanderer and his Shadow* he challenges the fundamental realist belief that the naming of something reveals its independent existence:

> The word and the concept are the most obvious reason why we believe in this isolation of groups of actions: we

do not merely *designate* things by them, we originally believe that through them we grasp what is *true* in things. Through words and concepts we are now continually tempted to think of things as being simpler than they are, as separated from one another, as indivisible, each existing in and for itself. There is a philosophical mythology concealed in *language*.[39]

In the *Twilight of the Idols* he exposes the origins of this mythology: 'Language belongs in it origins to the age of the most rudimentary form of psychology; we find ourselves in the midst of a rude fetishism when we call to mind the basic presuppositions of the metaphysics of language – which is to say, *reason*.'[40] From its earliest moments reason had noble aims, but soon took on the characteristics of the forces which gave rise to it:

If one needs to make a tyrant of *reason*, as Socrates did, then there must exist no little danger of something else playing the tyrant. Rationality was at that time divined as a *saviour*, neither Socrates nor his 'invalids' were free to be rational or not, as they wished – it was *de rigueur*, it was their *last* expedient. The fanaticism with which the whole of Greek thought throws itself at rationality betrays a state of emergency: one was in peril, one had only *one* choice: either to perish or – be *absurdly rational*.[41]

The result is that 'the "real world" has been constructed out of the contradiction to the actual world: an apparent world indeed, in so far as it is no more than a *moral–optical* illusion.'[42] This is not to say that Nietzsche – or his latter-day proponents – takes up an idealist position; rather, he is intent on dismantling the oppositional relationship with idealism from which realism derives its power and meaning. For it is within this destructive co-dependency that man takes revenge on life now and holds out for a better life later. In this modern condition the morality of idealism has little appeal and a limited power. This was made clear by his preamble to a passage quoted earlier in this essay:

Moral judgement belongs, as does religious judgement, to a level of ignorance at which even the concept of the real, the distinction between the real and the imaginary, is lacking: so that at such a level 'truth' denotes nothing but things which we today call 'imaginings.' To this extent moral judgment is never to be taken literally: as such it never contains anything but nonsense. But as *semeiotics* it remains of incalculable value: it reveals, to the informed man at least, the most precious realities of cultures and inner worlds which did not *know* enough to 'understand' themselves. Morality is merely sign-language, merely symptomatology, one must already know *what* it is about to derive profit from it.[43]

Nietzsche leaves the reader with no doubts about the disease lurking behind the symptoms: 'To divide the world into a "real" and an "apparent" world, whether in the manner of Christianity or in the manner of Kant (which is, after all, that of a *cunning* Christian –) is only a suggestion of *decadence* – a symptom of *declining* life.'[44]

From Hegel to Spengler, Kennedy to Fukuyama (and yes, to give credit to our own, from Gilpin to Mearscheimer) realists of various stripes have attempted to survey the future through the lens of historical and philosophical experience. Have they, however, 'understood' the 'moral–optical illusion' from which they view the world and envision a knowledge of it? I think not, and I think a genealogy of a forefather of realism can help us to understand why.

THE ETERNAL RETURN OF THE GHOST OF THUCYDIDES

There is of course no original realism to discover. But just as America needs its Columbus and 'founding fathers' to mythicize and legitimize the best and worst of its history, IR needs its seminal (they never seem to be 'embryonic') fathers (and never 'mothers') like Thucydides, Machiavelli, Hobbes, Weber, and so on. Robert Gilpin is most famous for giving voice and a disciplinary force to this sentiment ('Everything – well, almost everything – that the new realist find intriguing . . . can be found in the *History of the Peloponnesian War*'[45]), but it has often been repeated, either implicitly in the assumption of a self-reproducing 'tradition' of realism, or explicitly in the neo-realist notion of a scientific accumulation of knowledge.

In North American IR there are two periods usually deemed worthy of historical study in any detail, from which the origins and lessons of realism are then drawn and defended. The first is the Peloponnesian War, the second is the Cold War (which some will admit to require a smattering of knowledge of World War II). That both histories should be ideologically adducible for a contemporary balance of power, with the United States stepping into the role of hegemonic balancer is of no passing interest – but not the subject of this genealogy.[46] What is of interest is how the battle over Thucydides' shroud has recently revealed new fissures in the monolithic facade of realism, and helped to reconstitute new forms of realism.

Only an overview of the skirmishes that make up this discursive struggle can be reproduced here. Probably the most skilful and compact treatment of the debate comes from Michael Doyle, who surveys the field and argues that Thucydides the 'Minimalist Realist' wins out over the contending claimants, the 'Fundamentalist' and 'Structuralist Realist.'[47] Like many others in the field, Doyle exerts most of his intellectual efforts on a choice between parsimonious schools of thought rather than an appreciation of the interpretive forces that give rise to a plurality of meaning in Thucydides' text. Nonetheless, he ends on a useful cautionary note: 'Paternity suits tend to be messy.'[48]

This lesson is hammered home in the growing literature which treats Thucydides as a historically-situated thinker who acquired a transhistorical power for realism because of his skillful use of rhetoric and dramatic constructions. First out on this new interpretive form was Hayward Alker's 'The Dialectical Logic of Thucydides' Melian Dialogue.[49] Alker uses Nicholas Rescher's formalization of dialectics and Kenneth Burke's dramaturgical approach to present the case that the lessons of Thucydides are acquired and reinterpreted through an endless political argumentation.

This reclamation of Thucydides from formal modelers and structuralist neo-realists was further advanced by Daniel Garst's 'Thucydides and Neorealism.'[50] In this essay Thucydides is represented as a friendly ghost of political realism, rather than tortured – as those proto-scientists, the alchemists, tried to 'torture' lead into gold – into the family-line of neo-realism. Rather than claim some 'true' version of Thucydides as Author-God of realism, Garst interprets him as 'a contested terrain for realist and critical approaches to international relations theory.'[51] By focusing on the highest rhetorical moments of *The Peloponnesian War*, the speeches and debates, Garst produces new insights into the relationship of discourse and hegemony. He historicizes and opens the hermeneutic circle of realism without diluting its analytical power for our own times.

The latest, and certainly the strangest transfiguration of Thucydides, appears in a book on the Gulf War by the British philosopher Christopher Norris, *Uncritical Theory: Postmodernism, Intellectuals, and the Gulf War*.[52] Before the start of the Gulf War French social critic Jean Baudrillard published an article in the London *Guardian*, 'The Reality Gulf,' in which he argued that the Gulf War (as paraphrased by Norris) 'would never happen, existing as it did only as a figment of mass-media simulation, war-games rhetoric or imaginary scenarios which exceeded all the limits of real-world, factual possibility.'[53] At the end of the Gulf War he reiterated and defended his position in a provocatively entitled article in *La Liberation*, 'The Gulf War Has Not Taken Place.'[54] This was to be understood as a 'virtual' engagement, unlike any prior war. According to Baudrillard:

> The true belligerents are those who thrive on the ideology of the truth of this war, despite the fact that the war itself exerts its ravages on another level, through faking, through hyperreality, the simulacrum, through all those strategies of psychological deterrence that make play with facts and images, with the precession of the virtual over the real, of virtual time over real time, and the inexorable confusion between the two.[55]

Ignorant of, or perhaps choosing to ignore the ironic element of Baudrillard's critique, Christopher Norris took severe umbrage from these articles, and dashed off a polemic that draws from Derrida, Foucault, Lyotard and others to refute what he takes to be the excessive and flip postmodernism of Baudrillard. More important is who he channels for an alternative – realist as opposed to hyperrealist – interpretation of the Gulf War: yes, the ghost of Thucydides. Or rather the magical figure in J. Fisher Solomon's 1988 book, *Discourse and Reference in the Nuclear Ages*, who offers the hermeneutic key for understanding the perpetual war without referents – nuclear deterrence – through a 'potentialist realism.'[56]

This interpretive tug-of-war with Thucydides is sure to continue. But from the perspective of a semiology of realism, in the dual sense of a study of the symptoms of a disease and the sign-system of a powerful discourse, it is clear that the value of Thucydides increases in uncertain times, save perhaps, for those who take refuge in *idealist* forms like legal realism or technical hyperrealism. Again, Nietzsche says it best:

> My recreation, my preference, my *cure* from all Platonism has always been *Thucydides*. Thucydides and, perhaps, Machiavelli's *Principe* are most closely related to myself by the unconditional will not to gull oneself and to see reason in *reality* – not in 'reason', still less in 'morality' . . . One must turn him over line by line and read his hidden thoughts. *Sophist culture*, by which I mean *realist culture*, attains in him its perfect expression. . . *Courage* in face of reality ultimately distinguishes such natures as Thucydides and Plato: Plato is a coward in face of reality – consequently he flees into the ideal; Thucydides has himself under control – consequently he retains control over things.[57]

THE ENDLESS JOURNEY OF REALISM

There is a general consensus that realism in IR was first articulated in its modern form by E. H. Carr in his 1939 polemic, *The Twenty Years' Crisis*. Adopting a de-marxified historical materialism, Carr took on the inter-war idealists who were, according to Carr, in the grip of a Benthamite utilitarianism and a *laissez-faire* political economy. To simplify Carr's rich account, this caused the leaders of the time to mistake aspiration for analysis, appease when they should have confronted Hitlerism, and make possible if not certain the coming of World War II. If Carr provided the indictment against idealism, the horrors of totalitarianism and genocide delivered the verdict and sentence. This story of idealism's culpability, drowning out a well-documented contemporary argument made by A. J. P. Taylor that appeasement was the most realist of all possible options in the 1930s, became the historical *Ur*-text for traditional realists.[58]

It is not, however, the intent of this essay to challenge Carr's thesis, nor his reliance on a caricature of idealists that now makes the most notorious critics of realism seem magnanimous.[59] The aim of genealogy, semiology, and dromology is to understand how one realism emerged from a variety of forms to claim a natural identity based on a superior representation of the sovereign order of things. Some of the transformations and reductions of realism have been recent and profound. One took the form of a sea-change, as when Carr's and the emergent English school of realism was refigured as it traveled from Britain to the United States. Realism dropped the Augustinian language of providence and sin which was used by the Christians Herbert Butterfield and Martin Wight (and to a lesser extent by Carr who had been more under the influence of Marx than Reinhold Niebuhr, despite some claims to the contrary).[60] Realism as a counter-narrative was quick to take a new ideological baggage, with Cold War realists seeing in Stalin what the idealists had failed to discern in Hitler. Under the pressure of the behavioralist turn of the American discipline, and the allure of policy relevancy, it also began to take on a scientific identity, although cautiously and self-consciously at first. In *Politics among Nations* Morgenthau could assert that 'politics, like society in general, is governed by objective laws,' but then turn around in a sympathetic review of Martin Wight's work to criticize contemporary efforts 'to reduce international relations to a system of abstract propositions with a predictive function.'[61] The path of scientization that realism took is most evident in the work of Kenneth Waltz, who moved in *Man, the State and War* (1959) from the heavily qualified conclusions that he drew from political theory as well as game theory (of von Neumann and

Morgenstern), to a complete endorsement of microeconomic theory in *Theory of International Politics* (1979).[62]

There have been recurrent attempts to restore some flesh and blood to realism, most notably by Kenneth Thompson and a small but dedicated group acting as torch-bearers for political realism.[63] But for the most part the dominant story of realism in North American IR has been one of a sanitized reduction to minimalism, and a dialogue of the deaf between opposing schools. To borrow from literary examples of realism, it is as if the field moved from Honoré de Balzac's *La Comédie Humaine* to Bret Easton Ellis' *Less than Zero*. Philosopher Richard Bernstein provides, I believe, the best advice for when theory reaches such an impasse:

> We can never escape the real practical possibility that we may fail to understand 'alien' traditions and the ways in which they are incommensurable with the traditions to which we belong.... But the response to the threat of this practical failure – which can sometimes be tragic – should be an ethical one, i.e., to assume the responsibility to listen carefully, to use our linguistic, emotional, and cognitive imagination to grasp what is being expressed and said in 'alien traditions.' We must do this in a way where we resist the dual temptations of *either* facilely assimilating what others are saying to our own categories and language without doing justice to what is genuinely different and may be incommensurable *or* simply dismissing what the 'other' is saying as incoherent nonsense. We must also resist the double danger of imperialistic colonization and inauthentic exoticism – what is sometimes called 'going native.'[64]

However, there are positive signs, discernible in this collection of essays as well as in the recent efforts to reinterpret Thucydides and other classical realist texts, of what could be called a *Ulyssesian* realism.[65] It is 'Ulyssesian' in two senses. The Homeric sense captures the quintessential qualities of early North American realism. Even more so than in Europe, which had a long pre-history of a historical realism, realism in America emerged in opposition to a legalist–moralist tradition. The 'founding fathers' – men like Reinhold Niebuhr, Walter Lippmann, Hans Morgenthau, and George Kennan – were machiavellian, to the extent that they openly recognized the paramountcy of power in both domestic and international affairs. They were not, however, willing to subordinate their principles to the pressing demands of the Prince or to the passing desires of the public. They were 'Ulyssesian realists' in that they had early in their careers heard and survived the siren calls of power, wandered and been tested in the wilderness, and then returned to warn the public of grave dangers: of 'technocratic illusions' (Niebuhr), 'a new feudalism' (Morgenthau), and 'the sophisticated mathematics of destruction in which we have been entangled' (Kennan).[66] Most of them challenged conventional wisdom with nuanced positions of opposition at critical moments in American politics: Niebuhr criticized area bombing in World War II, Lippmann took on McCarthyism in the 1950s, Morgenthau early on came out against the Vietnam War, and Kennan opposed the Reagan arms build-up in the 1980s.

But another dimension is needed to equip the Ulyssesian realist for the journey into late modern times, for we witness a passage from heroic and epic to technocratic and hyperreal forms of governance. In spite of efforts by its earliest practitioners, realism was scrubbed clean of its original theologico–ethical rhetoric of tragedy and providence, justice and order, and neutralized by a nascent social science in search of a value-free discourse. In Homeric terms, the gift of knowledge took on a strictly academic use-value; its sacrificial exchange-value of symbolic communication and communalization were lost. Subsequently, the public philosophy of realism was handed back to the (Second) Cold War ideologues.

Now more than ever reality requires a new script: one that can match in representational power the demands of a new spatio–temporal matrix that can fit the world onto a single microchip and disappear it in a nanosecond; that can find a hybrid language for a multipolar, multicultural, deterritorialized world politics; and most importantly, that can imagine not an end to history but alternatives to the present. A realism stuck in the empirical prison of things as they really are encourages a denial and resentment towards things as they truly differ, for it is the will to reduce the other to the same and historical differences to objective laws that builds the traditionalist foundation of realism and divides the actual from the possible. Needed in its place is a critical realism that recognizes the tenuity of its singular reach, the instability of its antinomic foundations, and the necessity of an irreality beyond it. In short, recognition rather than colonization of the other.

But a critical and pluralist realism must be pragmatic as well, if it is to recognize and to discern the range of dangers posed by others beyond recognition. Whether mythically, naturally, or socially constructed, monsters from Sarejevo to Somalia can have violent and differing effects. Here the other Ulysses' encounter with the cyclops Polyphemous instructs. When asked his name by his captor, Ulysses (*oudeis*) word-plays and replies 'Nobody' (*outis*). Later, after using further guile to blind the cyclops, he makes good his escape when Polyphemous, helpless and in pain, shouts to his tribe that 'Nobody' is getting away. As is the case in other critical moments of his voyage, Ulysses eschews any notion of universal danger for the singularity of each threat, and chooses whenever possible cunning – and punning – over brute force as his first and last option. The first lesson of a Ulyssesian realism is that sometimes it is better (*more* real) to be Nobody (disembodied and deterritorialized) than Somebody (fungible, or worse, edible).

The second lesson comes from a later yet similar *Ulysses*, which traverses the self-imposed gap between the actual and the possible – and thus reveals the hole at the center of modern realism:

His [Bloom's] logical conclusion, having weighed the matter and allowing for possible error?

That it was not a heaventree, not a heavengrot, not a heavenbeast, not a heavenman. That it was a Utopia, there being no known method from the known to the unknown: an infinity renderable equally finite by the suppositious apposition of one or more bodies equally of the same and of different magnitudes: a mobility of illusory forms immobilized in space, remobilised in air: a past which possibly had ceased to exist as a present before its probable spectators had entered actual present existence.[67]

The final lesson of both Ulysses is, fittingly, a paradox: realism in late modernity requires counter-myths, not new essentialist truths. Without the reality of a universal subject (no-body), an immobile center (no-where), or a fungible power (no-thing), in short, without the surety of a self-same, sovereign identity, realism requires a voyage into the unknown, an affirmative leap into the imaginary, an assertion and recognition of otherness. The endgame of *Ulysses*, to ask and to will a yes from the other, represents the true beginning and just destination of realism. Otherwise we will not be.

Notes

1. *Economist* (March 6–12, 1993), p. 25.
2. *Newsweek*, (March 8, 1993), p. 22.
3. *Ibid.* See also *New York Times* (March 7, 1993), p. 39: 'Blast Shatters Illusion that US Soil is Immune From Terrorists': 'American targets have been attacked abroad but never before at home.'
4. *Sunday Times* (February 28, 1993), p. 10.
5. *New York Times*, 'Suspect in Trade Center Bombing Now Seen as Part of Conspiracy,' Ralph Blumenthal (March 11, 1993), p. 1.
6. *New York Times*, (March 2, 1993).
7. See Clifford Krauss, 'How US Actions Helped Hide Salvador Human rights Abuses,' *New York Times* (March 21, 1993), p. 1.
8. See J. Der Derian, *On Diplomacy: A Genealogy of Western Estrangement* (Oxford: Blackwell, 1987); and 'The Value of Security: Hobbes, Marx, Nietzsche and Baudrillard,' in *The Political Subject of Violence*, D. Campbell and M. Dillon (eds.) (Manchester: Manchester University Press, 1993).
9. Bertolt Brecht, quoted by Sandy Petrey, *Realism and Revolution: Balzac, Stendhal, Zola and the Performances of History* (Ithaca: Cornell University Press, 1988), p. xii.
10. I characterize the current assumptions of realism in IR as 'paraphilosophical' because they take on the dress (say, as Serbian paramilitary forces pose as a legitimate army) of a uniform realism without any intellectual engagement with the debates (especially of the last two decades) that have surrounded a mitotic body of thought. My particular point of purchase against the tradition is extrinsic and post-structuralist, and can be tracked from Wittgenstein and Austin to Barthes and Derrida (see below). But there has been another tributary (among others) of thought closer to the mainstream of philosophical realism that poses just as serious an inter-

nal challenge to many of the positivist as well as political assumptions of IR realism – one, I might add, that has suffered just as serious neglect in the field. I refer to post-marxist theorizing about the relationship of realism to idealism, materialism, and empiricism. For instance, the inter-war period produced a series of rich, aesthetic antinomies, most notably between Bertolt Brecht's agitprop expressionism and Georg Lukacs' essentialist formalism, and Walter Benjamin's romantic subjectivism and Theodor Adorno's psychoanalytic modernism, all of which in one form or another held up realism as a means to cut through false consciousness, 'defetishize' a reified reality, and provide a commonality of purpose and action. The emergence of the 'Frankfurt School' as well as the post-marxist phenomenological and structuralist critiques of Jean Paul Sartre and Louis Althusser attest to a diversity of realisms that have been ignored until quite recently by IR theory.

For a review of how some of these thinkers influenced debates over realism, see Frederic Jameson, *Marxism and Form: Twentieth Century Dialectical Theories of Literature* (Princeton: Princeton University Press, 1971); and Roy Bashkar, *Reclaiming Reality: A Critical Introduction to Contemporary Philosophy* (London: Verso, 1989). For arguments endorsing their significance for IR, see V. Kubàlkovà and A. A. Cruickshank, *Marxism and International Relations* (London: Routledge, 1985); Mark Hoffman, 'Critical Theory and the Inter-Paradigm Debate,' *Millenium*, 16(2) (Summer 1987), pp. 231–250; John Maclean, 'Marxism and International Relations: A Strange Case of Mutual Neglect,' *Millennium*, 17(2) (Summer 1988), pp. 295–320; and Jim George and David Campbell, 'Patterns of Dissent and the Celebration of Difference: Critical Social Theory and International Relations,' *International Studies Quarterly*, 34 (1990), pp. 269–293.

11. Nietzsche, *The Twilight of the Idols*, trans. R. J. Hollingdale (Harmondsworth: Penguin, 1968), p. 55.

12. *The Twilight of the Idols*, p. 38.

13. I cite Nietzsche and use the term 'semiology' here to provide a broad description of the 'linguistic turn,' that is, the various theoretical reactions to the loss of a pivotal center of meaning that has taken the form of structuralism, structurationism, or post-structuralism. Although they remain in the shadows (largely because their visage – not to mention verbiage – is not overly appreciated in IR discourse), two thinkers along with Nietzsche guide this semiology: Roland Barthes and Jacques Derrida. Particularly useful are two essays which engage historical and linguistic forms of realism: Barthes' *S/Z* (New York: Farar, Straus & Giroux, 1974), which takes apart line-by-line Balzac's *Sarrasine* – and many of the tenets of representational realism with it; and Derrida's *Limited, Inc a b c . . .* (Baltimore: Johns Hopkins University Press, 1977), which pushes beyond the limit the radical implications of J. L. Austin's speech-act theory through a critical, often polemical engagement with the philosopher of language, John Searle. An especially

useful bridging text between speech-act theory and later applications of structuralist and poststructuralist theories of representation is Sandy Petrey's *Realism and Revolution: Balzac, Stendhal, Zola, and the Performances of History* (Ithaca and London: Cornell University Press, 1988).

14. Semiology may be more resistant than other approaches to this inertia but it is not immune, as Roland Barthes, whose own career moved from a structural semiotics to an artful semiology, makes amply clear in an interview:

> [I] could say, however, that the present problem consists in disengaging semiology from the repetition to which it is has already fallen prey. We must produce something *new* in semiology, not merely to be original, but because it is necessary to consider the theoretical problem of repetition ... to pursue a general and systematic enterprise, polyvalent, multidimensional, the fissuration of the symbolic and its discourse in the West.

See 'Interview: A Conversation with Roland Barthes,' *Signs of the Times* (1971), reprinted in R. Barthes, *The Grain of the Voice* (New York: Hill & Wang, 1985), p. 129.

15. William E. Connolly, *Political Theory and Modernity* (Oxford: Blackwell, 1988), p. 169.

16. See Virilio, *Pure War* (New York: Semiotext(e), 1983); *Speed and Politics* (New York: Semiotext(e), 1986); *War and Cinema: The Logistics of Perception* (New York: Verso, 1989). A trivial but telling recent example of the primacy of time over space (and what fills that space) is the lead-in commentary on President Clinton's inaugural address: the three major networks and PBS put the emphasis on its 14-minute brevity.

17. See 'The (S)pace of International Relations: Simulation, Surveillance, and Speed,' *International Studies Quarterly* 34(3) (1990), pp. 295–310.

18. This mood and need was captured in a remark by Tom Brokaw, quoted in 'Being Whatever it Takes to Win Election,' Michael Kelly, *New York Times* (August 23, 1992):

> The news cycle has become as 24-hour-a-day thing, and it moves very fast all the time now. What happens is that a fragment of information, true or false, gets sucked into the cycle early in the morning, and once it gets into the cycle it gets whipped around to the point that it has gravitas by the end of the day. And, unfortunately, people are so busy chasing that fragment of information that they treat it as a fact, forgetting about whether it is true or not.

19. Virilio, interview, from *Art and Philosophy* (Milan: Giancarlo Politi Editore, 1991), p. 142.

20. For an explanation of the dangers and opportunities presented by the new 'antidiplomacy', see James Der Derian, *Antidiplomacy: Spies, Terror, Speed and War* (Oxford: Basil Blackwell, 1992).

21. The problem of defining 'realism' and 'idealism' in IR will be dealt with below. But at the starting gate it might be helpful to have some minimal, generic definitions. 'Realism' in general refers to a belief or doctrine that a physical world exists as a reality independent of how we might perceive or conceive of it. 'Idealism' is used here in the sense of the unity of intelligence and external reality in an idea, a metaphysical tradition that stretches from Augustine to Hegel to Marx. Of course the confusion between realism and idealism pre-dates current epistemological debates. We shall see how in our field it surfaces in E. H. Carr, who drew distinctions between a 'scientific' (i.e. marxoid materialist) realism and a 'utopian' (i.e. benthamite utilitarian) idealism. It is not a stretch to argue that Carr would find much of today's neo-realism – especially its reliance on a warmed-over utilitarianism – to be idealist. See below and E. H. Carr, *The Twenty Years' Crisis: 1919–1939* (London: Macmillan, 1939), pp. 5–30.

22. See n. 8 above.

23. Indeed, a good way to separate a hard-core realist from the rest of the IR pack is to ask whether the re-evaluation of realism is a cause or effect of its *Destruktion* as a self-evident concept and unified school of thought. '*Destruktion*' can be read in the Heideggerian sense of 'de-structuring' a term to retrieve its pre-metaphysical meaning; or it can be read simply (and less usefully) as the 'destruction' of a monological 'Realism'. For those wishing an elaboration of the first reading, see Hans-Georg Gadamer, '*Destruktion* and Deconstruction,' *Dialogue and Deconstruction*, D. P. Michelfelder and R. E. Palmer (eds.) (Albany: State University of New York Press, 1989), pp. 102–113.

24. Obviously it is possible and non-contradictory to be, in the manner of Hegel for example, both a philosophical idealist and a political realist. But since Hegel's failure to achieve a 'final solution' for the synthesis of both in a philosophy of totality, interpretive philosophers ranging from Thomas Kuhn and Alasdair MacIntyre to Michel Foucault and Jacques Derrida have argued that realism and idealism share more similarities than differences. They are both part of a rationalist tradition that no longer enjoys a natural *universality*. In effect, the whole idealist–realist debate has become in philosophical circles something of a side-show for the much more critical issue of a paradigmatic incommensurability opening up in Western philosophy, where the validity of fundamental truth claims of both idealists and realists have been called into question. In simple terms (that sacrifice the nuance and complexity of the issue), the contest between realists and idealists has been subsumed by a much larger battle between the Enlightenment project – in Richard Rorty's words, the 'Cartesian–Lockean–Kantian tradition' – and post-empiricist and post-structuralist philosophy in which neither side seems to share the same standards of rationality, values, language itself. Or rather, one side assumes universal standards for both, while the other denies any for either. This essay notes

but does not intend to enter this fray. Needless to say, I believe there is much be gained in IR theory – and in our understandings of world politics – by joining this debate. For a further exposition of the darker side-effects of the Enlightenment project (including Hegel's 'final solution'), see Zygmunt Bauman, *Modernity and the Holocaust* (Cambridge: Polity Press, 1989); Richard J. Bernstein, 'The Incommensurability and Otherness Revisited,' in *The New Constellation: The Ethical-Political Horizons of Modernity/Postmodernity* (Cambridge, MA: MIT Press, 1992); and Richard Rorty, *Philosophy and the Mirror of Nature* (Princeton: Princeton University Press, 1979).

25. Brent Scowcroft, 'America Can't Afford to Turn Inward,' *New Perspective Quarterly* (Summer 1992), p. 7.

26. Zbigniew Brzezinski, 'Selective Commitment,' *New Perspective Quarterly* (Summer 1992), p. 15.

27. The continued hegemony of realism in IR has been noted by many with differing attitudes and approaches to the subject. See for instance: Hedley Bull, 'The Theory of International Politics,' in *The Aberystwyth Papers: International Politics, 1919–1969* (London: RIIS, 1972) (see Chapter 8), pp. 38–39; Stanley Hoffmann, 'An American Social Science: International Relations,' *Daedalus* (Summer, 1977) (see Chapter 9); Robert Keohane and Joseph Nye, *Power and Interdependence* (Boston: Little, Brown, 1977); John Vasquez, *The Power of Power Politics: A Critique* (New Brunswick, NJ: 1983); Hayward Alker and Thomas Biersteker, 'The Dialectics of World Order: Notes for a Future Archaeologist of International *Savoire Faire*,' *International Studies Quarterly* (June 1984), pp. 121–142 (see Chapter 10); Richard Ashley, 'The Poverty of Neo-Realism'; William Olson and Nicolas Onuf, 'The Growth of a Discipline Reviewed', in Steve Smith (ed.), *International Relations: British and American Perspectives* (Oxford: Basil Blackwell, 1985); and Yale Ferguson and Richard Mansbach, *The Elusive Quest: Theory and International Politics* (Columbia: University of South Carolina Press, 1988).

28. The view that norms, values, 'truth' itself are produced through language has been part of a long debate that ranges from Wittgenstein and Austin to Barthes and Derrida. That this debate should still be ignored in IR, and worse, contested in ignorance (with a few notable exceptions) of the most important texts, is the equivalent of maintaining a Ptolemaic view of the universe in the physical sciences.

29. The best compendium of those differences remains *Neorealism and its Critics*, Robert Keohane (ed.) (New York: Columbia University Press, 1986), but for a remarkably lucid view from above the fray, see Richard Little, 'Structuralism and Neo-Realism,' *International Relations: A Handbook of Current Theory*, Margot Light and A. J. R. Groom (eds.) (London: Frances Pinter, 1985), pp. 74–89. For a more critical and complex views of the dependency of epistemic realism upon difference, see William Connolly, *Identity\Difference*, (Ithaca: Cornell University Press, 1991), pp. 36–63; and David

Campbell, *Writing Security* (Minneapolis, MN: Minnesota University Press, 1992), pp. 1–15.

30. Friedrich Heer, *The Medieval World: Europe 1100–1350* (Weidenfeld and Nicolson, 1961), p. 26.

31. Heer, *The Medieval World*, p. 277.

32. Carr, *The Twenty Years' Crisis*, p. 30.

33. See Der Derian, *Antidiplomacy: Spies, Terror, Speed, and War* (Oxford: Basil Blackwell, 1992), pp. 1–15.

34. See *Marx and Engels on Literature and Art*, L. Baxandall and S. Morawski (eds.) (St. Louis: Telos Press, 1973), pp. 30–32, 115–116, 150.

35. Georg Lukács, *Studies in European Realism* (New York: Grossert & Dunlap, 1964), p. 13. See also Lukács, *Essays on Realism* (Cambridge, MA: MIT Press, 1981).

36. *Realism and Tradition in Art, 1848–1900: Sources and Documents*, Linda Nochlin (ed.) (Englewood Cliffs, NJ: Prentice-Hall, 1966), pp. 33–34.

37. Nochlin, *Realism and Tradition*, pp. 38–39.

38. Martin Wight, *International Theory: The Three Traditions*, Gabriele Wight and Brian Porter (eds.) (London and Leicester: Leicester University Press, 1991), p. 258. Wight then goes on to list over a dozen novels that should be essential reading for every student of international relations.

39. F. Nietzsche, *The Wanderer and his Shadow* in *The Twilight of The Idols* (Appendices), p. 191.

40. Nietzsche, *The Twilight of the Idols*, p. 38.

41. F. Nietzsche, *The Twilight of the Idols*, p. 33. Elsewhere, Nietzsche finds rationality to be primitive and over-rated. In the *Will to Power* (1866) he states: 'Rational thinking is an interpretation according to a scheme which we cannot throw off' (quoted in Appendix to *The Twilight of the Idols*, p. 191).

42. *The Twilight of the Idols*, p. 39.

43. *The Twilight of the Idols*, p. 55.

44. *The Twilight of the Idols*, p. 39.

45. Robert Gilpin, 'The Richness of the Tradition of Political Realism,' *Neorealism and its Critics*, ed. Robert Keohane (New York: Columbia University Press, 1986), p. 308.

46. This interpretation has been persuasively argued by Justin Rosenberg, 'What's the matter with Realism?,' *Review of International Studies* (October 1990), pp. 285–304.

47. See Michael Doyle, 'Thucydidean Realism,' *Review of International Studies* (July 1990), pp. 223–237.

48. Doyle, Thucydidean Realism,' p. 237.

49. Hayward Alker, Jr., 'The Dialectical Logic of Thucydides' Melian Dialogue,' *American Political Science Review* (September 1988), pp. 805–820.

50. Daniel Garst, 'Thucydides and Neorealism,' *International Studies Quarterly* (March 1989), pp. 3–28.

51. Garst, 'Thucydides', p. 3.

52. Christopher Norris, *Uncritical Theory: Postmedernism, Intellectuals, and the Gulf War* (London: Lawrence & Wishart, 1992).
53. Norris, *Uncritical Theory*, p. 11.
54. Jean Baudrillard, 'The Gulf War Has Not Taken Place,' *The Guardian* (29 March 1991).
55. Baudrillard 'The Gulf War', p. 193.
56. J. Fisher Solomon, *Discourse and Reference in the Nuclear Age* (Norman and London: University of Oklahoma Press, 1988).
57. *The Twilight of the Idols*, pp. 106–107.
58. See A.J.P. Taylor, *The Origins of the Second World War* (New York: Atheneum, 1962).
59. On the reductionist interpretation of idealism, see David Long, 'J.A. Hobson and idealism in international relations,' *Review of International Studies* (July 1991), pp. 285–304.
60. For a fuller account of the development of British realism as well as its influence on their American counterparts, see Roger Epp, 'Power Politics and the Civitas Terrena: The Augustinian Sources of Anglo–American Thought in International Relations.'
61. Hans Morgenthau, *Politics among Nations* (New York: Knopf, 1985), p. 4; 'The Intellectual and Political Functions of Theory,' in *Truth and Power* (New York: Praeger Publishers, 1970), p. 251; and chapter 3.
62. See K. Waltz, *Man, the State, and War* (New York: Columbia University Press, 1959); and *Theory of International Politics* (Reading, MAL: Addison-Wesley, 1979).
63. See Alberto Coll, *The Wisdom of Statecraft* (Durham: Duke University Press, 1985); Michael Joseph Smith, *Realist Thought from Weber to Kissinger* (Dalton Rouge; LA: Louisiana University Press, 1986); and Joel Rosenthal, *Righteous Realists* (Baton Rouge, LA: Louisiana University Press, 1991). Another exception would be *The Logic of Anarchy: Neorealism to Structural Realism* (New York: Columbia University Press, 1993) by Barry Buzan, Charles Jones, and Richard Little, who construct a revisionist theory of neo-realism that is much more complex and historical than Waltz's.
64. R. J. Bernstein, *The New Constellation: The Ethical–Political Horizons of Modernity/Postmodernity* (Cambridge, MA: MIT Press, 1992), pp. 65–66.
65. This construction of a 'ulyssesian realism' is inspired by but not faithful to interpretations from the *Dialectic of Enlightenment* by Theodor Adorno and Max Horkheimer, and 'Ulysses Gramophone: Hear Say Yes in Joyce' by Jacques Derrida. See in particular the new translation of Adorno by Robert Hullot-Kentor of the second chapter, 'Odysseus or Myth and Enlightenment,' in *New German Critique* (Summer 1992), pp. 109–142; and the translation of Derrida by Tina Kendall and Shari Benstock, in *A Derrida Reader: Between the Blinds*, Peggy Kamuf (ed.) (New York: Columbia University Press, 1991), pp. 571–598.
66. See Rosenthal, *Righteous Realists*, pp. 160, 135, 118.
67. James Joyce, *Ulysses* (New York: Random House, 1986), p. 575.

Index

absolutism 352–4
acadeic community *see* scholars
action, human 330
  political 56
  rational 197
Adams, H. 32
aesthetics of existence 120–5
African world view 65
Alker, H. 283, 311
  dialectics of world order 242–78
  learning 298
  Thucydides 385
altercasting 159–60
analogies 329–30
  see also domestic analogy;
    historical analogy
anarchy 4, 30–1, 93.
  and power politics 130, 132,
    133–48; predation 144–8; self-
    help, intersubjective knowledge
    and 134–40; social construction
    of power politics 140–4
  and society 75–93; Hobbesian
    state of nature 81–90; universal
    state 90–3
anarchy problematique 7, 94–128
  Bull and domestic analogy 96–9
  domestication of global life
    102–25; active enclosure of
    history 104–5; aesthetics of
    existence 120–5; heroic
    practice and narrative of
    domestication 103–4; historicity
    of sovereignty 111–18;
    politicization of narrative of
    domestication 118–20;
    sovereignty of 'man' and
    centering of heroic
    practices 106–11
  post-structuralist attitude 99–102
Ancillon, J. P. F. 89
anthropology
  domestic analogy 85–6
  gender bias 343–4
Arendt, H. 221, 346, 356
  power 61, 356
argument from desperation 27–8,
  38

arms control 228
arms race 26, 206–7
  see also nuclear weapons
Aron, R. 189, 193, 214, 231, 247
  importance in international
    theory 228, 229
  reaction to *Peace and War* 218
art of life 120–5
artistic realism 377–9
Ashley, R. 6, 283, 311, 314
  history 298
  powers of anarchy 94–128
authority, final 352–4
autonomy
  insecurity, equality and 324–5
  of the political sphere 56, 58–9,
    67
Axelrod, R. 154

balance of power 20, 21, 42–3,
  229, 324
  society and anarchy 80, 85, 89, 90
  see also power
Balzac, H. de 379
Barraclough, G. 256
Baudrillard, J. 384
Beautiful Soul 358
Beauvoir, S. de 53
behavioral-scientific
  approaches 256
  global interdiscipline 244–5, 246,
    249–52, 266
  test of American
    parochialism 253–60
Bentham, J. 18
Berger, P. 135, 147
Berlin, I. 9, 354
Berlin settlement (1962),
  hypothetical 46
Bernstein, R. 387
bias, gender 343–4
Bloch, I. 28
Bolingbroke, H. St John 18
Boulding, K. 192, 198
Brailsford, H. N. 185
Brecht, B. 367
British Committee on the Theory of
  International Politics 6, 193